Fourth Edition

THE CONVERGENCE OF RACE, ETHNICITY, AND GENDER

MULTIPLE IDENTITIES IN COUNSELING

Tracy L. Robinson-Wood
Northeastern University

PEARSON

Boston   Columbus   Indianapolis   New York   San Francisco   Upper Saddle River
Amsterdam   Cape Town   Dubai   London   Madrid   Milan   Munich   Paris   Montreal   Toronto
Delhi   Mexico City   São Paulo   Sydney   Hong Kong   Seoul   Singapore   Taipei   Tokyo

Vice President and Editorial Director: Jeffery W. Johnston
Senior Acquisitions Editor: Meredith D. Fossel
Editorial Assistant: Andrea Hall
Vice President, Director of Marketing: Margaret Waples
Senior Marketing Manager: Christopher Barry
Senior Managing Editor: Pamela D. Bennett
Project Manager: Kerry Rubadue
Permissions Administrator: Rebecca Savage
Production Manager: Susan Hannahs
Senior Art Director: Jayne Conte
Cover Designer: Karen Salzbach
Cover Art: Fotolia
Full-Service Project Management: Anandakrishnan Natarajan, Integra Software Services, Ltd.
Composition: Integra Software Services, Ltd.
Printer/Binder: RRD/Harrisonburg
Cover Printer: RRD/Harrisonburg
Text Font: 10/12, Times

Credits and acknowledgments for materials borrowed from other sources and reproduced, with permission, in this textbook appear on the appropriate page within the text.

Every effort has been made to provide accurate and current Internet information in this book. However, the Internet and information posted on it are constantly changing, so it is inevitable that some of the Internet addresses listed in this textbook will change.

Library of Congress Cataloging-in-Publication Data
Robinson, Tracy L.
   The convergence of race, ethnicity, and gender: multiple identities in counseling/
Tracy L. Robinson-Wood.—4th ed.
      p. cm.
   Includes bibliographical references and index.
   ISBN-13: 978-0-13-261563-1 (alk. paper)
   ISBN-10: 0-13-261563-0 (alk. paper)
   1. Cross-cultural counseling.   I. Title.
   BF636.7.C76R583 2013
   158.3—dc23

                                                        2011044534

10 9 8 7 6 5 4 3 2 1

ISBN 10:   0-13-261563-0
ISBN 13: 978-0-13-261563-1

Dedicated to my darling daughters

PREFACE

I believe we must commit to learning to understand, from research in cross-cultural psychology and counseling, 'what works for whom, under what conditions, in which context.'

Farah A. Ibrahim

Much has been invested in equipping counselors and psychologists with tools to be culturally competent in multicultural contexts. A bounty of beautifully written articles, special editions, and tomes exists on multiculturalism and cultural diversity with the collective aim of improving the quality of our clients' lives. The quality of our teaching, research, and clinical practice has been enriched, and yet there is more we must still learn and unlearn.

New to This Edition

In this fourth edition, I have addressed many recommendations from reviewers and students. The following are new to this edition:

- Updated research literature has been added.
- There are many new clinical case studies that encourage students' growth as counselors-in-training.
- Several new storytellings highlight gender, race, and class inequity.
- There are fifteen chapters instead of seventeen. This new edition was reorganized to reflect the traditional 15-week academic semester.
- Data from the 2010 Census has been added.
- Dramatic changes throughout our world have been chronicled and included: the 2011 legalization of same-sex marriage in New York, the 2011 Arab Spring that brought revolution throughout the Middle East, and the 2011 ending of "Don't Ask, Don't Tell" (DADT) for gay military personnel.

CONVERGENCE OF RACE, ETHNICITY, AND GENDER IN COUNSELING

Historically, the multicultural counseling psychology literature has emphasized race. This is understandable considering the legacy and current reality of racism in America and the power people give to racial differences. The initial work on multicultural psychology and counseling was written by heterosexually-identifying men from diverse racial backgrounds who privileged race, ethnicity, and culture. As native-born people of color, immigrants, White men and women, gay people, and people with disabilities began writing from their personal and clinical experiences, gender, sexual, and disability identities were added to the literature. Increasingly, a focus on spirituality can be found. This expanded focus on disability, spirituality, sexuality, and socioeconomic class is crucial to an inclusive cultural paradigm. Convergence requires us to honor race and ethnic identities in our clients while simultaneously incorporating other identities. Concern about injustice, regardless of the constellation of our identities and even when we have membership in privileged groups, is a reflection of our commitment to diversity.

In 1989, as a new assistant professor, I began talking about "convergence." What I meant by convergence was the intersectionality of race, ethnicity, gender, and other primary identity constructs within the context of counseling. Each of these constructs is critical to a person's emotional and psychological development, and each intersects with other human dimensions. Fortunately, these intersecting identities have been receiving greater attention in the multicultural counseling literature. Prior to this, much of the literature focused on individual aspects of identity (most often race, culture, or ethnicity) and their subsequent influences on a cross-cultural counseling event in which the client was a person of color and the counselor was not. A consideration of how multiple identities, visible and invisible, converge simultaneously and affect development, behavior, and the counseling event itself was missing.

This new paradigm for imaging differences, both visible and invisible, allows us to engage in the never-ending process of growing in self-awareness as human beings with multiple and shifting identities. Differences are celebrated; the structural inequity that assigns power and privilege to immutable characteristics is not.

Multicultural counseling and psychology emphasize relational, cultural, ecological, and social justice frameworks. As professionals, we accept our responsibility to be agents of transformation by creating a more just and equitable world that reflects humane distribution of resources and opportunities. Multicultural counseling and psychology also recognize the way in which dominant cultural beliefs and values furnish and perpetuate feelings of inadequacy, shame, confusion, and distrust in clients in both the therapeutic process and within the larger society.

The response to the first three editions from colleagues and students has been uplifting. I am humbled by your support of my work. As detailed above, this fourth edition offers an updated format with revised chapters, case studies, and storytelling. New and existing research is discussed. In a spirit of *Umoja* (unity), I acknowledge and celebrate the contributions of "path walkers" who have gone before me. Our students continue to walk with us and point us in new directions.

A MESSAGE TO STUDENTS

The material presented in this book is intended to further your development as a multiculturally competent professional. Some of the information you encounter may provoke dissonance. It is hoped that you will honor your feelings and share them with your professors and classmates. Through your practica and internships, you will find that your clients will feel dissonance, confusion, anger, and a host of other emotions when exposed to a new insight or technique that will serve them long term but can be hard to take in the short term. Once the course is finished and you have your grade, it might be easy to retreat to more comfortable pre-multicultural class experiences. If you are willing to see a transformed way of being in the world, your thoughts, actions, behaviors, and beliefs about yourself and others will undergo transformation as well. The process of transformation is part of a social justice orientation and a lifelong commitment to using your power and privilege for good in the world.

I welcome you to this exploration. Please read the Storytelling and Case Studies, and listen to other people's stories—mine, as well as your own. Although growth cannot happen without dissonance, trust that you are being prepared to better appreciate the multiple layers and contexts that both you and your clients will bring to therapy. Your more informed sense of self will help you relate to your clients from their view of the world. This in turn will help you identify the questions to follow and avoid those that are better left unasked. As you process your own feelings and endeavor to make meaning out of new information, I hope you will have communities of support who listen, nurture, and, at the same time, challenge your positions. I also encourage you to accept that there may be individuals who will be unable to receive or support some of the new insights that you will take from this text.

A MESSAGE TO COLLEAGUES

Teaching multiculturalism is not easy. If successful, students will become aware of unearned skin color privilege and history denied and distorted. Hopefully, they will also become mindful of a dominant culture that esteems White or White-looking skin, masculinity, high-wage-earning persons, an able body, thinness, and heterosexuality. In coming to this awareness, there will be disillusionment, sadness, and anger—often directed toward you, the messenger. Faculty of color may be perceived as the ones who are best suited to teach diversity-oriented courses. Despite being well prepared and qualified to teach, White professors may be viewed suspiciously by students and faculty across race and ethnic groups. White students may fear that faculty of color are going to be punitive or make them feel guilty for being White. Students of color may feel the need to carefully weigh their words lest they offend their White professors and suffer from this power differential with an inferior grade. These matters are contextual; thus, there are White people and people of color, due to their proximity to socially constructed meanings about Whiteness, who regard White people as the most effective teachers of this material. Untenured professors of any race are naturally concerned about student evaluations, which can have positive and negative implications for promotion and tenure review. For this reason, I do not advocate junior faculty teaching this class by themselves initially—a co-teaching model with a senior colleague is recommended during the first few semesters. Senior faculty and department chairs need to understand these dynamics and act wisely, thus protecting vulnerable junior faculty. The politics are fierce and often unspoken, yet they represent the landscape of multicultural work.

With that said, the course is one where teachers are able to bear witness to students being changed at depth. This is a great gift and privilege. It does not, however, come without a price. It is important that you take care of yourselves and do the best work that you can. This is, after all, a calling. Watching students listen to other people's voices and coexist with different ways of being in the world allows us to contribute to meaningful change. At the same time, some students will receive excellent grades yet will not be significantly altered by their experiences in a multicultural class. Be prepared to read and hear racist statements from students. You must be prepared to hear that which is difficult to receive when you ask students to speak from their lived experiences. A question I ask students to consider is, how can the rain of racism fall throughout the land and miss your house? You have to trust that for some of your students, you are nurturing growth and change that you will not see by semester's end. I encourage new faculty members who have taken jobs away from home and other communities of support to have a ready list of people on whom to call and confide after a particularly difficult class that leaves them feeling drained and seriously questioning the decision making that led them to the place they now call home.

Finally, ask your students to buy world maps. You must not assume that they know geography. Although I have traveled the world, having a portable and laminated world map has been helpful.

OUTLINE OF CHAPTERS

The text is divided into three parts: *Imaging Diversity*, *Valued Cultures*, and *Converging Identities*. Every chapter has at least one Storytelling feature to honor the powerful oral tradition of storytelling that is alive in the world's cultures. To encourage the integration and application of the material, a case study that emphasizes counseling skills is presented in each chapter.

In this fourth edition, separate chapters are devoted to Native Americans, Latinos, people of African descent, people of Asian descent, and people of the Middle East. The reality of bicultural, biracial, and multiracial people as the fastest-growing demographic in the United States is recognized as well throughout the book.

Part One: Imaging Diversity Chapter 1, *Multiple Identities Defined*, provides an overview of culture, race, ethnicity, gender, sexuality, disability, socioeconomic class, and religion and faith. The U.S. value structure is touted as normal and superior to others. Given this, counselors' awareness of their attitudes about sources of differences is emphasized. Dominant cultural values are discussed as a way to orient the reader to core values that are not apparent, even to those of us born and reared in the United States.

Chapter 2, *Multicultural Competencies and Guidelines*, focuses on the knowledge, attitudes, and skills, both verbal and nonverbal, that are essential for the effective mental health professional to possess. Competencies from the American Counseling Association are discussed in depth as are American Psychological Association guidelines for teaching, research, practice, and organizational development. Information is provided on the integration of competencies in various settings, which includes the ability to know the limits of one's competence. Finally, ethical considerations are discussed within a multicultural context.

In Chapter 3, *Statused Identities*, gender, race, sexuality, religion, ability, disability, and class as sources of differences and status characteristics are explored. The intersections of identities and their contextual nature are discussed.

Part Two: Valued Cultures Chapter 4 focuses on Native Americans and Alaskan Natives. Chapter 5 explores Latinos. Chapter 6 focuses on people of African descent. Chapter 7 is dedicated to people of Asian descent, Native Hawaiians, and Pacific Islanders. Chapter 8 focuses on Arab Americans and people of the Middle East. A succinct overview of demographic characteristics, historical information, migratory patterns (where applicable), and cultural values are explored. The terms *people of Asian descent, people of African descent, Latinos, Native Americans and Alaskan Natives*, and *people of the Middle East*, are used for three reasons: to reflect the biracial and multiracial heritages reflected within and across racial categories; to respect the reality that people may live in America but hail from other parts of the world, such as the Caribbean or the continents of Asia or Africa; and to honor the reality that many people who have resided in America for many generations may not choose to self-identify as Asian American, Arab American, Latino American, or African American but by a particular ethnicity, such as Korean, Jamaican, Lebanese, Guatemalan, Cherokee, or Ghanaian.

In 1978, the Office of Management and Budget (OMB) adopted the term *Hispanic* to describe people who were perceived to have a similar ethnic background. Instead of *Hispanic*, *Latino* is used throughout this text because it is a self-defined term. Latinos can be of any race.

Part Three: Converging Identities Chapter 9, *Converging Race*, explores race from sociopolitical perspectives. Primary stage models of racial identity development and relevant research are presented. Via the case study, race, gender, acculturation, and assimilation are explored.

Chapter 10, *Converging Biracial and Multiracial Identities*, provides important definitions. Research is summarized that speaks to identity development. Clinical issues related to multiple racial and/or cultural identities are also presented by way of the case study that examines group affiliation and belonging.

Chapter 11, *Converging Gender*, discusses gender roles and gender identity and examines gender briefly from historical and biological perspectives. Sex and sex role typing are explored, and distinctions are made among terms. Female and male models of gender identity are discussed. Attention is given to gender socialization, the construct of physical beauty, emotion, and their influence on power and status.

Chapter 12, *Converging Socioeconomic Class*, focuses on class as a status variable both in society and within the therapeutic encounter. Class is inextricably linked to self-worth and income. The limited training that graduate students in counseling programs receive is discussed within the context of culture. Questions are provided to help students unravel the role of class in their own development and with respect to their perceptions of others. The intersections of power, powerlessness, gender, and race are considered.

Chapter 13 is titled *Converging Sexuality*. Often counselors and psychologists do not receive adequate training in sexuality, with respect to their own lives and those of their clients. The goal of this chapter is to expose readers to the heterosexual bias that exists in American culture and to increase sensitivity about the inherent danger to lesbian, gay, bisexual, and transgender clients in a climate of heterosexism. Greater attention is focused on transgender and intersexuality.

Chapter 14, *Converging Disability*, is focused on the able-bodied culture and its impact on perceptions of normalcy, beauty, and well-being. Counseling individuals with disabilities is emphasized, and demographic data are provided with respect to the number of people affected by disability, type of disability, poverty, housing status, and occupational participation.

Finally, Chapter 15, *Converging Spirituality*, defines religion and spirituality and provides the helping professional with insight into how to integrate spirituality into the therapeutic event competently and comfortably. A case study illustrates a therapist's skill at attending to a client grappling with a crisis of faith.

ACKNOWLEDGMENTS

Eighteen years ago, Mary Howard-Hamilton and I approached a publisher in the exhibition hall at an American Counseling Association convention. We told her of our desire and our dream: to write a book on multicultural issues in counseling that incorporated race, ethnicity, and culture as well as the muted topics of gender, socioeconomic class, and sexual orientation. We asked Linda Sullivan, an editor, if we could buy her a cup of coffee. She graciously accepted. Out of that conversation, her scrutiny of us, and our scrutiny of multicultural counseling and of ourselves as women, Black Americans, and academicians, an invitation was extended to us to develop a book prospectus which evolved into a signed contract for that first edition.

As I offer this fourth edition, I thank Mary for her invaluable contributions to the first edition of this text. I also want to thank my husband, children, friends, students, graduate assistants, and colleagues for inspiration, encouragement, welcome distractions, and love. Caroline Fernandes and Noreen Boadi, my graduate assistants, did an exceptional job of finding and organizing resources, including census data, books, and research articles—for this fourth edition. In the academy, our students are our greatest gifts.

Anybody can show up at the celebration party, but not everyone can walk with you on the journey. My children are my light and life. Geoffrey's love sustains me. Rita, Caren, Marilyn,

Sherry, Ro, Ann, Karen C., Janie, and Brookins have had their "I'm with you" shoes on forever. Your support gives me strength and direction. My angel mother and father have never left my side.

I want to thank the following reviewers: Malik S. Henfield, University of Iowa; Mona Robinson, Ohio University; Laura R. Simpson, Delta State University; Jose A. Villalba, University of North Carolina-Greensboro. I also want to thank Kerry Rubadue at Pearson for her invaluable support with this manuscript. Meredith Fossel has been a source of wisdom throughout the process. Books do not get to press without good editors. Both of you have been consistently available to me—thank you.

Tracy L. Robinson-Wood

BRIEF CONTENTS

CONTENTS

Multiple Identities Defined

Although it clearly is possible for patients to be harmed directly by psychotherapy, patients also can be harmed by the decisions that are made about psychotherapy.

SONA DIMIDJIAN AND STEVEN HOLLON, "HOW WOULD WE KNOW IF PSYCHOTHERAPY WERE HARMFUL?" *AMERICAN PSYCHOLOGIST.*

Identity constructs include race, ethnicity, gender, culture, sexuality, mental and physical ability, socioeconomic class, age, and religion. These and other dimensions of identity are sources of difference. Identities co-exist with one another, and they shift over time and within contexts. Some identities have more power than others and can take on different meanings. For example, my paternal grandmother, who had a 4th grade education, was regarded as a wise, prayerful, and godly woman in her small Baptist church community. Within the larger culture where education, Whiteness, and masculinity were valued, her education, race, and gender had less power. Within

1

therapy, identity affects the client's perspective about and orientation to her problem as well as the relationship between the client and her therapist.

A primary tenet of this work is that effective clinicians acknowledge sources of differences within themselves and among other people. Clinicians are aware of their feelings about differences, are mindful of their proximity to the many discourses about differences, and are able to confront themselves on their biases of, fears about, and prejudices against people. The multiculturally competent clinician receives help to improve their multicultural competence with people across age, ethnicity, ability, disability, gender, race, religion, sexuality, and socioeconomic class. There are discourses (e.g., Asians are good in math and science, or Arab men regard women as subordinate to themselves, or Black women are churchgoing Christians) that mental health professionals hold about people who are different from themselves. Discourses have to be confronted honestly and reflexively in order for therapy to proceed effectively.

A distinction exists between sources of difference among people and the socially constructed meanings about these differences. Being an elderly woman is a source of age and gender diversity—internalizing socially constructed meanings about old women as unattractive, lonely, and sexless is not the same as being a woman of age who is emotionally and physically healthy and who revels in her life exactly as it is.

Movements—such as the Asian rights movement, the Chicano moratorium, the civil rights movement, the women's movement, the gay rights movement, immigrant rights movement, disability rights movement, and Occupy Wall Street—are evidence of the ongoing struggle for human rights, social justice, access, and inclusion. Within a culturally diverse nation challenged by the concept of *equity for all*, this chapter explores implications for clinicians, counselors, psychologists, and other mental health professionals practicing within and across diversity. Historically, the focus of multicultural counseling was on race and culture. Over the past few decades, scholars in multicultural counseling and psychology have increasingly been privileging other dimensions of identity, both visible and invisible. These other dimensions include spirituality, class, disability, sexuality, and body size. Although invisible, unseen aspects of the self can be just as powerful as visible identities in the construction of identity. And although race intersects with other dimensions of identity, among people of color, sexuality or gender may be the clinical point of focus and represent a salient identity. Clearly, race and gender have been socially constructed to function as primary status or master traits, with race having grand-master status. Far too often, race eclipses the significance of other identities (Robinson-Wood, 2010). Similarly, Cose (1993) argued that race is never irrelevant.

Another primary tenet of this work is that although gender and race are characteristics into which people are born, they are not always visible. A client is done a disservice when the most visible aspect of the self is privileged over other identities. In this work, neither race nor the other dimensions of identity are essentialized. Essentialism boxes people into limiting and restricting behaviors based on preexisting and predetermined definitions regarded as natural. As Rosenblum and Travis (2006) said, "For essentialists, the categories of race, sex, and sexuality orientation, and social class identify significant, empirically verifiable differences among people" (p. 3).

Separating people into mutually exclusive racial and gender categories is not what this text is about. This text celebrates and recognizes that each of us has multiple identities that are fluid, sometimes invisible but nonetheless fundamental to personal identity construction. Within a color-conscious society, people are judged initially by immutable characteristics such as skin color and gender rather than acquired traits. Discourses associated with race, gender, and other sources of difference have far-reaching implications for one's income, place of residence, employment opportunity, educational quality, and access. This process of judging

Storytelling: The Inappropriate Professional

Throughout her thirties and forties, a woman had been receiving medication to treat her bipolar condition. She had been suffering with this condition for years and had tried many anti-depressants, anxiolitics, mood stabilizers, and anti-psychotic medications. Recently, a few of them had started working to help her manage her symptoms. She had stopped working once she discovered that working exacerbated her mood swings. The woman struggled with debilitating depression and panic. Work demands increased her symptoms. Consequently, her work performance suffered. The woman, married with children, also provided care to a parent who was showing signs of Alzheimer's. The patient had no desire for sexual relations with her husband but felt obligated to fulfill his needs, due to her religious upbringing. During a scheduled appointment with her psychiatrist, she mentioned her lack of interest in having sex. The psychiatrist leaned forward in his chair and said, "You have an obligation to have sex with your husband." The woman was dismayed by the comment but she believed him to be right; after all, he was her doctor and a man. She was also dependent on him to refill her prescriptions. By taking her medications regularly, she was able to stay out of the hospital. The psychiatrist gave advice to his vulnerable patient based on his personal values. His behavior was dictated by close proximity to discourses about societal gender roles: women are subservient to men and should meet their needs, regardless of their personal feelings. Being multiculturally competent means that as mental health professionals, we know when our values interfere with how we listen to our clients. It is also a basic tenet of good psychotherapy not to tell patients what to do.

by appearances is largely unconscious, yet it occurs throughout graduate education and within therapy. (See Storytelling: *The Inappropriate Professional.*)

MULTICULTURAL COUNSELING AND PSYCHOLOGY DEFINED

Multicultural counseling and psychology are not new. Often used interchangeably with diversity, "Multiculturalism recognizes the broad scope of dimensions of race, ethnicity, language, sexual orientation, gender, age, disability, class status, education, religious/spiritual orientation, and other cultural dimensions" (American Psychological Association, 2003). Dramatic demographic changes within the United States such as the "browning of America," a term used during the late 1980s, have alerted the profession to rethink assumptions about minority and majority status shaped largely by cultural discourses about power and powerlessness.

Weedon (1987) defined *discourses* "as ways of constituting knowledge, together with the social practices, forms of subjectivity and power relations which inhere in such knowledges and relations between them. Discourses are more than ways of thinking and producing meaning. They constitute the 'nature' of the body, unconscious and conscious mind and emotional life of the subjects they seek to govern" (p. 105).

As mental health professionals and students in training, we need to ask ourselves: What are the unconscious and/or unspoken discourses for me that frame or lie beneath socially constructed categories of difference? What do unspoken discourses mean within my therapeutic contexts and/or within my classrooms? Discourses may be unconscious in that people may not be aware of where they are located within and positioned by certain discourses. Location means "identifying where one resides in this society on a continuum from privilege to oppression in relation to various contextual aspects of the self, such as ethnicity, gender, sexual orientation, religion, and class status" (Vasquez & Magraw 2005, pp. 66–67). Discourses can be subtle yet pervasive throughout society, holding enormous power.

Within the framework of multicultural counseling and psychology, discourses about privilege, oppression, and difference often reflect confusion about what is meant and for whom. One of the discourses of cultural diversity is that it refers to people who are categorized as *other*: non-White, non-male, and non-mainstream. The disadvantage of this discourse is that it does not encourage people, regardless of group membership, to think about themselves as racial, cultural, and sexual beings. White people exist as persons who are not defined as racial beings, thus remaining invisible but defining and interpreting people of color.

A problem with the current state of multicultural counseling and psychology is the lack of clarity about the enormous difference between stigmatized/marginalized identities and internalized oppression. People possess both privileged and stigmatized identities simultaneously and across contexts. Some of these identities are immutable—people were born into them—and others were acquired. The presence or absence of a particular identity, in and of itself, is insufficient to determine what and how one feels or thinks. Each of us occupies a variety of statuses at any given moment. We may feel that one status is just as or more important than another, yet we do not always get to select which status is most important to others (Ore, 2006).

Multicultural counseling and psychology are respectful of multiple epistemological and philosophical perspectives and is to be contrasted with ethnocentrism, a belief that one's own culture and belief systems are superior to those who are culturally different from oneself. Ethnocentrism is in direct contradiction to the goals and aims of multiculturally competent counseling and psychology. Single-system or monoculturalism assumes that all people come from the same cultural plane and desire the values of the dominant culture dictated by those with the most racial and ethnic power (McIntosh, 1990). Multicultural counseling and psychology reaffirm comfort with and not mere tolerance of people. Differences are viewed as indispensable to a healthy society. Multiculturally competent counselors and psychologists strive to coexist with similarities and differences without defensiveness or denial. A dialectical or both/and approach to multicultural counseling and psychology supports complexity.

Embedded deeply in the fabric of daily life, culture is often rendered invisible, largely because of its pervasiveness. Dominant American cultural values include assertiveness, competition, convenience, Christianity, gender conformity, democracy, entitlement, educational attainment, equality, heterosexuality, individualism, materialism, meritocracy, productivity, the Protestant work ethic, Whiteness, and youth. For some people, culture is a dominant identity. Others are seemingly oblivious to it. Clinicians need to be sensitive to and respectful of the mighty role of culture in shaping the self. Many people are simply not conscious of the impact of culture(s) on their situation or problem in therapy.

Despite espoused values of democracy, diversity, and equality taught by schools, synagogues, mosques, church, political structures, and the family, Americans are socialized into an ethnocentric ideology. Ethnocentrism contributes to misinformation about people who are not legitimized by a culture. Students, across race, admit their ignorance about the enormous contributions from people of color to the United States and to the world. As racial and cultural awareness increase, as well as a social justice orientation, students might be confused and ask, "How could I have earned a bachelor's degree and have such limited and inaccurate knowledge about people who do not look like me or who do?" Just as curriculum materials are a reflection of what is valued throughout society, US history, too, is an institutionalized narrative. Loewen (1995) put it this way: "We are told that White plantation owners furnished food and medical care for their slaves, yet every shred of food, shelter, and clothing on the plantation was raised, built, woven, or paid for by black labor" (p. 95). Most of us also did not hear "America... derived its wealth, its values, its food, much of its medicine, and a large part of its 'dream' from Native America" (Gunn Allen, 1994, p. 193).

DIVERSITY: AN OVERVIEW

Since its beginning in 1776, the United States has been home to immigrants, documented and otherwise. According to the 2010 census, there are over 312 million documented people living in the United States. People here illegally are not included in this figure. If you are not one of the nearly 5 million Native Americans, then you or your ancestors came to America from somewhere else at some point in time, by boat, plane, train, car, or foot. Some of us or our ancestors came legally; some illegally, without a government-issued visa, passport, or other document granting entry. Others came voluntarily, and still others came against their will.

The designation "people of color" refers to individuals who are African American, Native American/Alaskan Native, Asian American, Latinos (who can be of any race), biracial, and multiracial. Sources of diversity include race, ethnicity, gender, size, sexuality, nationality, physical ability, mental ability, disability, socioeconomic status (SES), and religion. Nearly 32% of all Americans are persons of color. Over 9 million people in the 2010 census described themselves as being a member of two or more races (US Census Bureau, 2011).

The 2010 census reveals that European Americans were 72.4% of the population (they were nearly 74% just three years ago). Latinos have increased the most of any group and are 16.3% of the population; African Americans are 12.6% of the population, Asians are 4.8% of the American population, and Native Americans are less than 1% of the population (US Census Bureau, 2011).

As of the 2000 census, Latinos surpassed African Americans as the largest group of color sometime during the early part of the 21st century. Much of the racial and ethnic diversity in US society has been influenced by persons from Latin America and Asia, the areas from which the majority of current immigrants originate.

Since the recession that hit America in 2007, the workforce has deteriorated for all racial and ethnic groups. However, because of factors such as lower average amounts of education, concentration in urban central cities, employment in jobs that tend to have higher levels of unemployment, and discrimination in the workplace, Blacks and Latinos have been harder hit by unemployment than other ethnic groups (US Department of Labor, 2010). For example, in 2009, the unemployment rate was 14.8% for Blacks and 12.1% for Latinos, whereas it was 8.5% for Whites and 7.3% for Asians. The data do vary by gender. Among Latinos, the employment population rates were highest among men, at 73.5%. Latino men were most likely to work in natural resources, construction, and maintenance or production, transportation, and material movement. Asian men had the second highest employment population rate at 72.2%, with half of Asian men working in management, professional or related occupations. Black men, more so than other racial groups of men, were most likely to work in production, transportation, and material movement. Among women, Asians had the highest employment population rate at 56.7% and were more likely to be in management, professional, and related jobs. Conversely, Latinas had an employment population rate of 52.9%, with the greatest proportion of women, more so than among Blacks, Asians, and Whites, working in service-related, sales, or office positions. It is clear that many aspects of society are largely stratified by race and gender characteristics. Although persons who are more educated are less likely to be unemployed, in 2009, Blacks and Latinos at all levels of education were more likely to be unemployed than their counterparts in other ethnic groups.

In addition to changes in the workplace, US schools have undergone demographic shifts. In four states, Texas, California, New Mexico, and Hawaii, Latinos and Asians are not the minority, but rather the majority. Nationally, 22% of children under the age of 18 are Latino.

This is due to the nearly 60% growth rate among Latinos compared to 13% for the United States at large (National Center for Mental Health Promotion and Youth Violence Prevention, 2011).

Gender and sexuality are two other components of the diversity in the United States. Approximately 51% of the population is female and 49% are male—the male–female ratio is dictated by race and age. This topic will be discussed in greater detail in subsequent chapters. Human sexuality exists on a continuum and includes heterosexuality, bisexuality, and homosexuality (Robinson & Watt, 2001). The incidence of exclusive homosexuality is estimated to range from 2% to 10% for men and slightly less for women. It is clear that this is not an exact number. People who identify as transgender do not subscribe to a bifurcated male/female dichotomy. A person can be a biological female yet identify as male with respect to gender and sexual identities. The term *transgender* refers to the full spectrum of persons with nontraditional gender identities including pre- and post-transsexuals, transvestites, and intersex persons. Intersex persons may be born with ambiguous genitalia. Prior to any surgical intervention, intersex children are often assigned a gender after physicians have consulted with parents (Carroll & Gilroy, 2002). Such surgical interventions are highly contested among some who question the rationale for performing surgery on a normal child, particularly if there are no health risks associated with the genitalia that the child was born with. A large clitoris and a small penis are not life-threatening conditions.

Ours is an aging population. According to the 2010 census, the median age of Americans is 37.2. Between 2000 and 2010, the population 45 to 64 years of age grew 31.5% to 81 million, and this age group comprises 26.4% of the population. Even those 65 and older grew at a faster rate than most of the younger population groups. For example, in the same time period, people under the age of 18 grew 2.6% to 74.2 million comprising 24% of the population. There was less than 1% (0.6%) growth among those 18 to 44 years of age. Concerning age and race and/or ethnicity, African Americans and Native Americans have shorter life spans than do White Americans. Latinos and Native Americans have a lower median age than Whites.

A, B, AND *C* DIMENSIONS

As a means of conceptualizing human differences, Arredondo et al. (1996) referred to the characteristics into which people are born as *A dimensions* of personal identity. These include age, culture, sex, sexual orientation, language, social class, and physical disability. *C dimensions* are historical events that affect people's present and future lives and are grounded in historical, political, sociocultural, and economic contexts. Arredondo indicated that the C dimension "suggests there are many factors that surround us over which we have no control as individuals, but which will, nevertheless, affect us both positively and negatively" (p. 51). For immigrants, historical events can refer to political events that prompted departure from one'home country. The outbreak of diseases (such as polio, SARS, HIV), natural disasters such as hurricanes, tsunamis, and earthquakes, as well as terrorist events are examples of historical events that intersect with A and B dimensions. *B dimensions* are characteristics not necessarily visible to others but influenced by individual achievement; these include educational background, geographic location, income, marital status, religion, work experience, citizenship status, and hobbies. The B dimensions may represent the "consequences" of A and C dimensions. Arredondo et al. (1996) said, "What occurs to individuals relative to their B Dimensions are influenced by some of the immutable characteristics of the A Dimension and the major historical, political, sociocultural, and economic legacies of the C Dimension" (p. 52).

Understanding the convergence of multiple-identity constructs (A, B, and C dimensions) in people's lives is crucial to viewing clients holistically. Throughout this text, the intersections of race, gender, class, spirituality, disability, and sexuality (A and B dimensions) with historical events (C dimensions) and the social construction of difference are given primary focus.

CONCEPTUALIZATION OF THE SELF

A central focus on the individual is not typical of every culture. In many societies throughout the world, the self is conceptualized within the context of the collective or the community, not as a separate entity. The internalization of cultural values is influenced by acculturation, migration status, income, education, generational status, and racial/ethnic identity development.

Individualism and collectivism have roots in political and economic history, religion, and philosophy (Kagitcibasi, 1997). In **individualism**, the person is regarded as discrete from other beings and is considered the essential cornerstone of society (Kagitcibasi, 1997). Myers (1991) maintained that because Western society is philosophically oriented to individualism, individuals are the primary reference point and are separate from others. She saw fragmentation between spirit and matter (or *bifurcation of the self*) as an outcome of an individualistic frame of reference.

Enns (1994) stated, "Consistent with individualistic cultural values, the separate self values personal initiative, self-reliance, and achievement as coping mechanism and tends to take internal responsibility for both success and failure. In contrast, the collectivist is more likely to value making a contribution to a group effort, more likely to express modesty or self-effacement in the face of success and less likely than the individualist to make internal attributions for either success or failure" (p. 207).

Individualism influences and is associated with other core US cultural values such as empiricism. The scientific tradition in academia emerged from a positivistic-empirical model that emphasizes quantification, statistical measurement, and validation of reality by use of the five senses. In Western ideology, individualism, measurement, and control are cultural values, exerting powerful influence on the policies, programs, and politics of the United States, both past and present. The visible is legitimate and the invisible is suspect because it cannot be proven and counted. Yet Albert Einstein knew that "not everything that counts can be counted, and not everything that can be counted counts" (Harris, 1995).

Strangely enough, individualism may suppress individual expression. For example, external conformity and individualism appear to be in contradiction, yet these are two cultural values in the United States. Americans are encouraged to be autonomous, to be their own persons, and to do their "own thing". They are also told to maintain the status quo and "not rock the boat." There is almost an unwritten edict against extreme levels of individuality because this tends to be indicative of nonconventionality. US society espouses, "be all you can be," but conflicting messages are also given: "Do not cross the border of what is acceptable thinking and behavior." "Color within the lines and stay within the box!"

By not knowing the self or being able to ask and answer questions—"Who am I?" "What do I want to be?" "What and whom do I want?"—one is vulnerable to adopting others' answers to these questions. Although excessive forms of individualism can interfere with one's ability to live collectively and to ask for and receive help, individuality can play a critical role in forming an identity.

In addition to socialization factors, structural and economic factors mediate individualism. For example, when the United States's economy was agrarian-based and people were less mobile, interdependence was greater than it is in today's highly technological and mobile society in which people are often physically removed from extended family and community support.

IMAGES OF DIVERSITY

Culture

Culture is ubiquitous, central to each of our lives, and shapes the way we see the world. It has been defined as the myriad ways of people to preserve society and meet a range of human needs. Belief systems, behaviors, and traditions make up the essence of culture (Pinderhughes, 1989) as do people's relationships with time, nature, other people, and mode of activity (Kluckhohn & Strodtbeck, 1961). As pervasive as culture is, people are often oblivious to its impact on their and others' lives because of unstated assumptions and shared values that go unrecognized (Bronstein & Quina, 1988).

Enculturation refers to immersion in our own culture to the point where we assume that our way of life is "natural" or "normal" (Ore, 2006, p. 3). Enculturation is an impediment to effective multicultural work. Clinicians need to recognize and be willing to address their cultural biases. Dana (1993) identified an **emic perspective** as one that is respectful of and sensitive to the native culture's meanings for phenomena and native language and encourages recognition of persons on their own terms. It holds that the best place from which to help people of color is from their own perspective (Vontress, 1986). In contrast, an **etic perspective** emphasizes the observer's culturally driven meanings that are referenced as the standard for interpretation. Here, the focus is on similarities instead of cultural differences since a global view of humanity is taken (Vontress, 1986).

Acculturation appears to be a process of socialization into accepting and adapting to the cultural values of the larger society. Berry and Sam (1997) provided a definition of acculturation from Redfield, Linton, and Herskovits's (1936) definition: "Acculturation comprehends those phenomena which result when groups of individuals having different cultures come into continuous first-hand contact with subsequent changes in the original culture patterns of either or both groups" (pp. 293–294). Acculturation can take place at the expense of one's original cultural values as one internalizes the dominant society's values and traditions. Berry and Sam stated that *acculturation* is a neutral term in that changes may happen in both groups. Acculturation tends to bring about change in one group, which is referred to as the acculturating group. Two questions clarify the outcome of acculturation strategies:

1. Is it considered to be of value to maintain relationships with the dominant society?
2. Is it considered to be of value to maintain cultural identity characteristics? (Berry & Sam, 1997, p. 296)

Acculturation is not so much identification as it is internalization. Because this process is not always conscious (Sue, 1989), the possibility of cultural alienation from one's traditional culture is high.

Berry and Sam (1997) discussed four acculturation strategies: assimilation, traditionality, integration, and marginality. Although a dimension of acculturation, **assimilation** is different and describes those persons who do not desire to maintain their cultural identities and thus seek sustained interaction with other cultures outside their own. Sue (1989) discussed a similar phenomenon when describing assimilation. He said it refers to a conscious process in which the person desires to identify with the traditional society because its art, language, and culture are perceived to be more valuable than the person's own. Persons who are acculturated are viewed as being low in a knowledge of and appreciation for their own cultures while holding the dominant culture in high regard. The original cultures have been lost or relinquished, and persons have given up most cultural traits of their cultures of origin and assumed the traits of the dominant culture (Berry & Kim, 1988).

Traditionality describes persons who choose to hold on to their cultural connections and avoid interaction with others. Here, people have knowledge of and appreciation for their own cultures while holding the dominant culture in lower regard. When the dominant culture engages in these practices, the term is *segregation* (Berry & Sam, 1997).

Integration describes an interest in maintaining one's original culture while simultaneously seeking interactions with the other culture. According to Berry and Kim (1988), these persons are characterized as being *bicultural*. They are high in knowledge of and appreciation for their own cultures while esteeming the dominant culture as well. An integration of both an original culture and the dominant culture has transpired. Mental health and acculturation modality are related. Berry and Kim (as cited in Dana, 1993) stated that "mental health problems will be least intense with biculturality and progressively increase in severity with assimilation, traditionality, and marginality outcomes of acculturation" (p. 112).

Little interest in cultural maintenance and limited desire to interact with others from different cultures is defined as **marginality**. According to Dana (1993), "marginality will often occur when the traditional culture is not retained and the dominant society culture is not accepted" (p. 112). Emotional and psychological stress is associated with seeking to become acculturated within a given culture. Gloria and Peregoy (1996) discussed how alcohol and other drug abuse may be by-products of acculturation stress among some Latino populations. This connection between substance abuse and acculturation stress also seems to apply to Native Americans and other ethnic and racial groups in their attempts to contend with historical cultural devastation and the modern, ubiquitous, and subtle effects of institutionalized racism (Herring, 1992).

Race

Every human being is a member of the human race, of the species of *Homo sapiens*. Typical conceptions of race often refer to people of color (Christian, 1989); nonetheless, *race* refers to White people as well. Race is an extremely volatile and divisive force in this nation despite the heroic efforts of various movements (e.g., the Asian, Latino, and civil rights movements) that coalesced to create greater racial equity. Huge variations in income, occupational distribution, educational

Storytelling: Looking American

I participated in an Asian American literature book club some years ago. One of the men in the group, a native New Yorker, talked about how on a regular basis people ask him where he is from. He tells them New York—they then ask, "No, where are you really from?" He says, "New York City." "Which country were you born in?" they continue. He responds, "That would be America." People then ask him where his family is from and he says, "New York." This man's English sounds like mine and yet many people, based on the fact that he is Asian and looks Asian, assume he is foreign-born and not from here—not American.

levels, quality of and access to education, health care, and longevity can be seen between and within racial groups (Anderson, 2003). Race and skin color affect perceptions of nationality and citizenship. (See Storytelling: *Looking American.*)

What is race? To begin, there is no consensual definition of the term. According to some biologists, **race** (or subspecies) "is an inbreeding, geographically isolated population that differs in distinguishable physical traits from members of the species" (Zuckerman 1990, 1297). Healey (1997) said that race was "an isolated inbreeding population with a distinctive genetic heritage. Socially, the term is used loosely and reflects patterns of inequality and power" (p. 309).

The biology of race is heavily debated (Cornell & Hartmann, 1997; Healey, 1997). In fact, most biologists regard race as a social construct only. Even persons who appear very different from one another by virtue of skin color, facial features, body type, and hair texture are very similar genetically. The Human Genome Project discovered that 99.9% of our 30,000 human genes are shared by everyone (National Geographic News, 2010). Yet, phenotypical properties such as hair texture and the amount of melanin in the skin are typically the dimensions commonly associated with race (Lee, 2001). "Biological racial categories have more within group variation than between group variation" (APA, 2003, p. 1). Melanin is responsible for darker skin color hue and represents "an adaptation to a particular ecology" (Healey, 1997, p. 11). Although race is based on phenotype, these variables do not accurately reflect one's race but rather represent a basis for assigning people to a particular racial group. This issue is explored in greater depth later in this work. This text recognizes that race is a social construction and not biologically determined (APA, 2003).

Ethnicity

Race and *ethnicity* are used interchangeably by some authors and researchers; however, these terms are not synonymous. According to Pinderhughes (1989), **ethnicity** refers to a connectedness based on commonalities (e.g., religion, nationality, regions) in which specific aspects of cultural patterns are shared and transmission over time creates a common history and ancestry.

Ethnicity refers to commonality in which unique cultural aspects are shared and transmitted. Among some racial groups, *ethnicity* refers more to nationality and country of origin. For others, religion describes ethnicity or values and lifestyle (Lee, 2001). Ethnicity has been defined as the acceptance of the group mores and practices of one's culture of origin and having a sense of belonging (APA, 2003). Persons can be of the same ethnicity (e.g., Latino) but represent different racial backgrounds (e.g., White, Black, biracial, Asian). Persons can also be of the same racial group (Asian) but of differing ethnicities (e.g., Chinese, Southeast Asian Indian, Cuban, Filipino). When transmitted intergenerationally within the culture, language, dancing, dressing, singing, storytelling, ways of worship and mourning, quilt making, weaving, and cooking, for example, are ethnic behaviors (Alba, 1990).

Common discussions of ethnicity in the United States tend to include the "melting pot." This pot has been brewing and bubbling over for generations. Originating in 1910 at the University of Chicago (Steinberg, 1989), the term described the assimilating tendencies of the more than 1 million European immigrants who were entering the United States each year. Sociologists were interested in knowing how the more than 20 nationalities managed conflict. The melting pot theory differed from the theory of *ethnic pluralists*, who maintained that ethnicity was an enduring factor throughout American life. Yet the loss of native tongues, the decline of ethnic cultures, the dispersion of ethnic communities, the increase in ethnic and religious intermarriage, and the transformation of ethnic-sounding names to White Anglo-Saxon Protestant-sounding names were and continue to be examples of Americanization (Steinberg, 1989). In addition, the melting pot assailed the preservation of individual differences in that the pot was dominated by the majority (and thus most powerful) ingredient.

The process of assimilation among White ethnics differs greatly from that among people of color. Skin color and other phenotypical characteristics subject people of color to discriminatory treatment. Historical differences exist between race and ethnicity as a function of US policy. The 1790 Naturalization Law, which was in effect for 162 years, stated that only free "White" immigrants would be eligible for naturalized citizenship. This meant that general citizenship was denied Asians until the Walter-McCarran Act of 1952 (Takaki 1994). It was not until June 2, 1924, that Native Americans were granted citizenship through the Native Indian Citizenship Act signed by President Coolidge (NebraskaStudies.org).

When people lack an understanding of history, this misunderstanding can be the basis for ignorance about race and the perpetuation of racism. For example, Loewen (1995) informs us that Pilgrims did not introduce Thanksgiving; the Eastern Indians had been observing autumn harvest celebrations for centuries. Abraham Lincoln, in a move to bolster patriotism, proclaimed Thanksgiving a national holiday in 1863. Alba (1990) also referred to persons from Latin America as "new immigrant groups" (p. 1). During the late 19th and early 20th centuries, Europeans represented the largest group of immigrants to this nation. In 1848, Mexico lost half of its national territory, which included Texas, New Mexico, California, Arizona, Nevada, Utah, and half of Colorado, in the Treaty of Guadalupe Hidalgo (Novas, 1994). Awareness of historical inaccuracy is helpful; otherwise, it has the potential of misinforming and distorting our perceptions of people.

Gender

Traditional notions of gender reference non-males (Christian, 1989), yet *gender* refers to males, females, and transgendered individuals. Gender has socially constructed categories in terms of roles and behaviors based on a biological given of sex (Renzetti & Curran, 1992). **Gender** refers to the roles, behaviors, and attitudes that come to be expected of persons on the basis of their biological sex. Despite the advent of the women's and men's movements, in US society, men continue to be socialized to restrict themselves emotionally, function independently, value assertiveness and power, and equate sexuality with intimacy, manhood, and self-worth. On the other hand, women are socialized to be emotional and nurturing, and are groomed to direct their achievement through affiliation with others, particularly men (Mintz & O'Neil, 1990). In truth, men are emotional beings who rely on others, do not always feel strong, and desire to express a full range of emotions, including vulnerability. Women are leaders and providers, and can be extremely competitive and harsh with women and men.

Biological sex refers to the possession of an XY chromosome pair for a genetically healthy male and an XX chromosome pair for a genetically healthy female, along with the corresponding anatomical, hormonal, and physiological parts (Atkinson & Hackett, 1995). Some people are born with a variety of chromosomal configurations, such as Klinefelter's, in which a male person has an extra X chromosome or XXY. According to Newman and Newman (2010), this condition results in compromised sexual development, including enlarged breasts, small testes, infertility, and mental retardation. Support for the client's exploration of the ways in which life has been affected by biology and social constructions about normalcy displays multicultural competence.

Although not often related to chromosomal abnormalities, there are persons who are born with ambiguous genitalia. Physicians, in conjunction with results from appropriate endocrine tests and parental consent, affix a child's gender that corresponds with sexual reassignment. The ethics of this issue are hotly debated by the Intersexual Society of North America.

Sex and *gender* are terms that are easily confused. For instance, lactation and penile ejaculation are sex roles that are not biologically interchangeable for men and women, respectively. By contrast, diaper changing and car repair are not sex roles. They are socially constructed gender roles. There are no isolated genes for snow blowing or ironing, yet the arbitrary divisions of labor that society has constructed based on biological sex are stringent and far too often attributed to biology.

Psychological masculinity is not a biological phenomenon, yet it is often equated with characteristics of the US culture, such as rugged self-reliance, competition, and fierce individualism (Robinson & Watt, 2001). The characteristics often attributed to femininity, such as loving children, yielding, and nurturing, are not exclusive to the female sex or to heterosexuals of any gender. Communion continues to be viewed as feminine and agency as masculine (Good and Sanchez, 2010).

Androcentrism is a traditional systematic construct in which the worldview of men is used as the central premise of development for all individuals, including women (Worell & Remer, 1992). The central image underlying this concept is "males at the center of the universe looking out at reality from behind their own eyes and describing what they see from an egocentric or androcentric point of view" (Bem, 1993, p. 42). The many benefits associated with unearned privilege can distort one's vision of the disadvantages that accompany privilege. Both men and women alike suffer from the constricting consequences of socially constructed gender roles.

Sexuality

Sexuality exists on a continuum and encompasses homosexuality, bisexuality, and heterosexuality. There are different expressions of sexuality within and across the sexuality continuum.

All major mental health associations have affirmed that homosexuality is not a mental illness. There was a time when the American Psychiatric Association, the publishers of the *Diagnostic Statistical Manual*, viewed homosexuality as an indication of mental illness. Even today, the United States values heterosexuality and assumes it is normal. **Heterosexism** is the ideological system that denies, denigrates, and stigmatizes any nonheterosexual form of behavior, identity, relationship or community (APA, 2006). Heterosexism is institutionalized through law, religion, education, and the media and leads to homophobia (Pharr, 1988). Heterosexism has implications for the client–therapist dyad. Heterosexism could limit the type of advocacy a heterosexual or rapist might engage in with a gay, transgendered, or bisexual client. This is particularly true if the professional is extremely self-conscious about being labeled as gay because of affiliation with or advocacy for gays and lesbians.

Related to heterosexism, **homophobia** is the irrational and unreasonable fear of same-sex attractions and "persons whose affectional and erotic orientations are toward the same sex" (King, 1988, p. 168). It also applies to persons perceived to be gay or lesbian and emanates from the perception of homosexuality as an aberration of the correct social order. The term **homosexual** defines attraction to the same sex for physical and emotional nurturance and is one orientation on the sexual orientation continuum. The terms *gay* and *lesbian* are preferred to homosexual and used throughout this work. *Homophobia* comes from the Latin *homo*, meaning "same" (in this case, referring to same-gender attraction), and *phobia*, meaning "fear of."

As a reflection of changing times and sentiments regarding sexuality, some corporations and universities provide same-sex partner benefits (such as Northeastern University) for committed couples who are not married yet live together. Since the third edition of this text, the following states now issue marriage licenses to same-sex couples: Massachusetts, Connecticut, Iowa, Vermont, New Hampshire, New York, and the District of Columbia. Delaware, Hawaii, Illinois, and New Jersey allow civil unions. Civil unions provide state-level spousal rights to same-sex couples (National Conference of State Legislatures, 2011).

Disability

Section 504 of the Rehabilitation Act of 1973 and the Americans with Disabilities Act of 1990 (ADA) prohibit discrimination against individuals with disabilities. The ADA was signed into law 21 years ago on July 26, 1990. According to these laws, no otherwise qualified individual with a disability shall, solely by reason of his disability, be excluded from the participation in, be denied the benefits of, or be subjected to discrimination under any program or activity of a public entity. Disabilities can be physical, mental, psychological, and the result of injury, accident, illness, congenital, or organic.

According to the *Americans with Disabilities Act Handbook* (Equal Employment Opportunity Commission, 1991), an individual with a disability is a person who has a physical or mental impairment that substantially limits one or more "major life activities," or has a record of such an impairment, or is regarded as having such an impairment. Examples of physical or mental impairments include, but are not limited to, contagious and noncontagious diseases and conditions such as orthopedic, visual, speech, and hearing impairments; cerebral palsy; epilepsy; muscular dystrophy; multiple sclerosis; cancer; heart disease; diabetes; mental retardation; emotional illness; specific learning disabilities; HIV disease (whether symptomatic or asymptomatic); tuberculosis; drug addiction; and alcoholism. According to the US Census Bureau (2006), there are 51.2 million people, or 18% of the population age 5 and over, with a disability.

The nature of disabilities varies among people. The term *disability* is dynamic, given the open membership of this identity as a function of the natural aging process, injury, and/or disease. Numerous categories exist in describing persons with disabilities, from mild to moderate to severe. People need not be born into a disability. Whether it exists at birth or occurs at some juncture in life, it is, nonetheless, a biological reality. Disability is a lived experience for millions of Americans. Persons with physical and mental disabilities continue to face obstacles to access and experience discriminatory attitudes. Some of us have had the experience of going out to eat at a restaurant with a friend who had a visible disability only to find the waiter or waitress completely ignoring the person in the wheelchair and instead asking the person who appears not to have a physical disability what the person with the disability wanted to eat. Such attitudes are fueled by a societal perception that persons with disabilities are dependent, helpless, childlike, and incomplete. When people who are able-bodied disrupt this exchange and say, "Please ask her what she would like to eat," the discourse that disabled people are without capacity will be challenged and hopefully extinguished.

Disability has tremendous implications for socioeconomic class and quality of life. According to the US Census Bureau (2008), people with a nonsevere disability were less likely to be employed than people with no disability, 75.2% and 83.5%, respectively. The greatest disparity is seen among people who a severe disability, who were the least likely to be employed (30.7%). Among people who did not have a disability, 62.9% worked full-time, while only 48.1% of those with a nonsevere disability and approximately 16% of those with a severe disability worked fulltime.

Median monthly earnings for people without a disability was $2,530.00 in comparison with $2,250.00 for persons with a nonsevere disability and $1,458 for those with a severe disability. The poverty rate among the population 25 to 64 years of age with no disability was 9.1% compared with 12% for people with a nonsevere disability and 27.1% for people with a severe disability (US Census Bureau, 2008).

Disability is only one component of a person's overall identity. Fowler, O'Rourke, Wadsworth, and Harper (1992) said the term *disabled* "conveys a message of inability which overshadows other identity descriptors of the person and becomes the exclusive role for persons who are disabled" (p. 102). When visible, disability can function as a primary status trait and become regarded as the most salient dimension of a person's life. The therapist who associates the experience of being physically able and wealthy with power may perceive an unemployed client with a disability as pitiable. Despite the therapist's feelings, the client may feel psychologically empowered with access to emotional and spiritual resources that enable her to feel positive about her life (Robinson, 1999a), coming to regard unemployment as a transition and an opportunity to rest and regroup.

Socioeconomic Class

Socioeconomic class has traditionally referred to a person's or group's social and financial position relative to rank. Factors that affect one's socioeconomic ranking include educational level, employment stability, wages, marital status, income of spouse and/or other persons in the home, size of household, citizenship, and access to medical benefits. Exceptions exist, but increased education tends to be associated with higher incomes and less unemployment. According to the US Census Bureau in 2011, due to the economic downturn the overall poverty rate increased for everyone to 15.1%. Among non-Hispanic Whites, the rate was 9.9%; 12.1% for Asians, about 20% for Pacific Islanders, 26.6% for Hispanics, 27.4% for Blacks, and 24.6% for American Indians and Alaskan Natives (DeNavas-Walt, Proctor, & Smith, 2011; US Census Bureau, 2011). (See Table 1.1.)

Family constellation helps to explain poverty rates. In 2009, nearly half (44%) of Black families were headed by women, compared to 25% among Latinos, 15% among Whites, and 13% among Asians (US Department of Labor, 2010). According to the National Poverty Center (2011), 34% of Black children live in poverty, 30% of Latino children, 15% of White children, and 14% of Asian children. In America, one in five children lives in poverty.

Class intersects with gender and race. Black, Latino, Pacific Island, and Native American women have higher rates of poverty than do Asian and White women. Having resources to support

TABLE 1.1 2010 Poverty Rates by Race and Ethnicity

Group	Poverty Rate (%)
All	15.1
Asians	12.9
Blacks	27.4
Latinos	26.6
Pacific Islanders	20.0
Native Americans	24.6
Whites	9.9

one's livelihood affects the employee and those who rely on his or her salary. Sense of worth, access to health care, exposure to violence, a sense of personal safety, power, and agency, as well as access to fresh air and clean water are all associated with class status and income levels.

Self-construct—feelings of self-esteem and self-worth—are impacted by employment and socioeconomic class. It is not surprising that child-rearing practices would also be affected. Storck (1998) suggested that class has to be expanded to include psychosocial characteristics such as a sense of well-being. In their study of working parents, McLoyd and Wilson (1992) found that parents with fewer economic resources, in comparison to parents who were considered middle class, placed less emphasis on happiness as a goal while they were rearing their children. These parents were less likely to believe that childhood was a protected, carefree, and happy-go-lucky timeframe, or that it was their responsibility as parents to create such a climate for their children. The research presented by McLoyd and Wilson plus Storck's call for an expansion of the concept of social class suggest that class is not independent of other dimensions of one's personhood, such as one's mental health status and attention to happiness. Socioeconomic status has a substantial influence on health behaviors and health-related psychological processes, including physical activity, smoking, healthy eating habits and access to quality food, sleep quality, depression, cynical hostility, obesity, and chronic stress (Anderson, 2003).

Regardless of race, the last few years have not been favorable for many Americans and during the writing of this text, the Great Recession has occurred on the horizon. There are even concerns of a double dip recession, especially as Europe's debt crisis intensifies. At the time of the writing of this fourth edition, housing sales are depressed, with short sales and foreclosure having increased. The economic downturn that has impacted America needs to be examined within the context of corporate greed and corruption, race, gender, structural, and infrastructure issues such as the loss of manufacturing jobs in the United States and illegal immigration.

Spirituality

Across all age, race, and ethnic groups, religion and/or spirituality plays a part in many people's lives. The United States was founded on Christian principles. There exists much religious and faith diversity within and among religious and spiritual groups. Christianity is the largest religion worldwide and is purported to have 2.1 billion members, or one-third of the world's inhabitants. Included are Catholics, Protestants, Pentecostals, Latter-day Saints, Jehovah's Witnesses, and Quakers. Islam has approximately 1.5 billion members, or 21% of the planet's population, including Shiites and Sunnis. Persons who are secular nonreligious/agnostic/atheist number 1.1 billion and are the third largest group. They represent 16% of the world's religious population. Hinduism is fourth, with 900 million and 14% of religious followers. Chinese traditional religion is fifth with 394 million people; Buddhism is sixth with 376 million people; primal-indigenous is seventh and represents 100 million people. Included are African/Traditional/Diasporic religions, each representing 6% of the world's religious population (Adherents.com, 2007). Other world religions include Sikhism, Judaism, Bahai, Shinto, and spiritism. Religion, spirituality, and their various expressions are all affected by the identity dimensions of race, ethnicity, nationality, culture, gender, sexual orientation, class, and history.

Religion and spirituality are conceptualized differently. **Religion** may be measured by denominational affiliations (e.g., Baptist, Methodist), as well as by empirical, behavioral, or public indicators, such as churchgoing and avoidance of denounced (sinful) behaviors (e.g., alcohol consumption; cigarette smoking; foul language; the revealing of one's face or body; disobedience to one's family, culture, or husband; sexual intercourse outside marriage). **Spirituality** is often private and/or internally defined, transcends the tangible, and serves to connect one to the whole (other living organisms and the universe). Spirituality gives life direction and can help people maintain mental health (McDonald, 1990; Swinton, 2001). It is possible to define oneself as spiritual without being religious and to be religious but not spiritual (Burke & Miranti, 2001). Faith was defined by Fowler and Keen (1978) as being connected to but not the same as religion. It is "a person's or a community's way-of-being-in-relation to other persons and groups, and to the values, causes, and institutions that give form and pattern to life" (pp. 23–24).

IMPLICATIONS FOR COUNSELORS AND PSYCHOLOGISTS

Multicultural counseling and psychology recognize that differences exist among people. It views the assessment and understanding of one's proximity to discourses as critical. The development of multicultural competence among mental health professionals is a core value. Clinicians unwilling to interrogate themselves do not serve clients well. Clients need to beware of the clinician who will not seek personal therapy. Clinicians are encouraged to acknowledge their cultural and ethnic/racial development since attitudes and beliefs about differences affect the quality of the therapeutic encounter. Clinicians need to communicate effectively with their clients regarding the full range of the clients' values and the relationship between these values and their view of their situations and problem resolution. Because clinicians have biases, it is important to honestly gauge knowledge and feelings about sources of difference. (See Case Study: *Desperation.*)

To assist readers with the integration and application of the material to actual situations, a case study is included in each chapter.

CASE STUDY

DESPERATION

Mara is a 53-year-old, working-class Black woman living on her own in a large city in Maryland. She has been dating Jim for nearly one year. Prior to Jim, Mara had not dated anyone since she divorced 14 years ago. Although Mara would like to remarry, Jim has been slow to commit. Upon returning from a vacation with Jim, Mara is unbelievably tired—she is more fatigued now than she can ever remember—getting up in the middle of the night with her infant son years ago was not so fatiguing. After several weeks of catching up on her sleep, Mara continues to be exhausted and feels awful. On the insistence of her adult son, Mara goes to the doctor. Listening to her symptoms, and her dating relationship with Jim, her doctor informs Mara that she wants to run a complete blood panel, including Lyme disease and HIV. Mara does not see the need for either test but gives her consent for the HIV test. When her doctor inquired if Mara has been practicing safe sex, Mara said, "We are monogamous." "So you use condoms?" asked her doctor." "No" Mara replied. "We don't like them." Her doctor then said, "Then you are not practicing safe sex." Later that evening, Mara asked Jim whether he was seeing other people. He became defensive and said that he was not married, did not want to be tied down, and did not understand why Mara wanted to ruin a good thing. A few days later, Mara was asked to return to the office where her doctor somberly revealed that her test was positive for HIV. Her doctor provided her with prescriptions for her medications.

In addition, she recommended that Mara seek individual counseling and join a support group for women living with HIV. Mara is devastated by the news, so much that she leaves her car in the parking lot and calls her son to pick her up. After taking several days to call a community agency that provides crisis counseling, Mara is told that she is scheduled to meet with a female clinician. When Mara inquired about the clinician's race, she is told she is White. Mara wants to see a Black therapist—she is concerned that a White therapist is going to judge her, accepting the stereotypes about Black women being sexually promiscuous. She asks if there is a Black therapist available. There is one available, but Mara would have to wait a few weeks for an appointment. Mara reluctantly accepts an appointment to see Dr. Mansil.

QUESTIONS

1. Why are Black women disproportionately represented among those who are infected with HIV?
2. Where is a good place for the clinician to begin with Mara?
3. Should the therapist address Mara's concern that she initially expressed over the phone regarding her preference for a Black therapist, especially if Mara does not bring it up in the therapy session?

DISCUSSION AND INTEGRATION

The Client, Mara and the Therapist, Dr. Mansil

Interpersonal relationships are central to human beings' survival and well-being. Compared to other women, Black women across educational levels have higher never-married rates and higher rates of single parenting. Lower marriage rates, particularly when parenting solo, are associated with fewer economic resources and put large numbers of heterosexual Black women in the unenviable and stressful position of being more likely to be without a mate. Increasing rates of marriage between Black men and White women, as well as Black men's higher homicide and incarceration rates and their higher unemployment and underemployment rates, adversely impact Black women. This ultimately translates into fewer Black men being available as friends, dating, and marriageable partners (Robinson-Wood, 2009). Although Mara needs to accept responsibility for her choice not to practice safe sex, Mara's situation needs to be understood within this larger context of her racially gendered life. Nationally, Black women account for 66% of new HIV cases among women. More than heart disease and breast cancer, HIV is the leading cause of death among Black women ages 25–34 (Black Women's Health Imperative, 2011). Having unprotected sex with men who have sex with other men or who are intravenous drug users places unsuspecting women in peril. Mara had unprotected sex with Jim who was also having sex with other men.

Upon meeting Dr. Mansil, or Belle, Mara has many feelings. She is desperate to receive help. She is afraid to not get help. She fears being judged. She is uncomfortable about having to see a therapist; she is embarrassed, frightened, and enraged that she is HIV positive. She is afraid that she is going to die—so afraid that she has been having panic attacks, insomnia, and horrible headaches.

After completing an intake, Belle asks Mara what she would like to talk about. As a therapist influenced by a Narrative Therapy approach, Belle desires to listen to Mara's story

(Continued)

as Mara wants to tell it. Mara's body language tells Belle that she is terribly uncomfortable, defensive, and ashamed at having to be present. Belle is aware of Mara's initial reluctance to see her from information gathered during the initial phone call that Mara made to the agency. Belle actively listens for the problem saturation in Mara's story and where Mara continues to get stuck and see herself as the problem. Mara reiterates that she has HIV, that she can't believe that this has happened to her, that she is so angry at Jim for doing this to her, that she trusted Jim, that she feels so stupid. Belle shares with Mara that the problem is not Mara but HIV, and the problem is Jim's dishonesty, and the problem is difficulty with self-care that is prevalent among so many women. Jim's infidelity and high-risk behaviors along with Mara not protecting herself have infected Mara. Belle sees the benefit of certain psychodynamic techniques in her work with Mara, such as transference. Transference is "the unconscious process by which early unresolved relational dynamics or conflicts are unwittingly displaced or 'transferred' onto the current relationship with the clinician and then reenacted or expressed as though appropriate or 'real' in the moment" (Murphy & Dillon, 2008, p. 313).

Research supports the principle that transference strengthens the therapeutic relationship. In grounded theory research with 26 clients, it was discovered that the "transferential" process was described as positive and appeared to aid alliance building (Levitt, Butler, & Travis, 2006).

Belle says to Mara, "This is a very tough road you are on. I would like to walk with you during this rough time. Let's try this first session and see how you feel afterwards. Once our time is up and you decide that you would like a different therapist, I will help you to get an appointment sooner." After a hesitant start, Mara begins to talk. Belle listens. She validates her emotions, disappointment and rage, fear and extreme sadness. Mara also tells Belle that feeling like a tornado has touched down on only your house while the other houses are left unscathed is part of the avalanche of emotions she is feeling. Belle explains that releasing the emotions can keep you sane but she encourages Mara to suspend, for now, the need to gain insight into her situation. Slumped in her chair, Mara cries silently. Belle hands her a Kleenex and puts her hand on her arm. She does not avert her gaze as Mara cries so hard that she chokes and hyperventilates. Belle is unafraid of Mara's emotion—she is able to sit in the presence of it. She mines her own emotions and knows that she does not feel embarrassment or discomfort and is not overwhelmed. Instead she feels compassion and empathy for Mara. Belle is saddened by Mara's story and has cried with Mara in session. Therapists are not required to be robotic, but Belle knows that her tears are not incapacitating and do not render her ineffective. Showing compassion is different from losing professional objectivity.

A theme that has emerged with clients in therapy is that psychologists and counselors should explain to clients that therapy is a place where painful experiences are discussed and that they, the clinicians, do not need to be protected (Levitt et al., 2006). In addition to creating a safe place for Mara, Belle encourages her to find a good lawyer who can help her with legal aspects of her situation, particularly if Jim knew that he was HIV positive and knowingly had unprotected sex with Mara. At some future point, a support group may also be helpful to lessen feelings of isolation or feeling so different from others but not now. Mara is too embarrassed and ashamed of her status. After a few sessions, Belle brings to Mara's attention her observation that Mara wanted Jim to protect her and keep her safe. Mara discussed her own childhood with a father who died when Mara was 10; this was the root of her need to be protected and taken care of, contributing to her selflessness. Mara denies this initially but concedes that Belle is right. Discourses to which Mara has close proximity include these: others have your vested interest at heart and it is their responsibility to take care of you and to keep you safe; if you ask for your needs, your man may become uncomfortable and leave; silence is better as everything will somehow work out on its own. Belle asks Mara for an alternative ending to her situation. Mara says that Jim marries her and together they take their medication and love each other and have very long and happy lives.

Belle helps Mara confront a number of pressing issues such as the social stigma associated with HIV status. Existential concerns, such as loneliness, meaning-making, living life, and dying are issues that Mara reflects on. Mara is in a state of mourning. In terms of taking care of herself, she will need to engage in safe-sex practices. With the support of her therapist, Mara is not alone in walking a path that she did not plan. After a few years, Mara is eventually able to create an alternative story, an ending where she is healthy due to her medication compliance, is in a support group with other HIV positive women, and helping other women who find themselves newly diagnosed with HIV.

Summary

The various faces of diversity were discussed in this chapter, including culture, race, ethnicity, gender, sexuality, disability, socioeconomic class, and spirituality. The multiple identities in shaping psychosocial development were highlighted. A case study was presented to illustrate the textured life of a client in crisis and the skills that therapists can use to join with clients and help alleviate their suffering.

Multicultural Competencies and Guidelines

> *Culture should not be considered separate from the rest of human existence. Neither should it be viewed apart from counseling.*
>
> CLEMMONT VONTRESS

This chapter explores the development of multicultural competencies in counseling and the guidelines on multicultural education, training, research, practice, and organizational change for psychologists. Strategies for becoming a multiculturally competent counselor and guidelines on monitoring dissonance and measuring multicultural effectiveness are reviewed. A case study activity allows for an integration of the material presented.

Prior to a discussion of competencies and guidelines, a distinction is made between cultural competence and multicultural competencies. According to Chin (2003), cultural competence arose from a systems perspective to evaluate the quality of mental health service delivery programs for children of color. Multicultural competence emerged from a need to move beyond the traditional focus in psychology and mental health, which emphasized a Eurocentric and Western paradigm. The limitations of this paradigm were particularly apparent with clients of color.

MULTICULTURAL COMPETENCIES

Multicultural competencies (MCCs) have a 30-year history (Sue et al., 1982; Sue, Arredondo, & McDavis, 1992; Sue, Ivy, & Pedersen, 1996; Sue et al., 1998; Worthington, Soth-McNett, & Moreno, 2007). There are three competencies recognized by the American Counseling Association (ACA), appearing in bold in this section. Each competency is followed by parallel components: (1) attitudes and beliefs, (2) knowledge, and (3) skills.

Competency One: Counselor Awareness of Own Cultural Values and Biases

ATTITUDES AND BELIEFS   The first competency is counselor awareness of their own cultural values and biases. Counselors appreciate the significance and are aware of the values and beliefs of their own cultural heritage and its impact on them personally, psychologically, and on their decision-making. Counselors know the limitations of their expertise and are aware when their beliefs and attitudes may hinder service delivery. Culturally skilled counselors recognize their discomfort with differences between themselves and clients in terms of race, ethnicity, and culture. Counselors are mindful of ways to responsibly handle these differences. (See Case Study: *Client Identities* at the end of this chapter.)

KNOWLEDGE   Culturally skilled counselors know how their racial and cultural heritage informs their definitions of and biases about normality/abnormality in the process of counseling. In addition, culturally skilled counselors have knowledge of privilege and oppression in its many forms and its affect on them personally. They are aware of research on racism, ways to combat racism, racial identity development and measurement (Helms, 2007), and the relationship of these themes to counselors' professional development. Culturally skilled counselors know how they impact others socially. They are aware of power dynamics and how these interact with difference, across contexts and situations. Counselors are also clear about nonverbal communication styles within and among cultures.

SKILLS   Culturally competent counselors seek out educational and consultative training to improve their skills in working with culturally different populations. They actively seek to understand themselves as racial and cultural beings. They know when it is necessary to refer clients to other professionals.

Competency Two: Counselor Awareness of Client's Worldview

ATTITUDES AND BELIEFS   The second competency is counselor awareness of the client's worldview. Culturally skilled counselors are aware of the range of emotional reactions toward other racial and ethnic groups. Counselors are honest about stereotypes and their own biases relevant to certain racial, gender, class, sexual, ability, and ethnic groups.

KNOWLEDGE   Culturally skilled counselors know about their clients' cultural values and history, and the ways in which histories have been obscured and/or lied about. Culturally skilled counselors understand how race, culture, and ethnicity may affect personality development, vocational choices, psychological disorders, help-seeking behavior, and the relevance of counseling approaches. Counselors know about institutionalized racism, internalized oppression, poverty, and other forces impacting people within their communities.

SKILLS   The culturally skilled are mindful of the research in mental health and career issues that affect different cultural groups. Culturally skilled counselors engage in activities that both challenge preconceived stereotypes and encourage comfort with people across differences.

Competency Three: Counselor Use of Culturally Appropriate Intervention Strategies

ATTITUDES AND BELIEFS   The third competency is counselor use of culturally appropriate intervention strategies.

Culturally skilled counselors are able to identify aspects of spirituality relevant to wellness and healing. Culturally skilled counselors are able to integrate their efforts with indigenous helpers where appropriate. Culturally skilled counselors also recognize the value of bilingualism and the limits of monolingualism.

KNOWLEDGE   Culturally skilled counselors understand the context in which theories and the current counseling knowledge base have arisen. They are aware of the barriers to mental health service that low-income, persons with disabilities, and lesbian, gay, bisexual, and transgender populations may face. Counselors are able to suggest alternatives to traditional systems of helping and to communicate effectively with others about how to intervene appropriately.

Culturally skilled counselors are able to interpret assessment instruments in the context of a client's culture and are aware of existing bias in traditional systems of diagnosis. Counselors are aware of various resources within the community that can assist their clients while recognizing that culture can contribute to clients' decisions that are not culturally consistent with that of the counselor. Culturally skilled counselors are aware of discriminatory practices that impact clients' psychological welfare.

SKILLS   Culturally skilled counselors are able to send and receive both verbal and nonverbal messages accurately and appropriately. Counselors can help clients develop coping and resistance strategies and effective skills to deal with institutional discrimination. Counselors are aware of appropriate referrals within indigenous communities and are able to seek out the services of translators and are familiar with resources that provide appropriate language services to clients. Counselors are able to address the need for change and advocate from a social justice perspective. Counselors educate their clients about the process of psychological intervention, including goals, expectations, legal rights, and the counselor's theoretical orientation.

Arredondo and Arciniega (2001) added grounding principles to these competencies, which place the competencies within an ecological framework, encompassing multiple systems and environments. The first principle is of the learning organization. Namely, such an organization is teachable and open to change by questioning and challenging itself. The lone cross-cultural class that characterizes most graduate counseling training programs was criticized as not being representative of a learning organization or responsive to the research available on the significance of multicultural competence.

The second principle is a competency rationale, which provides the profession with guidelines as well as developmental benchmarks for attributes and characteristics that distinguish competent counselors from those who are not. Despite the greater attention given to multicultural counseling competence and research suggesting that multicultural education produces positive outcomes with respect to multicultural competencies (Worthington et al., 2007), how to effectively teach these to graduate students continues to be explored (Kim & Lyons, 2003). (See Storytelling: *I Fear.*)

Chao, Wei, Good, and Flores (2011) used a sample of 370 psychology trainees. The purpose of the study was to explore if multicultural training moderated racial/ethnic differences on multicultural counseling competence and changed the relationship between color-blindness and multicultural competence. The researchers found that at lower levels of training, trainees of color had significantly higher multicultural awareness than White trainees. At higher levels of training, significant differences were not found. More training served to increase the multicultural awareness of White trainees, but the same could not be said for the multicultural awareness of trainees of color. With respect to color-blindness and multicultural knowledge, the association was stronger at higher levels of multicultural training than it was at lower levels of training. Among those who had lower levels of color-blindness, the effect of training on strengthening multicultural knowledge was stronger than for those with higher color-blindness. *Color-blindness* refers to obliviousness about the social construction of race as well as the existence of racism in America. Those who endorse color-blind attitudes do not necessarily believe in racial superiority as much as they are just unaware of the existence of racism (Neville et al. 2000).

Storytelling: I Fear

Several years ago, I was talking with a friend and she asked, "How would our lives be different if we were not afraid?" I loved the question and thought about its relevance for counseling students within the context of multicultural counseling, where there is lots of fear. I asked my students, "What are you afraid of?" These were some of the answers I received on pieces of paper. I asked for no names.

1. I am afraid of people thinking that I am ignorant and don't know anything.
2. I am afraid of saying something insensitive to a person of color.
3. I am afraid that people of color will think I am racist.
4. I am afraid of not knowing what to say or do.
5. I am afraid that I won't be able to help someone.
6. I am afraid that I am racist.
7. I am afraid that people will think I won't have anything to offer them.
8. I am afraid that people will think I am the enemy because of the color of my skin.
9. I am afraid that I'm more like David (the middle-age man that the whole group spent an inordinate amount of time helping in the *Color of Fear* video) than I dare to think.
10. I am afraid of people's anger.
11. I am afraid of not knowing how to help problems that I've never encountered or have not heard about.
12. I am afraid that people will think that I am not only young but also dumb.

Students in training as well as seasoned clinicians will omit information deemed as fugitive or risky or avoid asking particular questions out of fear. They fear being perceived as ignorant, racist, insensitive, or discriminatory. Fear can disrupt the therapeutic event and interfere with the client's growth. Clients depend on the clinicians' awareness and initiative to bring difficult conversations into the room. Is it possible to help clients explore complex issues concerning sexuality, class, race, and cultural differences if clinicians are not actively engaged in this important work themselves? For some of us, explorations in diversity have not evolved since the single required diversity course in graduate school. Participation in personal introspection is a component of multicultural competence too. Bringing students face to face with their own stories and feelings is essential to multicultural education. Creating the space for the unspeakable to be spoken is empowering. Checking with students and asking how they are feeling, acknowledging the hard work they are doing, and honoring the emotions, including uncertainty, anger, and apathy, is important to training. Initially, such awareness can usher in feelings of powerlessness in the counselor-trainee, yet powerlessness is what many clients feel on a daily basis.

GUIDELINES

Six guidelines have been articulated by the American Psychological Association (APA). These guidelines to provide psychologists with the rationale for addressing multiculturalism and diversity in education, training, research, and practice; basic information, relevant terminology, and empirical research that support these guidelines; references to enhance ongoing education training, research, practice, and organizational change; and paradigms that broaden the purview of psychology as a profession.

Guideline 1: Psychologists are encouraged to recognize that they are cultural beings.

Guideline 2: Psychologists are encouraged to understand stigma and its relationship to marginalized identities.

Guideline 3: Psychologists are encouraged to become knowledgeable of different learning models and approaches to teaching multiculturally.

Guideline 4: Psychological researchers are encouraged to recognize the importance of conducting culture-centered and ethical psychological research among persons from ethnic, linguistic, and racial minority backgrounds.

Guideline 5: Psychologists are encouraged to apply culturally appropriate skills in clinical and other applied psychological practices.

Guideline 6: Psychologists are encouraged to use organizational change processes to support culturally informed organizational policy development and practices.

DIVERSITY TRAINING

Controversy surrounds which training model methods are the most appropriate for training counselors. Dinsmore and England (1996) stated that there is "no general consensus regarding what set of program characteristics constitutes a standard for multicultural program competence" (p. 59). There is considerable variety in counselor diversity training programs. Exposure to race and culture is standard in most courses on diversity, although issues of power and privilege may not be, Despite increased attention in the research to class, spirituality, and disability, not all programs expose students to these topics (APA, 2003). There has, however, been a greater emphasis on gender, and sexuality, and a growing focus has been noted on transgender issues and biracial/multiracial populations. Students tend not to have exposure to intersexuality and gerontology themes.

Faculty grapple with how to best teach multicultural counseling and psychology. Bowman (1996) concluded that "multicultural instruction should not be limited to one course but should be infused in all aspects of the training" (p. 16). A separate course on multicultural counseling does not allow the material to be incorporated into other core courses such as history and systems of psychology, psychopathology, and cognitive-affective basis of behavior. Mio (2005) suggests that courses build on each other in a heuristic fashion: for example, an introductory multicultural course, a second course on testing in multicultural issues, a third course on research, and a fourth course on clinical interventions.

Because society is very much segregated along racial lines, people need to be made aware that racism continues to exist (Mio, 2005). It is likely that many graduate students and their faculty do not have intimate friendships outside of their racial, sexual, and class groups. Bowman (1996) stated that "trainees need opportunities to examine the dynamics of establishing relationships with culturally diverse populations and to question how they apply what they know about self and others to successful cross-cultural interactions" (p. 23). To promote self-awareness and empathy, laboratory experiences may be helpful. As students encounter dissonance, they need safe places where they can ask questions and process newly encountered information. Faculty need to support students in their efforts at risk-taking while encouraging all students to be receptive to new, conflicting, and, in some cases, dissonance-provoking ideas from classmates, professors, course readings, and videos.

There are exercises that can facilitate student introspection and application of multicultural theory. Drawing one's culture with crayons and constructing a genogram to outline family history are two examples. Reading McIntosh's (1989) article "White Privilege: Unpacking the Invisible Knapsack" can be very thought-provoking. The unearned privileges associated with ability, gender, and sexual orientation can also be investigated as well as how White people who are gay, disabled, or low-wage earners receive privileges because of their skin color yet have stigmatized identities. Journals, personal narratives, participation in cross-cultural activities as a racial minority, and reading about power and oppression are critical aspects of multicultural training. Reading the text *Explorations in Privilege, Oppression, and Diversity* by Anderson and Middleton (2004, 2010) is an excellent way for students to gain exposure to personal narratives as they think about their own stories. One instructor encourages her students to write a comprehensive racial psychohistory, allowing them to document the role that race has played in shaping their life philosophies, personalities, and coping patterns (Kogan, 2000).

A variety of experiential activities, such as role-play, games, and films, are recognized as a means of educating counseling students about the counseling process. According to Kim and Lyons (2003), games, in particular, offer "optimal opportunities to gain multicultural counseling competence across attitudes, beliefs, knowledge, and skills" (p. 402).

To guide counselor education and counseling psychology departments in their training efforts, Ponterotto, Alexander, and Grieger (1995) developed a multicultural competency checklist. There are six themes, each with several items:

1. Minority representation
2. Curriculum issues
3. Counseling practice and supervision
4. Research considerations
5. Student and faculty competency evaluation
6. Physical environment

The first four items on the checklist seek to ascertain *minority representation*—whether 30% of faculty, students, and program support staff are visibly racially/ethnically diverse. Bilingual skills are also important. The second theme, *curriculum issues*, is covered across five items that reflect course work, pedagogy, and student assessment. For example, multicultural issues are integrated into all course work. All program faculty members can specify how this is done in their courses. Furthermore, syllabi clearly reflect multicultural inclusion. *Counseling practice and supervision* is the third area and contains three questions. The focus here is on students' practicum, supervision quality, and the "Multicultural Affairs Committee," which is recommended as a way to monitor multicultural activities. *Research considerations* have four questions concerned with a multicultural research presence in the program. Item 14 of the checklist asks if there is clear faculty research productivity in multicultural issues as evidenced by journal publications and conference presentations on multicultural topics. The four items in *student and faculty competency evaluation* emphasize proficiency in multicultural issues. Item19 asks whether students' "comprehensive exams reflect Multicultural issues." The final two items concern the *physical environment* and whether it reflects diversity in the faculty offices, reception area, and clinic area. The authors of this checklist recognize that very few programs will meet all the competencies in the checklist and suggest the development of one-, three-, and five-year action plans.

ASSESSMENT AND RESEARCH

One of the guidelines for counselors and psychologists affirmed earlier was the importance of conducting culture-centered and ethical psychological research among persons from ethnic, linguistic, and racial minority backgrounds. Multicultural research is defined as "the empirical examination of or inquiry into the experiences of individuals from diverse cultural backgrounds" (Utsey, Walker, & Kwate, 2005, p. 249). Not only are psychometric properties of instruments important to consider, but also flaws in methodological approaches, such as the tendency to aggregate groups instead of disaggregate them. An example is failing to disaggregate the data on Asian and Pacific Island populations (see Chapter 7). Their experiences are extremely different with respect to poverty, educational attainment, and income. Including people outside of the academy from the very cultures being investigated would add to multicultural variety and authenticity (Chang & Sue, 2005).

Sehgal, Saules, Young, Grey, Gillem, and Byrd (2011) developed an assessment of demonstrated multicultural counseling competence (DMCCC) of clinical psychology graduate students. DMCCC of clinical psychology graduate students was compared with multicultural competence of experienced psychologists. The researchers also assessed differences between the endorsement of appropriate multicultural competence strategies and the actual use of such strategies in clinical practice. Significant differences were noted between the DMCCC of graduate students and the multicultural competence of experienced psychologists. More education and professional experience was associated with greater DMCCC. DMCCC-should reflected the ability to recognize multiculturally appropriate strategies. For example, the participant believed these strategies should be used with clients of color. DMCCC-would referred to participant's willingness to use strategies in actual clinical practice with clients of color. MC experienced psychologists scored significantly higher on both DMCCC-should and DMCCC-would, relative to students.

In a study, Worthington, Soth-McNett, and Moreno (2007) reviewed and evaluated the content of the 75 articles and 81 studies done on multicultural competencies (MCCs). Their findings showed that (1) empirical research on MCCs has increased over the past 20 years, (2) a small number of researchers are producing the majority of research, and (3) the methods used in producing empirical research are narrow: 73% are from descriptive field studies and 25% from analogue research. In addition, most of the samples were convenience samples; this has implications for external validity.

Many traditional psychoeducational measures used for assessment and research purposes were not initially validated with diverse populations in their original sample groups and are based on individual performance or self-report or both. The appropriateness and validity of commonly used psychological and psychoeducational assessment instruments, when used with individuals and diverse populations, may be questionable. The APA (2003) stated, "culturally sensitive psychological researchers should strive to be knowledgeable about a broad range of assessment techniques, data-gathering procedures, and standardized instruments whose validity, reliability, and measurement equivalence have been investigated across culturally diverse samples" (p. 389).

The validity and reliability of assessment tools have implications for research and practice. Culturally insensitive research perpetuates the use of inadequate training models. According to Ponterotto and Casas (1991), one criticism of earlier research on people of color is that important intrapersonal and extrapersonal factors, such as client attitudes, client–counselor racial similarity, communication styles, acculturation, discrimination and poverty, were virtually ignored. Furthermore, this research had not considered or studied the tremendous heterogeneity in multicultural populations, which serve to foster and perpetuate ethnic stereotypes and global categorizations. Last, easily accessible subject populations (e.g., White psychology college students from large Midwestern universities) who tend not to be representative of the larger community have typically been selected as research populations. Overreliance on research using analogue designs, "whereby the subject pools have consisted of pseudo-clients (e.g., students) and pseudo-counselors (e.g., graduate students in counseling) instead of 'real' clients and counselors" (Ponterotto & Casas, 1991, p. 78), limits generalizability to actual client and counselor populations.

Researchers such as Ruelas (2003) and Worthington, Soth-McNett, and Moreno (2007) note limitations with multicultural competency measures, namely, their tendency to be self-report instruments, which tend not to be related to observer-rated multicultural competencies. Several instruments have been created to measure multicultural competencies. A study by Kocarek, Talbot, Batka, and Anderson (2001), explored the reliability and validity of three instruments: the Multicultural Counselor Awareness Scale (MCAS), the Multicultural Awareness of Knowledge and Skills Survey (MAKSS), and the Survey of Graduate Students' Experience with Diversity (GSEDS). With a sample size of 120 master's degree students from seven programs across the country, the reliability and validity of these instruments varied but for the most part held up, except for the awareness subscale of the MAKSS. The authors argue that a lack of consistency exists "between same-named subscales and high correlations between the Knowledge and Skills subscales" (p. 494). Subsequently, questions are raised about the development and meaning of the very constructs being measured. Chao (2004) examined multicultural competence, the counselor's race, ethnic identity, multicultural training, and color blind racial blind attitudes among 378 ACA and APA listserv members. She found that multicultural training, ethnic identity, and racial attitudes were significantly related to multicultural awareness. She used the Multicultural Knowledge and Awareness Scale (MCKAS) to assess multicultural knowledge and awareness.

Concern has also been raised over the validity and applied pragmatic utility of the many research findings appearing in the multicultural literature (Ponterotto & Casas, 1991). Client–counselor process variables have been overemphasized, and significant cultural as well as psychosocial variables that might affect counseling have been disregarded. In other words, important psychosocial variables (e.g., learning styles, communication patterns, racism, oppression, poverty), which may be more difficult to study but are vital to understanding the role of counseling with real clients, have been overlooked. A high degree of heterogeneity, such as demographic characteristics, class, and attitudes, exists within multicultural populations, yet these intracultural differences tend not to be noted in the research literature.

Qualitative research is also becoming increasingly popular, particularly as it relates to allowing voices to be heard that have traditionally been overlooked or silenced. In doing so, the researcher is not an objective entity but is actively engaged in the research through ongoing self-examination across multiple contexts (Choudhuri, 2005).

To demonstrate competence in multicultural assessment, conceptualization of presenting problems, establishment of appropriate interventions, development of client treatment goals, and the formulation of multiculturally sensitive research, psychological service providers and academicians will need to acquire cultural knowledge, information, and skills.

IMPLICATIONS FOR COUNSELORS AND PSYCHOLOGISTS

Current training programs may be lacking in their ability to help students take multicultural competence and translate it to actual practice with the client. Sehgal et al (2011), Saules, Young, Grey, Gillem, and Byrd (2011) argue that multicultural training has not changed much over the last decade. The result might be mental health professionals who demonstrate sensitivity to multicultural issues but lack multicultural competence.

Both the ACA and APA have voiced a commitment to training students to work competently with populations across sources of diversity. These professional organizations, to which the majority of counselors and psychologists belong, have great power, as do the boards affiliated with them that approve and accredit graduate counseling and psychology programs according to their adherence to program standards. Yet, how do APA-affiliated graduate programs with 100% White faculty receive a stamp of approval cycle after cycle from APA if racial diversity is more than an espoused value? This is an elephant in the room. One of the risks associated with expanding diversity to include other dimensions of identity is that some see this expansion as an opportunity to minimize race, bending diversity to satisfy gender and sexuality diversity while maintaining Whiteness as a non-negotiable construct or territory.

Unlearning practices that distance mental health professionals from themselves, clients, and students is lifelong work. Openness to being changed is crucial to developing nonracist, nonsexist, nonclassist, and non-homonegative identities. Being honest about the various emotions that reside within counselors and psychologists, even during the cross-cultural therapeutic event is essential. Abernathy (1995) said that "minimal attention has been devoted to addressing the anger that frequently emerges in cross-racial work" (p. 96). (See Case Study: *Client Identities*.)

Numerous books, articles, conferences, and associations are in the service of fostering a climate of multiculturalism and equity for all people. The ACA and the APA provide excellent resources for students, professionals, and practitioners who want to develop themselves and to connect with others who are like-minded in their focus on multicultural competence. Hartung (1996) noted the difficulty in developing cultural competencies among both faculty and students.

Knowledge of available resources does not replace genuine and authentic relationships— not just with colleagues who we may step out with for a coffee or lunch but with friends who are invited to each other's homes where honest talk can occur about our lives as racial, cultural, and gendered beings. This type of sharing and being together allows us to discuss, understand, and ultimately transcend the silence between racially different people around racial oppression. At the same time, acknowledging the shame experienced by many clinicians-in-training is a crucial beginning to understanding oppression and inequity. Such feelings are important and should be worked through as part of the multicultural training process (Parker & Schwartz, 2002).

CASE STUDY

CLIENT IDENTITIES

I routinely ask my students, during their psychosocial narrative assignment, to discuss any client identities that would present a challenge for them within a therapeutic encounter. I get a minority of students who admit to anticipating some difficulty working with someone who is mentally retarded, a sexual predator, or an elderly person. A few students have discussed their reluctance to work with someone who is a Nazi (blatantly racist) or who does not support women's egalitarianism (blatantly sexist or a traditional gender-conforming man or woman). For the most part, students indicate their willingness to essentially work with anyone, despite their characteristics. Part of this may be a desire to be open and accepting of all people. At the same time, building an awareness of oneself as a gendered, racial, and cultural being shaped by dominant race, gender, and sexuality discourses encourages multicultural competence. The maxim "Mental health professional, know thyself!" is still relevant.

QUESTIONS AND DISCUSSION

The following is a list of client identities. Take the role of therapist. Ask yourself the questions indicated. Then review the guidelines and competencies at the end of the chapter and, in small groups, add any others that apply.

1. **A woman actively committing adultery on her spouse and expressing no guilt or remorse**
   First, identify your feelings, then ask:
   a. If the client wept in therapy from feelings of guilt, would my feelings about working with the client change?
   b. If the woman had been cheated on initially by her husband, would my feelings about working with her change?
   c. If the husband had terminal cancer and had been given six months to live, would my feelings about working with the client change?
2. **A proud and out lesbian who is very feminine in dress and mannerisms**
   First, identify your feelings, then ask:
   a. If the client was less feminine (e.g., non-gender conforming) in appearance, would my attitude about working with her change?
   b. If the client was conflicted about her sexuality and felt guilty about her intimacies with women, would this impact me professionally?
3. **A man who will not allow his wife to work or leave the house without accompanying her**
   First, identify your feelings, then ask:
   a. If the wife supported her husband's position, would my feelings about working with her change?
   b. If the wife was very beautiful and attracted the attention of men whenever she left the house, would my feelings change about working with the husband?

(Continued)

(Continued)

4. **A pregnant mother who is abusing alcohol**
   First, identify your feelings, then ask:
   a. If the client's other children did not have fetal alcohol syndrome and she drank through her previous pregnancies, would my feelings about working with her change?
   b. If the client knew her baby had a genetic disorder and the child was most likely not going to survive after the first few days of life, would my attitude change?
   c. If the woman planned to give her child up for adoption to a caring and loving family who did not care how extensive the child's disabilities were, would my attitude about working with her change?

5. **A man on the down-low (in a heterosexual marriage but secretly having sex with other men)**
   First, identify your feelings, then ask:
   a. If the client's wife had a neurological disease which prevented her from being sexual with her husband, would my feelings change about working with him?
   b. If the client used condoms faithfully during sexual intercourse with men, would my attitude about his behavior change?
   c. If the client's wife had been badly burned in a house fire and was disfigured, would my feelings about the client's behavior change?

6. **A woman who is planning to leave her husband and two dependent children for another man**
   First, identify your feelings, then ask:
   a. If the client's husband had been beating her, would my feelings about her decision to leave her husband and children change?
   b. If the children were her stepchildren, would my attitude about her decision change?

7. **A man who announces he does not want to work with you because of your race**
   a. If the client had a negative experience in therapy with someone from my same racial group, would my attitude about working with him change?
   b. If the client was dealing with race-related issues that he needed to explore in therapy and he wanted a clinician of color who had expertise in this area, would my attitude about working with him change?

8. **A woman wants her African-born, school-age child tested for learning disabilities prior to finalizing the adoption**
   a. If the client had already adopted an African child with severe learning disabilities, would my attitude about her choice to do testing prior to the adoption change?
   b. If the child's biological mother was mentally retarded, would my attitude about working with her change?

Recommendations from *Guidelines and Competencies for Practice, Research, and Education* (APA, 2003)

1. Acknowledge your racial and/or cultural group's history in the oppression of other peoples.
2. Be able to recognize how your religious values affect your views about sex, drugs, death, marriage, and divorce.

3. Be aware of unearned able-body privilege and how this affects everything from driving, sexual activity, accessing buildings and mobility, and people's perceptions of another's attractiveness, intelligence, and moral character.

4. Know the limits of your multicultural expertise, and seek help when needed.

5. Acknowledge who is in your circle of friends, and if racial, sexual, and class diversity is lacking, ask yourself why you have been reluctant to develop friendships with people who are not like yourself.

6. Acknowledge feelings of guilt, shame, or resentment that arise as a function of your exposure to different types of diversity.

7. Realize that there are cultures that do not accept your attitudes about individuality, freedom, and women's rights—and they are not necessarily wrong or disadvantaged.

8. Ask yourself what the impact of your culture and ethnicity has been on your education, career, and/or mate choice.

9. Consider how much value you attach to consulting with healers who have not graduated from high school or did not go through a practicum or internship like you did.

10. Understand the potential bias of instruments and the cultural context in which they are normed.

Summary

This chapter offered an overview of multicultural competencies and skills. A brief review of diversity training programs for counselors in training was provided, as well as strategies for becoming a multiculturally competent counselor. The importance of attending to students' dissonance about their future multicultural effectiveness was discussed through Storytelling. The case study activity dealt with various counseling scenarios. The message was sent that identity profiles of our clients can be challenging and our feelings about these identities must not be ignored. We must acknowledge this exercise is not an assault on our professional identities but an opportunity to develop competence and overcome our fears of difference.

Statused Identities

*Efforts to prevent mental illness and promote mental health should build
on intrinsic community strengths such as spirituality, positive ethnic
identity, traditional values, educational attainment, and local leadership.*

MENTAL HEALTH: CULTURE, RACE, AND ETHNICITY.

US DEPARTMENT OF HEALTH AND HUMAN SERVICES

This chapter explores sources of human differences. The attitudes that mental health profession-als have about clients' identity constructs, particularly those that are visible, greatly impacts the therapeutic event. Via the Contextual and Social Construction of Differences Model, the social construction of identities within US society is conveyed. Implications for mental health profes-sionals and client populations are emphasized.

IDENTITIES AS STATUS: THE CONTEXTUAL AND SOCIAL CONSTRUCTION OF DIFFERENCES MODEL

Nearly 70 years ago, Hughes (1945), a sociologist, addressed dilemmas of occupational and ascribed status. He said that occupational or vocational status has a complex set of supplemen-tary characteristics that come to be expected of its incumbents. For example, it is anticipated that a kindergarten teacher will be a female. Such expectations are largely unconscious. People do not systematically expect that only certain people will occupy certain positions. Through a process of cultural socialization from the media, educational systems, clergy, and family, people "carry in their minds" the auxiliary traits associated with most positions in society. Persons who newly occupy prestigious positions contend with ongoing suspicions from those who have historically maintained these positions and from those who have observed such people occupying these positions. President Barack Obama contends with this dynamic. Chronic suspicions regarding his US citizenship, despite the presentation of his birth certificate, are largely race-based, although most of those who question his legitimacy would deny this.

At the base of people's thinking is the perception that new incumbents are not as qualified or worthy as those who preceded them and their incumbency is due primarily to affirmative action or other political processes, and not a result of qualifications, hard work, or merit. As new groups occupy positions that have been held almost exclusively by one racial and/or gender group, discourses do not completely disappear. Close proximity to dominant discourses means embodying a belief that quotas, unfairness, and luck are responsible for occupational success among people with stigmatized identities.

In the society about which Hughes spoke, race membership was a status-determining trait. Race tended to overpower any other variable that might run counter to it, such as educational attainment, a component of social class. Because racism, sexism, and homophobia are interlocking systems of oppression, membership in marginalized groups is associated with stigma. *Stigma* refers to "a bodily sign designed to expose something unusual and bad about the moral status of an individual" (Rosenblum & Travis, 2005, p. 27). Hughes's decades-old observations have contemporary relevance.

The **Model of Socially Constructed Discourses** suggests that human characteristics operate as status variables in society. (See Table 3.1.) The model maintains that in the United States race, gender, and class are socially constructed. From a constructionist perspective, these identities matter because society wants them to—this may not be right, but it is so. In both subtle and blatant ways, contextual and socially constructed discourses permit persons who hold membership in particular groups to have status within society, and this status makes them different from persons who do not hold membership in these groups. This stratification of race and other identities is a social construction—not an inevitability like the rising of the sun each day. (See Storytelling: *Colonizing Discourses* on page 49.)

Visible and invisible identities (e.g., race, gender, sexuality, religion, ability, and disability) are not oppressive. However, racism, colorism, sexism, homonegativity, able-body-ism, class elitism, and religious bigotry are oppressive and discriminatory (Robinson, 1999). A distinction exists between having an identity that is stigmatized (e.g., being a quadriplegic) and internalizing a sense of inadequacy or inferiority. The problem is discrimination against the disabled, not *being* disabled.

According to Reynolds and Pope (1991), a customary norm by which people are evaluated in the United States is based on proximity to being American. A discourse associated with being American is associated with Whiteness. Maleness, gender-conforming femininity, upper-middle class status, Christianity, heterosexuality, English-speaking, youthfulness, and mental/physical ability have been constructed to mean normativity. Economic exploitation, religious bias, homophobia, racism, able-bodyism, and other sources of discrimination emanate from this narrow and limiting construction of normalcy. The "other" refers to persons who are regarded as not only different from the norm but less than the norm.

TABLE 3.1 Model of Socially Constructed Discourses

Visible and Invisible Sources of Difference	Dominant Discourses	Consequences of Socially Constructed Meanings About Difference
Race	Whiteness is unexplored but is the basis by which people of color are evaluated.	Racism; obliviousness about one's status as a racial being, particularly among Whites
Skin color	White and white-looking skin is normative in ways that non-White skin is not.	Colorism
Sex	The masculine male experience is valued over women.	Sexism; unrealistic gendered expectations for women and men
Sexuality	Heterosexuality is valued over being gay, bisexual, lesbian, or transgendered.	Homonegativity
Ability	Physical and mental ability are esteemed and rewarded. Disability is an eventual reality for all people who are fortunate to grow old.	Ableism
Class	Upper-middle-class status is glamorized. Being working-class or poor is less valued.	Class elitism
Religion	Christianity is normative and privileged. Not having a religious orientation is devalued over non-Christian religions.	Religious bigotry

ASSUMPTIONS OF HIERARCHICAL SOCIALIZATION PATTERNS

The Model of Socially Constructed Discourses presents sources of differences as social constructions. The consequences of these social constructions are also detailed.

Sources of differences between and among people possess rank, have value, and function as primary status-determining traits. Characteristics perceived as normal are thought to be desired by and representative of all. For instance, students often have a difficult time understanding why a woman with a disability would not want to be able-bodied. Wouldn't her life be easier not having to deal with a scooter, walker, or wheelchair? Characteristics with less

Storytelling: Colonizing Discourses

A young woman was at the hairdresser. She and her stylist were talking about a popular singer who is African American. The stylist, also a young woman in her twenties, said, "She's pretty for a colored girl." The year was 2011 and the young woman who was having her hair done was shocked that this type of statement was made by a young person well into the 21st century. She was also surprised that the stylist used language that had not been used in over half a century to refer to African Americans.

rank (such as being old, or short, or fat) are held in lower esteem, are not regarded as desirable, and have less social power. Within this hierarchical framework, the most valued aspect of a person is not an achieved or acquired trait, such as compassion for others or being teachable, but an immutable quality, such as White skin.

Although human beings are more similar than they are different, a hierarchical framework, where differences have rank, inflates and distorts differences among people. In contrast, a system which honors our humanity deems people as worthy because they are alive and exist with "unique expressions of spiritual energy" (Myers et al., 1991, p. 56).

Racism

Racism involves a total social structure in which one group has conferred advantage over another group through institutional policies. **Racism** is a social construction based on sociopolitical attitudes that demean specific racial characteristics, as Pinderhughes (1989) makes clear:

> Racism raises to the level of social structure the tendency to use superiority as a solution to discomfort about difference. Belief in the superiority of Whites and the inferiority of people-of-color based on racial difference is legitimized by societal arrangements that exclude the latter from resources and power and then blame them for their failures, which are due to lack of access. (p. 89)

Discussing racism is unsettling and dissonance-provoking. White people are often reluctant to engage in dialogue about the realities of racism. Racism is a major part of this country's origins, but other terms can be used instead of racism, such as *manifest destiny*, *progress*, or *ambition*. Being committed to the process of transformation and social justice means not turning away from the truth. Ambition and racial exploitation should not be confused. Christopher Columbus was an ambitious explorer. He also ruthlessly exploited the Arawaks.

It has been said that America was built by taking land from a people and people from a land. Racially discriminatory practices were in progress when Africans built the infrastructure for major cities in the South and were not remunerated. White Americans perceived themselves as superior to Native Americans when, for centuries, they stole (there is no more appropriate term) the Native Americans' lands and destroyed their way of life. Americans behaved in a racist manner when scores of first- and second-generation Japanese Americans were interned during World War II. Small numbers of German and Italian Americans were interned also, but not to the same extent as were the Japanese. A racist ideology existed when the Southwest, which was once Mexico, was ceded to the United States by the Treaty of Guadalupe Hidalgo in 1848. People of Hispanic ancestry became "foreigners in their native land" that they had inhabited for centuries. A racist ideology existed when laws such as the 1882 Exclusion Act restricted Chinese from this country while White-skinned European immigrants flooded in. Racism was practiced when the 1790 Naturalization Law was in effect for 162 years; this policy reserved naturalized citizenship for Whites only (Avakian, 2002). There are current acts of violence and racism in countries we currently occupy, where children—who should never be held responsible for the actions and choices of adults—are vulnerable and live in fear. At various junctures in US history, laws forbade women across racial groups and men of color from voting, becoming literate, marrying White people, becoming educated at all-White institutions, owning property, working, and drinking water from public facilities. Such policies attested to the institutionalization of racism and sexism as blatant devaluations of women and non-White people. "The rationale of segregation implies that the 'others' are a pariah people. Unclean was the caste message of every colored water fountain, waiting room, and courtroom Bible" (Loewen, 1995, p. 163).

Racist attitudes portrayed in sentiments against racial intermixing were not simply between races but within ethnic groups as well. In the Nazi publication *Neues Volk*, it was written, "Every German and every German woman has the duty to avoid association with other races, especially Slavs. Each intimacy with a people of inferior race means sinning against the future of our own people" (cited in Rogers, 1967, p. 19).

Scientific notions about intelligence were developed against a biological and socio-political backdrop of racism. In *The Bell Curve*, Herrnstein and Murray (1994) examined ethnic differences on intelligence tests. They concluded that "for every known test of cognitive ability that meets basic psychometric standards of reliability and validity, Blacks and Whites score differently" (p. 276). These authors indicated that the differences are reduced once the testing is done outside the South, after age six, and after 1940. Herrnstein and Murray argued that even once socioeconomic differences are controlled for, the differences do not disappear, but class may reduce the overall differences in intelligence testing by about one third.

Grubb (1992) investigated the claim that Blacks are genetically inferior to Whites on intelligence testing. As a clinical psychologist specializing in the treatment of childhood and adolescent disorders, he examined 6,742 persons with developmental disabilities from three western states. If this argument that Blacks were genetically inferior to Whites was true, then he could expect to see a higher proportion of Blacks identified as having mental retardation, in comparison with Whites. Grubb found that, of the total population included in this project, 0.03% had developmental disabilities. This figure was consistent across racial groups. He concluded that the assumptions regarding heredity among the Black race were not upheld in this study, leading him to reject this line of reasoning.

Nisbett (1995) also challenged Herrnstein and Murray (1994). Nisbett argued that comparing high socioeconomic status (SES) Blacks with high-SES Whites is inherently flawed, given the higher income levels of Whites in comparison with Blacks. In addition, Nisbett stated that socialization and social factors affect ability levels. Claims by Jensen and other authors stating that "g-loaded" (g refers to general intelligence) tests differed between the races, with Whites having faster reaction times on complex maneuvers, was subjectively interpreted. According to Nisbett, "For skills such as spatial reasoning and form perception, the g-loading was relatively low and B/W gap relatively low" (p. 44).

During slavery, an institution steeped in dysfunction and deceit, two forms of psychopathology were common among slaves. The first, drapetomania, consisted of the single symptom of slaves running away. The second, dysathesia aethiopica, consisted of numerous conditions such as destroying plantation property, showing defiance, and attacking the slave masters. This second condition was also known as "rascality," and both were labeled as nerve disorders by reputable physicians (Bronstein & Quina, 1988). Liberty and the pursuit of happiness are explicit in this nation's charter, yet the desire for these entitlements among Blacks during slavery was regarded as pathological. Black people took care of White people, yet they were depicted as childlike, incapable of providing for themselves, and dependent on their benevolent White masters. Clinicians of the day interpreted 1840 census data that reported higher rates of psychopathology among Blacks to support the belief that "the care, supervision, and control provided by slavery were essential to the mental health of Blacks" (Bronstein & Quina, 1988, p. 39). This paradigm supported a false belief that Blacks were not only different but inferior. It was not possible to receive an accurate diagnosis when the psychological community perceived Black people to be chattel and inherently flawed. The current distrust of the mental health community in many communities of color cannot be adequately appreciated without an understanding of this history.

CONSEQUENCES OF RACISM FOR EUROPEAN AMERICANS   Racism, patriarchy, and classism are interlocking systems of both oppression and privilege (Landry, 2007). They operate in tandem with privilege and/or disadvantage people based on how they are socially situated with respect to immutable characteristics (race and sex). There are consequences of racism for people of color (e.g., stress, high blood pressure, disparities in access to health care). There are also consequences for Whites (Pinderhughes, 1989). The lie about racism is that White people are not affected, only non-White people. How can there not be consequences, given the pernicious nature of racism that affects all people?

Due to the social construction of whiteness in American society, White people lack understanding about the effects and consequences of race and racism on their own lives, due largely to "race," typically referring to non-White people. Not having an identity as a racial being contributes to misperceptions among Whites about the reality of racism, racial inequities, and discrimination against people of color. More White Americans than people of color believe there is equity for Blacks and Whites in this country and that Blacks are as well off as Whites in terms of jobs, incomes, health care, and schooling (Institute of Medicine, 2003). (See Storytelling: *It Had To Be You*.)

One way to facilitate a discussion of racism is through an examination of unearned White skin color privilege. McIntosh (1989) maintained that privilege is an invisible knapsack of assets an entitled group can refer to on a regular basis to negotiate their daily lives more effectively. Unearned skin-color privilege is a fugitive (McIntosh, 1989) subject for two reasons. First, privilege is something people are meant to be oblivious about. Second, non-Whites do not share in the privileges Whites take for granted but did not earn. Unpacking privilege produces dissonance among many Whites because it assails fundamental Western beliefs of meritocracy and justice while creating confusion about the meaning of being qualified and successful.

One consequence of racism for European Americans is that it limits emotional and intellectual development (Pinderhughes, 1989). Zetzer (2005) discussed her desire not to be a WMWP, or a well-meaning White person—defined as a White person who does not understand

Storytelling: It Had To Be You

A Black woman was at a park near her home. She sat with other parents as her pre-school age child played in the busy playground with other children. The woman soon learned that one of the mothers in the park could not locate her cell phone. The woman was asked if she had seen the lost phone. She replied no. She was asked this question repeatedly by the friends of the mother who could not locate her cell phone. The Black woman soon realized that the inquiries were accusations: they thought she had stolen the phone. Afraid for her and her young child's safety, the woman scooped up her daughter and proceeded quickly to her car. The woman of the lost phone and her friends began following the woman and her daughter, accusing her of stealing the phone. One of them said, "Use my phone to call your number—when it rings, we'll *know* she has it." The number of the lost/stolen cell phone was rung and a little tune was heard. The phone was in the pocket of its owner. No apologies were offered to the Black woman and her daughter who lived in the predominantly white neighborhood. Due to discourses about Blackness, the woman, a college professor, was perceived to be guilty of theft.

the social construction of race, the impact of daily racism on people of color, and their role in the perpetuation of inequity.

A growing area of research deals with the psychosocial costs of racism to Whites. Spanierman, Poteat, Beer, and Armstrong (2007) conducted research with 230 White undergraduate students using the Psychosocial Costs of Racism to Whites (PCRW) scale, with three subscales:

1. White Empathic Reactions toward Racism, such as sadness and anger
2. White Guilt
3. White Fear of Others

Five distinct cluster groups were also identified:

A. Unempathic and unaware
B. Empathic but unaccountable
C. Informed empathy and guilt
D. Fearful guilt
E. Insensitive and afraid

Spanierman et al. (2007) regard cluster C at the most desirable because participants had the greatest levels of racial awareness (lowest scores on the Color Blind Racial Attitude Scale (COBRAs) by Neville et al, 2000). This finding was interpreted as an understanding of institutionalized racism. Furthermore, these researchers see guilt as "not necessarily undesirable" (p. 439). Accountable guilt coexists with empathy and might predict antiracist activism. In more recent research, Spanierman, Todd, and Anderson (2009) conducted research with 287 White University freshmen. They found that appreciation of diversity and a critical consciousness of White privilege were both important for understanding the psychosocial cost of racism to Whites. Diversity appreciation was associated with more desirable PCRW types whereas being unaware of racial privilege was linked to types considered to be less desirable.

The consequences of racism in people's lives may be invisible, as are skin-color privileges. Two conditions might intensify obliviousness to unearned privilege. There is a lack of aware-ness about the circumstances that entitle groups to privileges. In addition, people have difficulty grasping that others who do not share immutable group membership also do not share privileges. *Non-seeing* can translate into reduced empathy during the therapeutic encounter. Mental health professionals are severely limited in their effectiveness when they are unable to empathize, as empathy is the most fundamental tool in counseling.

All of us have membership in groups that we have chosen: the gym, university, profes-sional organizations, families, etc. Each of us also has memberships that are not chosen but are nonetheless desired, (e.g., ability, race, gender). Social justice recognizes that people choose how to respond to earned and unearned privileges and will use privilege in its various forms to address disparities.

McIntosh (1989) identified several privileges that enabled her to negotiate her daily existence more effectively. She could choose not to teach her children about race or racism if teaching it would cause them some discomfort. The growing numbers of White women who are mothering non-White children are finding that this privilege is not afforded to them (Robinson, 2010). She could move to almost any neighborhood, confident that she would be treated well and welcomed (low-wage earning White people do not have this choice). She also knew that her children would be given school curricular materials that testified to the existence of their race.

Clearly there are benefits of privilege. Not having skin-color privilege does not leave a person bereft of hope, love, or moral fiber. This point is illuminated in the 2001 film *Honey for*

Ochun. The primary character is a Cuban man whose father lied to him and said his mother had abandoned him when he was a child. In truth, the father took the boy from his mother and brought him to Florida. As a man, he returns to Cuba in search of his mother, a dark-skinned Cuban woman who is portrayed in the movie as having lower class status. The colorism in the movie is evident but is a subtle aspect of the film. The man's persistence is rewarded as he finds his mother in a remote part of Cuba off of a little lake. The mother was committed to the truth. She knew she had not abandoned her son and believed that she would see her son again. Despite the colorism and class elitism, she resisted. Resistance refers to recognizing demeaning messages and replacing them with messages that empower.

Patriarchy

Patriarchy comes from a hegemonic or a ruling ideology (Rosenblum & Travis, 2005), wherein men have advantage conferred on them because of their prescribed rank or societal status. During the more than four decades of the women's movement, there have been increases in the college attainment rates of women and dramatic increases among women in the workforce. In fact, women under 25 are on par with men in labor participation. Amid these and other advances, gender inequity continues. In the United States, men earn $1.00 to women's $0.77, with $0.68 for Black women and $0.58 for Latinas (Fitzpatrick, 2010).

Patriarchy is intertwined with power and privilege. The ascribed status of sex is elevated as a primary status trait over achieved status. This system is inherently unjust. Biological sex is not chosen but is an extremely powerful determinant of how people are treated. Both women and men are necessary for society's maintenance, yet through an elaborate gender socialization process, expectations and behaviors are disseminated and internalized. These socialization practices, both blatant and subtle, maintain a system not only in the United States but in other countries throughout the world, where women are not as advantaged because of their less prominent status as females. Haider (1995) viewed this phenomenon globally and historically:

> In many cultures, the notion of male dominance—of man as woman's "god," protector and provider—and the notion of women as passive, submissive, and chaste have been the predominant images for centuries. In many cases, customary practices have been based on a pecking order that has not always been conducive to the well-being and personal development of those lower down the status line. (p. 53)

One consequence of patriarchy for men is that it contributes to a skewed emotional existence. Difficulty with experiencing and expressing a full range of emotions, such as fear, vulnerability, and uncertainty, is an outcome of patriarchy and a dichotomizing system that is polarizing. Patriarchy is a system of wide-scale inequity to which many people, including women, are oblivious.

Given the potential disadvantages of patriarchy for men, are there possible benefits of patriarchy for women? Patriarchy has its genesis in injustice. If any benefits of patriarchy result for women, they are temporary and elusive, primarily because the benefits would be dictated by women's adherence to the parameters of patriarchy and their compliance with subscribed gender roles. Does equality for women apply primarily to those women who subscribe to at least some but not to too many of the characteristics associated with masculinity (e.g., self-sufficiency, assertiveness, competition)? According to Bem (1993), any such benefits accorded to women are most likely a by-product of androcentrism, or male-centeredness, in which the male standard prevails.

In American society, men generally benefit over women. Male privileges do not bestow power on all men, but they ultimately deny all women. In fact, one benefit of the Men's movement is that it has called attention to the myth that women's powerlessness translates into men's power. Individual men may feel powerful, but not all men do. Swanson (1993) recognized this as the "new sexism" and noted, "Some men, rather than feeling like patriarchs, often feel like workhorses, harnessed with the burden of being family provider, trying to pull the family wagon up a muddy hill of financial debt" (p. 12). Men are conditioned to be providers, protectors, and ready for combat, yet they experience pressure from women to be nurturing, soft, and intimate (Skovholt, 1993). These messages are conflicting. Part of being a protector is not asking for help or appearing to be vulnerable, which is what intimacy and nurturance entail.

Many White men, men of color, or poor, disabled, old, and/or gay men do not share the same privileges that some economically privileged, able-bodied, and/or heterosexual men do. Thus, all men do not perceive a sense of personal power in that they do not possess crucial markers that society deems normative and valued. The presence of these critical markers does not ensure that individual men will automatically feel powerful. Because of the underlying assumption that persons who share gender are monolithic, use of the phrase *men in general* is problematic (Carrigan, Connell, & Lee, 1987). Making inappropriate attributions regarding clients' identity constructs is called a *miss*—for example, assuming a woman with a visible facial disability feels unattractive and is lacking in self-esteem.

Sexism

The women's movement challenged many traditional stereotypes about women, their work, and their place in society. That women wanted equal pay for equal work, respect in a society that too often reduced them to sexual objects, and denied them choice about their bodies and minds was the message echoed across numerous platforms. Women were encouraged to consider seriously the socialization experiences that contributed to their reliance on others for their emotional and financial well-being. **Sexism**, an institutionalized system of inequity based on biological sex, was brought to the nation's attention. Bem (1993), author of the Bem Sex Role Inventory, maintained that androcentrism responds to men as human and to women as other. Men thus enjoy certain privileges that women do not.

Another identity construct that can mitigate the privileges that certain groups have is sexuality. Some of the privilege associated with maleness has a qualifier of heterosexuality. Gay men who are "out" are vulnerable to experiencing violence from a homophobic society in the form of discrimination and physical aggression. Despite the disadvantages, being gay does not cancel privileges associated with being male or being White. Within a society where White skin is associated with unearned privilege, gay White men mediate the effects of homophobia with their White skin. Gay men of color receive male privilege yet contend with both racism and homophobia (Loiacano, 1989).

CONSEQUENCES OF SEXISM FOR MEN   Racism contributes to a dehumanizing stance and limits human development for people regardless of their race and ethnicity (Pinderhughes, 1989). Sexism adversely affects all people, men and transgender people included. The male gender role often results in men being restricted in their emotional expressiveness and promotes a limited range of behaviors available to them. "Restrictive emotionality involves the reluctance and/or difficulty men have in expressing their feelings to other people and may be related to their hesitancy to seek help from others" (Good, Dell, & Mintz, 1989, p. 295). Men are gendered and influenced by rigid and sexist discourses. They are oriented toward success, competition, and the need to be in control (Robinson, 1999). The danger in the male role is that it has been connected to "Type A" behavior patterns and to depression (Good & Mintz, 1990).

Homophobia

Homophobia emanates from the perception of homosexuality as an aberration of the correct social order. Discourses about gay people are that they are promiscuous, can be marked according to mannerisms and dress, are sexually aberrant, and are not to be trusted around young children.

CONSEQUENCES OF HOMOPHOBIA FOR HETEROSEXUALS   Men who engage in behaviors deemed "feminine" are suspected of being gay by other men and by women as well. One of the teachings of traditional masculinity is that anything associated with femininity is anathema. Heterosexual men may feel real fear in expressing physical affection with another man because of connotations of homosexuality. This concern may explain why upon greeting one another American men engage in roughhousing, evidenced by vigorous slaps on the back. Such behavior, however, is culturally dictated. In Ghana or in Egypt, for example, it is quite natural to see men holding hands while walking together. European men are often more demonstrative in their affectionate behavior. Affection and endearment, and their cultural expressions, support this behavior. In the United States, similar behavior might be interpreted as an indication of homosexuality.

Homophobia also interferes with the formation of cross-sexual orientation friendships out of fear that such interaction and proximity would be misinterpreted by others. In this context, heterosexual counselors can be inhibited in their ability to be allies to gay, lesbian, bisexual, transgender, intersexual, and questioning (GLBTIQ) clients.

Able-Bodyism

People with disabilities have a long history of being discriminated against. An understanding of this type of discrimination is enhanced by an assessment of the "mastery-over-fate" orientation descriptive of American society. The US culture places inordinate emphasis on youth and fitness and demonstrates a marked preoccupation with the body beautiful. A disability is seen as an imperfection, which is contrary to the culturally sanctioned values of control (fixing that which is broken or imperfect, overcoming, and domination).

Smart and Smart (2006) argue that the conceptualization of disability as "an attribute located solely within an individual is changing to a paradigm in which disability is thought to be an interaction among the individual, the disability, and the environment (both social and physical)" (p. 29). Despite this observation, a clear bias in favor of the able-bodied exists. Because most buildings have been constructed for able-bodied persons, persons without disabilities are often oblivious to their unearned privileges. How much thought do able-bodied people give to the accessibility of a house or other buildings? Having disabled friends or family in our lives, being temporarily disabled (e.g., after foot surgery), or negotiating sidewalks, narrow aisles, and closed doors with children in a stroller increases awareness. Architectural space and design are outgrowths of cultural attitudes and assumptions that are biased against the old and persons with disabilities (particularly women). As Weisman (1992) pointed out:

> Placement in barrier-free housing and rehabilitation services favors men...Disabled women are not usually thought of as wives and mothers who often manage households with children and husbands. The wheelchair-accessible two- and three-bedroom unit is a rarity. (p. 118)

The myth that people with disabilities are childlike, dependent, and depressed contributes to ignorance from the larger society and denial about the fact that, at any time, able-bodied people can and probably will become disabled if they live long enough. Multiculturally competent professionals have the ability to regard clients with disabilities as whole human beings wherein the disability is understood as a component of identity and not the entire focus of the counseling event or an exhaustive account of the client's essence (Fowler, O'Rourke, Wadsworth, & Harper, 1992). Facility at holding the client's multiple spiritual, occupational, sexual, and social identities is commentary about the professional's moral and ego development and multicultural competence.

CONSEQUENCES OF ABLE-BODYISM AMONG THE ABLE-BODIED   Society was created for persons who are able-bodied. Our society of concrete sidewalks and curbs is uninviting to persons with temporary and permanent disabilities.

Discourses abound regarding people with disabilities. One of the most pernicious is that persons with disabilities desire to be able-bodied. This mistaken belief is similar to the belief that people of color desire to be White or that women desire to be men. Equating the experience of having a disability with living a lesser life is problematic for two reasons in counseling and psychology. First, such an attitude does not embody the spirit of multicultural competence which embraces diversity in its many forms. Second, this attitude is psychologically restrictive for able-bodied persons. Clearly, having a disability in an able-bodied world can deflate a sense of self and depress self-esteem (Livneh & Sherwood, 1991), yet this is not the experience of all persons with disabilities.

Class Elitism

Much of the formal training counselors receive in traditional counselor education programs emanates from a middle-class bias. This bias is characterized by emphasis on meritocracy, the Protestant work ethic, Standard English, and 50-minute sessions (Sue & Sue, 1990). The difficulty with this type of partiality is that it can alienate counselors from poor clients. According to Liu and Arguello (2006, p. 9), no standard for training about social class and classism exists in counselor training. Because of this dearth, it is important that counselors in training seek out supervised experiences that allow them to explore their beliefs and attitudes about social class.

Persons who have limited access to material wealth in a materialistic culture are not perceived as being as viable as those with greater resources. Within our capitalistic culture, a dangerously close relationship exists between self-worth and income. The poor, regardless of their work ethic, tend to be perceived as being lazy and even immoral (Gans, 1992). Conversely, the rich are esteemed and admired, often independent of their moral or immoral conduct.

The relationship between class and power is dubious. Low-income status (even if the individuals in question are hard working) is not valued by a consumeristic society, and having membership in this devalued group can provoke feelings of powerlessness and depression (Pinderhughes, 1989). (See Storytelling: *Not Worth More*.)

CONSEQUENCES OF CLASS ELITISM   Because socioeconomic class converges with gender, race, ability, and personal power, as well as other identity constructs, it is simplistic to conclude that being able-bodied or male or having a high income is automatically associated with feelings of safety and security, a lesser tendency toward depression, and less pain. It is a mistake to assume that having membership in groups deemed by society to be high status is related to feeling more powerful.

Ageism

Ageism refers to discrimination against people because of their age. This discrimination is often aimed at the middle-aged or the elderly. Ageist terms vary and include primarily negative expressions. Examples are *crotchety*, *fuddy-duddy*, *fart*, *senility*, *golden-ager*, *graybeard*, and *Lawrence Welk generation*—this last phrase admittedly dated (Nuessel, 1982). Atkinson and Hackett (1995) stated that "delineating the elderly as being 65 and over is a purely arbitrary separation" (p. 192). This boundary's genesis is the decades-old Social Security system, which was instituted in 1935, when people did not live as long as they now do.

Ageism is compounded with other layers of discrimination. Until very recently, limited attention had been devoted to the study of breast cancer. On the surface, this lack of focus could be attributed to sexism; however, ageism is also at fault. Does the fact that the majority of women survivors of breast cancer are not in their twenties or thirties but rather in their forties and fifties contribute to the limited (but growing) research on this disease? Counselors and psychologists need to be aware of the consequences of intersecting layers of discrimination on their efficacy.

Storytelling: Not Worth More

I was speaking with my 26-year-old babysitter who was dog sitting and had several babysitting jobs in order to raise money for graduate school that was start in a few months. She told me of an opportunity to puppy-sit over a 24-hour period. I asked her how much money she was going to be making. She said she did not know. I suggested that she contact the owner of the puppy and ask. Not to do so was to depend on the pet owner's good graces as opposed to stating up front what she wanted to earn. We spoke about the difficulty women often have negotiating for pay in contrast with men, who engage in this practice quite frequently. I told her that some people will take advantage of women by paying them much less than what they would pay a man. My sitter called the woman and said that she wanted $5.00 an hour for the 24-hour period. The puppy had a special dog food that needed to be administered by hand and had to be let out twice nightly to potty. The puppy's owner initially agreed but a few minutes later called back and said that the young woman was asking for too much money. Instead she wanted to offer $50.00 for the entire 24-hour period, or about $2.00 an hour. The young woman decided to just stay about four hours with the dog, earning $5.00 an hour (i.e., all the owners would offer and the young woman needed the money). She could not believe how little the owner wanted to pay her. She said that she felt proud of herself for asking for what she wanted and would approach future jobs by clearly stating her salary requirements up front.

Elders ought not to be treated as monoliths. Doing so greatly impedes the delivery of effective services. Differences exist between a 65-year-old healthy person and a 90-year-old whose health has begun to decline. Atkinson and Hackett (1995) described the "young-old" and the "old-old" (p. 14). The young-old are in fairly good health with stable financial supports. The old-old are experiencing deficits in several psychological, physical, social, and financial resources.

Mental health professionals need to be mindful of the social supports available to the elderly client. Solid social supports with both friends and family can help elders to feel less dependent on others. Part of a counselor's assessment should be an examination of an elder's level of involvement in meaningful and purposeful social activity. The elder's sense of personal autonomy or control over life is also an important component of overall wellness. Some illnesses, such as Alzheimer's disease, will require working in sync with other caregivers to maximize the quality of living during a stressful and potentially chaotic time. Age biases contribute to some counselors seeing little merit in providing psychotherapy to aging persons. For example, one weakness of psychoanalytic theory is that it is not generally regarded as viable when started with persons aged 50 or older or for low-wage-earning people. Identifying a client's strengths, regardless of the presenting problem, is a crucial step in facilitating growth or bolstering coping abilities.

CONSEQUENCES OF AGEISM FOR THE NON-ELDERLY   Unlike most traditional cultures in which the elderly tend to be respected and valued, in the US culture, inordinate emphasis is placed on youthfulness. The societal significance attached to doing, productivity, and maintaining mastery over nature may explain this cultural preoccupation with youth and the herculean effort to defy and, in some instances, deny or defeat aging. Aging appears to be viewed as a loss of control and of diminishing power and beauty. Discrimination against a segment of the population that is composing a higher percentage of the total and of which all will be members, if they are fortunate, culminates in fear-based discourses about the experience of being an elder. It is heartening to see how a culture of menopausal women is redefining hot flashes as power surges and recognizing the "change" in life as a time of ascendancy and coming into one's own.

IMPLICATIONS FOR COUNSELORS AND PSYCHOLOGISTS

Not acknowledging the meaning of race can restrict the development of a racial self. This lack of clarity about a core identity construct adversely affects clinicians' empathy toward their clients. Counselors must also ascertain whether they are able to work effectively with a variety of clients. (See Case Study: *The Difference Class Makes*.) Despite an espoused value of diversity, American society socializes people into attitudes that are not honoring of difference. Professionals need to recognize these and other biases within themselves and not allow shame or guilt to fan denial. The process of unlearning these attitudes is ongoing, but it is possible.

Although professionals have an ethical obligation to refer clients to other professionals when they are unable to provide necessary assistance, the counselor who is highly judgmental of a White woman involved in an interracial relationship needs to be concerned if intolerance in one area of her life extends to persons who, for example, do not belong to her religious affiliation.

CASE STUDY

THE DIFFERENCE CLASS MAKES

Ms. Mary Cain is a 47-year-old unmarried White woman who resides in Massachusetts and lives in subsidized housing. She has a history of drug use but has been sober for a few years. Her 31-year-old daughter Ruby resides with her but was recently arrested for her fourth DUI and writing bad checks. Ruby does not work and is an alcoholic. Ruby's two teenage daughters, ages 14 and 16, reside in the home with their mother and grandmother. The 16-year-old has a three-year-old daughter, and the 14-year-old is pregnant. Ms. Cain was referred to a mental health agency by her doctor after he noticed her weight loss, insomnia, and other depressive symptoms. Ms. Cain presents to counseling 20 minutes late with her great-granddaughter. She travels to counseling via public transportation. She missed the first two counseling sessions she had scheduled with Julie; State policy does not allow agencies to charge a late fee to patients who receive the state's free behavioral health care (MassHealth). The therapist, Julie, is a 28-year-old Black Ph.D. student in Clinical Psychology. Julie was raised in a working-class family. Both of her parents are phlebotomists. Upon meeting Ms. Cain, Julie warmly refers to her as Mary. After the initial intake questions were asked and answered, Julie asked Mary if she was losing weight because she was depressed about her daughter's unemployment and addiction, as well as her grandchildren having children at such young ages. Ms. Cain responded, "I like a big family and my grandchildren are a blessing to me. I've lost my teeth but I want to eat. What I need is a dentist, but I don't have dental insurance." Ms. Cain has almost no teeth remaining. Julie asked, "Your place of employment does not provide dental insurance?" Ms. Cain replied, "I get public assistance and disability. With it, I take good care of my family." Julie suggested that Mary reduce her sugar intake and buy Ensure drinks so that she could receive nutrition in liquid form. Julie observes that Mary's great-grandchild is obese and has decaying teeth—Ms. Cain said affectionately, "She loves her bottle of fruit punch and macaroni sandwiches at night-night." Later, Julie tells her supervisor during supervision that she feels ineffective with this population and does not want to work with them once she is done with practicum. When asked why, she said "They have so many problems and they continue to make choices that worsen their situations. Really, what are they trying to do to help themselves? And when they don't show up, that's my time wasted and the agency can't even bill her for missing a session. I swear, I will not take 'Mass Health' once I'm licensed."

QUESTIONS

1. Why is Julie so reluctant to work with Ms. Cain and other poor people?
2. What are dominant discourses concerning people who are poor that contribute to Julie's desire not to work with the poor?
3. Does multicultural practice speak to Julie's disdain for working with the poor?
4. If Julie chose to work in a private agency where clients paid out of pocket for their mental health services because they could afford it, does this mean she is not committed to social justice?
5. Would a cultural assessment be of assistance to Julie in her work with Ms. Cain?

(Continued)

(Continued)

DISCUSSION AND INTEGRATION

The Counselor, Julie

There are some discourses that Julie espouses that disparage multicultural competency. One discourse is that in America, people have the freedom to impact their economic lives as they so choose. Another discourse is that people have the power to change not only their own economic outlooks but those of their children. Another discourse is that poor people are a burden, are difficult, and are not ideal patients due to the enormity of their problems. Julie believes in and values the myth of meritocracy. In her worldview, everyone starts at the same place with the same resources, privileges, and opportunities. Julie does not understand the multigenerational impact of systems on people and the psychological processes that can accompany systems, such as resignation, depression, hopelessness, or patterning one's life after other family members. Growing up with parents who worked very hard, often having two jobs at the same, Julie developed a consciousness of the societal inequities that exists due to class, skin color, gender, body size, age, and more. She was taught that if you want something, you have to go after it by getting a good education and keeping your nose clean. Although privilege keeps people oblivious to the ways in which immutable characteristics are rewarded and discriminated against. Julie is oblivious to the enduring impact of poverty intergenerationally, particularly among those who do not utilize education as a means to change one's class status. A prevailing discourse is those who find themselves in chronic poverty have themselves to blame for their lot in life. Julie defines life as being in control over one's fate, delaying gratification, making wise decisions, including when to bring a child into the world and choosing the most nutritious meals, irrespective of the cost. Julie has little patience for people who are not on time (regardless of the reasons). She also believes that having to depend on state assistance is an embarrassment. Julie seems to believe that mental health is a privilege that low income people should not have access to, and if they do have access to it, Julie is not the type of clinician to provide care. There is a fundamental lack of empathy and regard for Mary's strengths: sobriety, caring for her family, and commitment to therapy (evident through her travels via public transportation with a toddler in tow). With quality supervision, multicultural competence, as well as some life crises (sometimes a person can do all the right things and the undesirable still happens), Julie could learn to confront her biases about the poor and became an effective clinician for people across class statuses. Although a disconcerting thought, it is possible for students to have taken the one required diversity class, even in a doctoral program, without ever exploring their class elitism, power, and privilege. Those students who "made it out" of poverty may have the most difficult time extending empathy to people who are in poverty,

The Client, Mary

Mary typifies the chronic poor. It is possible to look at her life and say, "Well, if she would just learn a skill, she could get a decent paying job, and earn an income that would get her off of welfare—doing so would help not only Mary but her children, grandchildren, and great-grandchildren." Mary is actively caring for three generations of family members despite her history of drug abuse, singlehood, and poverty; she is able to love and hope despite a history of adversity and oppression.

By looking at the age of Mary's daughter, it is clear that Mary was a teenage parent like her daughter and granddaughters. Teenage parents are not likely to complete the education required to qualify for a well-paying job. They are also likely to be poor and to remain poor (National Campaign to Prevent Teen Pregnancy, 2010). Increasingly women and girls are represented among those incarcerated and yet, as Trotman Reid (2011) observes, policy has done little to offer hope for rehabilitation. A therapist needs to address the totality of Mary's life, not just a narrow focus on poverty, addiction, teenage pregnancy, obese children, and tooth decay. Mary needs to be seen as a client worthy of service. Instead of regarding Mary as pathetic, her commitment to a family that depends on her and her delight in her children, grandchildren, and great-grandchildren need to be considered.

A cultural assessment that encourages Julie to think about the contextual issues in Mary's life would be helpful to her. Mary is the provider for her entire family, yet her resources are limited. Mary experiences class elitism in a society that blames poor people for not being better off, Thus far, Julie is vulnerable to reproducing within the therapeutic event the dynamic of oppression that many marginalized groups endure on a daily basis (Comstock et al., 2008).

Summary

In this chapter, the presentation of human differences as status variables was explored through an examination of the Contextual and Social Construction of Differences Model. Hughes's (1945) work on the dilemmas and contradictions of status was also useful. The consequences of hierarchical socialization were presented, and the advantages of a model based on cultural pluralism were envisioned. The importance of counselors recognizing systems of inequity was articulated, and a case study allowed readers to apply the ideas presented.

Native Americans and Alaskan Natives

> *Snowflakes, leaves, humans, plants, raindrops, stars, molecules,*
> *microscopic entities all come in communities. The singular cannot*
> *in reality exist.*
>
> PAULA GUNN ALLEN

Harmony and Balance

Native American and *Alaskan Native* refer to people having origins in any of the original peoples of North and South America (including Central America) and who maintain tribal affiliation or community attachment (US Census Bureau, 2000). The origins of Native American/Alaskan Native people have been greatly debated. One of the most insightful theories regarding the people who occupied the New World was proposed by José de Acosta, a 16th century Spanish

Jesuit missionary. He theorized that North America, which was a continent clearly separate from Asia, had been settled before the birth of Christ by a group of hunters and their families who, in following animal herds, passed overland via an ancient land bridge that had formerly connected Asia to the Americas (cited in Hoxie, 1996). Anthropologists agree with de Acosta's theory. The debate rages over timing issues, as to whether the first people arrived in America more than or less than 15,000 years ago. DNA studies comparing Native Americans with other population groups found three distinct genetic mutations in Mongolia and Siberia, which suggests a separation as early as 30,000 years ago. It is widely accepted that the first Americans arrived in North America by way of the Bering Strait Land Bridge, or Beringia. Temporary ice melts for several thousand years most likely created natural passageways in the ice sheets for large game and their spear-wielding human predators (Waldman, 2000).

Native American Creation stories tell of being brought into existence by the Great Spirit or having come from the womb of Mother Earth. In writing of these origins, Gunn Allen (1994) honored Woman:

> There is a spirit that pervades everything, that is capable of powerful song and radiant movement, and that moves in and out of the mind. The colors of this spirit are multitudinous, a glowing, pulsing rainbow. Old Spider Woman is one name for this quintessential spirit, and Earth Woman is another, and what they together have made is called Creation, Earth, creatures, plants, and light. (p. 13)

HISTORY

It is estimated that in 1492, when Christopher Columbus arrived in the New World, there were approximately 1 million inhabitants within the continental United States (Russell, 1994). Columbus mistakenly thought he had landed in India and thus referred to the Native people as "Indios." The different European languages represented pronounced the word as "Indien" or "Indianer" (Brown, 1981).

The treatment of Native Americans and Alaskan Natives in the United States has been disgraceful. Within 400 years after the Europeans' arrival, the Native population had been decimated by wars, starvation, slavery, genocide, and disease, with typhus, smallpox, and measles being the greatest killers (Vernon, 2002). In 1790, the enactment of federal policies with the goal of displacing Native people began. The Bureau of Indian Affairs (BIA), which today is responsible for the United States' relationship with the 565 federally recognized Native American tribes and Alaskan communities, was created in 1824. The job of Thomas McKenney, the first director of the BIA, was to manage Native schools and administer Native trade. For many tribes, the BIA represented betrayal and broken promises. One Native person remarked, "They made us many promises, more than I can remember, but they never kept but one; they promised to take our land, and they took it" (Brown, 1981).

The Indian Removal Act of 1830 was enacted under the leadership of Andrew Jackson, the seventh president of the United States. This Act was intended to relocate Indians to a new Indian country west of the Mississippi (Hoxie, 1996; Russell, 1994). America's defeat of the British during the War of 1812 had helped create a nation with little concern for European alliances. The annexation of Spanish Florida in 1819 contributed to America's perception of Indians as hindrances to the expansionist interests of the millions of White European immigrants to America. The cultural and psychological violence aimed at Native Americans is evident in Jackson's Second Annual Message to Congress, given shortly after he became the president of the United States. In this message he announced the benevolent policy of the government with respect to Native people and its aims. Ultimately this policy removed Native people from Mississippi and the western part of Alabama, which according to Jackson would "enable those states to advance rapidly in population, wealth, and power." The policy was seen as kindly and Godly, saving Native people from themselves and allowing them to "cast off their savage habits and become an interesting, civilized, and Christian community." Jackson considered this act of removal to be benevolent because the government was funding the relocation. To the Native people, it was their "trail of tears" or the westward herding of the "Five Civilized Tribes" (Cherokees, Chickasaws, Choctaws, Creeks, and Seminoles) to Oklahoma. During the cold and brutal winter, people traveled by foot, horseback, wagon, and steamboat. They were hungry, cold, and sick, and hundreds died from starvation, exhaustion, disease, exposure, and accidents (Brown, 1981; Hoxie, 1996). Native resistance to removal was fierce, but their oppressors were opportunistic and destructive. For example, in New Echota, the capital of the Cherokee nation prior to their forced removal in 1830, the Georgia militia destroyed the printing press of the *Cherokee Phoenix*, a newspaper written in the Cherokee syllabary that Sequoyah had created (Waldman, 2000).

In 1934, the Indian Reorganization Act was passed, with a goal of ending restrictions against Native religions. Albeit for only 20 years, there was greater understanding and acceptance of Indian culture. World War II ushered in a period of greater attempts by the government to integrate Native people into American society. As had been typical of the past, more sacred lands were lost during this time and cultures were destroyed. During the 1970s, many traditional Indians were arrested for possessing sacred objects such as eagle feathers or for using peyote in religious ceremonies. Protests against this interference contributed to the 1978 passage of the American Indian Religious Freedom Act. Congress concluded that Native ways of worship were an essential part of Native life, and this law sought to protect and preserve such religious liberties (Hoxie, 1996).

Today, Native American and Alaskan Natives are a heterogeneous group, with 252 ribal languages and 565 federally recognized Indian tribes in the United States and in Alaska (US Census Bureau, 2011) . There are nearly 80,000 Alaskan Native tribal members that comprise the 229 Alaska region jurisdiction. This area stretches from Ketchikan in the Southeast Panhandle to Barrow on the Arctic Ocean and from Eagle on the Yukon border to Atka in the Aleutian chain (BIA, 2011). Native American and Alaskan Native tribes have tremendous diversity in customs, language, and family structure (Hoxie, 1996). Apache, Arapahoe, Arikara, Blackfoot, Catawba, Cherokee, Cheyenne, Chickasaw, Chippewa, Choctaw, Comanche, Coushatta, Cree, Creek, Crow, Erie, Eskimo, Haida, Hopi, Hupa, Iroquois, Lumbee, Osage, Mi'kmaq, Mohave, Narragansett, Navajo, Ottawa, Paiute, Pima, Potawatomi, Seminole, Seneca, Shawnee, Shoshone, Sioux, Tlingit, Tununak, Ute, Winnebago, Yaqui, and Zuni represent only a fraction of Native American and Alaskan Native tribal groups. The largest Native American tribes with populations of more than 100,000 are: Cherokee (819,105), Navajo (332,109), Choctaw (195,764), Mexican American Indian (175,494), Chippewa (170,742), Sioux (170,110), Apache (111,810), and Blackfoot (105,304) (US Census Bureau, 2011).

DEMOGRAPHY

The increase in numbers among Native people is a reflection of better census methods and wider acknowledgement of mixed ancestry. According to the 2010 census, there were 2.9 million people who indicated Native American and Alaskan Native ancestry alone, representing 0.9% of the total population (Humes, Jones, & Ramirez, 2011). Another 2.3 million people indicated American

Indian/Alaskan Native with another race. Since the 2000 census, there has been an increase of 1.1 million in the nation's American Indian and Alaska Native population. This represents an increase of 26.7% compared to a national growth rate of 9.7%. Almost half of the Native American population reported more than one race. Clearly, the majority of American Indian and Alaskan Natives have mixed backgrounds as biracial and multiracial people. A variety of phenotypic characteristics are found among Native American Indians.

The American Indian and Alaska Native population in California as of the 2010 Census was 723,225. In Oklahoma and Arizona, there were 482,760 and 353,386 Native Americans and Alaskan Natives, respectively. There were 15 states that had more than 100,000 Native Americans and Alaskan Natives during the 2010 census: California, Oklahoma, Arizona, Texas, New York, New Mexico, Washington, North Carolina, Florida, Michigan, Alaska, Oregon, Colorado, Minnesota, and Illinois (2010 Census Summary File 1, Table QT-P5). Alaska alone had the largest proportion of single-race American Indians and Alaskan Natives in its population: 13%. Wyoming and South Dakota had 3.4% and 3.2%, respectively, of Native Americans and Alaskan Natives in their populations. All other states combined represented 34% of the Native American and Alaskan Native population.

In 2010, there were 557,185 American Indian and Alaska Native families. Of these, 57% were married-couple families, including those with children. The average age of marriage for Native American and Alaskan Native woman was 26.8 and for men it was 29.6—these data are not significantly different for the general population. In 2004, the greatest percentage of Native American/Alaskan Native adults were married, at 40.1% (US Census Bureau, 2011).

Overall, about 68% of Native Americans and Alaskan Natives live in family households. Twenty percent of these families are maintained by a woman only with no husband present; 7% of family households were male only with no wife present. Nonfamily households comprised 31.8%. A *nonfamily household* is defined as people who live alone or people living with unrelated individuals.

In 2004, Native American/Alaskan Native women had higher rates of fertility than non-Hispanic White women. Forty-six percent of women in this group who gave birth in 2004 were unmarried, compared with 20.5% of White women. Similar to Blacks, Native American/Alaskan Natives are also more likely than non-Hispanic Whites to live with and care for grandchildren. About 7% of Native American/Alaskan Natives aged 30 and older were grandparents living in the same household with their co-resident grandchildren under the age of 18. More than half of grandparents (58%) were also responsible for the care of their grandchildren.

About 75% of Native Americans/Alaskan Natives aged 5 and older spoke only English at home, compared with 94% among non-Hispanic Whites. Roughly 28% of Native Americans/Alaskan Natives spoke a language other than English at home (US Census Bureau, 2011). The speakers of Inuit-Yupik-Aleut languages are primarily members of "First Nations" in North America. Some speakers live on the coast and islands of eastern Siberia. There are approximately 90,000 Inuit, Aleut, or Yup'ik speakers (www.sorosoro.org/en/eskimo-aleut-languages).

In 2010, there were 334 federal and state recognized reservations. About one-quarter of Native American and Alaskan Native elderly live on Native American Indian reservations or in Alaskan Native villages. In addition to earlier federal laws that played a role in the populating of urban areas with Native people, high unemployment on the reservations has contributed to the move of Native people to urban areas. Horse (2001) maintains that Native Americans are geographically dislocated from their homeland within a culture bombarded by the Internet, the US school system, peer pressure, and the mass media. Despite the reality of some Native people's cultural discontinuity, which refers to the gulf between mainstream expectations and Native people's cultural values, many Native people have learned to survive by becoming bicultural (Garrett & Pichette, 2000). Arndt and Davies (2011) discussed the PTSD that characterizes so many Native people contending with colonization and its many aftereffects.

SOCIAL, PSYCHOLOGICAL, AND PHYSICAL HEALTH ISSUES

Compared with the non-Hispanic White population, Native Americans and Alaskan Natives had a larger proportion of younger people and a smaller proportion of older people in 2004. Nearly 30% of this group is younger than age 18, whereas only 6.5% are 65 years or older. The median age is 29.5 years (American Indian and Alaska Native Population, 2010), which is more than 8 years younger than the median age for the non-Hispanic White population.

In 2010, the poverty rate for American Indians and Alaskan Natives was 28.4%, compared to 15.3% for the nation. This rate was higher than the poverty rates for non-Hispanic Whites, Asians, Pacific Islanders, and equal to that of Blacks (US Census Bureau, 2010). Among children under the age of 18, the poverty rate is 30.7%; that is, nearly one in three Native American children lives in poverty (US Census Bureau, 2007b).

In 2004, the median household income for Native American and Alaskan Natives was $35,062, or nearly $15,000 less than the median income for the general population. Income is related to status of housing. Although 54% of Native Americans and Alaskan Natives lived in owner-occupied homes, the percentage of renters is 44.5%. Nationally, 65% of Americans own homes (US Census Bureau, 2010). Among Native Americans and Alaskan Natives who own their homes, the median value is $95,000, which is $60,000 less than the median value of $154,000 for White owner-occupied homes.

Nearly one-third (32.8%) of Native Americans and Alaskan Natives do not have a usual or normal source of health care and are not regularly seen by a doctor or a clinic that can provide preventive care (Institute of Medicine, 2003). The lack of health insurance among the general population is 17.5%. As a result of treaty obligations, Native Americans receive their health services largely through the federal government and the Indian Health Service. Since 1955, a part of the US Public Health Service was to provide health care to all Native Americans/Alaskan Natives who belonged to federally recognized tribes and lived on or near the reservations throughout 12 service areas (Byrd & Clayton, 2003).

The number of Native-owned business has increased in the United States, as has the amount of money they contribute to the US economy. According to the US Census Bureau (2011), in 2007, there were 236,967 Native American and Alaska Native-owned businesses. This represents an increase of 17.7% from 2002. Also in 2007, Native American and Alaska Native-owned businesses generated $34.4 billion in receipts, representing a 28% increase from 2002.

More than half of the total Native American population resides in urban areas. Only 38% of Native Americans reside on federal trust lands. Although the federal government has played a key role in health care delivery for Native Americans, unlike other groups of color, the quality of and access to such care has been adversely affected by the way in which Native people are scattered throughout the country (Joe, 2003). In light of these and other data that reveal the poor quality of life for unacceptably high numbers of American Indian and Alaskan Native people, many American Indians and Alaskan Natives feel distrust for the dominant culture (Heinrich, Corbine, & Thomas, 1990).

Partly as a result of this legacy and continuing cultural conflict, alcoholism presents a social problem for many Native Americans, affecting family life, newborn health, and employment prospects. Co-morbidity is evident, given the relationship between substance addictions and mental health problems. Alcohol abuse is a substantial problem, with an estimated 12% rate of alcohol-related deaths for Native Americans (Frieden, 2011). The research is inconclusive regarding cultural identity and substance abuse problems. Venner, Wall, Lau, and Ehlers (2006) report conflicting findings about the protections against substance abuse that a bicultural identity offers. In addition to the adverse health effects of alcohol abuse on the body, alcoholism is linked to high-risk behaviors such as unprotected sex because it decreases inhibition. The use of black tar heroin on many reservations has contributed to an increase in substance dependency.

The number of reported Native American AIDS cases as of December 1999 was 2,132. Although this number seems low, AIDS is the eighth leading cause of mortality among Native Americans between ages 15 and 34 living on or near reservations (Vernon, 2002). Related to poor diet, diabetes ranges from 5% to 50% among tribes and Native communities, and colon and rectal cancer rates are the highest among any racial or ethnic group in the country (Institute of Medicine, 2003). As major causes of morbidity and premature death, these and other poor health outcomes contribute to nearly one in three Native deaths before the age of 45 (Vernon, 2002).

Many alcoholism treatment programs exist that have special programs for Native Americans, but there are no empirical, research-based findings on the efficacy of various treatments for alcohol problems among Native Americans (Thomason, 2000). The term *nativized treatments* refers to standard treatments that have been adapted to be more culturally appropriate for Native populations. These nativized treatments would include, for example, Native American cultural values and traditional healing techniques and ceremonies. A comprehensive program may be the best approach to treating Native clients with alcohol abuse issues. Such a program is descriptive, includes medical care, self-help groups, and purification ceremonies (Thomason, 2000).

Educationally, there have been increases in the high school graduation level, now at 77% among Native American/Alaskan Natives 25 years of age and older. This compares with 86% for the general population (2010 American Community Survey for the American Indian and Alaska Native alone population). Just over 13% had completed a bachelor's degree compared with 28% of the general population. Nearly 31 different tribal groups have established their own tribal colleges (Horse, 2001). Among Native American people who are more traditional and are not interested in leaving their reservations, lack of educational attainment may be a conscious decision, particularly in light of limited access and economic challenges (Rayle, Chee, & Sand, 2006).

About one-quarter of Native American/Alaskan Native workers are employed in management or professional occupations, compared with 38% among non-Hispanic Whites. Nearly 23% of Native Americans work in sales and office occupations, which is similar to non-Hispanic Whites (27%). Higher percentages of Native Americans and Alaskan Natives work in service occupations at 21.5% and in construction at 15%. Among non-Hispanic Whites, 14% are in service and 10% work in construction jobs.

American Indian people have been overlooked for their inestimable contributions to the Western world. Hoxie (1996) stated that across the Americas, Native people invented the hammock, the snowshoe, the blow gun, the bulb syringe, the kayak, the rubber boot. They also wove cloth from feathers, crafted animal and bird decoys for use in hunting, and used acid to etch designs onto shell.

Gunn Allen (1994) reminds us of the irrefutable influence of American Indian and Alaskan Native people. Elaborate systems of thought and governments based on egalitarianism, service, pacifism, and freedom characterized many tribal societies prior to the presence of patriarchy. In fact, Iroquois ideas were central to this nation's Constitution. Portman and Herring (2001) stated:

> Native American Indian women were integral to the economic and social survival of their nations and tribes. They also held positions of political importance. Native American Indians provided guidance and influenced governance decisions and served as leaders and advisers in many Native American Indian tribes and nations. (p. 187)

Among many Native Americans, a leader's influence was based on personal qualities. Authority within a group was derived from the ability to make useful suggestions and knowledge of traditional ways and tribal lore (Waldman, 2000).

CULTURAL PHILOSOPHIES AND VALUES

Despite chronic and contemporary challenges, a commitment to peoplehood, a spirit of resilience, and a strong sense of identity are evident among Native peoples. The tribe is a source of belonging and security for Native American and Alaskan Native people. Personal accomplishments are honored and supported if they serve to benefit the entire tribe or collective. Competition, the hallmark of the educational school system and a dominant cultural value rooted in individualism, is at odds with collectivism, a spirit of cooperation, and sharing of resources that belong to everyone.

Although values vary from tribe to tribe, Native American and Alaskan Native people believe in a Supreme Creator that is considered both male and female and is in command of all the elements of existence. Gunn Allen (1994) said, "There are many female gods recognized and honored by the Nations. Females were highly valued, both respected and feared and all social institutions reflected this attitude" (p. 193). Native Americans/Alaskan Natives also believe that all things in the universe are connected, have purpose, and exemplify personhood (Garrett & Garrett, 1994), "including plants (e.g., 'tree people'), animals ('our four-legged brothers and sisters'), rocks and minerals ('rock people'), the land ('Mother Earth'), the winds ('the Four Powers'), 'Father Sky,' 'Grandfather Sun,' 'Grandmother Moon,' 'The Red Thunder Boys'" (p. 138).

Honoring the Creator is sacred to Native American and Alaskan Native people and is central to Native Americans'/Alaskan Natives' harmonious relationships with nature and all things. Garrett (1998) said that "the wellness of the mind, body, spirit, and natural environment

Storytelling: Resistance is not Futile

1992 was the 500th anniversary of Christopher Columbus' arrival in the Western Hemisphere. That year, people across races and nationalities united with First Americans to reject the celebration and glorification of a man who was responsible for genocide, biological warfare, and oppression. The National Council of Churches asked Christians to refrain from celebrating the Columbus quincentennial. One teacher in Portland, Oregon, took a year off from his job to travel the country, helping teachers learn to tell the truth about the Columbus experience. A student climbed aboard a romanticized Columbus exhibit sponsored by the National Endowment for the Humanities called First Encounter. The student held a sign that read, "Exhibit Teaches Racism." Now thousands of teachers are telling the story of Columbus differently.

is an extension of the proper balance in the relationship of all things" (p. 78). In these cultures, sharing is valued over materialism because all belongs to Earth.

Elders are valued among Native American and Alaskan Natives "because of the lifetime's worth of wisdom they have acquired" (Garrett & Garrett, 1994, p. 137). Elders are accorded respect, and as they age, there is an increase in sacred responsibility for the tribe and family. They understand that their purpose is to care for and guide young people, yet a spirit of curiosity and openness to life's lessons prevails (Garrett & Herring, 2001).

Native American cultural values emanate from a spiritual center that emphasizes coexisting in harmony with nature. (See Table 4.1.) This entails a respect for Earth as natural medicine (Peregoy, 1993). Native people have always depended on the land, because it provided life, shelter, food, and medicine. The Paiute boiled sagebrush to relieve headaches

---

TABLE 4.1 Common Cultural Values among Native Americans and Alaskan Native People

Spirituality (Great Spirit)

Nature (Mother Earth)

The Sacred

Ritual

Tradition

Balance

Harmony

Explanation of natural phenomena according to the spiritual realm

Noninterference

Cooperation

Sharing

Extended and present time orientation

Hozhq (An expression of happiness, harmonious relationships, the beauty of the land)

Tiospaye (Shared responsibility, extended family, reciprocity)

Oral traditions

The extended family (The Tribe)

Selflessness

Deference to and respect for elders

Storytelling

Speak softly at a slower rate

Not holding direct eye contact to show respect

Time is always with us

and rheumatism. Even dandruff was cured by rubbing boiled willow leaves into the hair and scalp (Ballentine & Ballentine, 1993). "This harmony entails a holistic sensing of the state of continuous fusion among the elements of self with all life, including the creator" (Dana, 1993, p. 84).

Implicit in this value system is reverence for and acceptance of the gifts from the earth. In their reverence for the earth, a variety of plants, wild and cultivated, were used for both religious and practical purposes as well as for pleasure. Clearly some Indian people, particularly where agriculture was highly developed, used alcohol prior to contact with Europeans, but for the most part, drinking alcohol was a post-contact reality (Waldman, 2000). Native American people believe that to be human is a part of the Sacred, thus there is an acknowledgment that human beings make mistakes (Trujillo, 2000). Nature, in its natural, undisturbed state, is respected, and coexisting (not interfering) with nature is paramount as all things have spiritual energy. The universe, or Mother Earth, belongs to all people. For the Indian, the concept of land ownership was foreign and made as much sense as did carving up the sky (as defined national airspace boundaries have).

Honoring traditional ways suggests a respect for the past and the contributions of the ancestral spirits. According to Peregoy (1993), "The traditional Indian/Native's system of life is intertwined with the tribe and extends further into a metaphysical belief system" (p. 172).

Native American and Alaskan Natives see the extended family and the tribe as taking precedence over the self (Garrett & Garrett, 1994; Gunn Allen, 1994; Peregoy, 1993). Among many Native American and Alaskan Native people, the concept of self tends to be fluid and includes the individual as well as the tribe, the extended family, and even plants and animal spirits (Dana, 2000). A belief or knowledge in unseen powers and reference to deities and mystery is core to many tribal values, as is the importance of balance (Trujillo, 2000).

Respect for and coexistence with helpful animal spirits are enduring values found in nearly all Native American and Alaskan Eskimo societies. It was believed that the animals made themselves available to humans only for as long as there was respect from the hunters for the animal spirits. This involved ritual treatment of the animals so that the animals would, upon their death, return to the spirit world with a good report, which would ensure the success of future hunters. If a hunter was unsuccessful, it could be stated that the animal spirits had not been treated properly; therefore, proper rituals were needed to restore harmony and to correct the imbalance (Hoxie, 1996).

According to Garrett and Pichette (2000), there are verbal and nonverbal communication style differences between contemporary mainstream American cultural values and those of traditional Native people. More specifically, immediate responses, frequent interruption, and emphasis placed on verbal skills are characteristic of dominant US cultural styles. Delayed responses, less frequent interjection, and emphasis placed on nonverbal skills characterize Native cultural traditions.

ACCULTURATION

Most Native adults whose ancestry is both Native and non-Native retain their traditional values but also seek to live in the dominant culture (Garrett & Herring, 2001). According to Herring (1992), Native American/Alaskan Native people are "more unalterably resistant to assimilation and integration into mainstream society than are other minority groups" (p. 135); some, however, have become acculturated.

Acculturation and *assimilation* influence value structures and are important to an understanding of cultural adaptation. Garrett and Pichette (2000) identify five levels of acculturation among Native people:

1. Traditional
2. Marginal
3. Bicultural
4. Assimilated
5. Pantraditional

These levels exists on a continuum and are a function of a person's life experiences. The Traditional Native person may or may not speak English and will hold traditionally Native values, including tribal customs. The Marginal person identifies with neither mainstream values nor traditional values. The Bicultural person knows and practices both mainstream and traditional values. The Assimilated person holds the mainstream American values in high esteem to the exclusion of those Native. Finally, the Pantraditional person consciously seeks to return to the "old ways;" they attempt to embrace lost traditional values and beliefs and are often bilingual.

Garrett and Pichette (2000) offered a clear definition of acculturation in their discussion of Native American acculturation. It was stated that acculturation is "the cultural change that occurs when two or more cultures are in persistent contact... A particular kind of acculturation is assimilation, in which one culture changes significantly more than the other culture and as a result comes to resemble it. This process is often established deliberately through force to maintain control over conquered people, but it can occur voluntarily as well" (p. 6).

Acculturation may take place at the expense of one's original cultural values as one internalizes values and traditions. This process is not always conscious (Sue, 1989), and there is the likelihood of cultural alienation from one's traditional culture because the dominant culture is esteemed over one's own.

One dimension of acculturation is assimilation. Assimilation describes those persons who consciously do not desire to maintain their cultural identities and thus seek sustained interaction with other cultures outside their own. The original cultures have been lost or relinquished, and persons have given up most cultural traits of their cultures of origin and assumed the traits, behaviors, and attitude of the dominant culture (Berry & Kim, 1988).

Christianization was one way assimilation was accomplished among many Native Americans. Some Native Americans do not regard the two to be incompatible. In the Native American Church (NAC), Christian and Native beliefs coexist (US DHHS, 2001). In addition to the Spanish and French languages, European colonizers brought English to America. Language is a medium of culture, and English functioned as a way to deny the existence and relevance of Native languages. Such a policy existed in the US government-sponsored Indian boarding schools designed to mainstream American Indian youth. The first such school was established in 1879 in Carlisle, Pennsylvania, under the influence of General Henry Pratt. His motto was "kill the Indian and save the man" (Hoxie, 1996; Lesiak & Jones, 1991). In these colonizing contexts, children's hair was cut, traditional clothing was taken away, American Christian names replaced Native names, and only English was allowed to be spoken. The virtues of White American Christian traditions were extolled, and the Native ways were denigrated as uncivilized (Cameron & Turtle-song, 2003).

Native Americans and Alaskan Natives who possess a strong sense of heritage and honor tradition may be more likely to feel at peace on the reservation, where cooperation with others and respect for tribal values based on ritual are commonplace (Gunn Allen, 1994).

CASE STUDY

A WOUNDED MIND

Alana is a 46-year-old single woman who cares for her 71-year-old mother who has advanced Alzheimer's. The doctors have explained to Alana that her mother's condition is progressing and eventually she will need to enter into a care facility for people with Alzheimer's. Alana has vowed never to put her mother into such a facility, which she says is typical of White people who throw the old away after they have been used up and are of no use to anybody. During therapy with Connie, a 50-year-old Lumbee Indian counselor, Connie confronts Alana and discloses, "I'm like you, Lumbee. My father is in a nursing facility. He has Alzheimer's." Alana asks Connie how she could do such a thing, to which Connie replied, "I needed to put my father's needs above my own. His needs were greater than my ability to adequately care for him." Connie then told Alana that it is clear she is exhausted. Alana begins to cry and says she has not been sleeping well since her mother has started to either leave the house at night or roam about making noise and turning on the oven with empty pots on the stove. Alana locks the doors. Her mother has been undoing the locks and leaving the house. The doctors have told Alana that her mother will get to the point where she does not remember how to return home. Alana is also fearful her mother may start a fire. Alana told Connie that her mother forgets that she has eaten and does not remember how to eat—Alana has observed her mom shuffling the food around her plate without actually eating it. Alana also said that her mother resists having to bathe and is often unwilling to allow Alana to bathe her, despite having become incontinent. Alana admits to her fear that the people at the facility will mistreat and abuse her mother, that they will promise to do one thing but will not honor that promise. Alana asks, "How can I say that I love my mother and put her away?" Connie asks Alana if it is possible to show love for loved ones by putting them in the hands of caring people who will make sure she eats, keep her from leaving the house in the middle of the day and night, and attend to her personal hygiene needs. Connie suggests to Alana that in addition to seeing Connie, that she see a traditional healer for herself, not for her mother. Alana greatly appreciates the suggestion and receives a referral from Connie.

QUESTIONS

1. What are Alana's value orientations?
2. What are Connie's value orientations?
3. How do counselors and psychologists know when it is appropriate to confront clients and/or disclose personal information?

DISCUSSION AND INTEGRATION

The Client, Alana

Alana's relationship to her situation has to be considered. Collectivistic cultures tend to have a very different way of seeing themselves in relationship to self and others. The person from a collectivistic culture is likely to define "himself or herself in an interdependent fashion . . . Rather than emphasizing personal distinctiveness, this person is likely to stress his or her similarity to a group, view roles and obligations to a group as central aspects of self-definition, and value restraint and harmony" (Enns, 1994, p. 206). Alana also shows signs of fatigue and anxiety. She is not sleeping well and is bearing witness to losses/daily changes in her mother's thinking and behavior. Alana is also exhausted from caring for her mother and trying to work. Nonetheless, her commitment to caring for her mother is obvious.

IMPLICATIONS FOR COUNSELORS AND PSYCHOLOGISTS

Being from the same tribe or family does not mean people will endorse similar values—differences in cultural outlook can be seen between Connie and Alana. Much of the emphasis in cross-cultural and, more recently, multicultural counseling and psychology has been on helping counselors work effectively with clients who are different with respect to race, gender, class, disability, sexuality, and other sources of differences. What does it mean when clients and counselors are similar with respect to these identities and yet have different value orientations? Clearly, effective counseling depends on a sound therapeutic alliance (Vontress, 1986). It also depends on clients having a holding environment (Kegan, 1982) that is empathic and allows them to tell their stories while feeling validated (Rayle, Chee, & Sand, 2006; Murphy & Dillon, 2006). Mohatt (2010) commented that a challenge in psychotherapy is coming to grips with power and spiritual forces. He stated the healing process has been so secularly focused and "often reduced to the acquisition of skill rather than character, reflexivity, and spiritual intuition" (p. 240).

Connie is not afraid of mysterious aspects of healing. Alana appreciates that Connie, like many Native Americans, views wellness not only in terms of the body but also the spirit and the mind. Connie is able to use humor appropriately which is critical in integrating Native culture with psychotherapeutic healing (Garrett & Herring, 2001; Mohatt, 2010). Humor is also a way for Connie and Alana to maintain Native Culture and create unity, and, for Alana, it is a way for her to learn how to cope with a difficult situation (Garrett, Garrett, Torres-Rivera, Wilbur, & Roberts-Wilbur, 2005).

Portman (2000) found in her research with 505 American Indian women who took the Bem Sex Role Inventory (BSRI), that their scores were higher on the masculine role subscale than the White normative sample. The masculine subscale of the BSRI included phrases such as "acts like a leader," "assertive," "aggressive," and "defends own beliefs." Native women's masculine subscale scores were not higher than Latina and African American women's masculine scale scores who were part of the normative sample. Alana's decisiveness and strength can serve her—and yet Connie needs to help Alana come to understand that such coping styles can lock her into rigid patterns of behaving.

Connie chose to self-disclose or share some of her personal or demographic information with Alana (Murphy & Dillon, 2008). Connie felt that appropriate self-disclosure could be helpful and even therapeutic. Murphy and Dillon agree with this perspective and said, "We believe that judicious self-disclosure can help develop trust, especially for clients who are not comfortable with what may seem like artificial distance and anonymity" (p. 341). In addition, self-disclosure can be helpful when working with people from marginalized groups. Within the context of counseling Native Americans, Murphy and Dillon state that greater levels of trust may be present within the therapeutic relationship if clinicians use some self-disclosure and demonstrate cultural sensitivity prior to asking Native American clients personal questions. Clinicians should ask the following prior to disclosure:

1. Why am I choosing to self-disclose?
2. What is the impact of the disclosure on my clients?
3. Whose needs are being served by this disclosure, mine or that of the client?

As part of her assessment and treatment of Alana, Connie considers Alana's level of acculturation, her life off the reservation, and the fact that Alana honors more of the tribal (the presence of the medicine man and traditional ceremonies) than some of the mainstream customs (the Native American Church, which has been influenced by Christianity, and psychotherapy, in which the client is sharing personal information with a professional and a stranger).

Connie is aware that she is an insider. Alana told Connie that she would not counsel with a European or a Native person who has forgotten traditional Native ways. It bothers Alana that people take from the Native people, their traditions of healing (e.g., sweat lodges) without seeking permission from the elders. Sweat lodges have a long standing place in the traditions of Native people as a means of healing the body and the mind and seeking balance with the natural environment (Garrett et al., 2011). Connie understands the importance of continuing to strengthen the trust and rapport that she shares with Alana. Keeping with Native traditions where healing is understood within the context of the collective—one's caring and sustaining support network, Connie values working in conjunction with local and tribal resources (Dana, 2000; Trimble, 2010). Finally, Connie feels prepared to deal with the extent of Alana's pain and anger around generations of loss, transgression, and trauma (Olson, 2003; Arndt & Davis, 2011) that have resulted in treaty violations, loss of land, and broken promises between American and Native people.

Summary

This chapter provided a history of Native American and Alaskan Native people. Representation in the United States, demographic information, history, and common cultural values among American Indian/Alaskan Natives were provided. A summary of these values can be found in Table 4.1. A case study was provided for purposes of application of material and relevance to counseling.

Latinos

> *Intersectional approaches argue that occupying more than*
> *one disadvantaged social position leads to experiences*
> *with unique forms of discrimination.*
>
> CARLY FRIEDMAN AND CAMPBELL LEAPER

This chapter profiles Latinos, a racially and culturally diverse ethnic group. A brief look at history, cultural values, and demographic trends is included. A case study is provided for the integration of material in a therapeutic context.

THE SPANISH, PORTUGUESE, INDIANS, ASIANS, AND AFRICANS

The Western world's Latinos are *la raza*, which means "the race" or "the people." Places of origin among Latinos are diverse and varied: Puerto Rico (*Puertorriquenos*), Cuba (*Cubanos*), the Dominican Republic (*Dominicanos*), Central America, South America, Latin America, and Mexico (*Mejicanos*).

The federal government defines *Hispanic* or *Latino* as a person of Mexican, Puerto Rican, Cuban, South or Central American, or other Spanish culture or origin regardless of race (US Census Bureau, 2007). Novas (1994) clarified that for many Latinos, "'Hispanic' is merely a bureaucratic government census term." The term *Latino* or *Latina*, depending on gender, is widely used and refers to persons with Spanish ancestry. Many Latinos prefer to be called by their country of origin.

The racial diversity among Latinos is very old and connected to political movements, slavery, family, conquest, defeat, geographic movement, love, and war. The term *Hispanic* comes from España, or Spain, the country from which the conquistadors hailed. The Spanish encountered Native people across the various lands, including the Arawak, Maya, Aztec, and Inca. African people were brought involuntarily to the colonies, Mexico, the Caribbean and South America as slaves. They reproduced with the Spanish and the Native Americans. In the Philippines, the Spanish encountered Asian people and made their claim to the land in 1522; thus, Filipinos are categorized as Asian, but have Spanish ancestry. Also in 1522, the Spanish invaded Central America, including the future countries of Nicaragua, Honduras, El Salvador, and Guatemala, and conquered the region two decades later. During the colonial period, Spain ruled these countries. Other ethnic groups were considered of a lower social class. Class divisions were connected to skin color. Unions between the Spanish and the indigenous Indian people resulted in *mestizos*. Mestizos were not regarded as equals to the Spaniards but emerged as a higher class than pure Indians. Once Black African slaves arrived, new class and color configurations emerged.

During the 18th century slave trade, Europeans brought Black Africans to the Americas. The Garifuna people, a group of Africans believed to have come from Ghana, were taken to Central America. African slaves on the island of St. Vincent revolted and, led by Marcos Sanchez Diaz, fled to the island of Rotan in Honduras. From there the Garifuna or Black Carib people spread out along the Caribbean to Belize, Guatemala, and Honduras (www.worldtrek. org/odyssey/latinamerica).

Latinos can be of any race and represent a range of phenotypical characteristics, including white, brown, red, and black skin-color hues. Non-White Latinos experience discrimination that is politically, socially, and racially motivated (Hernandez, 1996). In addition to European, Indian, and African ancestries, some Latinos claim an Asian heritage (Santiago-Rivera, Arredondo, & Gallardo-Cooper, 2002).

DEMOGRAPHY

As of 2010, Latinos represent 16% of the US population, or 50.5 million people (Ennis, Rios-Vargas, & Alpert, 2011). Latinos continue to be the largest group of color. More than half of the population growth in the United States between 2000 and 2010 was due to the increases among Latinos. In this 10-year period, the Latino population grew 43%, or four times the total population growth rate of 10% in the United States (Ennis, Rios-Vargas, & Alpert, 2011). High rates of immigration, low median age, and high fertility rates account for this increase.

Mexican Americans increased the most of the other Latino groups, growing from 20.6 million to 31.8 million in 10 years. Mexicans are the largest single group of Latinos, representing 63% of the group. Puerto Ricans grew by 36% from 3.4 million to 4.6 million, and are 9% of Latinos. Cubans grew by 44% from 1.2 million to 1.8 million, and represent 3.5% of Latinos. Central Americans (people from Belize, formerly British Honduras; Costa Rica; El Salvador; Guatemala; Honduras; Nicaragua; and Panama) increased 137%, from 1.68 *million* to 3.99 million. They are 8% of Latinos. Of Central Americans, Salvadorians were the largest group at 1.6 million followed by Guatemalans at 1 million.

South Americans (people from Argentina, Bolivia, Brazil, Columbia, Chile, Paraguay, Peru, Uruguay, and Venezuela) increased 105%, from 1.35 million to 2.76 million. South Americans make up 5.5% of US Latinos. Columbians were the largest single group at 909,000, followed by Ecuadorians at 565,000.

Although Latinos can be of any race, in the 2010 Census, over half of Latinos reported their race as White alone. Over one-third (36.7%) stated they were some other race. Very small percentages of Latinos identified as one of the other racial groups: 3% identified as Black, 1% identified as Native American/Alaskan Native, 0.4% as Asian alone, and 0.1% as Native Hawaiian or other Pacific Islander.

Latino women have a higher fertility rate than non-Hispanic White women. In comparison to native-born Latinas, foreign-born Latinas have a higher fertility rate, with Guatemalan and Mexican women having the highest fertility rates of the specific Hispanic-origin groups and Cuban women having the lowest. There were 92.1 births out of 1,000 to Guatemalan women and 41.7 births out of 1,000 to Cuban women (US Census Bureau, 2007).

In 2004, 50.8% of Latinos were married while 35% were not married. Nearly 19% of households among Latinos were females with no husband present, whereas 9% of households were males with no wife present. Compared with the general population, there are higher rates of female and male households and lower rates of nonfamily households among Latinos. The lack of a wage-earning male present has enormous implication for economic stability. There are considerable inter-Latino group differences with respect to marriage and divorce. Divorce and widowed rates were lower at 7.5% and 3.3% respectively, compared with 10.2% and 6.1%, respectively, in the general population. Rates of separation were slightly higher, at 3.5% compared with 2.1%. Cubans have the highest rate of divorce, compared with Guatemalans who have the lowest: 12.4% and 4.1% respectively. Cubans were also the least likely to have never married at 25%, whereas Hondurans and Salvadorans were the most likely to never have married, both at 40%. Struggling with transition from one cultural context to the next and working long hours to support oneself and one's family in the home country can interfere with dating and looking for a mate. Regardless of specific group, Latinos tend to have larger household sizes at 3.4 compared with 2.6 for the general population. Guatemalans had the most people in their households (3.90).

The median age of non-Latinos in the United States is 37.2. Among Latinos, the median age is 27.4 years (Howden & Meyer, 2011). Mexicans have the lowest median age, 25.3 years, and Cubans had the highest, at 40.6 years. In fact, one-third of Mexicans, Puerto Ricans, Dominicans, and Hondurans are children. In 2009, 26% of children under the age of 5, were Latino (US Census, 2009). Among non-Latinos, the largest 5-year age group is 40- to 44-year-olds. Latinos have had the lowest proportion of elderly in each census.

GEOGRAPHY

Brazil is a South American country where the official language is Portuguese, but there are Brazilians who identify as Latino. Millions of Latinos from countries such as Argentina and Costa Rica are not of Spanish or Indian descent, but rather descend from European or Antillean nations (Beals & Beals, 1993). Some Britons emigrated to Latin America during the 18th century, and other Europeans went there during the 20th century to escape Nazi oppression (Santiago-Rivera et al., 2002).

Latinos in the United States are united by the Spanish mother tongue. There are dialect differences. Beals and Beals (1993) stated that the majority of Spain's citizens speak Castellano, whereas the majority of Chicanos (Mexicans) speak Pocho. According to Carballo-Dieguez (1989), many Latinos are fluent in both Spanish and English, others know very little English, others have limited knowledge of Spanish, and others speak "Spanglish," a mixture of both languages.

One of the discourses about Latinos is that they are brown, speak with an accent, and are foreign. Actually, the majority of Latinos were born in the United States, with most speaking only English at home or speaking English very well. In 2004, nearly 75% of Latinos were US citizens. In fact, 50% of Latinos voted during the 2008 presidential election. The 20th century witnessed the mass migration of Latinos to the United States, with most foreign-born Latinos entering in 1990 or later (US Census Bureau, 2007). Their points and periods of entry have differed from legal to illegal, from Castro's revolution for Cubans to citizenship status issues for Puerto Ricans, to the illegal and extralegal status of Mexicans and other Latinos who die daily en route to America. America has been enhanced, enriched, and transformed as a result of the presence of Latino people (Sanchez, 2002).

In 2010, 41% of American Latinos lived in the West and 36% lived in the South. In fact, representation in South Carolina grew the fastest, from 95,000 in 2000 to 236,000 in 2010. Alabama had the second fastest increase of Latinos. The Northeast and the Midwest accounted for 14% and 9% respectively of the Latino population. Over half of the Latino population resides in three states: California, Texas, and Florida. New York, Illinois, New Jersey, and Colorado are among the states that have Latino populations of 1 million or more. Mexicans are most likely to live in California, Texas, and Arizona; Puerto Ricans have the highest representation in New York, Florida, and New Jersey; Cubans are most likely to live in Florida, California, and New Jersey.

MIGRATORY PATTERNS FROM MEXICO

Mexico is one of the largest sources of new immigrants to the United States. A number of push and pull factors influenced the migratory patterns of Mexico's people to the United States. During the early 1900s, there was a great need for cheap labor to work in US agriculture. The harsh economic conditions in Mexico and high unemployment, along with Mexico's proximity to the United States, set the stage for large-scale migration (US Department of Health and Human Services, 2001).

The land that the majority of Americans now occupy was once Mexico. In 1821, Mexico won its independence from Spain, but this freedom was short-lived. In 1848, the signing of the Treaty of Guadalupe Hidalgo confirmed Mexico's defeat in the Mexican–American war that had begun in 1846. Through this formal agreement between Mexico and the United States, Mexico lost half of its territory. The cultural and geographic decimation was enormous. Mexicans who had lived on their own land, where their *almas* (souls) resided, now became migrant farm workers. Mexicans who had been landowners found themselves working for White men. Once Texas, New Mexico, California, Arizona, Nevada, and half of Colorado officially became United States territory, the Spanish language was ousted, with English becoming the primary and official mode of school instruction.

SOCIAL, PSYCHOLOGICAL, AND PHYSICAL HEALTH ISSUES

The diversity among Latinos is tremendous. Latinos are descendents of the oppressed and the oppressor with a history marked by social oppression, conquest, liberation, and struggle (Garcia-Preto, 1996). Among the diverse group of Latinos, differences exist across geography, country of origin, race, class, traditions, acculturation, and the time and sociopolitical circumstances in which persons entered the United States (Beals & Beals, 1993; Nicolau & Santiestevan, 1990). Stavans (1995) said, "We Latinos have an abundance of histories, linked to a common root but with decisively different traditions. At each and every moment, these ancestral histories determine who we are and what we think" (p. 20).

Variations are striking among ethnic groups with respect to educational attainment. More than one-quarter (27%) of Latinos have a ninth-grade education or less, compared with 5% of non-Hispanic Whites (US Census Bureau Current Population Survey, 2011). The high school graduation rate for all Latinos is 60%, compared with 88.6% for non-Hispanic Whites. South Americans (such as Peruvians, Columbians, and Ecuadorians) have much higher graduation rates (84.5%) than Central Americans (such as Guatemalans, Hondurans, and Salvadorans) with an average of 53%. Puerto Ricans have the next highest graduation rate at 71%. Mexicans have a graduation rate similar to Central Americans, at 52%. The college attainment rate among Latinos is 10% compared with 21.3% of non-Hispanic Whites (US Census Bureau Current Population Survey, 2011). Cubans have the highest college attainment rate at 23%, compared with 7% for Mexicans. In addition to geographic diversity, income varies as well. Latinos are more likely to be unemployed at 6.8%, compared with 3.4% of non-Hispanic Whites. Puerto Ricans have the highest unemployment rate at 8.1%, with 5.1% among Central and South Americans. When employed, Latinos are more likely to work in service occupations, at 19.4%, or in operator or labor positions, at 22%. Compared with non-Hispanic Whites, their participation in these positions is 11.8% and 11.6%, respectively. Non-Hispanic Whites are more than twice as likely to work in managerial positions at 33.2%.

Many of the male Latino workers who newly arrived in the United States now work in construction. These workers were also older and thus less likely to be low-wage earners. Nonetheless, many Latinos who are foreign-born are in poverty (Kochhar, 2007).

Over 26% (26.6%) of Latinos live in poverty compared with 15.1% for the general population (US Census Bureau, 2011). The poverty rate among Latinos is nearly triple the non-Hispanic White population, which is 9.9%. Thirty percent of Latino children under the age of 18 live in poverty. Among Latinos, Dominicans, Puerto Ricans, and Mexicans have the highest poverty rates at 28%, 24%, and 24%, respectively. Columbians have the lowest poverty rate at 11%. The poverty rate among Central Americans is 18%, which is higher than it is for South Americans (13%) (Census Bureau, 2007c). The percentage of Latinos who lacked health insurance in 2010 was 30.7% (DeNavas-Walt, Proctor, & Smith, 2011).

High poverty rates contribute to Latinos having the highest probability of being medically uninsured (Institute of Medicine, 2003). Despite the high poverty rates among Latinos, substantial income gains have been made. In 2010, the median household income for Latinos was $37,759, or nearly $12,000 less than the median income for the general population. Dominicans have the lowest median income at $29,624, and Ecuadorians had the highest at $43,788.

Income is related to status of housing. Latinos are more likely to own their homes than to rent them, but there is tremendous variation across ethnic groups. More than half (52%) of Latinos owned their homes in 2004, compared with 48% who rented. Only 25% of Dominicans own their own homes, whereas 61% of Cubans are homeowners. The median value of owner-occupied homes was $152,000, which was similar (a few dollars higher) to the general population. The median value of homes among Mexicans was $136,468 compared with nearly $300,000 among Ecuadorians. Along with African Americans and Native Americans, Latinos have greater incidences of illness and mortality due to diabetes compared with White Americans (Institute of Medicine, 2003). In addition, high blood pressure and obesity rates are also higher among Latinos (IOM, 2003).

The Epidemiologic Catchment Area (ECA) Study investigated rates of psychiatric disorders in five communities. Los Angeles was one of the sites studied, and Mexicans were oversampled. Mexican Americans born in Mexico were found to have lower rates of depression and phobias compared with those born in the United States. Another study examined rates of psychiatric disorders in a large sample of Mexican Americans residing in Fresno County, California. Lifetime rates of mental disorders among Mexican American immigrants born in Mexico were remarkably lower than the rates of mental disorders among Mexican Americans born in the United States. The length of time that Latinos spent in the United States was a factor in the development of mental disorders. Immigrants who had lived in the United States for at least 13 years had higher rates of mental disorders than those who had lived in the United States fewer than 13 years (US DHHS, 2001). "Recent immigrants of all backgrounds, who are adapting to the United States, are likely to experience a different set of stressors than long-term Hispanic residents" (US DHHS, 2001, p. 133). Acculturation, according to some epidemiological studies, may even lead to an increase in mental disorders.

Vulnerabilities among youth have been reported as well. A large-scale survey of primarily Mexican American teens in both Texas and Mexico found higher rates of depression, drug use, and suicide among Texas-based youth (US DHHS, 2001). Living in the United States was related to a higher risk of mental health difficulties than not living here. Texan youth were more likely to report high rates of depressive symptoms than Mexican youth, 48% compared with 39%. The rate of youth who reported illicit drug use and suicidal ideation in the last 30 days was also higher among Texas-based youth compared with youth who lived in Mexico. The number of Latino college students is growing, but the rate of acculturative stress and psychological distress has been little studied (Crockett, Iturbide, Stone, McGinley, Raffaelli, & Carlo, 2007).

The HIV/AIDS epidemic is a major threat to the Latino community. According to the Center for Disease Control (CDC 2011), Hispanic/Latino men made up three-quarters (76%) of new Hepatitis, STD, and TB infections among all Hispanics/Latinos. One in 36 Latino men will be diagnosed with HIV, as will 1 in 106 Latina women. In 2007, HIV was the sixth leading cause of death among Latinos aged 25 (The Henry J. Kaiser Foundation, 2011). In 2008, Latinos accounted for 19% of the more than 42,000 new AIDS diagnoses in the United States. Latinos are most likely to be infected with HIV as a result of sexual contact with men. Latino men who have sex with men (MSM) represent 72% of new infections among all Latino men. Among Latino MSM, 43% occurred in Latino MSM under age 30; the remaining 57% occurred in Latino MSM aged 30 and older. Latina women may not be aware of their male partner's risky behavior and ultimately how they are being adversely impacted. Latino youth are at higher risk for poor mental health outcomes, and they are more likely to drop out of school and to report feelings of depression and anxiety. Latino youth also represent 18% of juvenile offenders in residential placement (US DHHS, 2001).

MIGRATION AND ACCULTURATION

Given the disproportionately higher levels of poverty, stress, trauma of immigration and adapting to a foreign culture, and cultural isolation upon arrival, Latinos are in need of mental health services. Adjusting to a new environment, acquiring a new language, and contending with a host of internal and external demands, the stress may be much greater than previously thought, with chronic acculturation stress having enormous psychological implications (Santiago-Rivera et al., 2002). On average, Latinos have relatively low educational and economic status. Despite the fact that the United States is referred to as the second largest Latin American country in the world (Arredondo & Rodriguez, 2005), migration experiences and the psychological impact of these on mental health and well-being is an area of research that needs further exploration (Santiago-Rivera, 2003).

To have access to economic opportunity and to give their children a good life are the dreams of immigrants, regardless of their country of origin. Political instability, unemployment, wars, and devastation of a country's infrastructure often compel people in search of a better life to leave their homes. Although their homelands are rich in beauty, culture, and natural resources, economic and social development opportunities are often lacking (Suarez-Orozco & Paez, 2002). Feelings of personal loss and grief are part of the experience even when an individual's and/or family's economic outlook improves. Political turmoil may prevent some families from returning to their homeland. For some, there are fears of deportation if they return home. These circumstances can heighten a person's longing for home and the family and friends left behind (de las Fuentes, 2007). (See Storytelling: *I Quit*.) Acculturation or the process of adjusting to a nonnative culture (Miranda and Matheny, 2000) is a form of stress for many Latinos and there are multiple factors that contribute to this stress. The degree of acculturation, amount of coping with stress resources, facility with the English language, the degree of cohesiveness with family members, and the length of time that people have resided in the United States all impact acculturation stress for Latinos (Miranda and Matheney, 2000). Since September 11, 2001, xenophobic attitudes have increased, and Latinos found that attitudes and institutional structures impinged upon their lives. Acculturation stress is the emotional, physical disharmony and spiritual imbalance that is part of the acculturation process following immigration. Lack of a solid social network, limited facility with the English language, intergenerational conflicts, and overcrowded and unsafe living conditions and neighborhoods have been documented as part of the acculturation process (Arredondo & Rodriguez, 2005).

In working with Latinos, it is important to consider the client within the broader context of the family. A multidimensional ecological comparative model can help mental health professionals devise a relevant and respectful treatment approach. There are four domains to the model:

1. The impact of migration and cultural change
2. Family organization
3. The current ecological environment and the family
4. The family life cycle or transitions

(See Case Study: *Oblivious*)

Colorism refers to differential and often inequitable treatment because of skin color hue (Robinson & Ward, 1995). As with African American communities, colorism affects Latino communities. Sue and Sue (1990) indicated that "the more a person resembles an Indian, the more prejudice and discrimination he or she will encounter" (p. 298). A variety of hues—white, tan, black, brown, and red—compose the Latino population. This attests to roots from Africa, Asia, the Caribbean, Spain, and other parts of Europe, as well as Native American heritage. Research is needed to investigate the role of brown and black skin color hues among many Dominicans and Puerto Ricans and higher rates of poverty and family instability.

CULTURAL ORIENTATION AND VALUES

Cultural heritage commonalities are strong. Among most Latinos, cooperation rather than competition is stressed. The extended family and friendship networks are held in high esteem and are the basis of Latino culture (Gloria & Peregoy, 1995). (See Table 5.1.) Family members feel a sense of obligation to provide for and receive support from one another both emotionally and materially (Vasquez, 1994). *Familismo* (familialism) is considered to be one of the most important cultural values that Latino people have (Santiago-Rivera, 2003) and "involves the strong identification and attachment to nuclear and extended family. Loyalty, reciprocity, and solidarity among members of the family are associated with this attachment" (p. 50).

Latino cultures tend to be collectivistic, which means individual goals are subordinated to the larger group. Relationships in collectivistic cultures also tend to be more stable and even involuntary "because they arise from the fewer, yet closer knit, in-groups that permeate this orientation" (McCarthy, 2005, p. 110).

In many Mexican American families, the extended family is strong and includes *compradazgo*, or godparents, and among Puerto Ricans, *compadres*, or special friends, who often act as co-parents and receive a high place of honor, affection, and respect in the family (Santiago-Rivera et al., 2002). Gloria and Peregoy (1995) stated that more status is given to a person who honors family than to someone with material possessions.

Family structure and personal honor are highly valued. *Dignidad* is linked to both *personalismo* and *respeto*. *Personalismo* is an orientation in which the person is more important than the task. Warm and interpersonal relationships are valued (Santiago-Rivera, 2003). *Respeto* refers to "sensitivity to a person's position and creates a boundary within which conversations should be contained to avoid conflict" (Santiago-Rivera et al., 2002, p. 113). *Dignidad* encourages actions that cultivate pride for people independent of their position and refers to a strong sense of self-worth and personal dignity. A focus is also placed on being in the moment, with emphasis on the present.

TABLE 5.1 Common Cultural Values among Latinos
Personalismo (intimacy)
Dignidad (personal honor)
Familismo (faith in friends and family)
Respeto (respect)
Confianza (the development of trust and intimacy)
Simpatia (being a nice, gentle person)
Carino (a demonstration of endearment in verbal and nonverbal communication)
Orgullo (pride)
Loyalty to family
Collectivism
Service to others
Education as a means of development
Religion (for most, but not for all, the Catholic Church)

Family structures are often formal and hierarchical, practicing deference to elders and males. Although often misunderstood as related to men's sexual prowess and women's objectification and subjugation, *machismo* is a part of Latino culture that describes stoicism, the need for *dignidad*, or dignity, *respeto*, or respect, and in some instances, dominance within the family (Vasquez, 1994). Adherence to gender roles, such as males outside the home and females inside, represents another value orientation practiced by some Latino families (Arredondo, 1992). Preserving the Spanish language within the family is a common practice in many Hispanic homes.

In Latino culture, a premium is placed on personal relationships. *Personalismo*, or a desire to be close, to know one another intimately, and to communicate personally rather than impersonally, represents a value orientation common to many Latinos (Arredondo, 1992; Gloria & Peregoy, 1995). *Simpatia* refers to the value of smooth and harmonious interpersonal interactions (Gloria & Peregoy, 1995). It also speaks to the importance of harmonious and polite interactions (de las Fuentes, 2007).

Latino families are more likely to live within family units and, similar to Asian Americans and Pacific Islanders, are least likely to live alone. Children also tend to remain with the family (especially girls) until they marry. Demonstrated through loyalty for one's family, cultural pride is significant (Rendon & Robinson, 1994). According to Comas-Diaz (1993), the concept of *respeto* "governs all positive reciprocal interpersonal relationships, dictating the appropriate deferential behavior toward others on the basis of age, socioeconomic position, sex, and authority status" (p. 250). Within the concept of *respeto,* parents desire to raise children who are polite and well mannered (*bien educados*) as opposed to children who are not well behaved (*malcriados*) and is an indication of poor parenting (Arredondo & Rodriguez, 2005).

For most Latinos, the bond to Catholicism is strong. In fact, the concept of *Marianismo* "is based on the Catholic cult of the Virgin Mary, which dictates that when women become mothers they attain the status of Madonnas and, accordingly, are expected to deny themselves in favor of their children and husbands" (Vasquez, 1994, p. 202). Clearly, conflicts can emerge within this cultural value system, particularly for Latinas who may

Storytelling: I Quit

I went to college in southern California. One summer, I needed to find work to pay tuition. I found work in a factory where we made the telephone cords that went to landlines. We also detangled the cords as well. We used a chemical on the cords to clean them—this is what I and the other women in my particular area did all day long. Feeling bored, I decided to wipe these cords down while studying Italian—this did not go over well with the supervisor who told me to stop. Although I needed the money, I quit this job (I suspected that I was close to being fired). The smell of the chemical gave me a headache and made me nauseous. It was alarming that many pregnant Mexican women were subjected to this toxic chemical hour after hour every single day. I spoke to one of the women and told her that her job was dangerous to her health and to her baby's health. I remember that she looked at me like I was crazy. She said that she liked working and that she had a family. I soon came to realize that many of the women who worked at this factory were not in California legally. I was an American citizen, a college student, and needed summer work—I had no children to support. These women and their unborn children did not have the same privileges that I had.

be more acculturated. Overall, the church and faith play a crucial role and shape core beliefs, such as the importance of sacrifice; charity and service to others; and stoic suffering, even in the face of adversity (Sue & Sue, 1990). As is consistent with other groups who are more oriented toward collectivism than individualism, there is a holistic connection between the mind and body. *Curanderos,* or spiritual and herbal "folk" healers, who are primarily women, practice an ancient Native American art (Novas, 1994). They hold special status in many Mexican and Mexican American communities and often work in consultation on psychiatric cases with priests and other religious authorities (Arredondo, 1992). *Espiritistas* are spiritual guides, and *Santeros* (a reference to worshipers of Catholic saints and African gods) are consulted to diagnose conditions, both physical and psychological. Oils, prayers, holy water, candles, and special herbs are items used to perform rituals (Santiago-Rivera, 2003). For example, Aztecs have a rich history as herbalists, healers, botanists, and medical doctors (Padilla, 1984). That some of their descendants would have the gift of healing is understandable.

Communication styles represent a significant part of the way meanings are expressed and interpreted. Many Latinos tend to speak softly, avoid eye contact when listening to or speaking with persons perceived as having high status, and interject less. Often, the manner of expression is low-key and indirect (Sue & Sue, 1990). For many Latino youths and adults, being a linguistic minority represents a real barrier to education and employment. Families gather to celebrate holidays, birthdays, baptisms, first communions, graduations, and weddings. Latino families teach their children the importance of honor, good manners, and respect for authority and the elderly. Importance is given to physical appearance as a sense of honor, dignity, and pride. Formal attire is commonly worn to church, parties, social gatherings, and work.

Culture-bound syndromes are defined as "recurrent, locally specific patterns of a typical behavior and troubling experiences that may or may not be linked to a particular *DSM–IV* diagnostic category" (Shiarev & Levy, 2004, p. 244). Folk illness such as *empacho*, which is a bad upset stomach, *nervios* (nerves), and *mal de ojo* (evil eye) are often related to supernatural causes, particularly among Puerto Ricans, Cubans, and Dominicans. *Susto* refers to fright, and it originated from and is a combination of medieval Spanish, African, and indigenous beliefs (Santiago-Rivera, 2003). An expression of distress commonly linked to Latinos and Mediterranean groups is *ataques de nervios* or attack of nerves. Symptoms of an *ataque de nervios* include screaming uncontrollably, crying, trembling, heat in the chest rising to the head, and verbal or physical aggression. Death of a loved one, divorce, or interpersonal conflict can bring this syndrome about (Shiarev & Levy, 2004). Dissociative experiences, seizures, or fainting as well as suicidal gestures are known to occur in *ataques* (US DHHS, 2001).

Personal identity for Latino Americans is sociocentric in nature, with the self and self-interest often subordinated to the welfare of *la casa* and *la familia* (Becerra, 1988). The balance of group and individual prerogatives, however, depends on the individual manner of dealing with the culture in traditional, bicultural, nontraditional, or marginal terms. For traditional and bicultural persons, the balance will often be in favor of needs in the extended family. For nontraditional and marginal persons, the balance may favor more egocentric decisions and actions.

Traditional sex roles are clearly defined by *machismo* for men and *marianismo* and *hembrismo* for women (Becerra, 1988). *Machismo* is more than male physical dominance and sexual availability. It includes the role of a provider responsible for the welfare, protection, honor, and dignity of his family. *Marianismo* refers to the spiritual superiority of women and their capacity to endure all suffering, with reference to the Virgin Mary. After marriage, the *Madonna* concept includes sacrifice and femaleness, or *hembrismo*, in the form of strength, perseverance, and flexibility. These *hembrista* behaviors ensure survival and power through the children.

Personal identity is also associated with being strong. *Strong* refers to inner strength, or *fuerza de espiritu*, characterized by toughness, determination, and willpower (Dana, 1993). A strong person can confront a problem directly and be active in resolving it, thereby delaying the admission that help may be needed. *Controlarse*, or controlling oneself, is the key to being a strong person and includes *aguantarse*, or being able to withstand stress during bad times; *resignarse*, or resigning oneself and accepting fate; and *sobreponerse*, or imposing one's will or overcoming circumstance. A weak person will have little or no self-control and be less able to exercise responsibility or to display *orgullo*, or pride, and *verguenzza*, or shame. As a result, he is more easily influenced by people or events and is relatively unable to become strong.

The family name is very important to Latinos, with a man, along with his given name, adopting both his father's and mother's names. It is often expected, as well as encouraged, that family members will sacrifice their own needs for the welfare of the family (Goldenberg & Goldenberg, 1996). Thus, the family constellation is loyal, committed, and responsible to each other and has a strong sense of honor.

IMPLICATIONS FOR COUNSELORS AND PSYCHOLOGISTS

Among many collectivistic cultures, mental health services are not sought because in-group members' reliance for help comes from family or church. Persons who are members of the out-group might be viewed with mistrust and suspicion (McCarthy, 2005). Other barriers to counseling services for Latinos include mental health services that are culturally insensitive and a lack of Spanish speaking counselors. Spanish language skills, being an effective listener, engaging in intentional questioning, having empathy, and strong diagnostic skills, can make a big difference within therapy. Other considerations are just as important. For example, there is much informality in Western culture—everyone is on a first-name basis—but some clients of color as well as some White people are put off by a casual air because it feels disrespectful to them. This is a basic concept when working with clients who are older than the clinician. The concept of *falta de respeto* (lack of respect) is considered to be a major cause for breakdowns in communication across a number of relationship dyads (Santiago-Rivera et al., 2002). The Western view of the nuclear family is limiting for many Latinos and is connected to the cultural tendency to bifurcate and separate the self into discrete categories. Among many Latinos, family need not be defined through blood. It is important for counselors, then, to assess the clients' relationships within and outside the nuclear family (Schoulte, 2011).

An understanding of collectivistic frameworks and their influence on people's problem orientation and resolve can help a clinician serving Latino individuals. Many Latino families value close and intimate communication styles in which there is greater emphasis on the group and less on the individual acting as a lone agent. In many Latino families, the husband is the primary and only breadwinner, with gender roles well prescribed.

CASE STUDY

Oblivious

Zoe is a 23-year-old graduate student who has traveled to Guatemala with her college professor and other college students. Zoe was adopted as an infant from Guatemala. Through her travels, she is struck at how beautiful the country is. She also encounters the extreme poverty that many Guatemalan people experience daily—the skin color differences are striking to her as well—and she is aware that had she stayed in Guatemala, many opportunities might not have been available to her because of her dark skin color. Gender roles are well prescribed, and many women her age do not have an opportunity to get educated at the university. Zoe is angry at not knowing about her country of origin, sad at the discrimination, and confused at how she has remained oblivious to class, gender, and skin color issues, not only in Guatemala but in the United States. Zoe has always resented being mistaken for an African American—her adopted sister, who is also from Guatemala, looks European. Zoe has always preferred her sister's appearance over her own. Zoe never mentioned this to her mother. They never spoke about race or skin color in their home. Zoe resented it when people wanted to connect with her because of her race. Throughout her life, Zoe emphasized athletics (she won a softball scholarship to college because of her talents). She also emphasized her academic strengths, religion, and love for animals (she has two cats and a dog at home with her mother and sister). The trip has been life-changing for Zoe, who enjoyed long conversations with her professor, with local women, and with some of the students of color with whom she is traveling. Zoe observed the women in Guatemala see themselves within the context of their relationships. She is eager to return in order to find out more about herself, her birth mother and birth father.

QUESTIONS

1. Why was Zoe so unaware of her country of origin?
2. How could a therapist be effective with Zoe's confusion, anger, and sadness?

DISCUSSION AND INTEGRATION

Zoe

According to Falbo and De Baessa (2006), Guatemala is divided between Indian and non-Indian groups. The Indian groups, making up 40% of the population, are considered to be descendents of the ancient Mayans, who dominated the area during the first millennium AD. Beginning in 1523, the Indians were compelled to assimilate into the Spanish colonial system; this was typical of the colonizers' mindset, as they were determined to extinguish the indigenous peoples' language and ethnic identity. *Ladinos*, a term used to describe non-Indians, refers to a mix of the descendents of the ancient Mayans and Spanish colonists who are part of the dominant national culture. *Ladinization* is the process of shifting from Indian to Ladino. Although a diversity of experiences exist, Ladinos on average have higher social status than Indians (Falbo & De Baessa, 2006).

Like other Latinos, Guatemalans have a variety of phenotypes. There were African slaves in Guatemala, and some Guatemalans, due to their African roots, have dark skin and other Negroid features. Guatemala is home to more than 6,000 Black Guatemalans. A key ingredient to effective counseling is to wait and listen for valuable information that the client and the counseling process can and will reveal. In time, ask appropriate questions. Prior to her trip, Zoe knew that Guatemala was a Central American country. She also knew that Spanish was spoken, the dominant language of the conquistadores. She did not know about the Garifuna people or the Indian languages that are spoken as well, namely Kiché and Q'eqchi' (Falbo & De Baessa, 2006). Zoe knew that poverty rates were very high among in Guatemala, but she was unaware of the class/caste/color differences. Q'eqchi people tend to have less formal education and lower earnings than other Indian groups (Falbo & De Baessa, 2006). Her upbringing did not emphasize her country of origin; the focus was family- and community-centered. She was taught values of respect for elders, hard work, and honesty. She cannot recall a conversation with her mother about racism, racial pride, or racial socialization. An effective therapist would be able to listen extremely well to the range of emotions, to the confusion, and to the difficult work of identify formation and transformation: Who am I? Where do I come from? What do I love? Who do I want to be?

Summary

This chapter focused on Latinos. A demographical snapshot was provided and included information about representation in the population by ethnic group, the most populated states where Latinos reside, and educational attainment. Immigration was discussed, as were push and pull factors contributing to immigration. A case study was included, and cultural elements were discussed. An adopted Latina child and the confusion of learning about the meaning of race, color, and gender differences were addressed through the case study.

People of African Descent

> *Beah told me to say "thank you" to adversity because it gives you another perspective and makes you stronger.*
>
> LISAGAY HAMILTON, *FILMMAKER, ON BEAH RICHARDS,*
>
> POET, ACTIVIST, ACTRESS

This chapter is about people of African descent. The majority of Black people in this country are descendents of African slaves. The term *people of African descent* is used to recognize this majority as well as refer to people who have origins in any of the Black racial groups of Africa.

HISTORY, CE 500–1500

The skeletal remains of the earth's earliest human come from East Africa, representing all *Homo sapiens'* ancestors. According to Bennett (1982),

> Civilization started in the great river valleys of Africa and Asia, in the Fertile Crescent in the Near East and along the narrow ribbon of the Nile in Africa … Blacks, or people who would be considered Blacks today, were among the first people to use tools, paint pictures, plant seeds, and worship gods. (p. 5)

Between CE 500 and 1600, Africa had empires, governments, and systems of trade throughout the continent. The West African empires of Ghana, Mali, and Songhai emerged in the western Sudan and were in existence during that time (Christian, 1995). Each of these three states had a powerful king and was wealthy, with an abundance of gold, thriving agriculture, manufacturing, and successful international trading efforts. Ghana dominated the Sudan for three centuries and reached its peak in the early part of the 11th century. Mali rose in the 13th century, and Songhai was a formidable power in the 15th and 16th centuries. During this time, Timbuktu represented one of the world's greatest cities, with a reputation as the intellectual center of the Songhai empire.

The Slave Trade

The majority of African Americans trace their ancestry to the slave trade. The slave trade operated for four centuries. In 1501, for instance, the Spanish government authorized the use of African slaves in the Americas. Portugal was actually the first country to land a cargo of slaves in the Western Hemisphere (Christian, 1995) and remained the dominant slave trader well until the end of the 16th century (Stewart, 1996). In addition to the Portuguese, the Spanish, Dutch, British, and the colonies provided fierce competition for this lucrative industry, in which human beings were traded for gold, salt, sugar, wine, and tobacco. Nations that controlled most of the American waters controlled most of the trade. Slaves were shipped to Cuba, Spain, the West Indies, and to the colonies. The first American slave ship bound for Africa was called the *Rainbow* and sailed from Boston.

During the slave trade throughout Europe and the Americas, nearly 12 million people were taken out of Africa, mainly from West and Central Africa. Slave ships brought kidnapped Africans to the Western Hemisphere, which included the American colonies, Brazil, and the Caribbean. Most slaves came from an area bordering a 3,000-mile stretch on the West Coast of Africa. They hailed from different tribes, including the Hausas, Mandingos, Yorubas, Efiks, Krus, Ashantis, Dahomeans, Senegalese, and Fantins (Bennett, 1982).

It is estimated that as many as 2 million people perished at port, at sea, or upon arrival during the slave trade. The **middle passage** typically refers to the journey from Africa to the Americas, Europe, or the Caribbean. From roughly 1450 to 1600, about 367,000 Africans were removed from Africa, with this number increasing dramatically to more than 6 million during the 18th century.

Africans played a role in capturing other Africans for sale to White slave traders. Prior to European enslavement of Africans, slavery existed in the African states. This historical reality was used to justify the use of African slaves among Europeans. Although enslavement of any human being is morally reprehensible, there were two important differences between the slavery of Africans by other Africans and the slavery of Africans by Europeans. African slavery was not plantation or mining slavery. It did not strip African people of family linkage, nor was it based on racial hatred that reduced people's humanity. African slaves owned by other Africans would sometimes marry, own property, and become a member of the family (Zinn, 2003). The extent of Africans' participation in the selling of other Africans to Europeans depends on which version of history we read. According to Bennett (1982), there has been an attempt to overemphasize the degree of African involvement. Bennett said, "It is true that some Africans, corrupted by Europe's insatiable desire for human flesh, sold their countrymen. But many Africans, like King Almammy and Captain Tobba, loathed the whole business and forbade their subjects to take part in it" (p. 47). According to Stewart (1996), "Most of the Africans who became slaves were sold into slavery by other Africans ... A lucrative trade for European goods, especially weapons, facilitated the selling of slaves to the Europeans" (p. 10). Africans captured by other Africans and sold to White slave traders who sold them to the highest bidder in Virginia became part of the social structure of the colony (Christian, 1995).

The year 1619 is designated as the date when the first African settlers reached North America on a Dutch man-of-war in Jamestown, Virginia. This group of African indentured servants was not regarded as slaves. In exchange for their passage over, people sold their labor for a period of time. Thousands of Whites used this method as a means of coming to the colonies, and life for them was often similar to that of Black indentured servants. They worked alongside each other farming, clearing forests, and cutting tobacco. For these first forty years, Black settlers moved about with relative ease and had voting rights, and even—after surviving indentured servitude—purchased other Blacks. This system began to erode with the arrival of greater numbers of Africans, which made the profits from the slave trade escalate for both the slave trader and slave owner.

These servants were not, however, the first Africans to arrive in North America. Estevanico was the most important African explorer of the Americas and the first non-Native to discover the present-day Southwest. He was born in Morocco around 1500 and left Spain in 1527 as the slave of Andres Dorantes. These two were members of the expedition of Pánfilo de Narváez, the Spanish governor of Florida. Estevanico became the first foreign explorer of the southwestern United States and explored the area that became Arizona and New Mexico (Christian, 1995; Stewart, 1996). In 1539, Estevanico was murdered by Zuni Indians who were protecting their land.

During the latter part of the 1700s, southeast Native American tribes such as the Choctaws, Seminoles, and Creeks were slave owners, with the Cherokees having the largest number of slaves. Prior to Native people's removal to Indian Territory, Native Americans used Black slaves on their plantations in Georgia and Tennessee.

The slave trade was outlawed by the United States in 1808. At that time, there were approximately 1 million slaves. By 1860, there were close to 4 million, with Virginia having more slaves than any other state, followed by Georgia, Alabama, and Mississippi. Along with Texas, Louisiana, Tennessee, and Arkansas, these states were the cotton kingdoms, in which half of the US Black population lived and worked. Although the slave trade had been outlawed, slavery itself continued in the South until Lincoln, out of military necessity, signed the Emancipation Proclamation in 1863. The purpose of this document was to deprive the South of its slave labor power. Lincoln had no authority to free slaves in the slave states which had remained loyal to the Union, but only in those which had joined the Confederacy in rebellion. In 1865, on June 19th, a day better known as "Juneteenth," slavery was outlawed in Texas. Later that year, on December 18th, slavery became illegal with the passage of the 13th Amendment to the US Constitution.

RESISTANCE TO SLAVERY

A history of resistance and revolt characterize the African slaves. In 1526, at the San Miguel settlement in present-day South Carolina, slaves set fire to the settlement and fled to live among the Native Americans. Those slaves who managed to make it safely to the Gracia Real de Santa Teresa de Mose settlement, founded by escaped slaves, were granted their freedom by the King of Spain.

Slaves were required to work in tobacco, cocoa, sugar, and cotton fields. They also worked in gold and silver plantations, rice fields, in construction and timber industries as well as within the home. The resistance to slavery was multifaceted: it was political and literary, and it appeared on the pulpit as preachers spoke against this abomination to humankind. Many slaves ran away, often seeking to be reunited with loved ones and risking life and limb to escape their enslavement. The Black poet Frances E. W. Harper was born to free Blacks in Maryland. Some thought her to be a man or a White person with a black-painted face, given how intelligent and articulate she was (talk about discourses!). She protested the unequal treatment of people on the basis of gender and race. Her poem "The Slave Auction" appeared in her 1854 *Poems of Miscellaneous Subjects*:

> And mothers stood with streaming eyes,
> And saw their dearest children sold;
> Unheeded rose their bitter cries,
> While tyrants bartered them for gold.

Slavery was a barbaric institution supported by the government and often sanctioned by Christianity. The impact on and implications for Black people's mental health, self-image, psyches, and earning potential can never be truly assessed.

The ways in which Black people coped or resisted took on a number of different forms, with religion and spirituality being critical. "In the slave quarters, African Americans organized their own 'invisible institution.' Through signals, passwords, and messages not discernible to Whites, they called believers to 'hush harbors' where they freely mixed African rhythms, singing, and beliefs with evangelical Christianity" (Maffly-Kipp, 2000, p. 2). Negro spirituals had double meanings of salvation and freedom/escape. It was in this context that spirituals were created.

The only way for many Blacks to gain access to opportunity was to leave the South. Baltimore was considered a border city and represented a popular place for newly freed slaves to start a new life, after looking from town to town for displaced loved ones. In the same year the 13th Amendment was ratified, the Ku Klux Klan was organized in Pulaski, Tennessee. Its purpose was to undermine racial equality through acts of terrorism, which often went unpunished and, in some municipalities, were sanctioned by political officers who were themselves Klan members.

The 14th Amendment in 1868 extended citizenship to African Americans, whereas the 15th Amendment ensured the right to vote. Poll taxes, grandfather clauses, and literacy tests prevented Blacks from voting. ***De jure*** (by law) **segregation** replaced slavery—also known as Jim Crow. This inferior status of Blacks was supported by law, requiring Blacks to ride at the back of the bus, sit in different sections of movie theaters and sports stadiums, drink at separate water faucets, live in separate neighborhoods, and eat at separate restaurants.

After passage of the 13th Amendment, many Blacks sharecropped. Sharecroppers worked the landowner's land for a share of the profit once the crop went to market. Landowners kept the accounts. Keeping landowners honest was very difficult for sharecroppers who were mainly powerless and illiterate.

The majority of Blacks in the United States reside in the South. This percentage declined during the 20th century because of a series of events collectively known as the Great Migration. World War I created a huge demand for unskilled labor in the urban North; recruiters went to the South to bring Black workers to northern cities such as Pittsburgh, Chicago, Detroit, and Indianapolis. Between 1916 and 1919, 500,000 African Americans moved north (Stewart, 1996). During and after World War II, nearly 5 million Blacks went north between 1940 and 1960.

DEMOGRAPHIC TRENDS

As the second largest group of color in the United States, the 38.9 million people of African descent come from diverse cultures, including Africa, Haiti, the Dominican Republic, Jamaica, Central Europe, and North and South America. African Americans are 12.6% of the US population (Humes, Jones, & Ramirez, 2011). Outside of the White population, the Black population had the smallest percentage growth between 2000 and 2010, growing by 4.3 million people and grew slower than most of the major racial groups.

Of all African Americans, 8% are foreign born. About 66% of foreign-born Blacks come from Latin America, and 30% come from Africa. Of Black immigrants to the United States, 39% have arrived since 2000. Since the early 1980s more than 100,000 refugees have come to the United States from African nations (US Department of Health and Human Services, 2001). In Massachusetts, 1 in 4 Black people is foreign born.

The majority of Blacks in America reside in 10 states: New York, Florida, Georgia, Texas, California, Illinois, North Carolina, Maryland, Virginia, and Louisiana. In 2010, 55% of Blacks lived in the South, 18% in the Midwest, 17% in the Northeast, and 10% in the West (Rastogi, Johnson, Hoeffel, & Drewery, Jr., 2011).

States in the West have low proportions of Blacks in the population. Blacks make up less than 5% of the population in the West, and were less than 2% of the populations of Idaho, Utah, Vermont, New Hampshire, South Dakota, Maine, Wyoming, and Montana. A similar situation exists in most New England states, where Blacks are less than 1% of the population in Vermont, New Hampshire, and Maine. In the District of Columbia, 52% of the residents are Black. In Mississippi, Alabama, Louisiana, Maryland, Georgia, and South Carolina, more than 25% of each state's residents are African Americans.

SOCIAL, PSYCHOLOGICAL, AND PHYSIOLOGICAL HEALTH ISSUES

In 2010, the median age of the nation was 37.2 years (Howden & Meyer, 2011). The geographical area with the lowest median ages is the United States-Mexico border. Persons with the lowest median age are Latinos/Hispanics. The highest median ages are among Non-Hispanic Whites in Maine, Vermont, West Virginia, New Hampshire, and Florida. Although older than Latinos, African Americans are younger by about 9 years than the median age of non-Hispanic Whites. Persons between the ages of 15 to 44 are 44.1% of the population, followed by children under the age of 18 at 29.4%. Persons 45 to 64 are 23.4% of the population, with people 65 and older at 8.6% (US Census Bureau, Current Population Survey Annual Social and Economic Supplement, 2010).

In 2004, Black women had higher rates of fertility than White women. Over 60% (62.4%) of the Black women who gave birth in 2004 were unmarried, compared with 20.5% of White women. In 2010, the greatest proportion of Black people (36.5%) were in nonfamily households, A nonfamily household is defined as people who live alone or people living with unrelated individuals. Family households are defined as households in which at least one member is related to the person who owns or rents the occupied housing unit. Twenty-eight percent of Black households had women only with no male present; 29% were married couples, and over 6% (6.4) were male only with no spouse present. Blacks are more likely than Whites to live with and care for grandchildren. About 7% of Blacks aged 30 and older were grandparents living in the same household with their co-resident grandchildren under the age of 18.

Compared with the population at large, Blacks have higher rates of marital divorce, separation, and never-married status. Between the race and Hispanic-origin groups, Blacks have the lowest sex ratio, with Black females outnumbering Black males throughout every decade. In 2010, 46.8% of the Black population over the age of 15 had never been married, compared with 26.1% among Whites. Rates of separation are higher than those in the general population: 4.1% among Blacks compared with 3.3%for the total (US Census Bureau, Current Population Survey, Annual Social and Economic Supplement, 2010). In 2010 the poverty rate for African Americans was 27.4% (DeNavas-Walt, Proctor, & Smith 2011) compared with 13.2% for the nation at large.

Black children are more likely to live in female-headed households, which are disproportionately poor. Nearly two-thirds, or 66%, of Black children live in poverty. Black people are more likely to live in severe poverty in comparison to Whites. Blacks tend to have less money saved, lower rates of home ownership (54% of Blacks live in renter-occupied homes), and fewer investments (US DHHS, 2001; DeNavas-Walt et al., 2011).

Among Black people who own homes, the median value of their homes is $104,000, which is $50,000 less than the median value of White owner-occupied homes. There is another side to Black economic conditions. More than 30% of Blacks in America have incomes between $35,000 and $75,000. Nearly 32% live in the suburbs (US DHHS, 2001). Although there is a discernible middle class among African Americans, regardless of income, Black people in America tend to have fewer resources (e.g., public services, access to health care) and tend to be segregated in neighborhoods and have higher levels of health risks (Institute of Medicine, 2003). Compared with Whites, Black people are more likely to use public transportation to commute to work (12% of Blacks compared with 3% of Whites).

There have been increases in the high school graduation level, which is now at 84% among Blacks 25 years of age and older. This compares with 88.6% for non-Hispanic Whites (US Census Bureau Current Population Survey, 2011). Nineteen percent had completed a bachelor's degree (US Census Bureau, 2010). Under one-third, or 27%, of Blacks are employed in management or professional occupations compared with 38% among non-Hispanic Whites. Nearly 24% of Blacks work in sales and office occupations, which is similar to non-Hispanic Whites at 27%. Approximately one-quarter of Blacks work in service occupations, with 6% in construction jobs. Among non-Hispanic Whites, 14% are in service and 10% work in construction jobs. Higher percentages of Blacks are in production (13.1%) and transportation (11.7%) in comparison with Whites.

Compared with the general population, Black people are more likely to be exposed to violence, which has implications for mental illness symptoms such as depression and post-traumatic stress disorder (PTSD). More than 20% of Blacks do not have health insurance despite more than 8 in 10 African Americans being in working families (US Census Bureau, 2010). Access to mental health care is limited. Among Blacks who have health insurance, treatment-seeking behavior for mental health services does not automatically increase. Reluctance to seek mental health services is related to the stigmatizing attitudes that exist regarding mental health care.

One study found that the number of Blacks who feared mental health treatment was 2.5 times greater than the proportion of Whites who felt the same way (US DHHS, 2001). Other research found that Blacks were less likely than Whites to be properly diagnosed when suffering from affective disorders, such as depression. The tendency of clinicians, both Black and White, was to diagnose Blacks with schizophrenia (Good, James, Good, & Becker, 2003).

African Americans are approximately 13% of the US population, but they represent 41% of the incarcerated population in city and county jails and state and federal prisons (Harrison & Beck, 2005). Among Black males ages 25 to 29, 8.4% were in prison compared with 2.5% of Hispanic males and about 1.2% of White males in the same age group. Black women are two and four times more likely to be incarcerated compared to Hispanic and White women, respectively.

The higher rates of non-marriage and female-headed households among Black people need to be considered in context of socioeconomic data and the experience of so many Black men in America. According to the Washington-based research and advocacy group Justice Policy Institute (JPI), African American men are more likely to go to jail than to college. Between 1980 and 2000, the number of African American men in jail or prison grew three times as fast as the number in colleges and universities. The JPI report compared two decades of data from the Bureau of Justice Statistics and the National Center for Education Statistics and found that although states had plenty to spend on prisons, they had much less to devote to education (Schulte, 2002).

Health outcomes are related to lifestyle choices, such as smoking and nutrition. Blacks have myriad health challenges that must be examined in conjunction with the experiences of poverty, substandard housing, underemployment, unemployment, unequal access to quality health care, and chronic racial discrimination. Blacks suffer diabetes at a rate more than three times that of Whites, heart disease at a rate 40% higher than that of Whites, prostate cancer at a rate more than double that of Whites, HIV/AIDS at a rate more than seven times that of Whites, and infant mortality at a rate twice that of Whites (US DHHS, 2001). Relative to Whites, African Americans (along with Latinos) are less likely to receive appropriate cardiac medication (e.g., thrombolytic therapy, aspirin, and beta blockers) or to undergo coronary artery bypass surgery even when insurance status, income, co-morbid conditions, age, and symptom expression are taken into account (IOM, 2003).

Physical Appearance

Skin color has social power and status within the African American community (Okazawa-Rey et al., 1987). Mullins and Sites (1984) found that the inheritance of light skin color, which generally came from the mother, who tended to be lighter than the father, along with the mother's education, occupational attainment, and income, served to bolster a family's social position over time. Within a society preoccupied with skin color and where white skin is valued, the desirability of lighter-skinned women stems from their closer proximity to European beauty standards. Research has found that skin-color hue affects income, educational attainment, and perceptions of success (Rockquemore, 2002).

Intraracial conflict around **colorism,** or stereotyped attributions and prejudgments based on skin color, has been documented in the literature (Okazawa-Rey et al., 1987; Robinson & Ward, 1995; Rockquemore, 2002). As children, many African American women remember being cautioned by their mothers that unless their newly washed hair was "done" (which meant being pressed and curled or braided), they could not go outside. The implicit and sometimes explicit message in this statement was that a female's natural state was synonymous with not being presentable and looking unkempt. Among Black Americans, appearance is not solely linked to skin color but to a variety of phenotypical traits, such as body shape, facial features, and hair texture (Rockquemore, 2002).

Colorism is often manifested as a preference for lighter skin tones over darker ones. Color-consciousness is rooted in the social, political, and economic conditions that existed during and after slavery (Hall, 1992; Hall, 2005). During slavery, persons who were lighter in skin color received privileges that darker-skinned Blacks did not. Privileges included working inside of the house instead of outside or having educational opportunities. The color hue differences were due to mixed-race offspring who had White slave owning fathers and Black slave mothers. Colorism in the Black community may be a double-edged sword, affecting those who are seen perhaps as "too black" and those who may be seen as "not black enough." Discrimination against persons with lighter skin tones occurs as well. Robinson and Ward (1995) reported that African American adolescents reported high levels self-esteem, yet students who were at the extremes of skin color, lighter or darker than most African Americans, were less satisfied with skin color than students who were somewhere in the middle. Skin color attitudes are connected to several variables, including the particular ethnic group; group cohesiveness; the group's status in society; family, school, peers, and majority vs. minority status (Phinney, 1992). For instance, Harvey, LaBeach, Pridgen, and Gocial (2005) found that at a predominantly Black university, students placed more emphasis on skin tone than students at a predominantly White university. According to Ward (2000), unhealthy strategies of surviving racism include adopting hairstyles for the sole purpose of looking White and discriminating against other African Americans on the basis of skin color. She maintains that Black children and arguably adults must be taught to value their bodies for their strength and to appreciate the diversity of beauty found in Black people.

CULTURAL ORIENTATION AND VALUES

There is great diversity among people of African descent in country of origin, language, ethnicity, class, education, acculturation level, point of entry into America, and religious orientation. Despite struggle and hardship, values that transcend intragroup diversity are spirituality, persistence, forgiveness, resistance, humor, wisdom, and resilience (Exum & Moore, 1993). Spirituality is typically cited as a primary value in helping men and women survive prostate and breast cancer diagnoses and endure the strains of caregiver burden (Dilworth-Anderson, Boswell, & Cohen, 2007; Hamilton, Powe, Pollard, Lee, & Felton, 2007; Halbert et al., 2007). Black people are united by strong and rich spiritual traditions that infuse educational systems, cultural values, kinship networks, and political revolutions. Cultivating one's spirit and maintaining a strong connection with the church represent a foundation for the experience of most Blacks in America. Black people may not go to church or even have a church home, but they may still "pray to the Lord" (Boyd-Franklin, 2003, p. 270) when confronted with difficult times, such as illness, death, loss, and bereavement.

Historically, the Black church has been a focal point in the African American community and a force for advocacy and social and political change. The Black church played a prominent role in the civil rights movement, voter registration, fund-raising for college students, health promotion, and personal and spiritual development. Many musicians and other celebrities had their talents recognized and nurtured by participating in the choir, youth programs, and leadership forums. Although the majority of Blacks in American regard themselves as Christians, growing numbers of Blacks are Muslims, Buddhists, Jews, and agnostics.

Values common among many Blacks in America include the extended family, even including those who are not blood relatives. Collaborative relationships are valued over highly individualistic styles (Sue & Sue, 1990). Education as a means of self-help and a strong work ethic are often

Storytelling: She Didn't Really Love Him

Well over a decade ago, an almost 40-year-old Black woman married a man that she met online. She didn't really love him, but he said he loved her; he wanted to be a father; and she wanted to be a mom—and she thought her time was running out to find someone. She was overweight and did not feel good about her physical appearance. She wondered who else would love her and when she would ever have another opportunity at marriage and motherhood. Her dear friend said to her before the wedding, "You do not have to go through with this if you do not want to—it is never too late." The woman married the man anyway. They had children and loved them dearly. The woman was not truly happy in marriage. Her husband was extremely critical and she felt controlled. Although she was college-educated, she felt small, dumb, and insignificant in his presence. She eventually filed for divorce. The woman vowed to always, in the future, listen to her inner voice and not expect others to love her more than she was willing to love herself.

This story puts a face on the census data which documents the very high rates of non-marriage among Black women, across educational levels. Black women receive the same messages in society as do other women regarding the significance of marriage which can lead women to make desperate choices born more of fear than true love. A college education may mediate or attenuate the effects of sexism and other forms of oppression, but higher education does not indemnify one from oppression.

taught to children from a very early age. Communication patterns are not limited to verbal dialogue or to standard English—the Black dialect has survived rather well as has a sense of humor when dealing with injustice and all things ludicrous. Most Black people depend on nonverbal modes of communication patterns—*how* something is said rather than *what* is actually verbally spoken. Body movement, postures, gestures, and facial expressions represent dominant patterns of communication within the African American community. These tend not to be strictly linear as in Western society (Exum & Moore, 1993). Another value often manifested in the Black community is giving people status as a function of age and position. A present-time orientation is seen at church, parties, and other events. The event may formally begin at one time, but the majority of people may arrive at a later time. This fluid relationship with time varies by individual differences and acculturation levels. Value is also placed on the use of proverbs (e.g., "Every goodbye ain't gone") and spiritual wisdom ("If a door closes another one opens") to not only cope but to resist and to thrive. (See Table 6.1.)

According to Nobles (1972), African Americans' cultural traditions have been derived from several cultural and philosophical premises shared with West African tribes. Myers (1991) states:

> Afrocentricity refers to a worldview that believes reality is both spiritual and material at once...with highest value on positive interpersonal relationships between men/women; self knowledge is assumed to be the basis of all knowledge, and one knows through symbolic imagery and rhythm. (p. 19)

Within Afrocentric thought, the self is extended in unity with others and emphasis is on the collective. An African proverb, "I am because we are and since we are, therefore I am," summarizes the saliency of the collective. Among some African Americans, **consubstantiation**, or the sense that everything within the universe is connected as a part of a whole, is a way of seeing the world (Parham, 1992). Myers (1991) stated that, in the Afrocentric paradigm, spirit and matter are one and are a representation of one spirit manifesting good.

The *Nguzo Saba,* or classical African values, also provide insight into African American values (Karenga, 1980). The first and third principles are *Umoja* and *Ujima* and refer to unity and collective work and responsibility, respectively. These principles endorse solidarity, harmony, cooperation,

TABLE 6.1 Common Cultural Values among People of African Descent
Oral traditions
Reliance on proverbial wisdom
Spirituality and faith
Firm child-rearing practices
Education as a means of self-help
Collateral interpersonal relations
Formal communication styles with elders and authority figures
Respect for elders and authority figures
Nonverbal modes of communication
Extended family based on blood and strong ties
Unity and cooperation
Resistance
Purpose
Creativity
Fluid time orientation

and connection with others toward a common destiny. The second principle, *Kujichagalia,* means self-determination and naming for the self who the self will be, despite others' definitions. *Ujaama,* the fourth principle, refers to cooperative economics, in which resources are shared for the good of all. *Nia* or purpose is the fifth principle and benefits not only the self but also the collective, for which everyone has responsibility. The sixth principle is *Kuumba,* or creativity. Creativity is inextricably linked to imagination, ingenuity, and leaving the world a better place than it was when you first arrived. *Imani,* or faith, is the last principle and encompasses the past, present, and future.

Worldview refers to the way people make meaning. Adapted from Hilliard's work, Exum and Moore (1993) summarized elements of African American worldview. These include emphasis on the whole as opposed to the parts, preference for approximations over accuracy, focus on people rather than things, and acceptance and integration with the environment. In addition to these values is a respect for nature and emphasis on the group:

A theory of resistance is based on the Nguzo Saba principles (Brookins & Robinson, 1995; Robinson & Ward, 1991; Robinson & Kennington, 2002). The goal of resistance theory is to empower marginalized groups with optimal tools to name, confront, repudiate, and replace dominant and demeaning messages with knowledge of self and community (Ward, 2000). Resistance theory is an important response to the chronic stress of racism. There is limited research related to the use of specific modes of coping with perceived racism (Clark, Anderson, Clark, & Williams, 2002). African tradition includes a strong tie between the living and the world of the dead in defining the scope of community. J. A. Opoku (personal communication, April 3, 1994) said about Ghanaian culture, "The dead are still with us."

Robinson-Wood (2009) conducted research with 80 Black women, mostly students from a private, predominantly White university in Massachusetts and all 18–25 years old. They were administered the Africultural Coping Systems Inventory (ACSI). Of the ACSI's four coping modalities—cognitive emotional, ritual, collective, and spiritual-centered—collective coping was utilized most. Collectively centered coping reflects a reliance on the group and appears to be most similar to problem-focused/approach coping. It involves an awareness of what and how others have dealt with similarly difficult situations. Among many Black people, collective centeredness is central to being in the world.

There is great diversity among Black families, yet there are similarities independent of place within the Diaspora. According to Black (1996), people of African descent are set apart from other ethnic groups by the following:

1. The African legacy rich in custom and culture
2. The history of slavery and its insidious attempts to destroy people's souls while keeping their physical bodies in servitude
3. Historical and contemporary racism and sexism
4. The victim system, in which people are denied access and then blamed for their marginalized positions

African American families have demonstrated a stability and cohesive functioning that is often culture specific. Competencies among intact inner-city African American families include shared power, strong parental coalitions, closeness without sacrificing individual ego boundaries, and negotiation in problem solving. Many of these competent families are at risk because of economic conditions, appalling neighborhood conditions, violence, and uncertainty in employment status (Ingrassia, 1993).

As a result of economic conditions, families often do not include only blood relations but may have uncles and aunts, cousins, "big mamas," "play sisters," and "home boys and girls." In many Black American families, there is a three-generation system. The extended families encourage an elastic, kinship-based exchange network that may last a lifetime. These families exhibit spiritual strength, role flexibility, and interchangeability in which male–female relationships are often egalitarian because of the presence of working wives, mothers, and grandmothers (Hines & Boyd-Franklin, 1996; Staples, 1988). Members of the extended family may also exhibit "child keeping," using an informal adoption network.

Despite a feminist perspective that characterized large numbers of Black homes prior to women's liberation, African American men have identity as the nominal heads of households, tied in to their ability to provide for their families. Women often socialize their daughters for strength, economic independence, family responsibility, and daily accountability (Boyd-Franklin, 1989). Many Black mothers also raise their daughters with the responsibility of educating them about racism and sexism (Turner, 1997). Wilkinson (1997) said, "In the racially structured and multicultural evolution of this country, sex and gender alone have not been the principal determinants of the experiences or self-definitions of Native Americans or Americans, Mexican Americans, Japanese, and certainly not of African Americans" (p. 267).

African Americans, according to a recent study conducted by the Pew Charitable trust are "markedly" more religious on a variety of measures compared to other groups, including belief in God and miracles, daily prayer, and the importance of religion in their lives. In comparison with other racial and ethnic groups, African-Americans are among the most likely to indicate a formal religious affiliation. Eighty-seven percent stated they belonged to one religious group or another. Of this number, 59% had affiliation with a historically Black Protestant church, 15% were affiliated with Evangelical Protestant churches, 12% were unaffiliated and this group prayed nearly as often as the overall population of mainline Protestants; 5% were Catholic; 5% were other, and 1% did not answer. (Pew Forum US Religious Landscape Survey, 2008). Black women are regarded as possessing fortitude, perseverance, and strength during adversity. As such, women are also generally more religious than men and function to tie the family into a complete church-centered support system of persons in particular roles, activities, and social life (Boyd-Franklin, 2010; Hines & Boyd-Franklin, 1996). This culture-specific description of the African American family is not intended to suggest that all families are extended and nonconsanguineous in composition. Increasing numbers of Blacks are single, and many marriages have an increasing fragility as reflected in the higher rates of divorce and separation when compared with the general population (Boyd-Franklin, 1989; Ingrassia, 1993). Many African Americans are acculturated, identify with the dominant European American culture, and are more egocentric in lifestyle and less communal in orientation.

IMPLICATIONS FOR COUNSELORS AND PSYCHOLOGISTS

Multicultural competence requires knowledge of the psychological stress that is born of racism and oppression as well as clinical skills to improve mental health outcomes. Sutherland and Moodley (2010) discussed historical hostility which describes the collective psychology of Black people due to exposure to slavery, discrimination, and fears about unequal treatment. It is this historical context as well as contemporary realities of the ongoing and pervasive nature of racism that helping professionals need to be aware of and to know how to integrate this information into assessment, diagnosis, and intervention.

Part of our competence as mental health professionals is to realize our limitations. It is important not to get overwhelmed by the magnitude and sadness of clients' tragic stories. Listening, advocating, attendance, and empathizing are valuable gifts, particularly in times of crisis. These skills allow clients to feel cared for and held within a stable and nonjudgmental therapeutic environment. Such environments are not dictated by racial similarity between the client and counselor but from a connective capacity.

CASE STUDY

Anxiety Attacks

Vera is a 64-year-old African American grandmother who has cared for her two grandsons since they were 4 and 6. They are teenagers now. Her daughter died of a drug overdose, and the children's father is incarcerated for beating a man to death—an event his sons both witnessed. Vera continues to work as a public health department administrative assistant. She resides in the same home she has lived in for 33 years. Because of the need to get a second mortgage on her home in order to care financially for her grandchildren, her home is not yet paid for, making it necessary for her to work. Vera had breast cancer and had a bilateral mastectomy 8 years ago. At her last doctor's visit, routine blood work was done. The tests showed that Vera's cancer had returned. For several months, ever since the diagnosis of cancer once again, Vera has been experiencing heart palpitations and intense nausea. She also has tremendous headaches and at times feels like she can't catch her breath. Her doctor suggested she get counseling. Vera resisted at first and instead prayed about it, asking God to steady her nerves. She also called her "prayer warriors" from her Bible Study class. The panic attacks have worsened and are now interfering with her work performance. Vera reluctantly presents for counseling.

(Continued)

QUESTIONS

1. What might be helpful to Vera to encourage relaxation?
2. How might therapy help Vera's grandchildren?
3. How might a counselor help Vera to manage her anxiety and reduce her stress?

DISCUSSION AND INTEGRATION

The Client, Vera

Vera is distressed and is dealing with existential issues, facing cancer again, and the stress of raising the grandchildren who depend on her. She appears anxious. The *DSM–IV* defines Generalized Anxiety Disorder as

(1) excessive anxiety and worry (apprehensive expectation) occurring more days than not for at least 6 months,
(2) the person finds it difficult to control the worry,
(3) the anxiety and worry are associated with three or more of the following six symptoms:
    (a) restlessness or feeling keyed up or on edge,
    (b) being easily fatigued,
    (c) difficulty concentrating,
    (d) irritability,
    (e) muscle tension,
    (f) sleep disturbance.

Vera is in need of help. She has stepped up to the responsibility of caring for her grandchildren and now the disease that has taken her breasts and has returned. She has lymphoma. As a praying woman, Vera has important coping tools. According to research by Hamilton, Powe, Pollard, Lee, and Felton (2007), many breast and prostate cancer survivors believe that God is with them, healing and protecting them, and is ultimately in control of their lives. In another study by Dilworth-Anderson, Boswell, and Cohen (2007), 303 African American caregivers stated that their spiritual beliefs greatly helped them with giving care to others. Spiritual beliefs helped caregivers endure, experiencing a sense of reciprocity in giving back to those who had helped them, faith, and gratification to foster positive feelings about giving care.

After her grandchildren came to live with her, they had some of the classic symptoms of PTSD: avoidance of the stimuli associated with the trauma, nightmares, difficulty concentrating, and physiological reactivity on exposure to internal or external cues. There is tremendous stress associated with growing up in violence, and Black children are more likely to be exposed to it. As Boyd-Franklin (2003) stated, "many are acquainted from an early age with violence in their homes in the form of child abuse, sexual abuse, drug overdose, and AIDS" (p. 266). Vera's grandsons were diagnosed as hyperactive—they ran incessantly and stayed busy at all times. Vera did not accept the diagnosis and concluded that her boys just "needed to run all the chaos out of their systems." Vera was right. Children can experience difficulty with emotional and behavioral regulation when exposed to trauma (Rampage, Eovaldi, Ma, & Weigel-Foy, 2003). In time, her boys adjusted well at home and at school.

Vera is the only parent her grandchildren have; Black people are more likely than Whites to reside with their co-resident grandchildren. On one hand, the responsibility of being the sole provider of her grandchildren gives Vera the strength to go on. On the other hand, it fills her with fear.

A counselor is needed who can comfortably integrate Vera's need to pray prior to the therapy session. Vera may also want to discuss dreams or other messages that God might be giving her. Prayer could even be used as visualization to rid her body of the lymphoma. If Vera were to find comfort in speaking with the dead, including her deceased parents, the counselor needs to interpret this behavior within a cultural context—it is not unusual for African Americans to speak to the dead during times of loss, grief, and stress (Schoulte, 2011). Vera continues to be very active, despite her diagnosis, with work and caring for the children. Parham (1992) noted that among some African Americans, depression manifests not as psychomotor retardation but as increased activity in order to "keep on keeping on." Much of the Black experience in America is coping, surviving, and seeking to thrive. People have to function—go to work and school, feed the kids, and pay the bills despite the hardships.

As teenagers, Vera's grandsons have the task of growing up and dealing with their only parent's illness. They, too, could benefit from having a place to process their feelings and learn the truth of their grandmother's cancer.

The Counselor

Vera's therapist may consult Vera's minister about the spiritual aspects of healing. Doing so may provide the therapist with a sense of how to complement this core value of Vera's during psychotherapy. Vera's spirituality may also offer some clinical insight. The counselor says to Vera, "Think of a hymn that gives you the most comfort. What are the words that help you to feel peaceful?" Vera could be encouraged to become mindful of the worry thoughts and interrupt these thoughts with a song or a scripture. When a counselor can validate the meaning of spirituality in the lives of their clients, this can be enormously helpful to the client in making meaning out of their predicaments as well as finding peace (Nichols & Hunt, 2011).

Part of Vera's anxiety is not just for her own life but for those of two young men as well. She knows they "walk alone." It may be important for the therapist to challenge Vera's idea of what it means to walk alone. Perhaps her therapist could help Vera find a Big Brother program and inquire as to whether the church has a support group for teens. If not, they might start one. If there are no other extended family members to help support Vera through this difficult time, perhaps a family through the church or another civic/community group could be identified. Although increasingly common in our society, the idea of a single adult having the sole care of children and working a full-time job is not logical and does not allow the village to raise the children. The therapist must acknowledge that this is a difficult time for Vera and assure her that she will not have to walk this path alone.

Summary

This chapter provided history, demographic trends, and cultural values for people of African descent. A case study was presented for students to gain practice with integrating multiple issues: a grandparent raising her grandchildren and dealing with the reoccurrence of cancer, existential issues, and integrating spirituality into the therapeutic event. Counseling with people of African descent is discussed in the case study.

People of Asian Descent, Native Hawaiians, and Pacific Islanders

> *We are what we think. All that we are arises with our thoughts.*
> *With our thoughts we make the world.*

BUDDHA

This chapter is a focus on people of Asian descent. The diverse ethnic groups among Asians are highlighted. Demographic information, history, and cultural values are also presented.

Tremendous diversity is found within the Asian community. According to Humes, Jones, and Ramirez (2011), "Asian" refers to a person having origins in any of the original peoples of the Far East, Southeast Asia, or the Indian subcontinent, including Cambodia, China, India, Japan, Korea, Malaysia, Pakistan, the Philippines, Thailand, and Vietnam. It includes people who indicated their race(s) as "Asian" or reported entries such as "Asian Indian," "Chinese," "Filipino," "Korean," "Japanese," "Vietnamese," and "Other Asian" or provided other detailed Asian responses (p. 3).

Uba (1994) observed, "The term 'Asian culture' is technically a misnomer. The tenets of these belief systems are shared by many cultures—there are also significant differences among Asian cultures" (p. 12). More than 100 languages and dialects are spoken, and in some communities such as the Hmong and Cambodians, high rates of linguistic isolation exist, which explains the phenomenon of persons over the age of 14 not speaking English "very well" (US Department of Health and Human Services, 2001).

Ethnicity, nationality, migration or generational status, assimilation, acculturation, facility with the English language, political climate in country of origin, religion, socioeconomic status, occupation, transferability of skills, foreign credentials to the United States, and educational level provide some of the many sources of differences within the group (Sue & Sue, 1990; Tsai & Uemura, 1988).

MIGRATORY PATTERNS

The Chinese are the Asian ethnic group with the longest history in the United States and were the first Asian ethnic group to be recruited to the West Coast during the 1840s. At that time, there was a need for cheap labor to work on the transcontinental railroads (Tsai & Uemura, 1988). US policymaker Aaron H. Palmer predicted that with a connection to the East Coast, San Francisco would become the "great emporium of our commerce on the Pacific" (Takaki, 1993, p. 192). Chinese were perceived to be more suited for "cleaning wild lands and raising every species of agricultural product" (p. 192).

In 1863, Congress authorized construction of the US transcontinental railroad. The eastward track was laid from Sacramento, California, through the Sierra Nevada, and eventually into Utah. During the winter months, working conditions were often brutal, and snowdrifts would bury entire work crews. When spring arrived, their frozen bodies would be discovered. The westward track was built mainly by Irish immigrants and started in Omaha, Nebraska. Both the Irish and Chinese received a monthly wage of $31. Unlike the Irish, the Chinese worked longer days and slept in tents near the side of the road. The Irish worked 8-hour days and resided in boarding rooms.

Despite the harsh realities of work on the railroad, many Chinese were motivated to come to America. In China, floods were making it difficult to harvest crops. Political instability, such as taxation and ethnic conflict, was also a factor. Between 1865 and 1869, the total number of Chinese railroad workers increased from 50 to almost 12,000 (Avakian, 2002). Finding gold in California was also a dream of many Chinese (Cao & Novas, 1996).

Life in America was not only difficult for Chinese men. Chinese women were suffering as well. In 1860, it is estimated that more than 80% of Chinese women were prostitutes (Hirata, 1979), many of whom were teenage girls aged 15 and 16. As a result of slavery, kidnapping, and deception, Chinese girls found themselves on the auction block, where they worked as concubines or prostitutes, sexually serving both White and Chinese men (Avakian, 2002). Hirata (1979) speaks of two periods of prostitution concerning Chinese women in California. The first period was considered a period of free competition where the woman is said to have control over her "body service." This was estimated to be around 1849–1854. The second period was 1854–1925, considered to be a time of organized trade in which women were involved in a web of slavery similar to today's trafficking and exploitation of girls and women for sex work throughout America and the world.

In 1868, 141 Japanese men, women, and children arrived in Hawaii. The Japanese were recruited to work on the Hawaiian sugarcane plantations, along with the Koreans, Filipinos, and Puerto Ricans who came later, near the turn of the 20th century. The Japanese migrated to the United States during Japan's period of rapid modernization known as the Meiji Restoration (after Emperor Meiji). Because of tax increases levied to pay for sweeping reforms, Japan's peasant farmers suffered greatly from economic hardships and lost their land. Persons from the districts of Yamaguchi, Hiroshima, and Kumamoto were hit hardest by poverty and comprised the majority of immigrants hailing from Japan (Avakian, 2002).

Between 1885 and 1925, 200,000 Japanese left for Hawaii, and another 180,000 went to mainland United States. By the turn of the 20th century, 70% of Hawaii's sugar plantation labor was from Japan. In 1900, with the passing of the Organic Act, the US Congress voted to create the Territory of Hawaii. Despite the fact that Chinese and Japanese Hawaiians represented more than half of the population, they were not allowed to vote. Whites, the minority, represented the elite and ruling class. Fortunately, the Organic Act did allow laborers to have greater power in organizing themselves more effectively. Such resistance, led by the Japanese, encouraged planters to look for new labor sources, primarily from Korea and the Philippines.

Prior to the arrival of other Asians into the United States, Congress passed the Chinese Exclusion Act of 1882, which barred the "immigration of all Chinese laborers, lunatics, and idiots into the United States for a 10-year period" (Avakian, 2002, p. 51). This act allowed "only women who were native born, married, or born overseas to domiciled merchants to immigrate to the United States" (Hirata, 1979, p.11) and was the first and only law in US immigration that ordered an entire group of people of a specific nationality to be banned from the United States (Avakian, 2002).

On December 7, 1941, Pearl Harbor, a major base of the US Navy on the Hawaiian island of Oahu, was attacked by the Japanese. Bases in the Philippines, Guam, Midway Atoll, and other ports in the Pacific were also attacked. Nearly 3,000 soldiers, sailors, and civilians were killed. This surprise attack fueled existing anti-Japanese sentiments. With the passing of Executive Order 9066, signed by Franklin D. Roosevelt, wartime curfew and internment measures were enacted primarily against 110,000 West Coast Japanese Americans, three-quarters of whom were *Nisei*, or second-generation, American-born Japanese. The other fourth, the *Issei*, were born in Japan and thus barred from becoming American citizens (Zinn, 2003). Small numbers of Germans, Italians, and Eastern Europeans were also relocated to camps to safeguard the security of the United States. Although the order was a constitutional violation as well as a legal violation of due process (there were no warrants, indictments, or hearings), Japanese Americans were forced to leave their homes and move to cramped internment camps for three years (Zinn, 2003). The notice of Japanese Internment stated, "All persons of Japanese ancestry" are given two to five days notice to dispose of their homes and property and report to the "camps" (Chang, 2002).

The construction plans used for housing the internees were for unmarried army recruits, thus up to six families resided in long army barracks with very little privacy. The traditional diet of many Japanese people, such as fresh vegetables and fruits, was not available, and waiting in lines for meals and bathroom facilities was commonplace (Avakian, 2002).

Compared with the Chinese, Japanese, Koreans, Filipinos, and Asian Indians, the Vietnamese are the most recent immigrant group to arrive in the United States. Between April and December 1975, 100,000 refugees from Vietnam and Cambodia were admitted to the United States as parolees, as announced by the US attorney general (Avakian, 2002).

Southeast Asia represents the Asian subcontinent south of China and east of India. Persons from Vietnam, Laos, and Cambodia are neighbors. Indonesia, Malaysia, Thailand, Burma, Bhutan, and Bangladesh are also included. According to Sandhu (1997), more than 40 cultural groups comprise Asian and Pacific Islander Americans. Many of these groups are less researched and perhaps less well known than other groups who have lived in the United States for several generations. Asian newcomers speak hundreds of languages and dialects and practice a broad array of religions. Many ethnic Asian newcomers are more likely to identify with specific national or regional ties (e.g., Vietnamese, Korean, Hmong, Punjabi Sikh, Cantonese, Taiwanese). Pacific Islanders come from more than 22 islands, including Micronesia (Guam, Belau, and the Carolines, Marianas, Marshalls, and Gilberts) and Melanesia (Fiji).

The 20th century witnessed the migration of diverse groups of Asians to the United States. About one-third of foreign-born Asians entered during the 1990s, and about 17% arrived in 2000 or later (US Census Bureau, 2007e). Their points and periods of entry have differed and have been largely influenced by work (railroads, cotton, sugarcane, technology, medicine, and war—namely World War II, Korea, and Vietnam).

DEMOGRAPHY

In combination with Asian and some other race represented 6% of the population or 17.3 million people. "Other Asian" is a category that includes Bhutanese, Burmese, Indochinese, Iwo Jiman, Madagascan, Maldivian, Nepalese, Okinawan, and Singaporean (US Census Bureau, 2007e). There are 14.7 million single race Asians living in the United States (Humes, Jones, & Ramirez, 2011). Asians comprise 4.8% of the US population, yet from 2000 to 2010 they increased 43%, more than any other major race group. This group experienced the second largest numeric change, by 4.4 million, going from 10.2 million in 2000 to 14.7 million in 2010.

In 2010, 540,000 people reported being Native Hawaiian or other Pacific Islander, representing 0.2% of the US population. From 2000 to 2010, this group increased more than one-third, going from 398,835 to over 540,000. "Other Pacific Islander" includes Guamanians or Chamorros, Samoan, Tongan, or those of another Pacific island (Humes, Jones, & Ramirez, 2011). Pacific Islanders also encompass dispersed areas, including Australia, New Zealand (the Maori), Tasmania, Polynesia, Fiji Islands, the islets of Micronesia and Melanesia, and extending through New Guinea (US Census Bureau, 2000b). *Polynesians* are 63.5% of Native Hawaiians and other Pacific Islanders, including Samoans and Tongans. *Micronesians* are 25% of Native Hawaiians and other Pacific Islanders and include Guamanians, Marianas Islanders, Marshall Islanders, and Palauans. *Melanesians,* at 6% of this group, includes Fijians, Papuans, and Solomon Islanders (US Census Bureau, 2007f).

In 2010, over half of Native Hawaiians and Pacific Islanders, or 685,000 people, reported "more than one race," for a total of 1.2 million people who identified themselves as either Native Hawaiian/Pacific Islander or in combination with other races. In 2010, 1.6 million people reporting Asian and some other race were Asian and White, representing 18% of persons reporting two or more races. High rates of intermarriage between Asians and Whites, particularly among Asian women and White men, help to explain respondents' report of their biracial heritage. According to Wu (2002), "Among Asian Americans under the age of thirty-five who are married, half have found a spouse of a non-Asian background" (p. 263). In 2010, 165,690 biracial respondents reported they were Asian, Native Hawaiian, and other Pacific Islander; 185,595 were Asian, Black, or African American.

The Chinese are the largest group of Asians, representing 2.8 million, or 23% of the Asian population. In 2009, Asian Indians surpassed Filipinos as the second largest group of Asians, representing 19% of Asians at 2.6 million. Filipinos are the third largest group at nearly 18% with 2.1 million. Sixty percent of Asians are Chinese, Asian Indian, or Filipino. The fourth largest ethnic group among Asians is the 1.3 million Vietnamese who make up

10.5% of Asians. Koreans are the fifth largest Asian group at slightly under the numbers of Vietnamese, 1.2 million and 10.3% of Asians. Although the Japanese were the second group of Asians to enter America, more recent newcomers have surpassed this group in numbers. Other sizable groups are the Cambodian/Khmer, Pakistanis, Laotians, Hmong, Thais, Taiwanese, and Bangladeshi. California alone had 35% of the Asian population, which is highly concentrated in the West. Half of all Asians lived in three states: California, New York, and Texas. The seven other states with the largest Asian populations are New Jersey, 5%; Hawaii, 4.3%; Illinois, 4.2%; Washington, 3.2%; Florida, 2.9%; Virginia, 2.7%; and Massachusetts, 2.3%. Hawaii had the largest Asian proportion in its population, with Asians accounting for more than 40% of the state's total household population. In 2000, 9 of the 10 cities in the United States with more than 100,000 Asian residents were in California. The Northeast has nearly 18% of the Asian population. Less than 6% (5.7%, 5.6%, and 5.6%, respectively) of the Asian population reside in New Jersey, New York, and the South.

The median age among Asians of 35.3: The corresponding age for the population at large is 36.8 years (http://www.census.gov/popest/estimates.html). At the turn of the 20th century, the median age was approaching 40 years and was a function of the predominantly adult male migration to the United States from mainland China. Persons between the ages of 18 and 44 are 45.2% of the population, followed by people 45 to 64 at 23.5%. Children under the age of 18 are 23.6% of the population, with people 65 and older at 9.65% (http://www.census.gov/popest/estimates.html).

One of the discourses about Asians is that they are foreign-born. Although the majority of Asian Americans are US citizens, the majority were foreign-born. In 2004, 33% of Asians were native to the United States; 37% were foreign-born, naturalized citizens; and 30.5% were foreign-born, not a citizen. After Spanish, Mandarin Chinese was the most widely spoken non-English language in the home. Tagalog, Vietnamese, and Korean were each spoken at home by more than 1 million people (http://factfinder.census.gov).

Nearly 75% of Asians were US citizens (61%) or became naturalized citizens (11%). Among Pacific Islanders, 78% were native to America (US Census Bureau, 2007e).

SOCIAL, PSYCHOLOGICAL, AND PHYSICAL HEALTH ISSUES

Compared with the population at large, Asians have higher rates of marriage. In 2004, 62% of the Asian population over the age of 15 had married, compared with 57.3% among Whites. There is also much less divorce among Asians compared with the general population. Rates of divorce are less than half of those in the general population: 4.7% among Asians compared with 10.21% for the total population (US Census Bureau, 2007e). Approximately 10% of Asians are separated, widowed, or divorced compared with about 19% among non-Hispanic Whites. There are interethnic group differences. Asian Indians were most likely to be married, at 69%. People who were biracial (Asian and White) had the highest never-married rates, at 50.5%, as well as higher divorce rates, nearly 7% compared with less than 5% among Asian-only groups.

A different picture exists for Native Hawaiians and Pacific Islanders compared with other Asians. One-third of Pacific Islanders had never married in 2004. In addition, about one of every eight Pacific Islanders was separated, widowed, or divorced, compared with about one in five of non-Hispanic Whites (US Census Bureau, 2007f). (See Table 7.1.)

In 2004, Asian and Pacific Islander women had higher rates of fertility than White women, with respectively 59 and 78 births per 1,000 in the past 12 months preceding the survey. About

TABLE 7.1 Characteristics of Asians and Pacific Islanders

Characteristic	Asians	Pacific Islanders
Median age	35.3	29.9
Native-born	33%	78%
Total poverty rates	12.5%	15.1%
Poverty rates of children	13%	24.5%
Bachelor's degree	50%	14%
Never married	28%	33.3%
Marriage	62%	53%
Divorce	4.7%	7.3%
Median income	$56,161	$47,442
Median values of homes	$306,000	$230,000
Owner-occupied homes	57.6%	46.4%

36% of Pacific Islander women who had given birth were unmarried, compared with 8% of Asian women. Again there are group differences. Vietnamese and Asian Indian women have the highest rates of fertility, 74.5 and 72 births per 1,000, respectively. Chinese and Korean women have the lowest rates of fertility, 48.5 and 46 births per 1,000, respectively.

The greatest percentage of Asians lived in family households at nearly 75%. A nonfamily household is defined as people who live alone or people living with unrelated individuals. Sixty percent of households were married couples, 26% were nonfamily, 9% were female households only with no male present, and nearly 5% were male only with no female present. Unlike Blacks and Latinos, Asians were not more likely than Whites to live with grandchildren; however, Pacific Islanders were. About 10% of Pacific Islanders were living in the same house with co-resident grandchildren.

In 2010 the poverty rate for Asians was 12.1% (DeNavas-Walt, Proctor, & Smith 2011), compared with 13.2% for the nation at large. Asian children are more likely to live in married-couple households, although 14% of Asian children live in poverty—this is above the national poverty rate. Overall, Asians tend to have higher rates of home ownership at 58% in owner-occupied homes. Koreans were less likely than other Asian groups to own their homes (US Census Bureau, 2007e). Among Asians who own homes, the median value of their homes is $306,000, which is nearly twice the median value of White owner-occupied homes ($154,000).

Not surprisingly, the poverty rate for Pacific Islanders was much higher at 15.1% (2009 American Community Survey <http://factfinder.census.gov). One-quarter of Pacific Island children live in poverty. Among White children, the rate is 11% in married-couple households. Pacific Islanders have lower rates of home ownership compared with other Asians, or 46.4%. Among Pacific Islanders who own homes, the median value of their homes is $230,000, which is higher than the median value of White owner-occupied homes ($154,000).

Along with Arabs, Asians are among the most highly educated groups of color in the nation. Among Asians age 25 and older, 85% have graduated from high school. This compares with 865 for the general population. Consider that 27% of Latinos have a 9th grade education or less. Among Asians, 7% have a 9th grade education or less (US Census Bureau, Current

Population Survey, 2011). Half of all Asians (50%) have completed a bachelor's degree. Twenty percent of single-race Asians 25 and older had a graduate (e.g., master's or doctorate) or professional degree in 2009 compared with 10 percent for all Americans 25 and older (http://factfinder.census.gov). Educational attainment among Pacific Islanders is very different. Among Pacific Islanders age 25 and older, 86% have graduated from high school, but only fourteen percent of Pacific Islanders have completed a bachelor's degree and 4% had a graduate degree (http://factfinder.census.gov). Of all Asian groups, Asian Indians occupy the highest percentages of managerial and professional positions. In 2009, For Asian Indians, the median income was $90,429; for Bangladeshi, it was $46,657 (These figures represent the single-race population.) (http://factfinder.census.gov).

Based on 1997 data, 58% of Americans who descended from the Indian subcontinent (Bangladesh, India, Pakistan, and Sri Lanka) had undergraduate, graduate, or professional degrees (US DHHS, 2001).

Nearly half, or 46%, of Asians are employed in management or professional occupations compared with 38% among non-Hispanic Whites. Nearly 24% of this group work in sales and office occupations, which is similar to non-Hispanic Whites (27%). Comparable to the total in the general population, 15.5% of Asians work in service occupations, and very low numbers of Asians are in construction jobs (4%). Among non-Hispanic Whites, 14% are in service and 10% work in construction jobs.

Sue and Sue (1990) cautioned against acceptance of well-known myths and stereotypes concerning Asians in America as "model minorities" who do not face difficulties that other groups of color experience. (See Storytelling: *Activism and Peace*.) The model minority myth also denies the tremendous diversity that exists among individual Asian Americans. According to Takaki (1994), Asian-American "success" has emerged as the new stereotype for this ethnic minority. While this image has led many teachers and employers to view Asians as intelligent and hardworking and has opened some opportunities, it has also been harmful (p. 57). (See Storytelling: *Test Performance and Racial Representation*.)

Storytelling: Activism and Peace

I met a Black woman recently who was a native of the Solomon Islands, which is in the South Pacific east of Papua New Guinea and northeast of Australia. Solomon Islanders are Melanesians, one of the broad groups of Asian peoples. In 1999, a militia group called the Isatabu Freedom Movement, made up of indigenous Isatabus from Guadalcanal, expelled more than 20,000 Malaitans, or people from Malaita. The Malaitans had migrated to the Solomon Islands in search of employment. Many had jobs in the capital, which led to resentment from the indigenous people, the Istabus. The Mailitans formed their own group in response to the ethnic tensions. They were called the Malaita Eagle Force. Over the years, there was unrest, corruption, and instability. This woman became a peace maker. Although it was dangerous to speak to the men, many saw women as subordinate and inferior, she was courageous in her actions, taking her brother with her not only for protection but to have the status of a man with her. This resistance and activism is part and parcel of the experience of the diversity among Asian people worldwide, who are often given hope and ideas by the struggles of people in America. Many young Asians, including the Maori people in New Zealand, were inspired to develop a sense of ethnic pride and self-esteem when leaders in the Black Power movement encouraged African Americans to unify and define themselves on their own terms.

The model minority cannot be broadly applied. Wong and Halgin (2006) observed that the label cannot acceptably capture "the lives of all Asian Americans subsumed in this panethnic category" (p. 41). The model minority myth interferes with economically disadvantaged Asian American communities receiving the necessary emotional and financial resources and creates division among groups of color as one group is pitted against another (Wong & Halgin, 2006). Some suffer because of unemployment, and some newly immigrated groups, such as Vietnamese, have very high poverty rates and difficulties with social adjustment due to the trauma they experienced prior to immigration. In fact, Vietnamese Americans have an average family income that is about half that of Asian American Pacific Islander (AAPI) populations as a whole (Byrd & Clayton, 2003).

Pacific Islanders tend to have higher rates of poverty than other Asian groups, with Tongans and Samoans having some of the highest rates. (See Table 7.1.) Because of autonomous governments with a variety of political relationships with the United States, varying levels of health and health care exist for Pacific Islanders. For instance, Guam has a relatively high level of health care, with the Republic of Belau and the Federated States of Micronesia having older hospitals that provide a "generally poorer level of care" (Byrd & Clayton, 2003, p. 480).

Much of the literature that is available would suggest that Asian Americans, in comparison with the general population, consume less alcohol and drugs (Mercado, 2000). The myth of the model minority fuels this dearth of information. The truth of the matter is that Asians, like other groups, contend with substance addictions as well. There is research to suggest that substance abuse among Asians is on the rise (Zane & Huh-Kim, 1998). To best treat substance abuse issues, Mercado (2000) suggests a family counseling/therapy intervention. Respecting cultural values and understanding the extent of acculturation are critical to treating the client, even if the client is being seen alone (Chang, 2000).

Among refugees, such as Cambodians, Laotians, and Vietnamese, post-traumatic stress disorder and depression are common, given a history of war and poverty. Between 1975 and 1979, Pol Pot, leader of the Khmer Rouge, a communist guerilla organization, presided over Cambodia's "killing fields," an inhumane period of genocide during which one-third of Cambodia's population, or between 1.5 and 2 million Cambodians, were slaughtered. Anti-communists, students, intellectuals, the wealthy, and doctors were considered to be enemies of the state and tragically lost their lives (Avakian, 2002). One study found that Cambodian high school students had symptoms of PTSD as well as depressive symptoms. Among Cambodian adults who had been resettled in Massachusetts, 43% reported the deaths in Cambodia of between one and six children (US DHHS 2001). This distress produced an intense but invisible sadness.

Asians also suffer discrimination on the job, and career choices are skewed because of racial inequities. Educationally, some Asians have problems with the English language on standardized tests, and conflicts exist between American and Asian values. The stereotype of the model minority permeates the culture. Asian students who internalize this myth may find it extremely hard to ask for needed assistance or feel increasingly isolated in their attempts to achieve academic success (Gloria & Ho, 2003).

For some youth, the pressure to succeed academically can cause enormous stress. Chang's (1996) research on coping styles of Asian students is a welcome contribution to the literature, given the stress experienced by many Asian youth. He found in his study of 111 Asian college students and 111 White college students that Asian students used more problem avoidance and social withdrawal than the White students. Also, the Asian students, although more pessimistic in their orientations than the White students, were not less optimistic. Amid the expectation of negative events, the Asian students employed active coping styles.

The concept of talk therapy is foreign to many Asian American clients (Hong & Domokos-Cheng Ham, 2001). Asian Americans may be hesitant to discuss their feelings and problems openly and question the effectiveness of counseling. Some of the same attitudes that discourage Asian Americans from seeking mental health services discourage them, once in therapy, from discussing their problems. In spite of a lack of familiarity with psychotherapy, many Asian Americans might expect quick relief from their symptoms. Deferring to nonprofessionals, elders, and older relatives within the community (Yeh & Wang, 2000) is a way that Asian American communities deal with mental health challenges.

In addition to concerns about traditional coping strategies, there are other reasons that explain the reluctance among Asian Americans to discuss their problems. According to Uba (1994), it is not uncommon for Asian Americans to perceive talking about themselves or disclosing private personal information to a stranger as reflective of low maturity and lack of discipline.

Facility with the English language is one of the factors, from a study of Chinese Americans in the Bay Area of California, found to be associated with a more positive attitude toward help seeking for a nervous or emotional problem (Ying & Miller, 1992). In a study by Lin (1994) of 145 adult Chinese Americans, when qualified ethnic and language-matched therapists were provided, the Chinese Americans were found to stay in therapy as long as the general American public.

According to Dana (2002), "Somatization constitutes an attempt to communicate an experience of bodily symptoms and distress in response to psychosocial stressors often associated with depression and anxiety disorders, or worry and preoccupation with well-being" (p. 37). Research suggests that some groups of Asians may have higher rates of somatoform issues compared with the general population. Headaches are one way in which somatization is manifested.

Asian Americans typically have patriarchal families with authority and communication exercised from top to bottom, interdependent roles, strict adherence to traditional norms, and minimization of conflict by suppression of overt emotion (Kitano, 1988; Min, 1988; Tran, 1988; Wong, 1988). Guilt and shame are used to control family members, and obligations to the family take precedence over individual prerogatives (Kitano, 1988; Sue & Sue, 1990; Wong, 1988). Under the aegis of the family, discipline and self-control are sufficient to provide an impetus for outstanding achievement to honor the family. Negative behaviors such as delinquency, school failure, unemployment, or mental illness are considered family failures that disrupt the desired harmony of family life. In addition is the belief in external control, a fatalism that allows an equanimity and acceptance without question of life as it unfolds.

In China and the United States, absolute control by the family as a major ingredient in the formation of a traditional self-concept has not only diminished but is being openly questioned (Wong, 1988). Despite questioning of traditional filial identity, strong evidence suggests, at least among Hong Kong Chinese students, the continued presence of an extended self or collective orientation.

Similarly, in Japan the emphasis on the collective has been increasing, particularly in the form of corporate family effectiveness instead of intrafamily lineal authority or filial piety (Goldenberg & Goldenberg, 1996; Kitano, 1988). However, this collectivity may also be expressed in humanistic or socialist terms.

The primary tradition is **filial piety,** which is the dedication and deference of children to their parents (Goldenberg & Goldenberg, 1996). In the United States, problems faced by first- and second-generation Chinese may differ as a result of inability to express this tradition properly (Sue & Sue, 1990; Wong, 1988). Although first-generation men in particular are required to achieve and to be good providers for their families, sufficient achievement to fulfill family expectations has not always been possible for them. Second-generation individuals also may fail to be unquestioningly faithful to the traditional values of their parents. Their self-worth is increasingly defined either by dominant culture values or by pan-Asian values, in which a common response to racism and personal pride may take precedence over filial piety. As a result, individuals in both generations may experience considerable guilt and anxiety. It may be argued that the locus of loyalty within the Chinese community is in the process of shifting from the family, including ancestors, to other collectivities, including the pan-Asian community in the United States. Overall, the traditional Asian American family believes in loyalty and devotion to its values (Goldenberg & Goldenberg, 1996).

ACCULTURATION AND EXPERIENCES IN AMERICA

There are differences in the values expressed in Asian cultures and in the United States. Much of this difference, in addition to personality, is related to acculturation. Length of time in the United States, access to resources, English-language fluency, educational level, and employment status are factors that affect adjustment. Other moderator variables include generational status, age, neighborhood ethnic density, country of birth, kinship structures, and purposes of immigration. According to Berry and Sam (1997), cultural maintenance and contact and participation are important issues that groups and individuals consider in their interpersonal interactions. Two different immigrant streams are associated with huge diversity within the Asian and Pacific Island populations. The first stream represents people from countries that have large populations in the United States and tend to have better health. Included are Chinese, Filipinos, Koreans, and Asian Indians. The second stream consists of lower socioeconomic groups. Many refugees are included in this number (Frisbie, Cho, & Hummer, 2002).

Cultural maintenance refers to cultural identity characteristics that are considered important and for which people strive. **Contact and participation** refers to the extent to which groups deem it important to become involved with other cultural groups or remain primarily among themselves. **Assimilation** is defined as what takes place when persons do not wish to maintain their cultural identity and seek interactions with other cultures. **Separation** refers to what happens when the nondominant group places a value on holding onto their original culture and wishes to avoid interactions with persons from other cultures. **Segregation** is the term used to describe the dominant group's stance with respect to the nondominant group. **Integration** refers to the maintenance of cultural integrity while seeking to participate in the larger social network of a multicultural society. **Marginalization** is defined as little possibility or interest in cultural maintenance and little interest in having relations with others.

Recent research conducted by Chae and Foley (2010) looked at three separate Asian groups: Chinese, Koreans, and Japanese. The constructs of ethnic identity, acculturation, and psychological well-being were investigated. Among all groups, ethnic identity was a strong predictor of psychological well-being. Overall, bicultural identity had the greatest relationship with psychological well-being, more so than low or high acculturation; however, there were ethnic group differences with respect to acculturation and psychological well-being. Among Koreans, there was a significant inverse relationship between acculturation and psychological well-being. For this group, but not for Japanese where acculturation added little to the regression model or Chinese, high acculturation may be linked to lower levels of psychological well-being.

According to Kim (2011), there are approaches to increasing motivation for counseling among Asian clients. He stated that Asian American clients who avoid counseling due to fear of embarrassing their family, "the idea of confidentiality can be strongly and repeatedly emphasized"

(p. 271). He also advocated the use of cognitive-oriented therapeutic approaches over those that are emotion-oriented to accommodate Asian American clients who value emotional control.

Lee and Ahn (2011) conducted a meta analysis from 23 independent studies concerning Asian Americans. They produced 99 correlations. Researchers were interested in the relationship between racial discrimination and mental health. They found that the relationship between racial discrimination and mental health was statistically significant. More specifically, racial discrimination had significantly stronger correlations to depression and anxiety than to psychological distress. In relation to racial discrimination, Asians were equally as likely to suffer from depression and anxiety. Contrary to the emphasis on the collectivistic values of Asian people, this research found that individualistic forms of resources (e.g. personal constructs and strengths, coping strategies) appeared to have equal or stronger correlation to racial discrimination and mental health in comparison to collectivistic forms (e.g. social support and cultural identity).

Prior to arrival in the United States, most Asian immigrants and refugees have primary exposure to their own culture. Upon arrival, cultural adaptation is required, and a relinquishing of native aspects of their culture to function in school and work contexts is part of this process. In addition to the factors cited earlier that affect adaptation, age of migration (before or after the age of 12), reason for migration (economic development or political refuge), and mode of migration (with or without parents or family members) are critical issues (Tsai & Chensova-Dutton, 2002).

Among many Asians, arranged marriages are still practiced. Another practice is that of Asian-born children being adopted by primarily White American parents. During the Korean War, there were growing numbers of children in Korean orphanages. After the passage of legislation that made the adoption process easier, the practice became increasingly common in the 1970s. In addition to Korea, India, Vietnam, the Philippines, and Cambodia experienced upheaval that exacerbated poor living conditions. Vulnerable families relinquished their children for adoption. Between 1989 and 2003, according to the US Department of State, China sent 7,044 children to the United States, followed by Russia with 5,865 and South Korea with 1,716 (Le, 2008). The successes and creativity of many newly migrated groups from Asia have been attributed largely to the informal network system of valuing the group, being a member of the group, and attending to the needs of others through sharing financial and human resources, from employment information to housing, for the betterment of all (Chang, 1996; Sue & Sue, 1990). Among some Asian groups, even among newly arrived immigrants, a substantial number have higher education and extensive career experience. Much of the success in business noted among many Korean Americans can be explained by a system called *kae*, which is similar to the Chinese concept of *woi* and the Japanese system known as *tanomoshi*. These systems enable successful people to help newcomers through a lending and borrowing system. In addition, many of the Korean banks in America are under the authority of banks in Korea. In this way, newcomers face less discrimination than might be seen at an American bank (Avakian, 2002).

Storytelling: Test Performance and Racial Representation

Many years ago, a Japanese friend of mine recounted a story of not doing very well on the GRE. She shared her disappointing results to her highly successful aunt who said, "You are not Asian!" She took the test a second time and did much better, got into the graduate school of her choice, and has had a wonderful career. Her aunt was extremely supportive of her—once she performed in a way that her aunt felt properly represented Asian people.

CULTURAL ORIENTATION AND VALUES

Confucianism, Taoism, and Buddhism underlie many Asian cultural values. Founded in the 5th and 6th centuries BCE. by followers of Siddharta Gautama, later known as Buddha (Avakian, 2002), the basic teachings of Buddhism maintain that there is suffering, the first Noble Truth. Understanding the roots of suffering, the cessation of suffering, and being on the path to refrain from that which causes suffering are also emphasized (Nhat Hanh, 1998). Hinduism is older than Buddhism and dates back to 1500 BCE. Hindu beliefs are presented in two sacred books, the *Vedas* and the *Upanishads*. People are ranked into caste systems from the Brahmans (priests) at the top to the Shudras (peasants and laborers) on the bottom. Confucius, born in about 551 BCE, was China's most influential philosopher, and emphasized family loyalty, hard work, and respect for parents and elders. Like Confucianism, Taoism was also a religion in addition to being a philosophy. It emphasized harmony in nature and contemplation (Avakian, 2002). Such a philosophy is seen in the eighth chapter of the *Tao Te Ching*: "In dwelling, be close to the land. In meditation, go deep in the heart. In dealing with others, be gentle and kind. In speech, be true. In ruling, be just. In business, be competent. In action, watch the timing. No fight: No blame" (Lao Tsu, trans. 1972). *We wei*, which literally means "doing nothing" or inaction, was emphasized, but it could also refer to modesty, simplicity, and absence of ambition for power (Hong & Domokos-Cheng Ham, 2001).

Values common to Asian ethnic groups include emphasis on harmony in relationships, emotional restraint (emotional expression may be interpreted as a sign of immaturity), precedence of group interests over individual interests, extended family, deference to authority, obedience to and respect for parents, emphasis on hard work, fulfilling obligations, and high value associated with education (Sandhu, 1997; Uba, 1994). (See Table 7.2.) According to Ying (2002), "The primary objective of socialization is *tsuo jen* (which literally means to make/become human),

---

TABLE 7.2 Common Cultural Values among People of Asian Descent

Enryo (reserve, constraint)

Jen (benevolence, personhood, humanity)

Yuan (the influence of past relationships on present social relationships)

Face (concern for maintaining face)

Thrift

Interpersonal harmony in relationships

Ren qing (social favors exchanged in the form of money, goods, information—according to an implicit set of social rules)

Precedence of group interests over individual interests

Educational attainment and achievement

Obedience to authority

Marriage

Emotional self-control

Honor given to elders

Modesty and humility

Patriarchy

---

that is, to teach a child proper social rules of conduct and submission of personal desires to that of others in order to avoid interpersonal conflict and social disapproval" (pp. 174–175).

Among the Chinese, selflessness, obedience to authority, or deference to the collective unit is a primary value and is manifested in relations with elders or those in authority. Body parts are used to describe intimate relationships. For instance, biological children are referred to as bone and flesh and siblings are referred to as hand and foot (Ying, 2002). The concept of *jen*, or personhood, is emphasized. Jen is a Confucian virtue and is written with two strokes. Each represents one person and refers to responsibility for kin as expressed through respect, loyalty, and love (Dana, 1993).

Among collectivistic people, the self is conceptualized in a social way (Ying, 2002). In the West, the self is primary and exerts influence on expectations concerning psychological well-being. For instance, personal happiness is considered an inalienable right and an essential goal, almost an entitlement. In many Asian cultures, including Chinese but also Southeast Asian, achievement of personal happiness may be a less salient goal and constructed within a collectivistic framework because appraisal of the self is based on external social standards (Tsai & Chensova-Dutton, 2002).

Despite diversity among Asians, certain ethnic groups share some similarities, such as the Chinese and the Japanese. According to Sue and Sue (1995), in both cultures, the families are patriarchal and communication styles tend to be formal, well defined, and flow from the top downward. Relationships among family members are highly interdependent, with one person's actions reflecting on the entire family unit. Control of the children is maintained by fostering feelings of shame and guilt. Although parenting children in this manner may characterize many Asian families, it also applies to other cultures as well. Hsu (1953) observed that the most important issue to Americans is what parents should do for the children; to Chinese, what children should do for their parents is of greatest importance.

Family is given respect and honor. Among the Vietnamese, it is not uncommon for multiple generations to reside collectively in one home. Elders are honored, respected, and cared for because of the importance of family. Compared with other groups, Asian Americans are more likely to live in households comprised of family members only. They are less likely to live on their own and are characterized by low percentages of female-headed households. Pacific Islanders are also more likely to have larger families than most Asian Americans and Americans (Byrd & Clayton, 2003; US DHHS, 2001). According to McFadden (1993), Asians tend to believe that marriage is the most important event that can occur in a person's life and is perceived to be long-lasting, until the end of the person's life, with divorce being considered the greatest possible tragedy that could occur. "Most Asian cultures are historically patrilineal and patrilocal and favor male offspring over female. Consequently, women often grow up feeling devalued and suffer emotional and psychological consequences from these sexist customs throughout their lives" (Chang, 2000, p. 201).

Restraint of emotions represents a value for many Asian Americans. This is not to be confused with the absence of a sense of humor; however, *enryo*, or reserve and constraint, is important and represents a primary mode of communication. Uba (1994) said, "This syndrome may be manifested in a number of ways, as in a hesitancy to speak up in class or to openly contradict a person in a position of authority ... Another part of the *enryo* syndrome is a modest devaluation of oneself and one's possessions" (p. 18).

Humility is a cultural value, as is the notion of loss of face. Self-effacement and modesty are highly valued and reflect wisdom and function to increase social harmony (Ying, 2002). Leong, Wagner, and Kim (1995) stated that communication styles among Asians allow participants to maintain face. Therefore, direct communication styles, reflective of a Western style and involving confrontation and challenges, tend to be less desirable.

IMPLICATIONS FOR COUNSELORS AND PSYCHOLOGISTS

There is tremendous diversity among Asians with respect to nationality, language, immigration status, educational and occupational levels, and income. Despite this heterogeneity, the myth of the model minority for the entire group of Asians prevails. The disadvantages of ignoring this level of diversity among Asians is problematic. Monolithicizing a group reflects racism in its failure to honor important intragroup differences. In addition, the unique challenges and concerns that do not reflect success and achievement are obscured. Poverty, mental illness, gang affiliation, school failure, and racism are realities for many Asians. The stereotypes of Asians—China doll, Tokyo Rose, savage, mysterious, Charlie Chan, dragon lady, exotic, insolent, diminutive, mail order bride, and little brown brother (Zia, 2000)—are still with us today.

Although the median value of homes among Asians homeowners exceeds that of Whites, there was a time in this country when Asians could not own land. Known as the Alien Land Law, this law prohibited anyone of Asian ancestry from owning land. Internalized racism was also part of the experience of many Chinese after Pearl Harbor was bombed. Signs were seen posted in stores that announced, "This is a Chinese shop." Some people wore buttons that said, "I am Chinese" or "I hate Japs worse than you do" (Zia, 2000). Despite discourses that Asians are passive or politically safe, Asians have a history of resistance to oppression. The Japanese American Citizens League and the Chinese Consolidated Benevolent Association were centers of organization for equal rights and social justice. In a study investigating the benefits of Asian cultural values to Asian clients in counseling, Kim, Li, and Liang (2002) found that Asian American clients who had high adherence to Asian cultural values, as measured by the Asian Values Scale, perceived greater client–counselor working alliance and counselor empathic understanding than did clients who had low adherence to Asian cultural values. Such values representing related aspects of Asian cultural values included collectivism, conformity to norms, emotional self-control, family recognition through achievement, filial piety, and humility. The authors concluded, "Asian Americans who adhere to Asian cultural values try to be understanding, accommodating, conciliatory, and not directly confrontational, and they expect the same from others" (pp. 351–352). In providing mental health services to Asians, it is imperative to consider acculturation, facility with English, religious and cultural values, generational status, and social supports as part of diagnoses and treatment.

CASE STUDY

DUAL DIAGNOSIS

Jessica is a single, 36-year-old Japanese American. She is an Assistant Professor in Pharmacy at a large university in Georgia. She was born in California, and so were her parents and grandparents. Jessica comes from a family of professionals in health sciences. She has heard stories of her family's internment during World War II due to their Japanese ancestry. Her family has worked very hard and has dealt with racial discrimination. Her parents sacrificed to put Jessica and her siblings through school. Her sister is a nurse and her brother is a pharmacist. Her father is a physician's assistant and her mother is a physical therapist. Jessica has recently

(Continued)

(*Continued*)

learned that she has been denied tenure and promotion. Because of this denial of tenure, she will need to find employment elsewhere within the next year. Jessica is devastated and feels very ashamed. She does not know how to tell her parents the truth. They assume she has been awarded promotion and tenure and want to know when she is coming home to celebrate. Jessica has been extremely prolific and has presented the results of her research through the world. She was told that although she received many small grants, the university did not see the amount of money she brought in as adequate. Jessica has appealed the denial of tenure, but her appeal was rejected by a faculty committee. Jessica is a lesbian. She has not dated much during the last few years due to some rejections in dating and relationships. Jessica has not revealed her sexuality to her parents. She is concerned that such a revelation would contribute to distress and disappointment from both her parents and her married-with-children siblings. When Jessica was younger, her parents asked for grandchildren but have lately slowed their requests as Jessica ages. On the suggestion of a friend, Jessica seeks therapy. She has been weepy and irritable, and suffers from insomnia, vomiting, and hair loss. Jessica's longstanding but secret bout with bulimia has returned. Jessica's therapist is Naomi, a 40-year-old Latina psychologist.

QUESTIONS

1. Why is it so difficult for Jessica to tell her parents about her denial of tenure?
2. What is the influence of culture on Jessica's silence about her life?

DISCUSSION AND INTEGRATION

Naomi listens to Jessica, who is rather verbal during her initial intake. Naomi assumed that Jessica was reluctant to tell her parents about her sexual orientation due to the heightened stigma of heterosexism that many lesbian and gay people face. Although this is true for some, Moradi et al. (2010) conducted research that indicated similar levels of perceived heterosexism between lesbian, gay, and bisexual (LGB) people of color and White LGB. They stressed the importance of exploring perceived heterosexism among LGB people of color on an individual basis as opposed from a group perspective.

Jessica is a woman of color and a sexual minority. According to Friedman and Leaper (2010), lesbian, bisexual, and queer women experience discrimination based on their positions as sexual minorities and as women. The authors argue that "gendered heterosexism emphasized that sexual-minority women may experience discrimination that is qualitatively different from either sexism or heretosexism" (p. 153).

Jessica has been discrete regarding disclosure of her sexuality, which was consistent with Moradi et al.'s finding, that people of color who are LGB have lower levels of outness. Jessica wonders if being out to a few colleagues as work has cost her tenure. Naomi asks if Jessica thinks racism was involved in her denial of tenure. Jessica sighs and says that she does not know but she has wondered this for a while. Jessica had some dating experiences with White LGB members that felt very racist—some people were interested in her as a commodity. One woman she briefly dated said she "wanted to know what it was like to be with an exotic girl from the orient." Jessica also found that LGB people of color (mainly African Americans and Latinos) were surprised to find a "nice Asian quiet gay girl" in their midst. According to

Syzmanski and Sung (2010) LGBT (lesbian, gay, bisexual, and transsexual) Asian Americans experienced racism from the White LGBT community as well as internalized racism from LGBT communities of color. Both types of encounters are psychologically distressing.

Chow (1994), identified four cultural dilemmas facing Asian American women: (1) obedience versus independence, (2) collective (or familial) versus individual interest, (3) fatalism versus change, and (4) self-control versus self-expression or spontaneity (p. 186) that help Naomi in her approach to Jessica, particularly collective versus self-expression or spontaneity. When exploring this topic with Jessica, Naomi discovered that Jessica wanted to be a science fiction author, but her family, siblings included, thought such dreams were adolescent and inconsistent with the health science trajectories of her immediate family members.

Naomi aided Jessica in getting in touch with her anger at the tenure decision, the discrimination she has experienced from Whites and people of color in the LGBT community, and her family for being so prescriptive regarding her life choices. Her work with Naomi helped her to clarify future career steps as well as finding peace about continuing to not share her sexuality with her family but with supportive others from the LGBT community.

Jessica is not alone in feeling the burden of the inordinate emphasis on being thin, which translates into being pretty that exists in American society. Phan and Tylka (2006) conducted research on 200 Asian American women to examine whether several variables and paths included within one empirically supported model of eating disorder symptomatology were supported. More specifically, researchers examined ethnic identity, self-esteem, pressure for thinness, eating attitudes, and body shape. They found that Asian American women's perceived pressure for thinness slightly predicted their self-esteem and moderately predicted their body preoccupation both directly and indirectly. It was also found that Asian American women's body preoccupation strongly predicted their eating disorder symptomatology. What was most interesting and contradictory to previous research was that ethnic identity actually intensified the pressure for thinness. More specifically, "Pressure for thinness and body preoccupation were strongly related for women with high ethnic identity but moderately related for women with low ethnic identity" (Phan & Tylka, 2006, p. 45). It was hypothesized that within collectivism, a value often espoused by women who have high ethnic identity, Asian American women are more likely to be concerned about how their weight may have an adverse impact on significant others, which can then lead to body preoccupation.

Jessica espoused collectivism and had a strong ethnic identity, yet she struggled with disordered eating. Lee (2003) concluded from his research studies on two types of perceived discrimination (minority group discrimination and personal ethnic discrimination) that ethnic identity did not moderate or mediate the negative psychological effects of personal ethnic discrimination or minority group discrimination. He surmised, "It is possible that ethnic identity functions primarily as a psychological asset that contributes to well-being but it does not—in and of itself—protect against the effects of discrimination" (p. 139).

Naomi also has a history with bulimia and she was rightly concerned about countertransference. Vontress (1986) defined *countertransference* as psychological transposing. Although positive transference, which refers to fondness, tenderness, and respect, can contribute to a healthy therapeutic relationship, counselors need their own therapy in order to avoid countertransference, which stems from unresolved negative feelings that the clients' transference can stir within the counselor. Unresolved issues in counselors can be a source of countertransference. Naomi had personal therapy where she examined the multiple forces in her own life—cultural, familial, and institutional—that contributed to her eating disorder.

Summary

This chapter focused on people of Asian descent. A case study provided insight for counseling, where an Asian client who was a lesbian and had recently been denied tenure. She was working with a Latina therapist who had a history of an eating disorder. The therapist's negotiation of the therapeutic relationship required her to examine her own history with bulimia and the meaning of her clients' experiences with racism from both White and LGBT communities of color.

People of the Middle East and Arab Americans

The Africans, Asians, Europeans, and Arabs
Muslims and Arabs: Differences and Similarities
Migratory Patterns from the Middle East
Demography
Social, Psychological, and Physical Health Issues
Cultural Orientation and Values
Implications for Counselors and Psychologists
Case Study
Summary

> *I believe that the subjection of women within Islam
> is the biggest obstacle to the integration and progress
> of Muslim communities in the West.*
>
> AYAAN HIRSI ALI, *NOMAD* (160)

In 2011, the Middle East experienced the Arab Spring, a series of uprisings, demonstrations, gatherings, and revolutions that began in Tunisia and spread to Egypt, Yemen, Bahrain, Syria, Jordan, and Libya. At the time of this 4th edition, Libyan rebels (a group of students, bus drivers, doctors, and expatriates) have taken control of their country from Muammar Gaddafi, who ruled the nation for over four decades. Gaddafi is now deceased. Young people (ages 15–29), who represent 30% of the population in the Middle East (Forum One Communications, 2011), were pivotal to the uprisings, but people across age, nationality, race, and class were united. By word of mouth, the airways, the internet, poetry, and rap, voices of protest were lifted regarding a desire for democracy, decrying food inflation, low wages, high unemployment, state of emergency laws, corruption, police brutality, and censorship. In Egypt, the outcome was victory, and Hosni Mubarak was ousted. The world witnessed the power of civil unrest. Although lives were loss and there were injuries, the protests were largely peaceful yet transformative.

This chapter profiles Arabs and other people of the Middle East. A brief look at their history, cultural values, and demographic trends is included. A case study is provided for the integration of material in a therapeutic context.

THE AFRICANS, ASIANS, EUROPEANS, AND ARABS

The Middle East represents a region that encompasses southwestern Asia and northern Africa. It spans from Morocco to Pakistan and includes the Caucasus Mountains, which is a mountain system between the Black and Caspian seas that separates Europe and Asia. Spanning two continents, Africa and Asia, the Middle East is home to the beginning of civilization and all three monotheistic religions. The region's history has been influenced by Persians, Greeks, Romans, Crusaders, Mongols, Mamluks, Ottomans, Europeans, and many others. The majority of the countries that comprise the region only gained independence in the last century. The Middle East has been transformed by the discovery of oil, the creation of the state of Israel, the revival of Islam, the Iranian Revolution, the Iran-Iraq War, the Arab-Israeli conflict, the Persian Gulf War, and America's wars in Afghanistan and Iraq. The future of the Middle East is uncertain as it struggles to balance the importance of religion, development, and stability in an ever-democratizing global world (Middle East Institute, 2004; Dwairy, 2005).

The term *Arabs* originally applied to the Semitic peoples of the Arabian Peninsula. It is now used for populations of countries whose primary language is Arabic. Arabic was named as the sixth official language of the United Nations and is currently ranked as the fourth most widely spoken language in the world. A good command of the Arabic language is highly valued, as it is extremely difficult and grammatically complex (Dwairy, 2005).

The Arab League includes 22 countries: Algeria, Bahrain, Comoros, Djibouti, Egypt, Iraq, Jordan, Kuwait, Lebanon, Libya, Mauritania, Morocco, Oman, Palestine, Qatar, Saudi Arabia, Somalia, Sudan, Syria, Tunisia, United Arab Emirates, and Yemen. According to de la Cruz and Brittingham (2003), a person is included in the Arab ancestry if the person reports being Arab, Egyptian, Iraqi, Jordanian, Lebanese, Middle Eastern, Moroccan, North African, Palestinian, or Syrian. Some people from these countries may not define themselves as Arab, whereas people who identify as Arab may not have their country listed. Although Mauritania, Somalia, Djibouti, Sudan, and Comoros are part of the Arab League, the 2000 census did not consider people from these countries to be Arab. The U.S. Census Bureau included the following groups as Arab: Egyptian, Iraqi, Jordanian, Lebanese, Morroco, Palestinian, Syrian, and Arab (US Census Bureau, 2011). Iran, although located in the Middle East, is not one of the countries in the Arab League; its languages are Farsi and Persian. Bedouins are Arabs who reside primarily in Israel and who, until a few decades ago, had lived in the desert in a tribal social system. Now they reside in small villages (Dwairy, 2004).

The term *Palestinian* refers to people whose ancestors originated in Palestine prior to the establishment of the State of Israel in 1948. The majority of Palestinians who are Muslims are of the Sunni sect, whereas the majority of Christian Palestinians are Orthodox (Abudabbeh, 1996). Palestinians identify as Arabs and speak a dialect of Arabic that is shared with Syria and

Lebanon. Subsequent waves of Palestinian migration prior to World War I were made up of the highly educated and/or politically motivated—migrating because of loss of their homeland.

The Arab homeland covers 5.25 million square miles (the United States is 3.6 million square miles). Nearly three-quarters, or 72%, of the Arab homeland is in Africa, with 28% in Asia. Long coastlines give it access to vital waterways and include the Atlantic Ocean, the Mediterranean Sea, the Arabian Gulf, the Arabian Sea, the Gulf of Aden, the Red Sea, and the Indian Ocean (Dwairy, 2005). Another way to think about it is that 15% of Muslims live in the Arab world and another 25% in Africa.

MUSLIMS AND ARABS: DIFFERENCES AND SIMILARITIES

Islam is a younger religion than Christianity. It is the second largest in the world following Christianity with more than a billion followers and had its beginnings in the early 7th century (A.D. 610) in Mecca, a town in the western Arabian Peninsula. According to Islamic tradition, God (*Allah*) conveyed to Muhammad, a tradesman, a series of revelations that form the basis of Islam. *Islam* means submission to the will of God and comes from the Arabic word meaning "peace" and "submission" (Dwairy, 2005). A Muslim believes in the Islamic tradition, has submitted himself to Allah (meaning God), and acknowledges Muhammad as His prophet. The Prophet Mohammed called upon the people of the Arabian Peninsula to submit to God's will as expressed in the Qur'an. The Qur'an represents the "direct instruction from Allah and articulates the message that family members are expected to fulfill rules of behavior and family roles, such as husband, wife, child, etc without dissonance or disobedience" (Hall & Livingston, 2006, p.144). For Muslims around the world it is a way of life requiring absolute submission to the will of God. The Qur'an provides guidance to Muslims, just as the Bible provides guidance to Christians. A large percentage of the Arab world practices Islam, yet there is considerable overlap between Arabic and Muslim cultures (Nassar-McMillan & Hakim-Larson, 2003).

Sharia, or Islamic law, guides all aspects of Muslim life. Meaning "path" in Arabic, Sharia has influence on daily life, familial, financial and religious obligations. It is primarily derived from the Qur'an and the Sunna (the sayings, practices, and teachings of the Prophet Mohammed). Although there are varying interpretations of what Sharia law actually means, Sharia's impact on criminal law and personal status law is a source of controversy, as some interpretations are used to justify cruel punishments as well as the unequal treatment of women with respect to wealth, dress, and autonomy (Johnson & Vriens, 2011)

The three main Islamic sects are the Sunni, who comprise about 90 percent of all Muslims, the Shi'ites, and the Sufis. The Sunni are the largest branch in Islam and are sometimes referred to as "orthodox Islam." Their full name is Ahlus Sunnah wal-Jamaa'h. Although a fundamental creed is shared with the second largest division of Islam, the Shi'ite, the two divisions split regarding leadership after the death of Mohammed. The Shi'a of Ali, which literally means "the party of Ali," insisted that it was the Prophet's intention for his son-in-law, Ali, to succeed him. In contrast, the Sunni accept the legitimacy of the first four caliphs or successors to the Prophet. They maintained that the caliph should be elected and did not have to belong to the Prophet's family. Shi'ite legal tradition is generally regarded as more conservative than Sunni. Ali's followers insisted that a *caliph*, or imam, be a lineal descendant of Ali and his wife, Fatimah. There are also numerous small sects and subsects, such as Ahmaddis, Alawites, and Wahhabis, that differ in degrees of orthodoxy and practice. Sawy (2005) discusses the beauty of Islam and refers to it as a peaceful religion, saying there is an "element of poetry in a Muslim's everyday life. One says, 'Allah' or 'ma sha'a Allah' (as God wills) upon seeing something beautiful, like a sunset or a newborn baby" (p. 571).

The Five Basic Obligations of Muslims are the Pillars of Islam. The first pillar is oral testimony that there is only one God and that Mohammed is his prophet. The second pillar is that ritual prayer must be practiced five times a day with certain words and certain postures of the body. The giving of alms is the third pillar. Keeping a strict fast including no liquid or food from sunrise to sundown during Ramadan, is fourth. And the fifth pillar is the holy pilgrimage to Mecca once in a lifetime at a specific time of the year (Dwairy, 2005).

Many of the world's people who consider themselves to be Arabs are also Muslims, but being Arab does not mean the person is Muslim and being Muslim does not mean the person is Arab. Substantial parts of Asia are predominantly Muslim. For example, the largest population of Muslims in the world is in Indonesia, which is also the fourth most populous nation in the world. Indonesia is located in Southeast Asia and is not part of the Middle East. In addition, Indonesian, a standardized dialect of Malay, is the official language, not Arabic. However, Arabic script is used today in Indonesia, Afghanistan, Malaysia, sections of China, and in the Muslim areas of the Philippines and the former Soviet Union. Millions of people throughout Africa and Asia write their languages in the Arabic alphabet. Farsi, the language of Iran, and Urdu, the language of Pakistan and some parts of India, are written in the Arabic script. There are also significant Muslim populations in Europe and the Americas.

One of the dominant discourses in this country is that to be Arab means to be Muslim. However, the term *Arab* refers to a person's language and culture; it is not an ethnic origin (Abudabbeh & Nydell, 1993). The majority of Arab Americans are Christians, not Muslims. Approximately 14 million Arabs follow the Christian faith. Forty percent of Arab Americans are Catholic (Roman Catholic, Maronite, and Melkite), 23% are Orthodox, 23% are Muslim, and 12% are Protestant (**Arab American** Institute, 2006). The largest Christian denomination in the Middle East is the Coptic Orthodox Church. Orthodox denominations also include Antiochian, Syrian, and Greek. Lebanon contains the largest Christian population in the Middle East, as nearly half of that nation's citizens are Christian (Abudabbeh, 2006).

MIGRATORY PATTERNS FROM THE MIDDLE EAST

The first wave of people from the Arab homeland came to the United States between 1890 and 1940. Merchants and farmers emigrated for economic reasons from regions that were part of the Ottoman Empire. Ninety percent of this first wave were Christians from Syria and Lebanon. Lebanese families, like many other Arab families, are "traditionally patrilineal, endogamous, and extended, with wide and complex kin relationships that help to sustain traditional functions of the culture" (Simon, 1996, p. 365). Simon also pointed out, "Identity for the Lebanese does not exist apart from the family. In fact, the proper introduction of a Middle Easterner does not end with the announcement of his name—his family group must also be established" (p. 365).

The second wave came after the World War II, after the creation of the State of Israel in 1948. Unlike the first wave, those coming later were mainly people with college degrees or those seeking to earn them. People came with an Arab identity and were from regions of post-European colonization as well as from sovereign Arab nations. The third wave to the United States came after the 1967 Arab-Israeli war and included people from various Arab countries. Like many immigrants from around the world, people were seeking refuge to escape political unrest in their home countries. Lebanese immigrants and Iraqis following the Gulf War were also included. Nassar-McMillan and Hakim-Larson (2003) maintain that Arab Muslims have a more difficult time assimilating into mainstream society than Arab Christians.

DEMOGRAPHY

Arab Americans number almost 4 million and are one of the fastest growing immigrant groups, mainly due to war and political unrest in the Middle East. (Rice, Weglicki, Thomas, & Hammad, 2006). In 2010, 1.69 million people reported Arab ancestry according to the US Census Bureau (2011), 2009 American Community Survey).

In 2000, this number was 1.2 million, representing an increase of 29%. Nearly one-third of those reporting an Arab ancestry in 2010 were Lebanese or 504,000. Armenians closely followed the Lebanese at 485,000. The next largest group was Arabs at 286,000. Egyptians and Syrians were next at 197,000 and 159,000 respectively. Over 350,000 (351,000) people reported other specific Arab ancestries, including Palestinian at 104,000; Iraqi, Moroccan, and Jordanian populations were at 101,000, 78,000, and 68,000 respectively. Arabs live in all 50 states and are evenly distributed across the country with 25% living in the Northeast, 27% in the Mid-West, 24% in the South and 23% on the West coast. Arab Americans are very diverse geographically, religiously, and linguistically. Over 800,000 (845, 396) people speak Arabic in the home (US Census Bureau, 2011). In addition to Arabic, Arab Americans speak many languages in addition to such as Farsi, Persian, Urdu, French, and Kurdish. One third of Arab Americans reside in California, Michigan, and New York and two-thirds reside in 10 states. The top six metro areas where Arab Americans reside are: Detroit Michigan, Los Angeles, California, New York, Chicago, Illinois, Washington, D.C., and Northeastern New Jersey (Arab American Institute Foundation, 2011). According to the US Census Bureau (2000), 30% of Dearborn, Michigan, is Arab.

SOCIAL, PSYCHOLOGICAL, AND PHYSICAL HEALTH ISSUES

There are variations among Arabs and people of the Middle East as a function of gender, education, level of acculturation, income, phenotype, and geography. For example, life expectancy is lower in poor Arab (e.g., Somalia) and Muslim (e.g., Afghanistan) countries compared with rich Arab (e.g., Kuwait and UAE) and Muslim (e.g., Malaysia) countries.

Arab countries have the highest level of extreme poverty in the world, with one out of five people living on less than $2 per day, with Saudi Arabia, Qatar, United Arab Emirates, and Bahrain being wealthy countries from the oil that was discovered in the middle of the 20th century.

Although Arabs in America are more likely than the general population to have a college education, two-thirds of illiterate Arabs are women. Adult literacy in the Arab world is about 60%, compared with 79% in the world at large. Approximately 85% of Arab Americans have a high school diploma, and more than 4 out of 10 Arab Americans have a bachelor's or higher degree—this is compared with 24% of the American average. Twice as many Arab Americans as Americans have postgraduate degrees (Abudabbeh, 2005a). According to a Pew Research Center (2011) survey of 1,033 Muslim Americans, 59% of adult Muslims are between the ages of 18 and 39, compared with 40% of adults in the general public. Twelve percent of Muslim adults are ages 55 and older; This is compared to 33% of all US adults who are 55 or older. Foreign-born Muslims are somewhat older than native-born Muslims. In general, immigrants tend to arrive as adults and then start families in the United States.

Nearly two-thirds (64%) of Arab Americans are in the labor force. Among workers, 42% are in management and professional positions; 31% in sales, office, and administrative support; 12% in service industries; 10% in production, transportation, and material moving; and 5% in construction, extraction, and maintenance (Arab American Institute, 2006).

Storytelling: Racial Profiling

Her son is now 21. Prior to his arrival into the world in 1991, his mother, a very pregnant African American Christian woman in her last trimester, was dressed in a head scarf and a long coat. As she walked alone down the street, a White man in a business suit quickly approached her. Upon passing her, he stared directly into her face and angrily uttered the words, "Sand Nigger Bitch!" He then spat on her. Terrified, she stumbled away as quickly as her body would allow. This impeccably dressed stranger had verbally and physically abused her. Due to her light skin and head wrap, the man assumed she was Muslim and an Arab, which meant something to be hated during America's involvement in the Persian Gulf War. There are countless stories like this that happen to Latinos, African Americans, Asians, Indians, and Arab Americans since 9/11, illuminating the terror and threat surrounding groups who are marked and targeted.

The median income for Arab Americans in 2008 was $56,331 compared with the National median of $51,369.

Arab Americans have a tendency to display emotional distress in terms of physical complaints. This somatization may be partially explained by the mind-body connection descriptive of many people from collectivistic cultures. Many Arab Americans come from Middle Eastern countries where tobacco use is high. On average, 45% of the men and 5% of the women in the Middle East smoke cigarettes. Tobacco use by women in the Middle East was traditionally very low, but it is now on the rise. The Middle Eastern nations with the highest adult cigarette-smoking rates include Iraq (40%), Yemen (45%), Lebanon (58%), and Tunisia (60%) (World Health Organization Tobacco Free Initiative, 2005b).

According to Abudabbeh and Nydell (1993), some of the mental health problems presented clinically by the Arab immigrant population are physical abuse, identity confusion, loss of extended

TABLE 8.1 Common Cultural Values among Arab Americans
Hospitality and generosity in giving and spending
Respect for elders and parents
Wealth and preeminence of male children
Subordination of women to men
Modesty and privacy
Intensive religiosity
Marriage
Group values over individual interests and career
Equality of all human beings
Health and strength
Communication patterns dictated by authority, age, and gender
Family cohesion
Loyalty

family support system, adjusting to a lower social and economic status, intergenerational value conflicts, changes in the role of family members, and parenting problems.

Given that sexuality discussions are regarded as taboo for many people of the Middle East, where does the Arab homeland stand in the fight against HIV/AIDS, given that sexual transmission remains one of the primary ways to contract the virus? Estimates by the World Health Organization (WHO) and the joint United Nations program on HIV/AIDS show that HIV prevalence is low in the Middle East and North Africa region (0.2%). The most recent estimate of the number of people living with HIV/AIDS in the Middle East and North Africa is a half million. It has been suggested that the low prevalence of HIV in these regions is linked to Islam and its influence on the behaviors that affect the transmission of HIV (Obermeyer, 2006). Traditional Muslim approaches tend to be conservative; some even regard HIV as divine punishment for deviance, whereas religion is regarded as a protection.

Certain risk factors increase the spread of the epidemic such as unprotected extramarital sex, war, migration, and the population of intravenous drug users who may constitute a "bridge" to the general population. Compared with sub-Saharan Africa, HIV rates in the Middle East and North Africa are relatively low. Low alcohol intake as well as male circumcision may also account for this low prevalence rate. Governments in several countries are breaking the silence and allowing information about prevention and treatment to be disseminated.

A cultural context exists where marriage is universally expected. A high value is placed on virginity, which means unmarried young women are subject to judgment and stigma from health workers if they try to obtain contraception (DeJong & El-Khoury, 2006). Moreover, women are pressured to have children as soon as they marry. Tunisia is cited as the only Middle Eastern country that has legalized abortion; however, unsafe induced abortion occurs throughout the Arab world.

Following the events of September 11, 2001, many Arabs were personally subjected to discrimination or knew someone who had experienced discrimination because of anti-Arab attitudes. In research with 108 Arab Americans, the constructs of discrimination, self-esteem, and personal control were examined. A direct link was found between perceived discrimination

Storytelling: American Dreamers

The Pew Research Center recently conducted a survey with 1,033 Muslim Americans. The general public's perceptions of Muslims differ from reality. For example, a majority (56%) of Muslim Americans say that most Muslims who come to the United States want to adopt American customs and ways of life. Only 20% say that Muslims in this country want to be distinct from the larger American society. The general public, however, said that just a third (33%) of Muslims in the US today want to assimilate. Muslim Americans embrace the American Dream more so than the general public. Nearly three-quarters (74%) of Muslim Americans endorse the idea that most people can get ahead if they are willing to work hard; just 26% say hard work is no guarantee of success. Among the general public, somewhat fewer (62%) say that most people who work hard can get ahead. US Muslims are about as likely as other Americans to report household incomes of $100,000 or more (14% of Muslims, compared with 16% of all adults). They also reported similar levels of satisfaction with their financial situations. Nearly half, 46% say they are in excellent or good shape financially; among the general public, 38% say this. Muslim Americans are as likely as the public overall to have graduated from college (26% of Muslims vs. 28% among the general public). About one-in-three (33%) say they have worked with other people from their neighborhood to fix a problem or improve a condition in their community in the past 12 months, compared with 38% of the general public.

events and psychological distress (Moradi & Hasan, 2004). This study also found that "perceived discrimination events were related to lower levels of perceived control over one's life and lower perceived control in turn was related to lower self esteem and greater psychological distress for Arab American individuals" (p. 425). (See Storytelling: *Racial Profiling*.) The discourses associated with *Arabs or the Middle East* include potential Muslim extremist, terror suspect, foreign-born and foreign-looking, oppressive toward women due to patriarchy and sexism, and non-Christian. Research suggests that such discourses are damaging and affect the psychological well-being of Arab Americans, who represent an understudied group. As multicultural competence is developed through workshops, classes, supervision, and continuing education, clinicians will hopefully become mindful of their proximity to these and other discourses.

CULTURAL ORIENTATION AND VALUES

According to Abudabbeh (2005a), the Arab family can be described as "patriarchal, pyramidically hierarchal with regard to age, sex, and extended" (p. 427). (See Table 8.1.) Communication styles are restrained and formal, making it difficult for an Arab client in therapy to disclose personal feelings and problems to someone outside of the family. Persons who are subservient to authority by virtue of age or gender communicate accordingly. In terms of communication between parents and children, Abudabbeh also says that children respond to parental authority by censoring themselves, crying, or withholding information. An Arabic saying goes, "to satisfy God is to satisfy parents" (Hall & Livingston, 2006, p. 144). For the majority of Arab people, the family is the primary means of support. Men have specific duties toward their wives and children. Similarly, wives are given instructions regarding the proper treatment of their husbands and children. Muslim law allows a woman to be contracted for marriage by her guardian. In most cases, this is the woman's father (Abudabbeh, 2005a). The more education a woman has, the older she is likely to be when she marries. A collectivistic orientation prevails in that the good of the family is elevated above the fulfillment of personal and individual needs and wishes. Talking negatively about the family is unacceptable. Sexuality is a taboo subject (Abudabbeh, 2005a).

Cultural values recognized by the Qur'an include hospitality and generosity in giving and spending, respect for elders and parents, wealth and preeminence of male children, subordination of women to men, modesty, intensive religiosity, equality of all human beings, and health and strength (Hall & Livingston, 2006). In addition, final authority rests with the father. Individualistic pursuits in the West, such as when and where to go to graduate school and who to marry, are seen as selfish. Privacy is primary and is connected to honor and the good name of the family. Family structures are often formal and hierarchical, in that deference to elders and males is practiced. Because of the central place of family, going outside the family to seek help for personal problems may be seen as disloyal or a threat to group honor. There is a concern of being seen as *manjun* or crazy (Shiraev & Levy, 2004).

According to Dwairy (2004), women's treatment is inferior in the Arabic world. More specifically, their freedom is limited, as is their mobility, social behavior, and decision making. Currently, women are not allowed to drive in Saudi Arabia. Domestic violence at the hands of brothers, husbands, and fathers is a reality for many. In countries struggling to keep their integrity because of war, famine, upheaval, and corruption, mental health needs are not a priority for women or men (Souter & Murthy, 2006).

Traditional Islamic law allows men four wives; however, polygamy is rare in modern Arab societies. Men are also instructed by the Qur'an to not marry more than one woman unless they are able to treat all wives equally. Tunisia forbids the practice of polygamy, whereas some Arab countries require the man to secure a court's permission to take on a second wife, which is the case in Iraq. In some countries, such as Lebanon and Morocco, a woman can insist on a premarital contract that allows her to divorce her husband if he decides to marry a second wife (Abudabbeh, 2005a).

IMPLICATIONS FOR COUNSELORS AND PSYCHOLOGISTS

The Western view of the nuclear family is limiting for many Arabs and other groups of color in that there is a cultural tendency to separate the self into discrete categories. Interventions with Arab clients need to be considered within the context of the family, the extended family, community, and even tribal background (Al-Krenawi & Graham, 2000). Krenawi and Graham (2000) identified that clients of Arab origin tend to have a negative view of mental health service delivery and may even mistrust it. Clients may even expect the therapist to provide them with solutions to their problems and see the mental health provider as an authority figure. Treatment can be enhanced if the therapist is willing to relinquish traditional approaches (Abudabbeh, 2005a). Therapists are encouraged to use didactic and structured therapies, calling other family members personally if they refuse to present for therapy, and be willing to accept gifts and invitations to their home. Refusal may be perceived as rude. Therapists should also remember that some topics are taboo, such as sexual problems or homosexuality. Flexibility to accommodate the client and the family's needs is an important therapeutic skill. Among Arab Americans, distrust of outsiders is not uncommon. Many Arab clients tend not to see the origins of illness from a biomedical point of view but rather as stemming from an external locus of control. The intervention of supernatural elements such as spirits and angels is a belief held by some within the culture, as is a belief in fate. Thus, some Middle Eastern clients turn to fortune tellers, priests, imams, physicians, and Koranic healers for assistance with mental health issues (Nassar-McMillan & Hakim-Larson, 2003).

Informality is an aspect of western culture. For example, children and adults are on a first-name basis. Some Arab clients as well as members from White European groups may be put off by a casual air that can feel disrespectful. Al-krenawi and Graham (2000) maintain that "an assessment of the client's personal background and level of acculturation will alert the sensitive practitioner to potential cultural conflicts with regard to treatment" (p. 12). Among first-generation immigrants who are attempting to adjust to a new environment, acquire a new language, and deal with a host of internal and external demands, the stress may be much greater than previously thought, with chronic acculturation stress having enormous psychological implications. Finally, an Islamic concept of predetermination or fate can make primary prevention a challenge (Nassar-Mcmillan & Hakim-Larson, 2003).

A premium is placed on the family as a core unit. Gender socialization and roles are often prescribed with the fathers having a level of authority and centrality in the home. Girls are raised to exercise discretion and modesty in their interactions with others and through their styles of dress—a lesson America could borrow given our penchant for showing undergarments and body parts (e.g., low-rise jeans) that strangers really have no business seeing. Boys are socialized to be leaders in the home and to be head of their household by showing strength and Godly direction.

A host of factors have been found to predict the mental health of Arab Americans and include age, gender, income, and education, variables such as age at migration, length of time in the United States, religion, and discrimination experiences. It is important that counselors assist Arab-American clients to develop skills for recognizing and confronting the negative effects of racial and religious discrimination (Aprahamian et al., 2011).

CASE STUDY

PERCEPTIONS OF DANGEROUSNESS

Yasmin Ahid is a 19-year-old college student. His parents were born in Morocco. Yasmin was born in Illinois. He and his family are Muslims. Yasmin is very active in college—he is involved with the Psychology Club and is president of the Middle Eastern Club. His girlfriend, Amina, is also from Morocco—he grew up with Amina (her parents immigrated to the States shortly after his parents did). Yasmin is fluent in Arabic, English, and French. He has been accepted to be a Resident Assistant next year and he is very excited about being a student leader. Yasmin was attending an orientation for future Resident Assistants. The group facilitator presented a case of a male student with alcohol problems, poor academic performance, and behavioral problems (e.g. getting into arguments and fights with other males). The facilitator asked attendees to discuss methods of effective intervention. One student said that it is important to show empathy and a willingness to listen to the students' problems and to know when to refer the student to the campus Counseling Center. Yasmin stated that one of his concerns when dealing with combative residents was related to how his religion and physical appearance might intensify existing feelings of anger that the student may already have. Yasmin has brown skin with dark eyes, and dark curly hair—he likes to say with a smile that he looks like a very handsome Middle Eastern man. A few of the students, including an African American woman and a Chinese man, stated that his concerns were unfounded and that students only care about the quality of leadership. Yasmin stated that he has personally experienced racism on and off campus. He recalled an encounter when he was at a local pub with other students. Some of the patrons appeared uncomfortable with his presence and kept giving him looks. One man began hurling racist comments at him, particularly after the CNN news commentator discussed the recent death of American troops in Afghanistan killed by insurgents who used a rocket propelled grenade to bring their helicopter down. The same students who dismissed Yasmin's claims of discrimination blamed the man at the pub's behavior on too many beers and a loss of inhibition. Yasmin said that he is not imagining racism but it is a reality and that people who don't experience racism should maybe listen to those who actually experience it. A few of the White group leaders now have concerns about Yasmin's appropriateness given his inability to tolerate multiple and diverging perspectives. They also have concerns about his claims of racism, particularly in light of the denial of racism from students of color who were in attendance.

QUESTIONS

1. What are the factors that influence Yasmin's outlook about racial and religious discrimination?
2. What prevents students and administrators from validating what Yasmin is saying?

DISCUSSION AND INTEGRATION

Yasmin

Yasmin's identity and orientation has been shaped by multiple influences. These include his nationality, acculturation levels, skin color, US citizenship, his parents' immigrant status, religion, education, and personality. Yasmin has a high ethnic identity—he is president of the Middle-Eastern Club. Awad (2010) conducted research with 177 people from the Middle

East/Arab Americans. He looked at the constructs of acculturation, ethnic identity, and religious affiliation. Awad found that ethnic identity was a predictor of perceived discrimination. Persons who were Muslims also reported higher levels of discrimination than did Christians. It was also found that Muslims who were more highly acculturated to dominant society were more likely to perceive discrimination whereas Christians who were highly acculturated were less likely to perceive discrimination. Yasmin is a Muslim man who has a high ethnic identity and is somewhat acculturated Awad's research serves to explain some of his experiences with racial discrimination. According to a recent study by the Pew Research Center (2011) in which over 1,000 Muslims were surveyed, Muslims in the United States continue to reject extremism by much larger margins than Muslims in most other nations surveyed this year by the Pew Global Attitudes Project. Although contrary to dominant discourses about Arab Americans, Muslim Americans expressed concern about the possible rise of Islamic extremism, not only in the United States but throughout the world.

Yasmin is a Muslim man from a collectivistic and pyramidic culture. A person from a collectivist culture is likely to define himself "in an interdependent fashion; the self may vary across situations or contexts. Rather than emphasizing personal distinctiveness, this person is likely to stress his similarity to a group, view roles and obligations to a group as central aspects of self definition, and value restraint and harmony" (Enns, 1994, p. 206). It is not surprising that some of the students of color could not relate to Yasmin's claims of racism. Not all students of color perceive discrimination. This could be a function of racial identity levels that encourage their obliviousness to discrimination. Regarding the group facilitators present, it is common for White people not to understand the reality of racism, if they do not have people of color in their lives who share such experiences or if they are not familiar with the literature that addresses racism in the 21st century.

Summary

This chapter focused on Arab Americans and people of the Middle East. A demographical snapshot was provided and included information about the Arab homeland, distinctions between Muslims and Arabs, religion, and the most populated areas where Arab Americans are from and now reside. The three dominant waves of immigration were discussed, as were the factors contributing to immigration. A detailed case study was included that featured a Muslim college student leader who shared his experiences of racism with other student leaders who dismissed such allegations. Emphasis was on understanding the reality of racism among people from the Middle East, particularly those who are Muslim and have high levels of ethnic identity.

Converging Race

The Social Construction of Race
Race and Science
Origins of Racial Groups
Racial and Ethnic Identity Development
Implications for Counselors and Psychologists
Case Study
Summary

... oppression is as American as apple pie.

AUDRE LORDE

Race intersects with other dimensions of identity and across situations and contexts. For most clients, and for some people of color, race does not exist as a source of clinical exploration. Throughout this chapter, racial identity theory is discussed. The discussion expands race beyond the limiting and essentializing dimensions of phenotype and skin color.

THE SOCIAL CONSTRUCTION OF RACE

Historically, the literature of multicultural counseling and psychology has emphasized race. This is understandable considering both the legacy and current reality of racism in America and the power that people give to racial differences to privilege, stratify, and stigmatize. Omni and Winant (2006) argued that although particular meanings, myths, and stereotypes about race can and indeed do change, "the presence of a system of racial meanings and stereotypes, of racial ideology, seems to be a permanent feature of U.S. culture" (p. 23).

Written predominantly by heterosexually identified and racially diverse men, the initial writings on cross-cultural counseling and psychology emphasized race, ethnic, and cultural identities. As US-born women and people of color, racially and ethnically diverse immigrants, transgendered people, gay people, and people with disabilities began writing from their personal and clinical experiences, gender, sexual, and disability identities were added to the literature. Increasingly, a much needed emphasis on spirituality is found. This expanded focus on disability, spirituality, sexuality, and socioeconomic class is crucial to a more integrated cultural paradigm.

To what extent are recently added identities perceived to trespass on the rightful terrain and turf of race and ethnicity? It is important to ask what the legitimate and perceived illegitimate dimensions of diversity are. Convergence asks that we honor race and ethnic identities in our clients while simultaneously incorporating other identities that are just as legitimate in the never-ending process of meaning-making (Robinson-Wood, 2010b).

Within the discourse of diversity, who is included? The current discourse suggests that it is not White people. Although whiteness is unremarkable and unexamined (Newman, 2007), it is against whiteness that discussions about diversity occur. Lipsitz (2005) said "whiteness is everywhere in American culture, but it is very hard to see … As the unmarked category against which difference is constructed, whiteness never has to speak its name, never has to acknowledge its role as an organizing principle in social and cultural relations" (p. 402).

When White people choose to get up close to their skin color privilege, they are perceived by other Whites, as well as some people of color, as noble and exalted in ways that people of color are not when they tackle similar issues. The discourse is that Whites are special when they challenge racism, particularly because they do not have membership in the group that is usually the target of racism—people of color. It is presumed that people of color would naturally focus on race, women would logically be interested in gender, and gay and lesbian people would devote their time and attention to sexuality. Regardless of the constellation of our identities and membership in privileged groups, a concern about social justice is a reflection of commitment to diversity.

How do discourses about whiteness and other race discourses show up and affect the profession, our students, clients, and clinicians? Where do White people who are not gay, female, or disabled go to explore their whiteness? More importantly, what is the motivation for doing so? Without being named in the dialogue, White people who do not have a marginalized identity are given a message that it is not necessary for them to be engaged in and embraced by the work of diversity. We know this to be untrue.

Despite the tremendous heterogeneity among racially similar groups and homogeneity across different racial groups, race functions as a master status in society. As a social construction, race has the power to eclipse other identities that are just as potent in identity construction. Race, then, is not only a master status, but is a grand-master status. A recent study found that African Americans were less likely than Whites to receive grants from the National Institutes of Health. Data from more than 40,000 researchers were analyzed. Among researchers, more than 80,000 grant applications were submitted to NIH between 2000 and 2006. About 16% of applications from Blacks were approved, compared with about 29% of those from Whites. Asian applicants appeared to be slightly less likely than Whites to get grants. That gap, however, disappeared when researchers matched equally qualified White and Asian US citizens. Hispanics were about as successful as Whites Ginther, Schaffer, Schnell, Masimore, Liu, Haak, & Kington (2011).

The social construction of race is sociopolitical and looms large. Racial categories contribute to race labeling. **Race labeling** is a function of phenotype and skin color characteristics to assign people to categories that are castelike in nature. **Race** typically refers to appearances, such as skin color, hair type (straight, curly, kinky), skin hue, eye color, stature, body size, nose, eyes, and head shape. Clearly, these characteristics alone do not accurately assign a particular racial classification or negate the larger biological similarities that *homo sapiens* are destined to share.

Representations of race are used by police, mortgage lenders, judges, teachers, employers, potential suitors, health care professionals, federal grant agencies and the public at large to categorize people into racial groups. (See Storytelling: *Silence is not Benign.*) Socially constructed discourses about race contributes to differential treatment. Compared with Whites within a similar income bracket, Blacks and Latinos are given loans with higher interest rates and are not provided the same quality of health care treatment. In sum, race and ethnicity discourses affect the nature of people's daily experiences. (See Table 9.1.)

At the time in US society when the US Census Bureau listed five races, to be *colored* (Black or mulatto) was not just a source of difference. Race functioned as a status variable. More specifically, the experience of being "colored" meant no voting rights, no educational access to predominantly White institutions, nonexistent or woefully inadequate health care, extreme vulnerability to being lynched, and no protection under the law. Yet the mere classification of race was not solely responsible for differential treatment. Attitudes about race were pivotal to the creation of a social structure

TABLE 9.1 Dominant Race and Ethnicity Discourses

Whites	Blacks and Maori	Arab (men)	Latinos	Asians
Middle-class	Low-income/poor	Monied	Low-income/poor	Successful
Qualified	Special affirmative action admit	Terroristic	Lots of children	Model minority
Oblivious about Whiteness; unsure allies in ending racism	Emotionally unrestrained (angry, loud)	Conservative, suspicious	Brown (monolith, e.g., Mexicans)	Emotionally restrained (quiet, not angry like Black people and Latinos)
Smart, capable, successful	Not intelligent as Whites, Asians; Blacks "sound or act White" if articulate	Intelligent; Sneaky	Non-English-dominant and in need of remediation	Brilliant in math and science; smarter than White people
Beneficiaries of God's grace	Spirituality among women; dangerousness among men	Muslim extremists	Catholics	Buddhists
Hardworking	Gang bangers among youth	Terror suspect	Gang member	Studious, hardworking
Normal Americans	Diverse; urban	Foreign-born	Foreign-born	Foreign-born
Necessary	Lazy; oppressed	Women as inferior	Illegal/immigrant	Scientists
In-charge, powerful	Great athlete; good dancer; fine entertainer	Sexism among men	Sexism among men	Exoticism among women

Storytelling: Silence is not Benign

A former student of mine taught Cultural Diversity courses for years. Although she knew the material and was very committed to teaching, she was often met with suspicion from students. My former student was White, and among some students, her skin color contributed to their doubts about her legitimacy or whether her lived experiences provided sufficient insight into the topics germane to a Diversity course: inequity, experiences with racism, power imbalance, and privilege. When she spoke with me about this dynamic, I asked her how she came to know what some students were thinking and feeling about her. She said that some students, each semester, mentioned this during their anonymous evaluation of her course. I asked if she had raised this issue in class. She said she did not because she did not know how, and she was annoyed that some students would feel that way about her, given her academic qualifications. I told her that there are also students who question a faculty member of color's legitimacy to teach certain course material, such as statistics. I told her that not speaking to the issue did not allow her to bring this unsettling but substantive topic out of the shadows. This was not fair to her or the students. I reminded her of Audre Lorde's quote: "Your silence will not protect you."

in which institutional policy bestowed privilege and conferred disadvantage on persons because of race (Cornell & Hartmann, 1997; McIntosh, 1988; Pinderhughes, 1989). The 2000 census, for the first time, enabled people to select more than one race as a way of describing themselves. Of the 309 million Americans who responded to the 2010 census, 2.9% indicated that they belonged to more than one race—that is, over 9 million people. The 2010 Census also revealed that 7.5 million people claimed a White identity while reporting one or more other race. The majority at 24.5% stated they were White and African American (Hixson, Hepler, & Kim, 2011)

In an effort to address racial and gender inequity, affirmative action was created through the provision of opportunity for groups that had been targets of historical discrimination. Takaki (1994), a scholar on race and ethnicity, stated that:

> Affirmative action is actually designed to address the legacy of past racial discrimination and existing inequality by training and identifying qualified individuals of excluded racial minorities and allowing them greater access to equality and opportunity in education and employment. (p. 7)

That affirmative action seeks to impose quotas resulting in unqualified people (meaning people of color and women) taking jobs away from those who are qualified (meaning White males) is a myth. The goal of affirmative action was to encourage college admissions and employers to create opportunity for people of color, given their exclusion throughout history and in present-day America. Eventually, this provision extended beyond racial classification to include gender, sexual orientation, physical disability, and religion.

RACE AND SCIENCE

A substantial portion of the dialogue about race includes conceptual frameworks that attribute inferior yet inherent biological deficiencies to African and Semitic people. In October 2007, Dr. James Watson, a 1962 Nobel Prize recipient for his role in discovering the structure of DNA, found himself in trouble for making statements that were interpreted as racist. He stated that he was "inherently gloomy about the prospect of Africa because all our social policies are based on the fact that their intelligence is the same as ours, whereas all the testing says not really" (Nugent, 2007). Watson later apologized for his remarks.

Charles Darwin's 1859 work *On the Origin of Species by Means of Natural Selection* was used to support the genetic intellectual superiority of Whites and the genetic inferiority of non-Whites, who were referred to as the "lower races." There are claims regarding racial purity and racial superiority, but these are bogus and represent a false hope (Cooper, 2002). Everyone comes from the same source (Zuckerman, 1990). Still, outdated racial categories such as Negroid (Black), Mongoloid (Asian), and Caucasoid (White) remain. Human beings are products of migratory patterns and world conquests throughout the centuries; thus, a "pure race" does not exist (Dobbins & Skillings, 1991).

The recently completed Human Genome Sequencing Project has confirmed what scientists have known for a very long time—humans do not fit into the biological criteria that define race. The widely held belief in the biological differences between racial groups is simply incorrect (LaVeist, 2002). "Any way you measure, the amount of divergence between people is essentially zero," according to Joseph L. Graves, an evolutionary biologist. He went on to say that "the scientific case for the nonexistence of human race is overwhelming" (Graves, 2003).

As early as 1870, the US Bureau of the Census divided the US population into five races: White, Colored (Black), Colored (Mulatto), Chinese, and Indian (Root, 1992). Since this time and in even the present day, controversy among biologists, anthropologists, and other scholars has surrounded the topic of the number of races.

For instance, Gossett (1963) recognized the diversity of opinion and observed the following:

> Linnaeus had found four human races; Blumenbach had five; Curvier had three; John Hunter had seven; Burke had sixty-three; Pickering had eleven; Virey had two "species," each containing three races; Haeckel had thirty-six; Hurley had four; Topinard had nineteen under three headings; Desmoulins had sixteen "species"; Deniker had seventeen races and thirty types. (p. 82)

Zuckerman (1990) sought to clarify misconceptions surrounding racial similarity and difference. He reported that, in his analysis of 18 genetic systems (blood groups, proteins, and enzymes) in 40 populations within 16 subgroups around the world, "the major component of genetic diversity is between individuals in the same tribe or nation; it accounts for 84% of the variance. Of the remaining variance, 10% is accounted for by racial groupings and 6% by geographic regions" (p. 1300). The existence of definable groups or races is not self-evident, although human variation is (Cooper, 2002).

Alan Goodman, dean of natural science at Hampshire College, said that depending on which trait is used to distinguish races, "you won't get anything that remotely tracks conventional race categories" (cited in Begley, 1995, p. 67). Spickard (1992), a scholar on biracial identity, argued, "The so-called races are not biological categories at all. Rather, they are primarily social divisions that rely only partly on physical markers as skin color to identify group membership" (p. 17). (See Storytelling: *Internalized Racism.*) Scientists studying the human genome have announced that the DNA of human beings is 99.9% alike. According to the US Department of Energy Office of Science, Office of Biological and Environmental Research, Human Genome Program:

> DNA studies do not indicate that separate classifiable subspecies (races) exist within modern humans. While different genes for physical traits such as skin and hair color can be identified between individuals, no consistent patterns of genes across the human

Storytelling: Internalized Racism

In Henry Louis Gates' documentary *Blacks in Latin America*, the ruler of the Dominican Republic from 1930 to 1961 was highlighted. Although General Rafael Leonidas Trujillo Molina had Haitian ancestry, he ordered the army in 1937 to murder thousands of Haitians living on the Dominican side of the border. In this event, known as the Parsley Massacre, it is estimated that over 15,000 Haitians were killed over a six-day period. To hide their murders, the soldiers used machetes, hence the term *el corte* (the cutting) in the Dominican Republic. The soldiers interrogated persons with dark skin, using the shibboleth *perejil* (parsley) to distinguish Haitians from Dominicans. The "r" of perejil was difficult for Haitians to pronounce. As a result of the massacre, the Dominican Republic agreed to pay Haiti US$750,000, which was later reduced to US$525,000. Trujillo was assassinated in 1961. The general came to be known for his use of White powder to to whiten his face.

genome exist to distinguish one race from another. There also is no genetic basis for divisions of human ethnicity. People who have lived in the same geographic region for many generations may have some alleles in common, but no allele will be found in all members of one population and in no members of any other (http://www.nowpublic.com/world/human-genome-project-announces-race-does-not-exist#ixzz1fu89nel9).

ORIGINS OF RACIAL GROUPS

Considerable uncertainty surrounds racial origins. Rogers (1967), a historian, wrote that "for us of the present day, the earliest history of all peoples and nations is lost in a fog" (p. 21). Agreement among reputable historians and archaeologists is that the color of primitive humans was Black. Zuckerman (1990) concurred and wrote, "Although there is considerable speculation on the origin of races, little can be proved other than that a species, *Homo sapiens*, gradually evolved from its predecessor *Homo erectus* about 200,000 years ago in East Africa and spread through Africa and Eurasia" (p. 1297). It had been thought until recently that *Homo habilis* was a direct ancestor of *Homo erectus*, but evidence now shows they were sister species, living side by side. For about 500,000 years, *Homo habilis* and *Homo erectus* co-existed side by side. A 1.5-million-year-old skull and jaw bone found in Kenya have given rise to a rewriting of early man/woman.

Early humans are thought to have been of "small stature, probably from four and a half to five feet tall. Their nearest living descendants are believed to be the Bushmen of South Africa; the Mincopies of the Andaman Islands off the coast of India; the hill-folk of Southern India; the Tapiro of New Guinea; and the Negritos of the Philippines" (Rogers, 1967, pp. 28–29).

Given that the origins of the human race are Black, White racial characteristics result from a lack of pigmentation, lost over time because it was not needed in cold environments. Sergi, of the University of Rome, stated that European man was African man, *Eur-African*, transformed by European environmental effects. There are three categories of *Eur-African*: "(a) the African with red, brown, and black pigmentation, (b) the Mediterranean or brunette complexion, inhabiting the great basin, including part of Northern Africa ... and finally, (c) a Nordic variety of blond skin and hair, blue or gray eyes, most universally represented as Scandinavia, North Germany, and England" (Rogers, 1967, pp. 29–30).

RACIAL AND ETHNIC IDENTITY DEVELOPMENT

The importance of and a search for racial and cultural understanding is a tenet of racial identity development. Nonetheless, the need to develop a racial identity is coupled with the oppression of racism (Gillem, Cohn, & Throne, 2001), wherein stigma is attached to people of color and privilege is embodied in whiteness.

Racial identity theory assumes that individuals at early levels of development have the potential to change over time as they encounter dissonance to existing cognitive schema (Robinson, 1999a). The models reflect movement and change over time. By integrating racial identity with a discussion of race, a focus is placed on development, an achieved characteristic, and not solely on skin color, an immutable one.

Until recently, within the past 15 years, the racial identity development literature has focused primarily on White, Black, and other monoracial groups. Helms's (1995) work on a model of racial identity for people of color and the earlier racial/cultural identity development model (originally called the minority identity development model) by Atkinson et al. (1983) are exceptions. A problem with traditional racial identity models is their failure to include people who are biracial and/or multiracial. Chapter 10 is devoted to an in-depth discussion of biracial and multiracial issues with a goal of becoming familiar with models of racial identity for people with more than one racial identity. In addition, a focus on identity moves the discussion of race beyond the narrowness of phenotype traditionally associated with race.

Experiences with racism differ among groups of color and within groups of color. A number of factors may moderate the experience of racism for people of color, such as physical appearance or skin color hue and class markers (e.g., income, occupation, country of origin, and facility with the English language).

Pieterse and Carter (2007) conducted research with 220 Black American men, recruited primarily from barbershops in New York City and Washington, DC. The purpose of the study was to examine the influence of perceived racism-related stress on psychological health and to explore the predictive quality of racism-related stress on psychological health when controlling for general life stress. All of the men reported experiencing some type of racist incident in the prior month and year. Although racist events were stressful, racism-related stress did not seem to influence the well-being of working-class men. The researchers concluded that for Black men in particular, "social mobility encompasses hidden costs, one of which could be a greater sensitivity to experiences of racism and discrimination" (p. 106).

Ancis, Sedlacek, and Mohr (2000) studied 578 African American, Asian American, Latino, and White college student responses to a questionnaire assessing perceptions and experiences of the Campus Cultural Climate Questionnaire (CACQ). This scale has 100 statements regarding campus climate. The 11 factors include racial tension, fair treatment, cross-cultural comfort, racial pressures, comfort with own culture, and lack of support. The researchers found racial differences among respondents. African American students reported more negative experiences in comparison with Asian American, Latino, and White students. More specifically, Black students experienced "greater racial-ethnic hostility, greater pressure to conform to stereotypes, less equitable treatment by faculty, staff, and teaching assistants, and more faculty racism than did the other groups" (p. 183). The Asian American and Latino students reported experiences of stereotyping and prejudice. They indicated limited respect and unfair treatment by faculty, teaching assistants, and students and pressure to conform to stereotypes. Compared with other racial groups, Latinos experienced the least racism and a campus climate relatively free of racial conflict. Compared to African Americans, White students reported less racial tension, few expectations to conform to stereotypic behavior, an experience of being treated fairly, a respectful and diverse campus climate, and the most overall satisfaction.

Rowley, Burchinal, Roberts, and Zeisel (2008) investigated changes in racial identity, cross-race friendships, same-race friendships, and classroom racial composition on changes in race-related social cognition from third to fifth grade for 73 African American children. Three major findings were found. First, there was a decline in expectations for discrimination from third to fifth grade. Second, having more African American friends was associated with expecting more discrimination in cross-racial interactions from third to fifth grade. Third, increases in racial centrality were related to increases in discrimination expectations. Increases in public regard were associated with decreases in discrimination expectations. Racial identity includes the extent to which a person defines himself or herself in terms of race (racial centrality). A person's sense of pride in group membership and evaluation of the merits of the group refers to private regard. Public regard involves beliefs about how others view the group.

Ethnic Identity

Because there are conceptual differences between ethnicity and race, it makes sense for there to be a difference between racial identity and ethnic identity. *Representations of race* typically refer to phenotype or genetic heritage, whereas *ethnicity* is defined as sociocultural heritage. There has not traditionally been a difference in the psychological literature between racial and ethnic identity. Recently, Cokley (2005) argued that confusion exists among racial identity, ethnic identity, and Africentric beliefs. Ethnic identity refers to the extent to which a person identifies with his or her ethnic group—"it is the meaning, strength, and salience of one's ethnic identity" (Cokley, 2005, p. 517).

In the early days of ethnic identity, Phinney (1990) acknowledged that there was no widely agreed upon definition of ethnic identity. At the same time, the components of ethnic identity include self-identification as a group member, a sense of belonging to the group, attitudes about group membership, and ethnic involvement (social participation, cultural practices, and attitudes) (Phinney, 1990).

Ethnicity is often presented as a subset or is subsumed under race, although people can be of the same ethnicity while representing different races. An example is the Dominican ethnic group, in which there is considerable ancestor-based skin color variation. People can be from the same race and have different ethnicities. There are people of African descent who are Nigerian; some are Cape Verdean, some are Jamaican, whereas others are US born.

At adolescence, ethnic identity has particular relevance given the pressure of peer groups and the upheaval associated with identity search across multiple levels of identity, including sexuality, gender, and race. In her study of 669 American-born African American, Latino, and White high-school students, Phinney (1997) found that ethnic identity was clearly an important contribution to an adolescent's sense of self and that this finding was consistent across ethnic groups. Among Black and Latino teens, being an American was not closely tied to the sense of self. American identity had no contribution to their self-esteem. For White students, however, ethnic identity and American identity were strong predictors of global self-esteem. Many African American and Latino teens may feel ambivalent about being American given their uncertainty around the meaning of American and the discourses about American actually referring to White people. (See Table 9.1.)

A challenge with the concept of ethnic identity is its confusion with acculturation. *Acculturation* "deals broadly with changes in cultural attitudes, values, and behaviors that result

from contact between two distinct cultures" (Phinney, 1990, p. 501). In other words, acculturation speaks to changes that occur over time when two cultures not only come into contact but
stay in continuous contact (Phinney & Flores, 2002). Acculturation is mentioned with ethnic
identity due to the importance of considering the ethnic group member's relationship with the
dominant group. Ethnic identity can be approached as a state in terms of the self-defining labels
that a person may use to label himself or herself at a given point in time. Stages of ethnic identity
chart changes over time in a person's way of identifying as an ethnic group member.

Phinney's research (1989) was instrumental in providing a framework of ethnic identity
development. Ninety-one American-born Asian American, Black, Hispanic, and White tenth-
grade students, all from integrated urban high schools, were interviewed. The subjects were also
given questionnaires to measure ego identity and psychological adjustment. On the basis of the
interviews, the minority subjects were coded as being in one of three identity stages: diffusion/
foreclosure, moratorium, and identity achieved. Among children of color, nearly one-half of the
subjects had not examined their ethnic identity, which was conceptualized as diffusion and foreclosure. *Diffusion* referred to a lack of interest in or concern with ethnicity. *Foreclosure* reflected
the views and opinions held by others (Phinney, 1990). In Phinney's (1989) work sample, about
one quarter were considered to be in *exploration* or *moratorium*, understood as seeking to understand the personal meaning of ethnicity for oneself. One-quarter were identified as *ethnic identity achieved* in that they had explored and were committed to an ethnic identity and had a clear
and confident sense of their own ethnicity. This last group had the highest scores on a measure
of ego identity and psychological adjustment. Although identity development was similar across
the three groups of color, the issues specific to each group differed.

Several racial identity development models are discussed in the following sections. Core
differences exist within groups rather than between them. As such, differences in racial identity and value orientation are to be expected among racially similar individuals. Racial identity
development theory underscores the reality of psychological differences within monoracial and
ethnic groups.

Native American Identity

Bryant and LaFromboise (2005) conducted research with 103 Native American Lumbee high
school students using the People of Color Racial Identity Attitude Scale (PCRIAS) by Helms
(1995). This instrument was developed to provide a measure of racial identity attitudes among
Asians, African Americans, Latinos, and Native Americans. There are four stages. *Conformity*
represents conformance to the dominant ideology and a devaluing of a person's own racial group.
Dissonance reflects confusion about a person's racial group. *Immersion* describes identification
with and even idolization of a person's racial group. Lastly, *internalization* refers to commitment to a person's group and an ability to integrate a person's racial identity into his or her life.
Internalization attitudes were dominant among this group, followed by immersion, dissonance,
and conformity.

Bryant and La Fromboise concluded that the internalization findings "suggest they possess a positive American Indian racial identity and also have the ability to acknowledge the
positive aspects of White society" (p. 86). In addition, immersion attitudes may suggest some
level of psychological as well as physical retreat into the Lumbee American community. Given
the students' level of awareness about the impact of race on a daily basis, the conformity and
dissonance attitudes may reflect some confusion, albeit minimally, about the sociopolitical constructions of race. Scholl (2006) had similar findings in his research with 121 Native American

college students. Internalization attitudes were dominant and conformity (or preencounter) attitudes were least likely to be represented.

Ethics, or the principles or moral values that guide people's actions, provide Horse (2001) with a clear conceptualization of Indian identity. Part of this ethic is within the context of a collective consciousness. Consciousness requires memory, which Gunn Allen (1994) remarked is not encouraged in the West. "The American idea that the best and the brightest should willingly reject and repudiate their origins leads to an allied idea—that history, like everything in the past, is of little value and should be forgotten as quickly as possible" (p. 192). According to Horse, consciousness is influenced by multiple issues: the degree to which someone is grounded in the native language, tribe, family, and culture; the worldview that is embraced; recognition as a member of an Indian tribe by the government of the tribe; and the validity of a person's genealogical heritage as an Indian. Concerns over human-made laws, such as blood quantum amounts (Wilson, 1992), is not as relevant as is someone's consciousness and identity as an Indian.

Asian American Identity Development

Myriad challenges face Asian people, as a heterogeneous group, in America. One of the most pervasive is related to the psychological conflict around racial identity. This conflict is connected to the experience of institutional racism, which is often subtle but damaging nonetheless to people who are targeted as inferior due to being different from a standard of White acceptability (Kim, 2001). According to Kim, "At some point in their lives, many Asian Americans have either consciously or unconsciously expressed the desire to become White, and tried to reject their identity as Asians" (p. 70).

Very few studies exist on Asians and racial identity development (Chen, Le Phuoc, Guzman, Rude, & Dodd, 2006). Research was conducted on 344 self-identified Asian American adults recruited through Asian American electronic mailing lists, professional organizations, and snowballing. The study authors investigated racial identity profiles, racial attitudes, and racism-related stress among Asian Americans using the PCRIAS, the CoBRAS (a measure of Color-Blind Racial Attitudes), and the ASRRSI (or the Asian American Racism-Related Stress Inventory). Within the context of other groups of color, the social construction of race is such that Asians occupy an intermediary position in the racial hierarchy, with Whites on the highest rung and Blacks on the lowest (Chen et. al., 2006).

Kim (2001) identified grounding principles of an Asian American identity development model:

1. The predominance of White racism and its impact on Asian American identity development must be acknowledged.
2. Internalized racism has to be unlearned unconsciously.
3. A healthy identity requires the transformation of a negative racial identity into a positive and healthy one.

The proposed stage model is sequential but not linear. This model is influenced by other racial identity development theories, yet takes into consideration the unique experiences of Asian Americans.

Stage One: Ethnic Awareness This first stage represents the period prior to children's entry into the school system. The social environment and reference group consists largely of family. The extent of participation in Asian-oriented activities can bolster a sense of positive ethnic awareness.

Stage Two: White Identification This stage is marked by children's painful awareness that they are different from White people and that this difference is not regarded as a good thing. Feeling a sense of shame for being Asian can result in desperate attempts by Asian children to fit into White society. To compensate for feelings of inferiority, many Asian children will seek leadership in organizations and excel academically. Active White identification refers to the Asian student not consciously perceiving herself as different from Whites, thus there is a desire to alienate herself from and not be regarded as Asian. Passive White identification Asians enter this stage during their later years and are buffered by early exposure to predominantly Asian communities that nurtured self-esteem. The distancing from Asians and seeking to pass for White is not evident here, but fantasizing, (e.g., "I wish") about being White does occur.

Stage Three: Awakening to Social Political Consciousness A shift from personal to social responsibility for racism allows Asian Americans to understand racism and transform their negative sense of self into a positive one. At this stage, White people are no longer the reference group and Asians do not regard themselves as inferior. The person essentially asks the question, "Why should I be ashamed of who I am?" There is a connection to other people of color.

Stage Four: Redirection to an Asian American Consciousness In this stage, the sense of self as a minority is crystallized into a sense of being Asian. There is often an immersion into the Asian experience, and the ego is centered on Asian things and people. Racial pride is experienced as is a positive self-concept. In addition to pride, people feel angry at the way in which the dominant White culture perpetuates racism and cultural violence.

Stage Five: Incorporation A person's racial identity is blended into other social identities. The self is seen as whole, with race representing only one aspect of social identity. The immersion of the previous stage is relaxed. A clear Asian American identity has been achieved, yet people in general are the person's reference group.

African American Racial Identity

Cross's (1991) theory of racial identity development, called the **Negro-to-Black conversion experience**, or **Nigresence**, is the most widely used racial theory about African Americans. It presumes a sociopolitical perspective and refers to the process of developing healthy racial collective identities as a function of discrepancies in sociopolitical power across racial groups. In Cross's work, a distinction is made between *personal identity* (*PI*) and *reference group orientation* (*RGO*). The former refers to self-esteem and interpersonal competence; the latter refers to racial identity and racial self-esteem. Cross's work on Black racial identity has been extremely influential in the development of models related to other aspects of identity, including racial and cultural identity models for other groups of color and the womanist identity model (see Ossana, Helms, & Leonard, 1992).

Within Cross's (1991) theory, identity development is a maturation process whereby external negative images of the self are replaced with positive internal conceptions. Cross's five-stage Nigresence model—preencounter, encounter, immersion and emersion, internalization, and internalization and commitment—refers to "a resocializing experience" that "seeks to transform a preexisting identity (a non-Africentric identity) into one that is Africentric" (p. 190). Robinson and Howard-Hamilton (1994) discussed **Africentricity** as a conscious ideology with a strong connection to spirituality and kinship via African culture, culminating in the shared belief, "I am because we are and since we are, therefore I am." An optimal Africentric worldview can be measured by an instrument called the Belief Systems Analysis

Scale (BSAS), developed by Fine and James-Myers (1990). Africentrism involves an awareness of Black identity, knowledge of cultural customs and traditions, liberating psychological resistance strategies, and an understanding of oppression and strategies to resist it (Dana, 1993; Robinson & Howard-Hamilton, 1994).

Cross developed the Cross Racial Identity Scale (Vandiver, 2001) to measure the revised dimensions of his 1997 Nigrescence model. Vandiver reviewed the Cross Racial Identity Scale (CRIS), a 40-item, 7-point Likert-type inventory, to measure Cross's revised theory of Nigrescence. Reference group orientation and race salience are also assessed. There are six scales: Preencounter Assimilated (PA), Preencounter Miseducation (PM), Preencounter Self-Hatred (PSH), Immersion/Emersion Anti-White (IEAW), Internalization Afrocentriocity Black Nationalist (IA), and Internalization Multiculturalist Inclusive (IMCI). The psychometric properties of the CRIS report acceptable Cronbach alphas: PA = 0.85, PM = 0.89, PSH = 0.85, IEAW = 0.85, IBN = 0.79, IMCI = 0.76.

At *preencounter*, the acculturated African American views the world through the lens of the White dominant culture. Essentially, race has low salience. When people are asked to describe themselves, identifiers other than race, such as work, church, profession, and club affiliation, surface as key descriptors. Cross (1991) maintained that many preencounter African Americans are psychologically healthy and that anti-Black attitudes among African Americans in this stage are rare, although they do exist. Despite indices of psychological health among African Americans at this initial stage of racial identity, Cross stated, "Preencounter Blacks cannot help but experience varying degrees of miseducation about the significance of the Black experience" (p. 192). African Americans in this first stage are more likely to operate from a Eurocentric cultural perspective in evaluating beauty and art forms.

According to Jones, Cross, and DeFour (2007), the assimilation subscales measure pro-American and assimilationist attitudes (e.g., "I think of myself as an American, and seldom as a member of a racial group"). The miseducation subscale taps into the extent to which the respondent adheres to negative stereotypes about Black people as a group (e.g., "Blacks place too much importance on racial protest and not enough on hard work and education"). The racial self-hatred subscale assesses racial self-hatred attitudes (e.g. "When I look into the mirror at my Black image, sometimes I do not feel good about what I see").

At the *encounter* stage, a person's new view of the world, as a result of a shocking personal experience, is inconsistent with the old. According to Cross (1991), the two aspects of this stage are experiencing an encounter and personalizing it. In every year of a person's life, myriad encounter experiences could encourage movement from preencounter to encounter. If the experiences are not internalized and personalized, however, movement up to this next stage cannot occur. Other identity constructs, such as religion, class, and education, can delay racial identity formation, particularly when similarity with the referent group (e.g., being Christian, middle class, academically gifted) is encouraged and differences (e.g., race) that may be perceived as threatening or divisive are ignored (Robinson, 1999a).

In the *immersion and emersion* stage, the focus is on being Black to the exclusion of others, particularly Whites. Cross (1991) indicated that this is a transitional stage with respect to identity transformation: "The person's main focus in life becomes a feeling of 'togetherness and oneness with people'" (p. 207). The anti-White subscale assesses dislike for White people and culture (e.g., "I have a strong hatred and disdain for all White people").

The fourth stage of Cross's model, *internalization*, is characterized by more peace and calm. At this juncture, dissonance regarding an emerging identity has been resolved, evidenced by high salience attached to Blackness.

Internalization and commitment persons seek to eradicate racism for all oppressed people. According to Cross, this stage is similar to the internalization stage but is reflective of sustained long-term interest and commitment, as opposed to a brief period in that person's life. Here, the African American is more able to reconceptualize the self across multiple identities. At initial stages, the African American has little awareness of racial oppression, because race has minimal importance. The Afrocentric and Multicultural subscales assess this internalization stage. The Afrocentric subscales measure Black Nationalist attitudes characterized by empowerment (e.g., "I see and think about things from an Afrocentric perspective"). The Multicultural subscale measures Blacks' acceptance and connection with others from diverse cultural contexts (e.g., "As a multiculturalist, I am connected to many groups").

Jones, Cross, and DaFour (2007) administered the CRIS, the Rosenberg Self-Esteem Scale (RSE), the Schedule of Racist Events (SRE), and the Center for Epidemiologic Studies Depression Scale (CES-D) to 118 African American and 144 self-identified Caribbean women. They discovered that racist stress events and racist stress appraisal play a role in negative mental health, particularly depression. In their sample, multicultural identity attitudes lessened the negative mental health impact of racist stress events and racist stress appraisals, particularly as they related to depression. There was an increase in depression scores as racist stress appraisals increased, but "not to the same degree as those with multicultural identity attitude scores 1 standard deviation below the mean" (p. 222).

Latino Identity Development

That Latinos can be and are of any race is often confusing and difficult for counseling students to grasp. When students are told that Latinos are not a racial group but an ethnic group with different ethnic and racial subgroups, the confusion magnifies. When I make the point to students that sharing race does not mean sharing ethnicity and sharing ethnicity does not mean sharing race, I often draw a Venn diagram or say something like: "A White-skinned woman with blond hair and blue eyes might identify herself ethnically as Cubana, but racially she considers herself to be White. Is she Latina?" Yes. At the same time, a sister Cubana may have African roots, dark skin, and very curly hair. Ethnically, she is also Cubana but considers herself racially Black. Cubans hail from Africa, Europe (Spain), or Asia (Chinese) and/or are indigenous. The difficulty with understanding Latinos both racially and ethnically is related to the dichotomization of racial categories. A bifurcation of people—"you are either this or that"—has had implications for a racial/ethnic identity development model for Latinos. The dialectic embraces a "both/and" way of being in the world and is needed to appreciate multiple identities within and across groups of people. In addition, the existing models of racial identity cannot be applied to Latinos. Latinos are not a racial group.

According to Ferdman and Gallegos (2001), there are key dimensions involved in defining a nonlinear Latino identity: how a person prefers to identify herself, how Latinos as a group are seen, how Whites are seen, and how race fits into the equation.

Latino Integrated Persons who are Latino integrated are able to embrace the fullness of their Latino identity and integrate this into other identities, such as class, profession, and gender. A dialectic, as mentioned earlier, is characteristic of the Latino integrated. This person is comfortable with all types of Latinos as there is a broad lens used to see themselves, White people, and others.

Latino Identified This group has more of a pan-Latino identity, with a view of race, *la raza*, as uniquely Latin. There is a deep and abiding understanding of a history of political struggle and a desire to be united with other Latinos in racial unity. Despite the awareness of and vigilant stand against institutional racism, Latino-identified persons may see Whites, Blacks, and other groups in rigid ways.

Subgroup Identified Persons of this group see themselves as distinct from White people but do not necessarily identify with other Latinos or with people of color. The broad pan-Latino orientation discussed in the previous orientations is not reflected here. Other Latino subgroups may be viewed in an inferior way. People's allegiance to a particular subgroup is nearly exclusive. Race is not a central or clear organizing concept, but nationality, ethnicity, and culture are primary.

Latino as "Other" Persons with this orientation see themselves as people of color. This may be a function of biracial or multiracial status, ambiguous phenotype, or dominant constructions of race. In certain contexts, persons see themselves as minorities and not White. There is no identification with Latino cultural norms or with White culture, and an understanding of Latino history and culture is missing.

Undifferentiated Persons with this orientation regard themselves as simply "people" with a color-blind eye. The emphasis on racial classification is not a part of their framework. The desire to associate with other Latinos is not prominent because contact with others is distinct from a person's race or ethnic identity. Life is lived apart from attention to and thoughts of difference.

White Identified White-identified persons perceive themselves as White and thus superior to people of color (*non-White-skinned people*—emphasis mine). Assimilation into White culture is a possibility, as is connection primarily to only one other group (e.g., light-skinned Cubans) while denying connection to other subgroups. There is an acceptance of the status quo and a valuing of Whiteness to the extent that marrying White is preferred over marrying dark. Latinos with this orientation are *mejorar la raza* (i.e., improve the race).

The strength of this model is that it helps counselors and clients ascertain identity development for Latinos who differ greatly across acculturation level, skin color, national origin, and political ideology. This is also not a linear model; nonetheless, it is clear that there are orientations more conducive to unity with others across race and skin color wherein people are valued because they are human and not because of what they look like.

Umaña-Taylor (2004) studied ethnic identity and self-esteem among 1,062 Mexican-origin adolescents who attended one of three schools: predominantly Latino, predominantly non-Latino, and balanced Latino/non-Latino. Phinney's Multigroup Ethic Identity Measure was used to assess ethnic identity. Rosenberg's Self-Esteem Scale measured self-esteem. A significant relationship emerged between ethnic identity and self-esteem for adolescents attending the predominately non-Latino school, the balanced school, and the predominantly Latino school. This finding suggests that the relationship between self-esteem and ethnic identity may not be context specific. Maternal education was higher among students at the predominantly non-Latino school. Students attending the predominantly non-Latino school were more likely to have been born in the United States than students at the balanced school. Finally, students at the predominantly non-Latino school reported higher levels of ethnic identity than teens at the predominantly Latino and balanced schools. These data suggest that "ethnic identity appears to be more salient for Mexican-origin adolescents when they are in a minority context than in a majority context" (p. 144). However, the relationship between self-esteem and ethnic identity did not differ across schools. Predominantly Latino school students are a minority in the larger society, irrespective of their majority presence at school, which may account for this finding.

White Racial Identity Development

Traditional conceptions of race refer to people of color, but European Americans are also racial beings and experience racial identity development. As racial beings, White people are shaped by the construct of race in their and other people's lives, affected by both skin color privilege and the adverse consequences of racism (Robinson, 1999a).

It is an infrequent experience or encounter that would encourage a White person to assess her attitudes about being a racial being (Pope-Davis & Ottavi, 1994). In a society where unearned skin color advantages are conferred, European American counselors need to develop a positive racial identity that does not emanate from oppression and domination. This transformation may be difficult for two reasons:

1. It is possible for White people to live in US society without having to acknowledge or give much consideration to the meaning of being White.
2. Denial about one's own race impedes self-awareness, a crucial factor in racial identity development.

Helms (1995; Helms & Parham, 1984) has been the predominant voice in the development of White racial identity theory. Hardiman (1982, 2001) developed the White identity development (WID) model, which was the first model on White racial identity development. Helms's (1984, 1995) White racial identity development model (WRID) has six statuses. The term *status* is preferred over *stage* in that the latter is more reflective of a fixed state. Helms believed that people could be characterized by more than one status at a given time. These statuses are contact, disintegration, reintegration, pseudoindependence, immersion-emersion, and autonomy. Helms's revised model includes information-processing strategies for each of the six statuses.

A person enters the *contact* status from encountering the idea or actuality of Black people. Family background and environment affect whether the attitude toward Black people is one of trepidation or naive curiosity. In contact, the European American automatically benefits from institutional and cultural racism without the conscious awareness of doing so. The identity ego status and information-processing strategy for contact is obliviousness. White people are satisfied with the status quo and are fairly oblivious to the role of racism and their involvement in it.

White people in the contact status tend to have positive self-esteem. They are idealistic about the equal treatment of African Americans; however, in actually interacting with Blacks, they may experience some anxiety or arousal. Through interaction with African Americans, the European American realizes that clear distinctions exist in the treatment of people across race, independent of economic conditions.

Continuing to have socialization experiences will move the person into Helms's second status, *disintegration.* Entry into disintegration is characterized by conscious conflict that has its origins in dissonance. Here, the White person realizes that people are treated differently as a function of race. The identity ego status and information-processing strategy for disintegration are suppression and ambivalence. White people in this status are truly confused by anxiety-provoking racial moral dilemmas that require them to choose between own-group loyalty and humane behavior.

The third status is *reintegration*, which is entered as the White person realizes that, within the dominant culture, the covert and overt belief of White superiority and Black inferiority exists. The desire to be accepted by the White racial group is very strong. It is important in reintegration that a racial identity be acknowledged. Here, White privilege is protected even though it is unearned. People of color are not entitled to privilege because they are morally, socially, and intellectually inferior. Because honest dialogue about race between racially different people does not often take place, it is fairly easy for a person to fixate here. A jarring event can trigger movement into the fourth status, *pseudoindependence*. The identity ego status and information-processing strategy for reintegration are selective perception and negative out-group distortion. White people are idealized, while others are not tolerated well at all.

According to Helms (1990), "Pseudoindependence is the first stage of redefining a positive White identity" (p. 61). This status is primarily one of intellectualization, wherein the person acknowledges responsibility for White racism. The negativity of the earlier stages does not exist; nonetheless, White norms continue to be used to interpret cultural or racial differences. Socially, the person is met with suspicion by both Whites and Blacks. Discomfort with their ambiguous racial identity may move the person into the fifth status. The identity ego status and information-processing strategy for psuedoindependence are reshaping reality and selective perception. The commitment to racism is largely intellectual. The goal is to reach out and assist other racial groups.

This fifth status, *immersion-emersion*, is characterized by the replacement of old myths and stereotypes with accurate information. It is a period of unlearning. Here, the person may participate heavily in White-consciousness groups in which the goal is to help the person abandon a racist identity. The focus is not on changing Black people but rather on seeking to change White people. The successful resolution of this status requires that the individual recycle or re-experience earlier emotions that were distorted or repressed. The identity ego status and information-processing strategies for immersion-emersion are hypervigilance and reshaping. There is a diligent search for the personal meaning of racism and the ways in which people can benefit from racism.

Autonomy, the sixth and last status of Helms's model, is an ongoing process. In this status, a primary goal is internalizing and experiencing new ways of being racial that were learned from previous stages. Race, your own and other people's, is not a threat. The identity ego status and information-processing strategy for autonomy are flexibility and complexity. Internal standards are used for defining the self, and there is a capacity to relinquish the privileges of racism. Helms (1990) stated that the second phase, development of a nonracist White identity, begins with the pseudoindependent status and ends with the autonomy status.

Watt, Robinson, and Lupton-Smith (2002) conducted a study of ego identity and Black and White racial identity among 38 graduate students (30 White, 6 Black, and 2 Middle Eastern) at the beginning, middle, and end of their counseling training in a program that included student counseling, community agency, and school counseling tracks. The researchers used the Washington Sentence Completion Test to measure ego identity and used Black and White versions of the Racial Identity Attitude Scale. It was hypothesized that the ego developments of students enrolled in Prepracticum (a second-year class) would be higher than the ego development of students enrolled in Theories and Cross-Cultural (both first-year classes). It was found that students in Theories had lower ego development than students in Cross-Cultural and Prepracticum; however, there were no differences in ego development between students in Cross-Cultural and students in Prepracticum. It was also found that students enrolled in Theories had a lower mean score at the pseudoindependence status than did the Prepracticum students. In addition, the racial identity status of students enrolled in Cross-Cultural was higher than the racial identity status of students enrolled in Theories. These data are important in understanding ego and racial identity development for students at different developmental stages in their programs. The study needs to be replicated with a much larger and racially and culturally diverse sample.

Leach, Behrens, and LaFleur (2002) make a distinction between white racial identity and white racial consciousness. They define White racial consciousness as the ways that White people think about people who are not White or the racial out-group. The model "attempts to identify commonly held constellations of attitudes and attempts to determine, which, if any best characterize the racial attitudes held by White individuals" (p. 69).

Seven types of attitudes have been grouped into two categories: achieved, which is the result of personal consideration and commitment to some set of attitudes about racial material (four types), and unachieved, or lack of exploration or commitment or both with respect to racial attitudes (three types). Unachieved attitudes include

1. Dependent, or attitudes determined by a significant other
2. Dissonant, or uncertainty about attitudes
3. Avoidant, which is attitudes that ignore and/or minimize racial issue

Achieved attitudes include

1. Conflictive, which describes fairness but where rugged individualism is strong
2. Dominative, which describes ethnocentric or pro-White attitudes
3. Integrative, which reflects positive and pragmatic attitudes
4. Reactive, which are strong pro-groups of color attitudes

Yep, Settles, and Pratt-Hyat (2011) used a community sample (rare in counseling research) of 161 African American adults. Their constructs included racial identity (public regard, private regard, and centrality), racial membership, and life satisfaction. Two identity functions, belongingness and discrimination mediated life satisfaction. The researchers found that when African Americans have high race salience, In that they define themselves more in terms of race, view their own racial group positively, and believe other groups view their racial group more positively, they report greater satisfaction with their lives. Among women but not men, belongingness was related to greater life satisfaction.

Optimal Theory Applied to Identity Development

Myers et al. (1991) developed a theory of optimal identity that is neither linear nor categorical. In criticizing some psychosocial identity models, they observed that the models have limited the role of the individual in the identity process, did not consider people with multiple identities, and were based on a Eurocentric worldview. Myers et al. maintained that the dichotomy of the spirit world and matter within American society make it difficult to attain a positive self-identity in the United States, regardless of race, because self-worth is based primarily on external validation. Persons who turn outside themselves for meaning, peace, and value have adopted a suboptimal worldview. According to Myers et al., within an optimal perspective, self-worth is intrinsic in being. Thus, the purpose of life is becoming clearer about how the self is connected with all of life. Spiritual development is an integral part of identity development.

In Phase 0, known as *absence of conscious awareness*, the person lacks awareness of being. This is regarded as an infancy stage. Phase 1 is *individuation*. Here, the world is the way it is in that people simply lack awareness of any view of self other than the one to which they were initially introduced. They rarely assign meaning or value to the various aspects of their identity. Phase 2 is *dissonance*: persons begin the exploration of their true self and effectively explore dimensions of the self that may be demeaned by others. In Phase 3, *immersion*, persons' energy is focused on those who are regarded as similar. Phase 4, *internalization*, occurs as people feel good about who they are and have successfully incorporated feelings of self-worth. Phase 5, *integration*, happens as people's deeper understanding of themselves allows them to change their assumptions about the world. The self is more secure internally, and peaceful relationships are a manifestation of this. The final stage, Phase 6, is *transformation*. The self is redefined toward a sense of personhood that includes ancestors, the unborn, nature, and community. The universe is understood as benevolent, orderly, and personal.

IMPLICATIONS FOR COUNSELORS AND PSYCHOLOGISTS

In a survey conducted by the Kaiser Family Foundation (US Department of Health and Human Services, 2001), it was found that 12% of African Americans and 15% of Latinos, compared with 1% of Whites, felt that a doctor or health care provider would judge them unfairly or treat them with disrespect because of their race or ethnic background. There is a climate of mistrust around race. Poor Black families are often stigmatized as disorganized, lazy, and deprived (Boyd-Franklin, 2003).

Part of multicultural competence is knowledge of these sociopolitical dynamics and resources for counteracting them. Day-Vines et al. (2007) introduced the concept of **broaching**, which refers to the initiation on the part of the clinician to bring issues of race and diversity, often regarded as fugitive topics, into the therapy room. The purpose of doing this is to encourage the client's exploration of these difficult topics. Due to fear of being perceived as ignorant, insensitive, or racist, counselors will avoid asking particular questions. This fear can paralyze the therapeutic event and interfere with the client's growth. Leadership requires therapists to introduce conversation about difficult and sensitive topics. A source of resistance may be an internal reluctance to talk about race, even after taking the required graduate-level cross-cultural diversity course.

The therapeutic relationship is influenced by a client's racial identity development in that it can directly affect the client's preference for a counselor. Clients of color in preencounter (Black), White identified (Latino), or White identification (Asian) are more likely to prefer a White counselor over a counselor of color. The belief exists that "Whites are more competent and capable than members of one's own race" (Sue & Sue, 1990, p. 108). In this scenario, if the counselor is White, the client will typically be overeager to identify with the counselor. If the counselor is non-White, then the counselor will experience feelings of hostility from the client even if the client and the counselor are of the same race. Independent of the counselor's race, the counselor has a responsibility to help reeducate the client as they work together through the client's conflicts. Regardless of race, counselors who choose not to face their biases are not appropriate candidates for the mental health profession.

During the encounter and dissonance stages, clients are preoccupied with questions concerning the self and identity. They may still prefer a White counselor; however, counselors can take advantage of clients' focus on self-exploration toward resolution of identity conflicts. During the immersion/emersion and resistance and immersion stages of racial/ethnic identity, clients of color tend to view their psychological problems as an outgrowth of oppression and racism. In this stage, clients of color are prone to prefer counselors of their own race. In fact, people of color may tend to perceive White counselors as enemies. Thus, it is important for White counselors to not personalize attacks from clients of color. Statements regarding the unjust sociopolitical nature within the United States have legitimacy. It is also wise for counselors to anticipate that resistance/immersion clients will test their clinicians, as this stage is one of great volatility. Finally, counselors are apt to be more effective with a client when they use action-oriented methods aimed at external change.

Clients of color at more integrated phases of racial identity often experience an inner sense of security. They are able to choose therapists, not necessarily on the basis of race but on the basis of the professional's ability to be empathic and understanding of the issues clients bring to counseling. Sue and Sue (1990) stated that "attitudinal similarity between counselor and client is a more important dimension than membership-group similarity" (p. 112). Nonetheless, clients at higher stages of racial identity may accept a counselor of a different race while preferring one of their own racial, ethnic, or gender group. This preference need not be an indication of discriminatory attitudes but may instead reflect a desire or need for a cultural connection that may or may not occur.

All mental health professionals need to acknowledge their biases and assess their personal readiness prior to engaging in counseling across sources of diversity. (See Storytelling: *Requests for Same-Race Therapist.*) Not to do so is to place the client in jeopardy. If need be, licensed professionals may want to contact a supervisor at parallel or more integrated levels of racial identity to facilitate their racial identity progression (Ladany, Brittan-Powell, & Pannu, 1997).

Richardson and Molinaro (1996) found that the reintegration therapist may be impatient toward clients of different races and less likely to establish rapport with these clients. Cook (1994) suggested that White counselors may also engage in ethnocentric behavior if they operate at Helms's reintegration stage and recognize their own race as standard for "normal" behavior of the client. Not until the immersion/emersion stage do White clinicians acknowledge clients' race, respect cultural influences, and examine the sociopolitical implications. At the pseudoindependence stage, the White counselor will discuss racial issues but only when interacting with persons of color (Cook, 1994). Ethnocentric assumptions still frame people's thinking.

Storytelling: Request for Same-Race Therapists

I recently received requests from two Black female colleagues, one a graduate student and the other a working adult, looking for Black clinicians to work with them. These women specifically asked for professionals of color. Fortunately, there were licensed professionals available to whom I could refer these women. It does not surprise me that some Black clients prefer other Black professionals, particularly when issues of racism or microaggression are at the core of the presenting issue. Preference for a counselor on the basis of race can and does occur. An agency or practice or group may not have an appropriate match but may have gender compatibility. The literature is inconclusive regarding the link between racial identification and counselor preference (Pope-Davis, Liu, Toporek, & Brittan-Powell, 2001). Being a therapist of color or a woman or both does not ensure that one is able to work effectively with women clients of color. Wilkinson (1997) pointed out that Black educators and mental health professionals internalize racism and the negative scripts around race just as White people do. This in turn can have two impacts. First, it can contribute to Black professionals' ignorance about class discrimination and its influence on people's lives (p. 271). Secondly, internalized racism among Black people may contribute to Black people's inability to relate to other Blacks who are of a lower income bracket or who were born on the African continent. Despite this reality, a same-race counselor has often had "similar emotional and physical experiences with racism, and more of a willingness to confront this external barrier" (Washington, 1987, p. 198). It is important for multiculturally competent White therapists to broach the topic of race and explain to their clients that discussions of race and racism are welcomed—that the focus of therapy is on the clients' healing, not on protecting the therapist from topics of White racism. Part of the everyday experience of Black people is comporting themselves so as not to offend or censuring themselves in order to get along. Therapy should not reproduce these experiences. Multicultural competence is an awareness of sociopolitical issues such as structural inequalities that affect people's attempts to be agentic and have control over their economic lives. Knowledge and assessment of proximity to race and ethnic discourses, skills about broaching difficult topics, referral, and advocacy, and an understanding of racial identity development and multicultural terminology are all skills of multiculturally competent counselors (Holcomb-McCoy, 2000).

Ultimately, our beliefs and attitudes will inform the quality of our listening and our talking. Delpit (1997) eloquently said, "We do not really see through our eyes ... but through our beliefs. To put our beliefs on hold is to cease to exist as ourselves for a moment—and that is not easy ... but it is the only way to learn what it might feel like to be someone else and the only way to start the dialogue" (p. 101).

CASE STUDY

TEACHING PRIVILEGE TO THE PRIVILEGED

There are a host of emotions that accompany undergraduate and graduate students' awareness of unearned privilege. Guilt, anger, minimization, rationalization, humor, sadness, and confusion are common emotions. The following themes are intended to assist instructors with teaching privilege to the privileged. This discussion is relevant for skin-color privilege as well as gender, ability, class, religious, and sexuality privileges.

QUESTIONS AND DISCUSSION

1. Realize that unearned privilege and entitlement go hand in hand. Entitlement is the belief that one has the right to be acknowledged, protected, respected, and rewarded. When denied any of these, shock and anger emerge.
2. Respect the difficult feelings that accompany the unpacking of the invisible knapsack. Allow yourself and students to feel their feelings, knowing that such feelings are necessary for change and growth. Most students have been taught that society is fair and just, and White people tend to not confront the role of racism in their own lives (Tatum, 1992).
3. Although race, gender, class, and sexuality are identity constructs that have status, race in America is a grandmaster status and often eclipses and overwhelms other markers, such as class. Working-class Whites are often quick to invoke their modest class origins and may attempt to compare their class oppression with racism. Skin color is an immutable characteristic and is not fluid as class often (but not always) is. Universities are filled with White professors whose families of origin were low-wage earning and working class and yet, unless people identify this as part of their life history, how do we distinguish this group from those whose parents and grandparents were academics? Finally, working-class status among whites and working-class status among Blacks and other groups of color is different. Being low-income and Black represents two marginalized identities, not one.
4. Not having White skin-color privilege or other sources of privilege does not render a person powerless. Having White skin-color privilege does not necessarily result in people feeling powerful, competent, or peaceful.
5. "Counselors need to enhance themselves personally and professionally by reading and exposing themselves to various artistic art forms" (Lee, 2001). Reading newspaper articles and attending films and other culture-specific activities can inform a professional's sense of another person's culture.
6. Engage in an inventory of your life. Who are the people you invite into your home? What level of comfort do you feel with certain groups of color compared with others?

(Continued)

(Continued)

Culture-free service delivery does not exist; therefore, it is impossible to help clients examine cultural identity and self-esteem issues if counselors and psychologists have not done this important work for themselves (Pinderhughes, 1995, 1989).

7. Encourage narrative with students as well as their exposure to others. Psychosocial narrative questions that I ask students include:
   a. What does it mean to be the race(s) you are?
   b. What impact has spirituality had on your development as a counseling professional?
   c. What did your parents teach you about race and skin color?
   d. What are the privileges and oppression in your life?
   e. How do you feel about the presence and/or absence of privilege and oppression in your life?
   f. Tim Wise (2005) suggests this question for White students, "What does it mean to be White, especially in a nation created by people like you, for people like you?" (p. 2)
8. Healing racism is an evolving but important process. Ellis (2004) wrote that healing promotes self-discovery. Healing also enables a person to rest from frequent race-based encounters.
9. Multicultural competencies and guidelines encourage counselors and psychologists to understand how gender, race, class, sexuality, ethnicity, and nationality intersect in the lives of their clients (Salazar, 2006).

IMPLICATIONS FOR COUNSELORS AND PSYCHOLOGISTS

Therapists attempting to develop a process that will take into account the impact of culture could follow Hanna and Brown's (1995, p. 101) assessment questions of racial and cultural factors. Some of the questions are also used in my psychosocial narrative assignment:

1. How does your racial/cultural/religious heritage make your family different from other families you know?
2. Compared with other families in your cultural group, how is your family similar?
3. What did your parents teach you about gender, race, sexuality, and class?
4. What are the values that your family identified as being important parts of your heritage?
5. At this particular time in your (family's) development, are there issues related to your cultural heritage that are being questioned by anyone?
6. What is the hardest part about being a person of color in this culture? In your family?
7. When you think of living in America versus the country of your heritage, what are the main differences?
8. What lesson did you learn about your people? About other people?
9. What did you learn about disloyalty?
10. What are the privileges and/or oppressions in your family? How does your family feel about their presence and/or absence of privilege/oppression?
11. What were people in your family negative about?
12. Does your spirituality and religion differ from your family's?
13. What might an outsider not understand about your family's racial/cultural/religious background?

Summary

This chapter examined race as a social construction and a status variable. Other constructs were considered in relationship to race in an effort to provide an understanding of the saliency of race as an identity construct that intersects with other multiple identities. Also discussed in this chapter were racial and ethnic identity development models for people across race and ethnicity. Both qualitative and quantitative methodologies were highlighted. Race and ethnic discourses were identified as were strategies for instructors of diversity courses.

Converging Biracial and Multiracial Identities

I will not live a slave, and if force is employed

*to re-enslave me, I shall make preparations to meet
the crisis as becomes a man.*

J. W. LOGUEN, SON OF A SLAVE MOTHER AND HER WHITE OWNER,

IN RESPONSE TO THE FUGITIVE SLAVE ACT OF 1850

This chapter on converging biracial and multiracial identities explores race as a shifting construct in American society. In doing so, demographic data reflecting increases in biracial and multiracial populations are reviewed. A case study is provided, relevant research is discussed, and stories are presented that emphasize the narrative tradition.

Storytelling: Mum

One of the New Zealand mothers in my research with White mothers of non-White children witnessed racism that her Maori/White daughter was facing. Her daughter was about 21 at the time and looking for a flat. Her daughter was also pregnant and single. She had brown skin, curly hair, and dark eyes. She was beautiful. One day her daughter approached her mother and said, "Mum, you come with me so that I can get the flat." The mother accompanied her daughter to look for an apartment. Her daughter was offered the first apartment she and her mother looked at together. Prior to this, the daughter had searched day after day looking for an apartment but could not get one. The daughter knew that having her mother with her as she looked for an apartment would result in success. The mother, however, had no idea that her daughter was being discriminated against in this way. She wept bitterly as she told this story of injustice.

DEFINITIONS

Racial purity is myth; For the purpose of clarity, definitions are provided. The child described in Storytelling: "Mum" is *biracial*—she is of Maori (Polynesian) and New Zealand/Pakeha (British) heritage. Her mother is White and her father is Maori. As a group, biracial people are also referred to in the literature as "biracials." There is considerable *intraracial* diversity among people from the same racial group. The daughter and her mom are part of an *interracial* family. Their college student neighbors are *monoracial*. One of the men is White—from Australia. His roommate is from Fiji and considers himself one of the indigenous Melanesian people; he has dark skin. This student is *bicultural* in that he speaks **Fijian,** which is an Austronesian language. He also speaks English and some Hindustani, because of the large Punjabi population in Fiji. He celebrates his Fijian culture as well as the cultures of many immigrant groups, including Punjabi and Chinese. His girlfriend is Chinese and White. If he marries his girlfriend and they have children, their children will be multiracial, with African, Asian, and Caucasian ancestry.

People may choose an identity that may be inconsistent with others' perceptions. In addition, identities are fluid and can change over time. It is our hope that the world in which these children live will become increasingly *multicultural*.

DEMOGRAPHY

The U.S. Census Bureau documents the reality of increasing numbers of persons who are biracial and multiracial. For the second time since the 2000 census, in 2010, people were asked to report one or more of the following races: White, Black or African American, American Indian or Alaskan Native (AIAN), Asian, Native Hawaiian or other Pacific Islander (NHPI), and some other race (SOR).

According to Humes, Jones, & Ramirez (2011), the two or more races population was one of the fastest-growing groups between 2000 and 2010. This population increased approximately one-third between 2000 and 2010. There were 9.1 million, or 2.9% of the U.S. population, reporting more than one race. About 92% of the people reporting more than one race reported having two races. Eight percent reported three or more and less than 1% reported more than four races (Humes, Jones, & Ramirez, 2011). The combinations are listed in Table 10.1. The largest multiple race categories were among four groups: White and Black at 20.4%; White and some race (SOR) at 19.3%; White and Asian at 18%; White and Indian

TABLE 10.1 Two or More Races Population by Combination: 2010	
White and Black	1.83 million
White and some other race	1.74 million
White and Asian	1.62 million
White and Indian/Alaskan Native	1.43 million
Black and some other race	314, 571
Black and Indian/Alaskan Native	269,421
Asian and some other race	234,462
Asian and Hawaiian/Pacific Islander	165,690
White and Black and Indian	230,848
White and Black and Asian	61,511

or Alaskan Native at 15.9%. In 2000, children under the age of 18 represented nearly 42% of the two or more race population (Jones & Symens Smith, 2001). Nearly half of the American Indian and Alaskan Native population and more than half of the Native Hawaiian and other Pacific Islander population had the highest percentages reporting more than one race.

People who reported more than one race were considerably younger than the total U.S. population. The median age for two or more races was 23.4 compared with 35.4 for the total U.S. population. Among those reporting two or more races, 25.2% were under the age of 10 compared with 14.1% in the total population. White and Black races were particularly young, with 71% of the population under the age of 18 compared with 25% in the general population. More than 2 million Hispanics, or nearly one-third of two or more races in the population, reported more than one race; 43% were under 18. Among non-Hispanics, the comparable rate was 24% (Jones & Symens Smith, 2001). The median age for White and Black races was 9.7 years. The next youngest was White and Asian, with a median age of 18.1 years.

Only 5% of two or more races were 65 and older compared with 12.4% in the total population. There are differences between groups. Among the White and American Indian/Alaskan Native population, 7.5% were 65 and older. This group has the highest median age among the two or more races, at 32.9. Among two or more races, there were similar numbers of males per 100 females, while the U.S. population had more females than males (Jones, 2005).

About 27% of the total population 15 years of age and older had never been married. Among two or more races, 37.3% had never been married. The group with the lowest never-married rates was White and Native American/Alaskan Native, at 28.3%. Among two or more races, 45.6% were married, compared with 54.4% in the total population. Asian and Native Hawaiian/Pacific Islanders and Whites and SOR had higher than average rates of marriage among this group, 50.6% and 50.4%, respectively.

More than one-half (52.5%) of all households in the United States were maintained by a married couple, compared with slightly less than one-half (46.6%) of households with two or more races (Jones, 2005). Two or more races had slightly lower than average separated, widowed, and divorced rates than the total population, 17.1% compared with 18.5%. There was, however, a greater likelihood of female householder families among two or more races compared with the total population. The average is 11.8% compared with 16.3% among two or more races. White and Asian races have lower female householder rates, at 10%.

The highest is among Black and American Indian/Alaskan Native (29.8%), Black and SOR (26.5%), and White and Black (25.6%).

People who reported two or more races were more likely to be foreign-born at 24%, compared with 11% of the U.S. population that is foreign-born. Nearly 40% of people aged 5 and older who reported more than one race in the 2000 census spoke a language other than English at home, compared with less than 20% of the U.S. population. Three of the combinations involving Asian (Black and Asian, White and Asian, and Asian and Pacific Islander) had about 25% to 35% of individuals who spoke a language other than English at home.

Nearly 20% of people who reported two or more races had attained a bachelor's degree or higher compared with 24.4% of the total population. White and Asian races had the highest percent, 34.8% with a bachelor's degree or higher. Asian and SOR were the only group with 25% or more of people in the same group with less than a high school diploma and 29.5 with a bachelor's degree or higher. American Indian and SOR had the highest rates of less than a high school diploma at 43.8%, compared with 19.6% in the total population.

Compared with the U.S. population 16 and older, the two or more races population had a larger proportion employed in service occupations but a smaller proportion employed in management, professional, and related occupations. White and Asian and White and Black and American Indian/Alaskan Native individuals were the most likely to hold management, professional, and related occupations at 36.8% and 35.7%, respectively. The group with the highest proportion working in service occupations was Black and SOR at 27%.

A range of median annual earnings exists between the two or more races population and across gender. Although the average earnings for all working males were $37,057, they were $31,035 among men of two or more races, $37,055 among White and Asian men, and $24,665 among American Indian/Alaskan Native/SOR men. The average earnings for all working females were $27,194, about $10,000 less than for men. They were $25,399 among women of two or more races, $29,973 among White and Asian women, and $29,988 among American Indian/Alaskan Native/SOR women (Jones, 2005). White and Asian households had a median family income of $52,413, which was higher than the average for the total population. The next highest were Asian and Native Hawaiian/Pacific Islander at $51,664 and White and Native Hawaiian/Pacific Islander at $45,758.

The poverty rate for children under the age of 18 in the two or more races population was 19.9%, compared with 16.6% for all children. (See Table 10.2.) For people aged 65 and over, the poverty rate was 16.9% for the two or more races population, compared with 9.9% for the U.S. population (Jones, 2005). Among children, Black and American Indian/Alaskan Native and Black and SOR combinations had higher poverty rates than children in other race combinations. White and Asian was the only population in which a larger proportion of the elderly than children lived in poverty, 16.6% compared with 7.5% among White/Asian children.

In the United States, about two-thirds of occupied housing units were owner-occupied, compared with 46.6% of those occupied by individuals who reported more than one race. Four of the race combinations had home ownership rates of 50% or higher, which is greater than that of the total two or more races population: White and American Indian, 59.6%; Asian and Pacific Islander, 51.9%; White and Pacific Islander, 51.4%; and White and Asian, 50.5%. Black and SOR and White and Black householders were the most likely to be renters, at 69.3% and 65.1%, respectively.

Because race is a social construction, it is possible that the 2010 census might have yielded a different estimate of the size of the biracial and multiracial population had an alternative measure been selected than the one given, which was to report one or more of the following

TABLE 10.2 Characteristics of Two or More Races and Total Population

Characteristic	Two or More Races	Total Population
Median age	23.4 years	35.4 years
Native-born	76.5%	88.9%
Poverty rates of elderly	16.9%	9.9%
Poverty rates of children	19.9%	16.6%
Bachelor's degree	19.6%	24.4%
Never married	37.3%	27.1%
Marriage	45.6%	54.4%
Divorce	17.1%	18.5%
Median-income women	$25,399	$27,194
Median-income men	$31,035	$37,057
Owner-occupied homes	46.6%	66.2%

races: White, Black or African American, American Indian or Alaskan Native, Asian, or Native Hawaiian or other Pacific Islander (Harris & Sims, 2002). In other words, who in the household completed the census? Who identifies as multiracial on a daily basis? Whose ancestors come from more than one racial group?

In the 2010 Census, just over one-third of the U.S. population reported their race and ethnicity as something other than non-Hispanic White alone. The states with more than 40% minority populations were Arizona, California, the District of Columbia, Florida, Georgia, Hawaii, Maryland, Mississippi, Nevada, New Jersey, New Mexico, and Texas (Humes, Jones, & Ramirex, 2011). California led the nation with the largest minority population (22.3 million). Texas (13.7 million), New York (8.1 million), Florida (7.9 million), and Illinois (4.7 million) round out the top five states with the largest minority populations (Humes, Jones, & Ramirez, 2011). People with two or more races were most likely to reside in the West, at 40%, with 27% residing in the south, 18% in the Northeast, and 15% in the Midwest.

THE ONE-DROP RULE

The **one-drop rule** emerged in the South during slavery and is traditionally understood as disallowing a White identity to anyone who had one-sixteenth Black ancestry, regardless of physical appearance. People were considered Black or Negro not only if either of their parents was Black but also if their only Black ancestor was a great-grandparent. People who were not considered to be White were classified as Negroes and other races. During this time, race was not simply a social construction, but was steeped in biology. Spickard (1992), a scholar on biracial identity, argued, "The so-called races are not biological categories at all. Rather, they are primarily social divisions that rely only partly on physical markers as skin color to identify group membership" (p. 17).

A castelike naming system existed. Whites had the most social power, followed by mixed-race and often light-skinned Blacks: mulattos, quadroons, and octoroons. Darker-skin Blacks were on the bottom rung of this ladder (Brunsma & Rockquemore, 2001). Mulattos had one

Black parent and one White parent, usually a Black mother and a White father. Quadroons had one-quarter Black blood with one Black grandparent. Social privileges such as indoor housework instead of field work in the hot sun and educational opportunities were provided to offspring of White fathers, which served to create division in the Black community and gave rise to colorism. Octoroons had one-eighth Black blood or a Black great-grandparent. They were classified as non-White regardless of their phenotypical presentation. "Passing" was an option; that is, presenting as White, as long as the person did not maintain contact with family members who were counted as and/or identified as Black.

Sharfstein (2007) argues that the one-drop rule did not automatically make all mixed-race people Black. Communities co-existed with contradiction and allowed people to "cross-over" the color line—not because they were liberals or abolitionists, but because the individual doing the crossing may have held segregationist and anti-Black attitudes as well. Defining and demarcating race is shifting, as is the discourse on race. White college students, in contemporary times, claim a Black identity to get into college. Others do not claim a Black identity despite knowledge of Black people in the family. There are increasing numbers of White and multiracial people with biracial and multiracial children who represent the fastest growing groups of children.

Despite changes, in how people identify racially, the one-drop rule is still alive; however, it is not as pervasive as it used to be (Rockquemore, 2002). Increases in biracial and multiracial populations and different, hybrid identities of race in a post-civil rights age contribute to the lessening grip of this antiquated way of defining people's racial identities. Nonetheless, society has difficulty with multiracial individuals' alignment with more than one racial identity. Rigid and binary notions of race are being contested, and the cultural dimensions of race in the United States are shifting (Brunsma, 2006). Biracial and multiracial identities do not obfuscate the construct of race, but they do challenge the one-drop rule that denies a claim to a White identity if a person is also Black.

For some, a denial of multiple aspects of their racial and ethnic identities is likely to occur when a monoracial identity is claimed. Within the Black community, biracial and multiracial identities have existed since slavery. The one-drop rule, which is cloaked in a racist ideology that assumes racial purity, disallowed other than a Negro identity for people with both White European and Black African ancestry. Thus, mulattos were considered Black due to the concept of *hypodesent*, or the process wherein biracial people were assigned to the social group with less social status (e.g., the Black mother during slavery). Due to the violence of slavery, the Black/White offspring conceived during this time were predominantly between Black slave women and White slave-owning men, but such was not always the case.

Biracial and mixed-race identities have existed in the Black community for centuries. What has not always existed, and is still highly contested, is whether Black/White biracial identities occupy a space that is different but not altogether separate from blackness. Claiming a biracial identity is neither a rampant negation of African ancestry nor an unbridled introjection of whiteness, but this is not collectively known or believed. Today, many people of color resist multiracial identity claims among Black/White people.

The elevated social status associated with lighter skin, a characteristic among many monoracial and biracial people, has served to pit Black people in this country, and arguably throughout the world, against one another. Some people of color believe that a single racial definition reflects unity and power, while some political groups oppose a multiracial category. There are multiple concerns: that allocations for school and social-based programs will be adversely affected by a multiracial designation (Schwartz, 1998), that a biracial identity might lead to further divisions among Black people, resulting in a loss of political clout. Finally, there is concern that a biracial identity might be interpreted by the dominant society as biracial people's rejection of blackness.

THE FLUIDITY OF RACE

Confusion exists as to who is considered multiracial. How past generations racially identified, phenotype, social contexts, and self-identification have all been used to define multiracial people. Among Native Americans, blood quantum has been considered. The concept of race as fluid suggests it, like class, social experience, and custom, is not static, is shaped by social circumstances, and extends throughout the developmental life (Hall, 2001; Lou, LaLonde, & Wilson, 2011).

Shih and Sanchez (2005) maintain that several approaches exist for understanding multiracial people. One approach is the problem approach, which sees non-monoracial groups as marginal, susceptible to poor psychological outcomes such as low self-esteem and an inferiority complex, lability in mood, and hypersensitivity. The equivalent approach argues that after 1970, there were social movement shifts in the form of civil rights and racial politics. Racial pride was invoked and miscegenation was outlawed. Although racial identity models for monoracial groups were in development, their application to biracial people was deemed appropriate; in reality, this was shortsighted. They did not account for being able to identify with more than one racial group simultaneously.

The variant approach is the most recent approach and views "multiracial identity as a unique category, separate from any monoracial category (e.g., Asian, White, or Black)" (Shih & Sanchez, 2005, p. 571). It seems that such an approach is interdisciplinary in focus, drawing on sociology, psychology, anthropology, literature, and feminist studies, and encourages the perspective that multiracial people have multiple understandings of their racial identities (Brunsma & Rockquemore, 2001).

Race as a fluid construct is fundamentally different from passing. What does the fluidity of race mean, across contexts (home, school, and work), if biracial or multiracial persons were not denying any one identity or were not choosing to pass as something they were not but identified according to contexts? Harris and Sims (2002) examined data from Wave 1 of the National Longitudinal Study of Adolescent Health (Add Health), a school-based, longitudinal study of health behaviors for youth in grades 7 through 12 collected in 1994 and 1995. More than 83,000 in-school interviews were conducted with students from 80 high schools and 52 middle schools. In addition, in-home interviews were conducted with more than 18,000 youth from the school sample. Finally, in-home interviews were conducted with a primary caregiver of each of the youth interviewed at home. All children who identified as Hispanic were excluded, as Hispanicity is deemed separate from race. The sample was also restricted to youth sampled both at school and at home.

Great variation in patterns of expressed internal race for multiracial populations was found. Among White/Black, 0.6% identify as White and Black at home and at school. White and Asian students did not differ between the school and home interviews in terms of their identities. However, White/Native American youth were different. More than 2% identified as White and Native American at school, yet a smaller share (1.5%) claimed a White/Native American identity at home. The researchers concluded that with "respect to racial self-identification, there is not a single multiracial experience" (Harris & Sims, 2002, p. 618). That racial identities are fluid was concluded: only 87.6% of adolescents expressed identical racial identities across contexts. Furthermore, 8.6% of youth reported being multiracial at home and 1.6% identified as multiracial in both contexts, across home and school. Geographical context is important to consider. In the south, White/Black youth were less likely to select White as their best single race. Other people's interpretation of biracial people's appearance places parameters on their own racial self-understandings (Brunsma & Rockquemore, 2001).

BIRACIAL AND MULTIRACIAL IDENTITY DEVELOPMENT

Brunsma and Rockquemore (2001) conducted research with 177 White and Black biracials (people with one Black parent and one White parent) to assess racial identification. Four identities were identified in previous research by Rockquemore (1999):

1. Singular identity
2. Border identity
3. Protean identity
4. Transcendent identity

Respondents were asked: which of the following statements best describes yourself exclusively?

1. I consider myself Black (or African American).
2. I sometimes consider myself Black, sometimes my other race, and sometimes biracial depending on the circumstances.
3. I consider myself biracial, but I experience the world as a Black person.
4. I consider myself exclusively as Biracial (neither Black nor White).
5. I consider myself exclusively as my other race (not Black or biracial).
6. Race is meaningless; I do not believe in racial identity.
7. Other

Phenotype (skin color), appearance, and interactional experiences (preadult racial composition and negative treatment from Whites and Blacks) were queried.

The majority of respondents (56.2%), despite a variety of skin color hues, defined themselves as "ambiguous though most people assume I am Black," (Brunsma & Rockquemore, 2001, p. 38). Seventeen percent stated they "appear Black, most people assume I am Black" and nearly 17% stated, "ambiguous, most people do not assume I am Black." Ten percent said they "appear White, I could pass as White." The majority of the sample considered themselves to have border identities, in that they understood themselves as neither Black and White but as exclusively biracial. Although this is the case, most of the border biracials said they experience the world as a Black person. Their experience as exclusively biracial is not validated by others in interactions. Only 14% of the sample saw themselves as exclusively Black. The same percentage did not apply racial labels to themselves and is considered to be a transcendent identity or with no racial self-understanding. Five percent saw themselves shifting among Black, White, and biracial identities, depending on the circumstances. This is referred to as a protean identity. Nearly 4% saw themselves as singularly White.

Wijeyesinghe (2001) presented a factor model of multiracial identity (FMMI) developed from a qualitative study of African American/European American multiracial adults. This model is nonlinear and represents factors or dimensions of identity. These dimensions include:

- Racial ancestry or family tree
- Early experiences and socialization, which includes exposure to culture, such as food, music, holiday, dialect, and language
- Cultural attachment that may influence racial designation
- Physical appearance, which includes skin hue, body shape, and hair texture
- Social and historical context, such as the presence of other multiracial people or the 2000 and 2010 census allowing people to choose more than one box to designate themselves racially/ethnically

- Political awareness and orientation, which is connected to the awareness of race and racism within a larger sociopolitical context
- Other social identities, such as sexual orientation and social class
- Spirituality or being guided by spirit, which fosters connection to others and allows people to transcend the divisions of race and ethnicity

Kich (1992) developed a three-stage biracial model for Japanese and White Americans from semistructured interviews with 15 biracial adults. The first stage is awareness of differentness and dissonance between self-perceptions and the perceptions from other people. Biracial people are seen as different. Dissonance or discomfort about this difference can occur when the comparison process is regarded as devaluation. The second stage, struggle for acceptance from others, can extend into adulthood and often occurs in the context of school or community settings. In cases where a biracial person is the only one in a particular context, the question "What are you?" may be asked, especially in light of differences in the person's name or phenotype.

The final stage is self acceptance and assertion of an interracial identity. Kich (1992) says, "The biracial person's ability to create congruent self-definitions rather than be determined by others' definitions and stereotypes may be said to be the major achievement of a biracial and bicultural identity" (p. 314).

Kich (1992) also discussed the ways in which biracial Japanese Americans achieved a sense of identity development. Some traveled to Japan and learned the language. Others met and spoke with extended family members who may have been less emotionally available in the past. Others who had endorsed the European American community exclusively may have explored their Japanese heritage anew or for the first time.

It is not uncommon for biracial persons to struggle with reconciling their various identities. According to Mass (1992), Japanese people in Los Angeles had higher rates of out-marriages compared with other Asian groups. In a study conducted among interracial Japanese Americans, Mass sampled 53 college-age White Japanese respondents and 52 monoracial Japanese American college students. She measured ethnic identity, acculturation, self-concept, and the Japanese American ethnic experience and then administered a personality inventory. No differences in the psychological adjustment and self-esteem of the two groups were found. However, it was discovered that interracial Japanese Americans showed less identification with being Japanese than monoracial Japanese Americans. Japanese Americans who were raised in parts of the country (Hawaii and certain California communities) where there were larger numbers of Japanese Americans tended to have few or no problems with race.

Poston (1990) proposed a model of biracial identity development with five linear stages: (1) personal identity, (2) choice of group categorization, (3) enmeshment/denial, (4) appreciation, and (5) integration. Stage 1 is the initial step in identity process and is seen among young children who have not developed group self-esteem. Choice of group categorization (Stage 2) consists of persons choosing a racial group to identify with. Ethnic background, neighborhood, and social support are factors that can influence this choice. Stage 3 represents upheaval and confusion about choosing a group with which to identify. Feelings of being betwixt and between can characterize people who may not feel acceptance from either group. Learning to accept their multiple identities describes Stage 4, and Stage 5 is an integrated place where people are able to celebrate all of who they are.

Research and Biracial and Multiracial Populations

Although more research is being conducted, there is a dearth of empirical research on multiracial populations (Herman, 2004). Shih and Sanchez (2005) observed that much of the work done was on investigating the psychological impact of having a multiracial identity and the difficulty that multiracial people had in defining a racial identity. There have been difficulties with sample size, methodological issues such as randomization in sampling, and problems with self-report inventories (Herman, 2004). Qualitative research may be best suited for research on biracial and multiethnic populations given that it allows the researcher "to enter the subjective world of other people and groups through interviews and rich descriptions, which is not achieved through quantitative methods" (Jourdan, 2006, p. 330).

Ho, Sidanius, Levin, & Banaji (2011) examined whether the rule of hypodescent, whereby biracial individuals are assigned the status of their socially subordinate parent group, would govern perceptions of Asian–White and Black–White targets. Across five experiments using speeded tasks, a face morphing program, and a family tree, the researchers confirmed the rule of hypodescent which reflected the racial hierarchy in the United States. Lou, Lalonde, & Wilson (2011) conducted a study to explore biracial people (Asian/White and Black/White) within a multidimensional framework using Rocquemore (1999) types. The researchers found variation in identity selection within each of the Asian/White and Black/ White subsamples. The highest proportion of the Asian/White group (30%) held a protean identity, followed by the validated (28%) and unvalidated (20%) border identity options. A validated identity refers to consistency between external validation from others and one's personal sense of identity. An validated identity speaks to conflict between one's internal construction of their identity and that of the public. Among the Black/White research participants, the validated border identity was the most common (42%) and the unvalidated border identity was the next most common (at 34%). Compared to Asian/White participants, few Black/White participants (10.5%) selected the protean option.

Theoretical sampling is a critical concept in qualitative research and refers to the research participants' contribution to the study with less emphasis on numbers. Qualitative methodologies, such as semistructured interviews, are ideal for research with multiracial populations in that they allow for a broader and more in-depth exploration of mixed-race people's life experiences while allowing the researcher to develop hypotheses for future studies from a contextual and cultural perspective (Collins, 2000).

Biracial Identity Development

The majority of the research conducted on biracial populations has focused on children and teens. Until recently, this literature has been scarce. Concerns about identity diffusion, low self-esteem, academic difficulties, and heightened risk of problem behaviors among multiracial children have been feared, found, and/or predicted (Choi, Harachi, Gillmore, & Catalano, 2006; Kerwin, Ponterotto, Jackson, & Harris, 1993; Gibbs & Hines, 1992).

Although the focus was on adults, Miville, Constantine, Baysden, and So-Lloyd (2005) conducted a qualitative investigation with ten self-identified biracial and multiracial individuals. People were asked to describe their experiences with growing up, a time when the person first became aware of racial group membership, general observations about monoracial and multiracial people, and joys and hardships related to being multiracial. Four essential themes related to identity development were found:

1. Encounters with racism
2. Racial identity label and/or reference group orientation
3. The "chameleon" experience
4. Identity development in context

Encounters with Racism This research found that all participants had encounters with or experiences of racism that facilitated their understanding of racial group membership. Being asked the question "What are you?" was common fare for these participants, as were encounters with "monocultural" racism through work or other contexts.

Reference Group Orientation Participants discussed their racial or ethnic label, such as Puerto Rican or Asian, but also saw themselves as multiracial. Identification as a person of color facilitated community building, racial intimacy and pride, and social support networking. Some participants also talked of feeling alienated by groups with whom they were unable to fit.

The Chameleon Experience The importance of strategies to negotiate their multiple racial identity was a finding from this research. The ability to be flexible across and cross rigid social boundaries was seen as an advantage, although a sense of not belonging to any group was echoed by some.

Identity Development in Context: Critical People, Critical Places, Critical Period Parents were cited as the most influential people in participants' lives regarding the expression of their racial identity. The authors said, "In general, it seemed that participants adopted the racial-ethnic label of the parent to whom they felt emotionally closest or whom they viewed as most dominant in the household" (Miville et al., 2005, pp. 512–513). Social settings were identified as possibly playing a major role in the development of a positive racial identity with respect to acceptance or tension. Critical periods were connected to elementary school, high school, and college.

Rockquemore (2002) conducted in-depth, loosely structured, qualitative interviews with 16 Black/White biracial respondents. The primary theme that emerged was negative interactions with monoracial African Americans. (See Storytelling: *Hostile Assumptions*.) Women were more likely than men to report negative interactions. The content of these encounters was typically related to physical appearance, such as skin color, body size, and eye color. Competition for Black men was discussed. That Black women have few eligible suitors given that successful Black men are just as likely to marry inside and outside of their race has to be considered within the context of this finding. The internalization of negative messages among some of the biracial women in the sample was identified. Black people were broadly characterized as being on drugs, without jobs, and ill-mannered. Many of the respondents were raised by White women, given that White woman/Black man is the most common dyad for Black/White marriages.

Interview respondents raised by White mothers frequently reported dealing with a White parent's explicit racism and dealing with the racialized negativity that the White parent had for the respondent's Black father. Rockquemeore (2002) cited that a cognitive dichotomy can emerge when a Black father is abusive or addicted and in contrast a friend's White father is attentive and involved. Blackness can be conceptualized as betrayal and Whiteness as goodness. Rockquemore concluded by saying that for women of African descent, skin color acts as a microlevel manifestation of oppression with respect to the conflicted and contested relationship between Black and biracial women.

Storytelling: Hostile Assumptions

One of the mothers in my research with White mothers of non-White children, along with her husband, had adopted two Black/White biracial children. She was at the grocery store one day with her children and noticed that the check-out clerk, a young Black woman, seemed to be hostile toward her. She chalked it up to a bad day. The same experience occurred when she took her children to buy school clothes. She reflected on these events during our interview and said that it actually happened a lot. I asked her if she thought the women had made an assumption that she was the biological mother of these children, which meant their father was a Black man. She nodded and concluded that this may explain their attitude. This issue of hostility from Black and Maori women toward White mothers, even women who have adopted children or single lesbians, has been discussed in my research.

Skin color is no small issue within society and impacts dating, mating, money, and politics. Hochschild and Weaver (2007) noted that Americans across and within racial or ethnic groups attribute more favorable characteristics to people who have lighter-skin tones and often believe that others also deem light skin as more attractive than dark skin. They also note that dark skinned Blacks in the United States have "lower socioeconomic status, more punitive relationships with the criminal justice system, diminished prestige, and less likelihood of holding elective office compared with their lighter counterparts" (p. 643).

CASE STUDY

DENIAL OF SELF

Zach is an 11-year-old boy. He lives with his father, Ben. His mother, Sheila, lives elsewhere with two of her other children. She told Ben that he needed to take care of Zach, as she had other children to raise. Zach's siblings have a different father than Zach. Ben is White and Sheila is Black. Ben took Zach to counseling because his behavior changed dramatically once his mother stopped caring for him—she did not call him on the phone. Zach's grades have fallen—to the point where the teacher has told Ben that Zach will most likely have to repeat sixth grade. Zach has also been caught vandalizing cars—he and his friend throw rocks at expensive cars that are painted black. Zach deeply resents when someone refers to him as being Black. When asked about his race, he says he is Italian since his dad is Italian. Some children at school have accused Zach of lying about his race. Zach does not like to speak about his mother during therapy. When he does mention her, he does so with great disdain and anger. Leah, the counselor, is Japanese American. Leah's husband is white and she has biracial children. Ben was attracted to Leah as a counselor given her clinical emphasis on biracial children, interracial families, and identity development. Leah senses some hostility from Zach. Ben reacts with embarrassment when his son is rude to Leah. Ben says he does this with his teachers. Zach interjected, "Not all of them." Ben mentioned that Sheila has a problem with alcohol and that if she keeps it up, she will lose custody of her younger children. Ben told Leah that Sheila's alcohol problem was responsible for their relationship failing.

(Continued)

(Continued)

QUESTIONS

1. What are the implications for therapeutic effectiveness when the counselor is the same race as the young client's mother with whom he has an estranged relationship?
2. What are the factors that contribute to Zach's denial of his African American heritage?
3. Are race related issues relevant in therapy when working with children?

DISCUSSION AND INTEGRATION

The Client, Zach

There are multiple issues in Zach's life. He feels rejection from his mother. He is understandably angry at his mother for choosing her other children over him to raise. He may have difficulty identifying with the parent from whom he feels alienated and estranged. Robinson-Wood (2010a) found that some biracial children had difficulty racially identifying with a parent who had left the family or who had been violent within the family. Leah realizes that underneath Zach's anger is enormous sadness—from feeling rejected by his mother. His hostility toward her is reflective of transference (and his unresolved feelings of anger towards his mother, also a woman of color). Although Zach is young, he can be helped to explore his feelings about race. Leah senses that his target of Black cars is connected to his anger at the disruption of the maternal bond when Sheila abandoned him and sent Zach to be raised by his father.

The term *double* is not applicable to Zach. "Double denotes those who have a positive reflection of their identity based on the coexistence of their ethnicities" (Collins, 2000, p. 126). Zach has not yet created an identity that is more than the sum of its parts regarding his White and African-American identities. Part of this can be explained by age as well as the trauma associated with his mother choosing to raise her other children and not him. Lee and Beal (2007) conducted interviews and found that multiracial blacks were not as likely as Asians and Latinos to identify multiracially largely because of other people's ascription. This in turn can influence the range of choices that a person has regarding their identities.

The Therapist, Leah

Japanese American women have the highest rates of marriage to Whites among all other Asian ethnic groups (Le, 2007). More than 38% of Japanese women have White spouses, compared with 27% of Filipino women, 23% of Korean women, 14% of Chinese women, and 11% of Vietnamese women. Asian Indian women at 4.3% are the least likely of all Asian groups to have a White spouse. According to Passel, Wang, and Taylor (2010) among all newlyweds in 2008, 9% of whites, 16% of blacks, 26% of Hispanics and 31% of Asians married someone whose race or ethnicity was different from their own. The authors noted that gender patterns in intermarriage vary widely. Some 22% of all black male newlyweds in 2008 married outside their race, compared with just 9% of black female newlyweds. Among Asians, the gender pattern is altogether different. Forty percent of Asian female newlyweds married outside their race in 2008, compared with just 20% of Asian male newlyweds. Among whites and Hispanics, by contrast, there are no gender differences in intermarriage rates. Leah does not take a color-blind approach to life. Color-blindness refers to the denial, distortion, and/or minimization of race and racism (Neville, Spanierman, & Doan, 2006). In her research with the Color-Blind Racial Attitudes Scale (CoBRAS), Neville and her colleagues found that although there are different types of color-blindness, this phenomenon has been related to higher levels of fear about people of color, lower levels of White guilt, and less anger and/or sadness about the existence of racism.

To competently respond to clients' issues associated with race as a personal identity and social construct, Leah's awareness of her own racial identity is a benefit. Her understanding of the literature regarding biracial children and clinical issues that can arise for them is also a plus to Zach and Ben and the other families she serves—many who are interracial families with biracial and multiracial children. Leah has a developed sense of who she is as a Japanese woman and understands that as a woman, irrespective of her race, Zach will transfer his feelings about his mother onto her. Collins (2000) found in her qualitative research with Japanese/White individuals who grew up in predominantly White neighborhoods, that they did not acknowledge their Japanese ethnicity, did not have the opportunity to socialize with other biracial children, and their self-definition was thus devalued. As children grow and seek to belong to others, exclusion from groups may become an issue. Physical appearance, stereotyping, or being given a message that you are excluded from a desired group can provoke dissonance about where a person belongs and even encourage attempts to belong to the excluded group (Ahnallen, Suyemoto, & Carter, 2006). This is information that is helpful to Leah as she processes Zach's relationship to race.

Root (1998) investigated 20 sibling pairs. She found that hazing was reported as an experience among many of these siblings. Root referred to hazing as "an injunction to prove one is an insider through a demeaning process of racial and ethnic authenticity testing" (pp. 242–243). Although children are believed to benefit when parents discuss race as a component of identity, (Root, 1998) stated that there are times when family dysfunction (abuse and addiction) result in racial themes not being salient. This is the case with Zach's parents.

Leah's children are biracial, and they are being raised to be bicultural. Biculturally identified people take pride in cultural traditions from both ethnic and racial groups. Despite differences in her sons' appearances, Suzuki-Crumly and Hyers (2004) state that Asian/White biracials may be less noticeably non-White and more ambiguous in their appearance than Black/White biracials. Leah notes that Zach looks like a child of color, which makes his attestations of being Italian, despite the dark features of many Italians, to be a source of confusion for some children. In time, she plans to disclose to Zach that she has children who have parents of different races.

Implications for Counselors and Psychologists

Some of the early research suggested that biracial children had a high incidence of academic and behavioral problems presumed to be connected to identity conflicts and related challenges (Gibbs, Huang, & Associates, 1989). Santiago-Rivera, Arredondo, and Gallardo-Cooper (2002) encourage parents of bicultural children not to impose their culture on the child, particularly adolescents. It is suggested that children will internalize a variety of experiences and beliefs into their own value system that encompasses multiple identities and worldviews.

(Continued)

(Continued)

Shih and Sanchez (2005) cautioned researchers who study clinical samples to apply these findings to nonclinical samples. In their review of multiracial literature, multiracial persons in the general population were not more dissatisfied, unhappy, or uncomfortable with their racial identity. In their analysis of Add Health data comparing mixed-race adolescents to single-race adolescents, Udry, Li, and Hendrickson-Smith (2003) concluded adolescents who identify with more than one race were at a higher health and behavior risk when compared with adolescents identifying with only one race. The risk may be related to the stress associated with identity conflict. Without direct evidence, the researchers cautioned against jumping to conclusions.

Schwartz (1998) observed that the racial identity development of multiracial youth is more complicated than for monoracial youth. Herman (2004) affirmed the ethnic identity research, which suggests there are opportunities associated with identity development. Although there is societal racism (negative feelings about interracial marriages) and families that do not emphasize race, children come to see prejudice and racism in society. In addition, some children may feel enormous conflict about choosing one racial identity over another based on the child's phenotype, neighborhood, or, in the case of divorce, the race of the custodial parent. Socialization of children to embrace a biracial or multiracial identity communicates to a child the value and importance of all of his or her racial and ethnic identities. Although more complicated, the experience of identity formation can be a positive and affirming experience (Herman, 2004). Treating race as a social construction as opposed to a biological one was found by Shih, Bonam, Sanchez, and Pick (2007) to help buffer people from stereotype threat effects.

Summary

This chapter provided several definitions, including *biracial, multiracial, bicultural, interracial*, and *interracial*. Research on biracial and multiracial populations was highlighted, and a discussion of research methodologies was examined. The political nature of the topic of race and biracial identities was a theme throughout the chapter.

Converging Gender

> *A woman is nobody. A wife is everything.*
>
> ELIZABETH CADY STANTON

Black men and women brought to the Americas as slaves suffered an oppression that lasted over two centuries and continued after slavery was abolished. White women suffered from oppression as well. Legally, albeit immorally, they were denied their own wages and were unable to vote, and were treated as objects. It was even against the law to have a child outside of wedlock. Women were not allowed to speak publicly and were encouraged to be compliant, hospitable, and chaste. Laws from the English that were unduly influenced by Christian doctrine dictated women's place. Women won the right to vote in 1919, but had cried out against their inequality since the 18th century. Women resisted their subjugation and demanded to be seen as equals, spoke out in churches, refused to take their husbands' names, organized meetings, received medical degrees, resisted slavery, founded schools, created clothing for women (e.g. bloomers), wrote books, and poetry. It was a long struggle of resistance and persistence. Lucy Stone, Elizabeth Cady Stanton, Lucretia Mott, Elizabeth Blackwell, Dorothea Dix, Harriet Tubman, and Sarah and Angelina Grimke were some of the courageous heroines who resisted society's refusal (men and women alike) to honor their voice and vote. According to Zinn (2003), prior to the signing of the Declaration of Independence, Abigail Adams wrote to Thomas Jefferson, and said, "In the new code of laws which I suppose it will be necessary for you to make, I desire you would remember the ladies, and be more generous to them than your ancestors' (p. 110). Jefferson underscored his phrase, "all men are created equal" and stated that women would be "too wise to wrinkle their foreheads with politics" (p. 110). The majority of today's college students are women who often have no sense of the struggles that women have endured in order for them to vote, wear shorts, choose who they wish to marry (if at all), or buy a home in their own names and live in it by themselves.

In this chapter, gender is emphasized as both a social construct and a status characteristic. It is acknowledged that gender differences exist both between men and women and within groups of women and men. This truth is neither refuted nor regarded as problematic. However, the way gender inequity is perpetuated as a primary status characteristic within society is examined. Selected literature is presented that examines relationships with the self and others as a function of gender, gender roles, and sex role typology. The subsequent impact on gender identity is also investigated, as is gender from a biological perspective. Myths about biological differences between males and females are exposed.

GENDER DEFINITIONS

Sex roles and *gender roles* differ. Typically, **sex roles** are behavioral patterns culturally approved as more appropriate for either males or females (Worell & Remer, 1992); however, in this work, *sex roles* refer to roles related to the function of one's biology, such as erection, ejaculation, menstruation, ovulation, pregnancy, and lactation. **Gender roles** are a consequence of society's views regarding appropriate behavior based on one's biological sex, such as diaper changing, snow removal, leaf blowing, bill paying, and primary breadwinning. Gender labels are applied to people, and, once done, people behave toward an individual based on a set of expectations held for persons who have the same label. A *role* is a cluster of expectations for behavior of persons within a specific category. The meaning of **gender** varies among different cultures and changes throughout time (McCarthy & Holiday, 2004). The most common definition is the culturally determined attitudes, cognitions, and belief systems about females and males. Haider (1995) said, "The focus of gender is on social roles and interactions of women and men rather than their biological characteristics which is sex … gender is a matter of cultural definition as to what is considered to be masculine or feminine" (p. 35). The male gender role affirms masculine identity around qualities such as self-reliance and success, while that of women affirms feminine characteristics traditionally associated with noncompetiveness and care of others. The negative consequences of gender role restriction is termed **gender role conflict** (Lane & Addis, 2005) and "describes the detrimental consequences of gender roles either for the person holding them or for those associated with this person" (Mintz & O'Neil, 1990, p. 381).

Masculinity refers to traditional societal roles, behaviors, and attitudes prescribed for men, whereas **femininity** references traditional societal roles, behaviors, and attitudes prescribed for women (Mintz & O'Neil, 1990). Masculinity is construed with hegemonic power and men's dominance over women; however, men are dependent on women and perceive women as having expressive power over them or the power to express emotion (Pleck, 1984). Another form of power that women are perceived to have over men is *masculinity validating power,* or men's dependence on women to affirm their masculinity and validate their manhood. A system of this nature reinforces homophobia and heterosexism in its dependence on rigid adherence to gender and sex role-appropriate behaviors that operate exclusively in the context of heterosexuality (or the semblance thereof) and gender conformity.

Androcentrism refers to males at the center of the universe, looking out at reality from behind their own eyes and describing what they see from an egocentric—or androcentric—point of view (Bem, 1993).

GENDER AND BIOLOGY

Confusion arises when the sex category to which one is assigned is ambiguous. With the application of rigorous criteria that are socially derived, people are placed within categories as male or female, man or woman (West & Zimmerman, 1991). West and Zimmerman said, "Not only do we want to know the sex category of those around us (to see it at a glance, perhaps), but we presume that others are displaying it for us in as decisive a fashion as they can" (p. 21).

In each human cell, chromosomes are the genetic material carried. Except for the reproductive cells (sperm and ova) and mature red blood cells, each cell has 46 chromosomes arranged into 23 pairs. Twenty-two pairs of chromosomes, called **autosomes,** are matching sets in both males and females. The 23rd pair, called **sex chromosomes,** differs between the two sexes. Among genetically normal males, the sex chromosomes are XY; among genetically normal females, they are XX (Moir & Jessel, 1991).

From conception to about the sixth week in utero, all human embryos are anatomically identical. During the sixth week, sexual differentiation begins. The genetic information in the Y chromosome stimulates the production of a protein called *H-Y antigen,* which promotes the change of the undifferentiated gonads into fetal testes. The fetal testes synthesize myriad hormones known as **androgens.** Two important androgens are *Mullerian inhibiting substance (MIS)* and *testosterone.* MIS is involved in the degeneration of the female duct system (Renzetti & Curran, 1992). Testosterone promotes further growth of the male Wolffian duct, the duct system that leaves the testes. Testosterone is often referred to as the aggression, dominance, and sex hormone (Moir & Jessel, 1991).

In the eighth week, the hormone dihydrotestosterone encourages the formation of external genitals. It is suggested that, for the female, the lack of testosterone may prompt the undifferentiated gonads of an XX embryo to transform into ovaries around the 12th week of gestation (Renzetti & Curran, 1992).

THE SOCIAL CONSTRUCTION OF GENDER

Gender is a crucial part of our daily lives. It takes deviation from gender conformity to get people to notice the undoing of gender. Gender influences what we believe about ourselves and others. Across race, class, culture, disability, and sexuality, common gender themes seem to exist for men and women. Among people of color, gender is often obscured by race, in that race vies for more attention as the salient identity construct.

Gender is a status characteristic that manifests in dominant and multiple ways (See Storytelling: Caring for Children). For the most part, males tend to enter into the world as the preferred sex and are accorded power within a patriarchal society. Because gender intersects with sexuality, class, and race, some men in society have more power than others and less power than some women. Clearly, not all men feel powerful and exert power over all women within a system of male supremacy. There are women, who by virtue of their race, nationality, skin color, able-body, and class privileges, exert power over some men and other women. Men operate as both the oppressed and the oppressor (McCarthy & Holliday, 2004). An androcentric culture exists and dictates for both women and men images and standards of acceptability that influence body image and self-esteem.

The devaluation of women and the esteem given to men is culturally rooted. Saucier (2004) noted that "women are set up to fail in a system that defines success for men in terms of productivity and accomplishment and designates beauty and sexiness as the measure of success for women" (p. 420). The process of preparing boys to be masculine men and girls to be

Storytelling: Caring for Children

I know a woman who hired a babysitter to care for her young children while she was attending a staff meeting. The sitter sat with the children in the hallway outside the meeting. One of the children was fussy, so the mother brought the child into the meeting. The child played quietly. Eventually, the mother took the child to the sitter, but the other child began to fuss, so the woman brought this child in. The sitter remained in the hallway with the first child. Several of the woman's co-workers commented on how quiet the children were. This was the second of nearly 50 staff meetings to which the woman had brought her children. The woman received the following email from her male supervisor two days later. The year is 2011:

I would like to give you some feedback regarding childcare during meetings, and I hope that you will take my feedback as constructive, rather than critical. I believe it must be a challenge balancing childcare and work responsibilities. I noticed that you have brought your child or children to several meetings on campus (e.g., meeting with me, or more recently staff members. I think in general it is a good practice to communicate about your childcare plan with the faculty members with whom you are meeting, or at least the chair of the meeting, prior to bringing your child(ren) to the meeting. The advance communication and request will be respectful for all. As for me, I would prefer not to have children present when I am having formal meetings with staff. I also think that it is not appropriate to have children at our monthly staff meeting. I hope that you are able to find childcare help during those meetings, and I suggest that you look into what the company has to offer regarding childcare. I understand that this feedback likely is not pleasant to hear, when you have to juggle with so many things. I do hope you understand that meetings involve other people, and we want to be mutually respectful and productive in meetings. Please let me know if you have any question or concern. Thank you for listening.

In sharing the email with others, the woman heard stories. One woman had been criticized for taking too much time for prenatal visits; she eventually resigned her job. Another woman, during her third trimester of pregnancy, asked her professor if he would get a laptop so that she could participate in classroom discussions via Skype because her doctor did not want her traveling the lengthy distance between home and school. The professor stated that the department did not have the resources to accommodate her request, and he neither tried to help nor did he offer solutions. A fellow student helped the woman via Skype every class. Another woman talked about how a colleague of hers brought her young child to meetings. She said, "Nobody minded—we understood that she was taking care of her child and working. We supported her—the child didn't bother anything or anybody."

feminine women is largely an unconscious one within the culture. The family influences children in their most important identity formation, the gender role. Socializing influences include parents, grandparents, the extended family, teachers, the media, other children, and textbooks. Evans and Davies (2000) found in their examination of first-, third-, and fifth-grade literature textbooks that despite publisher's guidelines and Title IX, males are still portrayed in stereotypical ways, as aggressive, argumentative, and competitive. It is not uncommon for couples with girls to keep trying for a male child. This information needs to be contextualized. There are families with boys who will keep trying for a female child as well.

An individual's personality develops through the interplay of both biological inheritance and social experience. At birth, males and females are ascribed certain roles, characteristics, and behaviors associated with explicit values and expectations according to a constructed gender role that is socially generated (Haider, 1995). Society places men's work on a higher level for remuneration and recognition. (See Storytelling: *Maiden Name*.) Even in female activities, male involvement reflects their expertise.

Once upon a time, before satellite and cable television, high speed Internet, cable, iPhones, iPads, BlackBerries, video games, Xboxes, PlayStations, and play-dates, children went outdoors and played with other children. Store-bought toys were available, but often imagination and improvisation were used and children made up their own games or toys. As was the case both then and now, parents ensured that children were exposed to games, activities, and household chores compatible with children's gender. Children were rewarded for acting appropriately and punished when there was deviation from that standard. Rewards were in the form of toys, accolades, encouragement, playing with other children, or offering advice and instructions. Punishments were in the form of ridicule, denial of privilege, or removal of an offensive object (e.g., a Barbie doll for a little boy). Pressure was put on girls to be obedient, nurturing, selfless, dependent, and trustworthy (McBride, 1990). A relationship exists between these types of gender socialization experiences and girls' tendency to attribute their success to luck as opposed to skill (Sadker, Sadker, & Long, 1993). In a study of 392 college women, a lack of problem-solving confidence predicted depressive symptoms, which predicted eating disorder symptoms (VanBoven & Espelage, 2006).

Dealing with novelty or the unexpected can be a challenge for girls because they tend to be protected and sheltered. Boys are taught to be outgoing, independent, and assertive. This is not to say that all boys are assertive and powerful and that all females are passive and powerless. Race, class, sexuality, disability, and immigrant status are all factors that mediate the impact of privilege and oppression on people's gendered lives. Fortunately, the study of femininity and masculinity is increasingly focused on cross-cultural contexts (Wester, Kuo, & Vogel, 2006). For instance, immigrant women in the United States experience oppression from xenophobia, racism, class discrimination, and sexism (Yakushko & Chronister, 2005). Research was done with 60 male participants at a school in Massachusetts and 45 male participants at a large public university in Costa Rica. The research was investigating culture, gender role conflict, and likelihood of help-seeking for two different problems from a variety of potential help providers. The Costa Rican men were more likely to report higher levels of restrictive affectionate behavior between men and lower levels of conflict between work and family than were U.S. men. The researchers surmised that the two groups of men might experience similar levels of success, restrictive emotionality, power, and competition but the meaning and importance of these constructs might vary between the cultures (Lane & Addis, 2005).

Leaper and Brown (2008) conducted research with 600 girls, ages 12–18. What they found was disturbing. Nearly the entire sample (90%) of girls had experienced sexual harassment at least once. A few girls reported sexual harassment that had occurred several times. Most frequently cited were inappropriate and unwanted romantic attention, demeaning comments related to gender, teasing about one's appearance, and even unwanted physical contact. The results are disturbing because sexual harassment can make girls vulnerable to developing negative images about their bodies; self-esteem can also be adversely affected. Finally, many girls expect demeaning behaviors to be normative in heterosexual relationships. Thus, they may be at risk for future abusive relationships. The study found that male peers were the most likely perpetrators of academic and athletic sexism.

Girls can become rather conflicted when boys are disapproving of their technical skills or athleticism. Consequently, some girls may minimize their competencies in athletics and/or math and science, which hinders subsequent achievement in these areas. Other girls were another common source of perpetrators of sexism. Same-gender peers are powerful players in gender socialization. Sadly, "teachers were among the most common sources of negative comments about girls' academic abilities" (p. 697).

Good and Mintz (1990) found that boys' games, although rule-governed, rewarded creativity, improvisation, and initiative and involved teams comprised of a larger number of peers while encouraging both cooperation and competition. In addition to being socialized to play with other boys on teams, boys are also prepared to engage with and explore the world and to play by themselves. In doing so, they develop improvisational and problem-solving skills and are given important practice in the art of negotiation. Achievement and success are emphasized for boys, which may explain why boys enter an activity with the assumption that they should master, create, and influence.

The instrument commonly used to measure masculine role conflict is the Gender Role Conflict Scale (GRCS). It is based on the notion that the traditional gender socialization of boys asks more than what is possible to give. To be regarded as masculine, men are expected to acquire power, compete with one another, demonstrate control over themselves and their environment, and dominate women. Vulnerability is frowned upon, as is weakness and irrationality. The inability to shoulder all of these expectations ushers in distress. Gender role conflict was associated with psychological distress, such as paranoia, psychosis, obsessive-compulsive disorder, depression, and interpersonal sensitivity.

One consequence of the male socialization pattern that emphasizes strength, self-reliance, and independence is restrictive emotionality. **Restrictive emotionality,** the socialized practice of men not expressing their emotions, is one of the subscales on the Gender Role Conflict Scale. According to Good et al. (1996), four behavioral patterns emerge when men experience gender role conflict. The first behavioral pattern is *restrictive emotionality,* which refers to men's reluctance or difficulty in expressing their emotions. *Alexithymia* describes symptoms that include a decreased ability to label and communicate affect, confusion of affective and somatic symptoms, and externally oriented thinking. Alexithymia may be linked to a variety of both psychological and physical disorders, including depression (Carpenter & Addis, 2000).

The second behavioral pattern is *restrictive affectionate behavior between men.* Men may be afraid of sharing a full range of emotions for fear of being seen as gay (Good, Dell, & Mintz, 1989). Gertner (1994) said that men may also be limited in how they express their sexuality and affection to others.

Obsession with achievement and success is the third behavioral pattern, which references a disturbing and persistent preoccupation with work, accomplishment, and eminence as a means of demonstrating value. Seeking help may be experienced as the antithesis of being in control and having power. This may explain why men remain less likely than women to seek therapeutic assistance (Gertner, 1994). Women are not more psychologically disturbed than men, but men's socialization patterns do not encourage them to seek needed psychological help. Feeling sad or depressed may be viewed as unmanly (Good et al., 1989).

There has been greater emphasis in the past few decades on *coaching*, defined as an ongoing professional relationship that helps people produce extraordinary results in their lives, careers, businesses, or organizations (McKelley & Rochlen, 2007). Coaching may appeal to men, particularly those who are averse to receiving professional help. Its emphasis on a collegial relationship (perhaps less of a power differential) and on the teaching of human relationship skills to successful executives over addressing psychological deficits has been cited as the appeal.

Balancing work and family relations is the fourth behavioral pattern. Because men are socialized to focus on achievement, other areas of life, such as home and leisure, can easily be ignored or sacrificed. These four behavioral patterns have been related to depression (Good & Mintz, 1990). Gertner (1994) added homophobia and health care problems to this as well.

A study which investigated gender role conflict and the supervisor working alliance was done involving 103 master's- and doctoral-level male interns in Association of Psychology Postdoctoral and Internship Center (APPIC). The main finding was that men high in restrictive emotionality tended to deal with a loss of power by turning against themselves in the form of negative perceptions of their own counseling efficacy. This study revealed that counseling students were not immune to internalizing gendered behavior, even if doing so was linked to negative consequences (Wester, Vogel, & Archer, 2004).

Another way of understanding restrictive emotionality on men's lives is by comparing an underused muscle to the difficulty many men have in receiving assistance during emotional stress or accepting responsibility when necessary. In a study with 207 college students (17% non-White), men were found to experience shame, guilt, and externalization (Efthim, Kenny, & Mahalik, 2001). **Externalization** was defined as the act of shifting blame outward for negative events and is a defensive maneuver in dealing with shame and guilt (Skovholt, 1993). Men's tendency to avoid expressing affection toward other men is associated with increased likelihood of depression, as is their reluctance to seek psychological help.

The psychological distress experienced by women occurs within the context of unfair treatment due to their biological sex (perceived discrimination) and subsequent and negative personal views of women as a group (private collective self-esteem) and of themselves as individuals (personal self-esteem) (Fischer & Holz, 2007).

Storytelling: Maiden Name

When you call the credit card company and speak to a representative to check on your balance, request a credit line increase, or request a lower interest rate, the password is your mother's *maiden* name. Every time I get asked this question, I complain—ultimately to the representative, who has no power to make or change policy but only to enforce it. Heterosexist, racist, and sexist discourses are loaded in the question. First, it is assumed that people's mothers married—some mothers have a child or children without marrying the father. Nonmarriage is not a negation of a child's birth. A large percentage of women of all races, but particularly among Black women and Latinas, are single parents. Second, it is assumed that a woman is heterosexual and thus married a man and had sex with him. Third, the credit card company policy assumes that upon marriage, all women renounce their birth names and take their husband's names. This practice is antiquated.

UNDOING GENDER

Western philosophy holds that the construction of masculinity and femininity as mutually exclusive or dichotomous. Common language used when referring to the two genders is "the opposite sex," or reference is made to one's partner as "the other half." Masculinity in the Western worldview is associated with an instrumental orientation, a cognitive focus on getting the job done, or problem solving. Femininity, in contrast, is associated with a concern for others and harmony with the group. Until gender roles ascribed by society change and the inherent sexism is transformed, men and women alike will be constricted to and suffer from the consequences of inequities based on biological sex and socially constructed roles (Gertner, 1994). Although there are serious consequences associated with rigid sex-based gender roles that limit the range of affect, behaviors, and cognitions perceived to be available to people, they are adopted and perpetuated. This issue was explored by psychologist Sandra Bem, who developed the concept of androgyny. She also designed the Bem Sex Role Inventory (BSRI), which has been used in hundreds of research studies on *gender role socialization* and androgyny. *Androgyny* is from the Greek *andro*, meaning "male," and *gyne*, meaning "female" (Bem, 1993). Androgyny is consistent with the notion of people as gendered beings fully developing without restricting and confining sex roles.

Androgynous refers to persons who are high in both feminine and masculine psychological and behavioral traits, not to persons' biological, male or female, physical characteristics. According to Bem (1993), an individual can be both masculine and feminine; expressive, instrumental, and communal; and compassionate and assertive, depending on the situation. Limiting oneself to one domain could be costly to human potential in that individuals may be required to mitigate agency with communion and strength with yielding. Bem stated that balance is necessary because extreme femininity untempered by a sufficient concern for one's own needs as an individual may produce dependency and self-denial, just as extreme masculinity untempered by a sufficient ability to ask for help from others may produce arrogance and exploitation. An individual with both masculine and feminine characteristics would arguably be more flexible and function more productively than a sex-typed individual. Androgynous persons demonstrate a lack of statistically significant differences between masculinity and femininity scores, thus showing a blend of both dimensions.

Psychological differences between the sexes are not biological destiny but rather are learned after birth through the sex role socialization process (Cook, 1987). Although this is the case, a *uniformity myth* tends to make sex synonymous with gender roles. Men are connected with masculine characteristics that are instrumental, agentic, and goal-oriented in nature. Emphasis is placed on self-development and separation from others. Masculine characteristics are associated with goal directedness, achievement, and recognition by others for one's efforts. Highly valued traits within the culture of the United States are also deemed masculine—competitiveness, assertiveness, high achievement, and individualism (Burnett, Anderson, & Heppner, 1995). Saucier (2004) observed that most positive traits associated with masculinity increase with age (e.g., competence, autonomy, self-control, and power). Not only are males elevated, but masculinity also has greater "social utility" than femininity. This, according to Burnett et al. (1995), is known as the masculine supremacy effect. "This position suggests a cultural bias toward masculinity such that individuals who are masculine receive more positive social reinforcement and hence develop higher self-esteem" (p. 323). Masculinity was viewed as more valuable not only for men but also for women. Women who were low in individual masculinity were at greater risk for decreased self-esteem. There is, however, a flip side. Women who demonstrate too much masculinity are regarded as aggressive and bitchy, whereas boys and men who exhibit an excess of feminine qualities are ridiculed and called derogatory names, such as "fag" and "sissy"

(Haddock, Zimmerman, & Lyness, 2003). Femininity may influence how others respond to a person, but masculinity is strongly related to various indexes of psychological health (Burnett et al., 1995). Masculinity had a more positive impact on how one sees oneself. Conversely, women are associated with the feminine characteristics of expressiveness and communality, with a focus on emotionality, selflessness, sensitivity, and interpersonal relationships.

The challenges with measurement of masculinity and femininity were echoed by Hoffman (2001):

> There are numerous instruments that are widely used today by a range of individuals from researchers in counseling, psychology, and education to human resource personnel. Unfortunately, what is being assessed is often given only cursory consideration by researchers and consumers alike. (p. 472)

Despite the murky waters of masculinity and femininity, these terms are popular within the culture. Sex role typology, which references a psychological dimension, is not predicated on biological sex. Masculinity or femininity refers to behaviors, not physical makeup. Men can be psychologically feminine and women can be psychologically masculine. Sex-typed persons (e.g., men ascribing to a strictly masculine role, women to a feminine role) have internalized society's sex-appropriate standards for desirable behavior to the relative exclusion of the other sex's typical characteristics. The traditional masculine role, which has been found to be unhealthy on many indexes of functioning, is related to status, toughness, success, achievement, emotional stoicism, and anti-femininity (Lane & Addis, 2005).

Sex role rigidity contributes to narrow and restricted behaviors. An example of this was seen in research conducted by Stevens, Pfost, and Potts (1990). They found that "masculine-typed men and feminine-typed women reported the most avoidance of existential issues, with sex-typed persons indicating the least openness to such concerns … the findings also complement evidence of behavioral rigidity among sex-typed individuals" (p. 48).

Spence and Helmreich (1978) developed the Personal Attributes Questionnaire (PAQ). Like the BSRI, the PAQ identified four groups: feminine, masculine, androgynous, and undifferentiated. This model recognized that masculinity and femininity coexist to some degree in every individual, male or female. The androgynous person, less bound to the restrictive, sex-appropriate standards for behavior, is theoretically able to develop psychologically to the fullest and respond receptively to a wide range of situations, perhaps in ways that the less integrated person is unable to do.

Cross-culturally, the concepts of *masculinity* and *femininity* have been represented as complementary domains, traits, and behaviors for thousands of years. The yin-yang theory of the harmony and balance of forces in nature is based in Confucian thought and Chinese cosmology. Uba (1994) said that the yin is feminine, negative, inferior, and weak, whereas the yang is masculine, positive, superior, and strong. "If this supposedly natural balance is upset (e.g., if a wife domineers over her husband), the equilibrium within the family would be disrupted" (p. 29).

Good and Sanchez (2010) investigated gender conformity, self-esteem, and affect among 401 women and men. It was found that investment in living up to a societal gender ideal (feeling that it is important to be like society's ideal mean or woman) was associated with pressured motivation for gender-conforming behavior—this negatively impacted self-esteem. Private regard was defined as a subset of collective self-esteem that captures positive feelings regarding one's particular gender group or having a sense of pride in being a woman or a man. It predicted autonomous motivation for gender-conforming behavior which positively predicted self-esteem. Valuing one's gender was not shown to be directly costly for the person, but instead it influenced self-esteem by encouraging gender-conforming behavior. The authors conclude that it is possible that individuals who receive greater rewards (sanctions) for gender typical behavior may be more likely to behave in accordance with gender norms due to society's ideals, and thus experience pressured gender motivation.

SEX AND GENDER ROLES

Several models describe women's development (Enns, 1991). These models seek to highlight the relational strengths that women embody and, according to Enns, attempt "to correct the inadequacies of mainstream theories and conceptualize women's experiences in their own terms" (p. 209). Evans, Kincade, Marbley, and Seem (2005) reviewed the historical aspects of feminism and feminist therapy in women and men's lives. Feminist therapy skills, an emphasis on social justice and change, and the relationship between the client and the counselor were all highlighted.

Erikson (1968), one of the early and essential voices in identity development, has been criticized for focusing the majority of his attention on the masculine version of human existence. However, the primacy of men in the human life event reflects the sexism of the time (Horst, 1995). Women's psychosocial development is different from men's. Gilligan (1982) criticized major identity development theorists who depict women as inferior to men because of important gender differences. According to Gilligan, women's development "relies more on connections with others, on relatedness rather than separateness" (p. 271). Recently, other psychologists have written about the unique experience of womanhood on development. Jordan (1997a) and Nelson (1996) commented that relational skills are highly functional and involve a complex array of competencies essential to preserving family and culture.

Compared with men, women may emphasize relationships, and the importance of autonomy for women cannot be underestimated. McBride (1990) argued that **autonomy** refers to being able to define oneself, rather than being defined by others. This definition is not seen as an isolated and extremely individualistic self. Rather, autonomy refers to interdependence, mutual cooperation, and individuation. McBride stated that **instrumental autonomy** refers to the ability to act on the world, carry on activities, cope with problems, and take action to meet one's needs. **Emotional autonomy** is the freedom from pressing needs for approval and reassurance. Women are often unaware of how much energy they invest in doing things for others versus developing healthy interdependence. The capacity to commit to concrete affiliations and partnerships and to develop the ethical strength to abide by such commitments, even though they may call for significant sacrifices and compromises, is a source of strength. It is questionable as to whether such commitments and mutuality can be achieved when there is a considerable power differential (Haddock et al., 2003).

GENDER AND EMOTION

The history of gender relationships in this country is steeped in patriarchy and inequality. Elizabeth Cady Stanton, one of the cofounders of the first Women's Rights Convention held in 1840, observed the burden of caring for everyone other than oneself on the faces of women. She said,

> The general discontent I felt with women's position as wife, mother, housekeeper, physician, and spiritual guide, the chaotic condition into which everything fell without her constant supervision, and the wearied, anxious look of the majority of women, impressed

me with the strong feeling that some active measures should be taken to remedy the wrongs of society in general and of women in particular. (cited in Zinn, 2003, p. 123)

This socialization process of selflessness contributes to women equating self-care with selfishness. Women who sacrifice their own development to meet the needs of others often inhibit the development of self-expression, self-knowledge, and self-esteem (McBride, 1990). Yet the culture encourages women to sacrifice their development and needs for the benefit of others' needs, usually men's. Depression is associated with the behavior of women constantly putting others' needs first and discounting their own needs. It is important, then, not to pathologize women for behaving in this manner. Women who are selfless and sacrificial have had cultural, institutional, and relational reinforcement (Lemkau & Landau, 1986). Choosing to care for the self might be perceived as an unacceptable proposition, because it is likened to the denial of others (McBride, 1990). When women feel that they have failed to be in nurturing and sustaining relationships, there is a sense of shame. Gender socialization is riddled with shame for women and men. There is not enough room in this book to address the shame heaped upon transgendered people due to nonconformity with gender socialization processes and practices.

Researchers found that shame proneness among women was the dominant affective response related to living up to female gender role norms (Efthim et al., 2001). For shame to be experienced, a person appraises the self as having violated group norms or as having failed to live up to the standards of the social group. Five factors of the Female Gender Role Stress (FGRS) Scale examined women's gender role stress:

1. Emotional detachment (e.g., having others believe that you are emotionally cold)
2. Physical unattractiveness (e.g., being perceived by others as overweight)
3. Victimization (e.g., having your car break down on the road)
4. Unassertiveness (e.g., bargaining with a salesperson when buying a car)
5. Failed nurturance (e.g., having someone else raise your children)

In the Efthim et al. (2001) study, five factors of the Male Gender Role Stress (MGRS) Scale examined men's gender role stress and reinforced the dimensions of masculinity:

1. Physical inadequacy (e.g., losing in a sports competition)
2. Emotional inexpressiveness (e.g., admitting that you are afraid of something)
3. Subordination to women (e.g., being outperformed by a woman)
4. Intellectual inferiority (e.g., having to ask for directions when lost)
5. Performance failure (e.g., being unable to become sexually aroused when you want to)

Many men leave intimacy to women. Consequently, the requirement for intimacy in adult relationships, to join in mutuality and to surrender to another, is a tremendous source of conflict and anxiety for men (Jordan, 1997b). Men need to be educated on the benefits of emotional expression. As human beings, men have basic needs to love and to be loved, to care and to be cared for, to know and to be known, but socially prescribed gender roles tend to require men to be inexpressive and competitive with one another. Evaluating life success in terms of external achievements rather than interdependence is emphasized.

In the Newman, Fuqua, Gray, and Simpson (2006) study, the relationship between gender, depression, and anger was investigated in a clinical sample. There were 65 men and 74 women in the study, with a median age of 31. People were in the low-to-moderate income range and were predominantly White. Despite previous research that women are more likely to be depressed than men, this study found no difference between men and women on any of the affective scales, including depression. Both men and women had high Beck Depression Inventory scores. A significant finding was that 38% of the variance in depression was related to the five anger scales used in the study: state anger, trait anger, anger-in, anger-out, and anger control. The relationship between anger and depression was substantial for both men and women. The emphasis on quantitative methodologies and homogeneity in race and ethnicity represent severe limitations to this research, and yet the findings help us see the benefit of focusing on clinical samples and not relying on and applying findings from nonclinical samples to clinical ones.

Wester, Vogel, Wei, and McClain (2006) provide one of the first studies to examine race and male gender role conflict. In their sample, 130 Black male college students completed the GRCS, the Cross Racial Identity Scale, and the SCL-90 to measure psychological distress. A Bonferroni correction was done to address the multiple independent *t* tests performed on gender role conflict subscales. Black men's GRCS scores were predictive of their psychological distress. Black men who internalized a racist understanding of themselves as men of color suffered more from their attempts to navigate the male gender role than did men who internalized a racial identity based on an appreciation of their African American heritage. Internalized racism served as a vehicle through which internalized sexism (gender role conflict) affected quality of life. Racial identity partially mediated the effects of gender role conflict on psychological distress. The negative consequence of internalized racism was associated with racialized gender behavior.

Healthy male development can be accomplished with the expansion of gender roles. Skovholt (1993) said that "this narrow funnel of acceptable masculinity may give males a solid sense of gender identity, but it can, in time, also become a prison that constricts personal growth and development" (p. 13). Men are fearful of being perceived as or labeled feminine, which is part of the narrow funnel through which they must conduct their lives. From a psychosocial perspective, this fear stems from the arduous tasks men must complete: separating from their mothers and developing their male identities (Skovholt, 1993). This particular socialization process dictates that men should never engage in opposite-sex behaviors and attitudes.

Men travel through their developmental paths unduly conflicted yet trying to maintain power over women and other men (Pleck, 1984). A key task of the men's movement was to articulate the male experience of power and powerlessness, which assumed that female powerlessness translates into male power (Swanson, 1993). It is clear that the wounds of patriarchal power and control are damaging to men and women (Brown, 1994). The roles for men need to be transformed so that men become "acutely aware of their power to influence self and to break the bonds to patriarchy, emotional handcuffs in the form of assumptions and interpretations that favor patriarchal values above the worth of human beings and the meaning of their experiences" (Brown, 1994, p. 118).

GENDER AND THE BODY

Cultural values of independence, thinness, physical strength, and athleticism pervade U.S. society. Both print and audiovisual advertisements are a primary medium for the transmission of images. Chronic dieting and preoccupation with bulk and speed among men and women to the point of damaging the health of one's body with steroids and from anorexia and bulimia are epidemic within the culture. Cultural values must be considered when tracing the etiology of gender-based practices. (See Storytelling: *Barbaric Practice or Cultural Rite?*) For instance, health behaviors may manifest masculinity. Men "anticipate their world from the experiences of being males in their respective cultures (e.g., being told to be tough, self-reliant, violent, promiscuous) and take (or not take) certain actions based on their understanding of their

Storytelling: Barbaric Practice or Cultural Rite?

When traveling in Tanzania, our group had the privilege of staying with the Masai—a nomadic people who eschew modern conveniences like electricity and plumbing. We were told that circumcision for women and men is a prerequisite for marriage, and girls know they will not be marriageable (deemed worthy of a Masai man's hand in marriage) without doing so. We were told that women did not fear circumcision; they anticipated it as part of the preparation for marriage. Chung (2005) states that female genital mutilation (FGM) is a standard cultural practice in preparing for marriage and adult status in sub-Saharan Africa, Egypt, United Arab Emirates, Bahrain, Oman, Indonesia, South Yemen, Pakistan, Malaysia, and some parts of Russia. It also occurs in immigrant and refugee communities in the Americas and Europe.

world (e.g., ignore pain, refuse help, become violent, engage in risky sexual practices" (Mahalik, Lagan, & Morrison, 2006, p. 192). These behaviors have their genesis in culturally laden images that privilege physical power.

In the United States, more than 90% of persons suffering from **anorexia nervosa,** or self-starvation of the body, are young females (Andersen, 1986; Anorexia Nervosa and Related Eating Disorders, 2011). Pursuit of the thin beauty ideal has meant different things for women. One percent of the 10- to 20-year-old American female population has anorexia nervosa. It is estimated that 4% of college-age women have bulimia nervosa, but this could be higher given the secret nature of binge eating. Ten percent of anorexics and bulimics are men. About 72% of alcoholic women under the age of 30 also have eating disorders (ANRED, 2011). Disordered eating is far too often associated with becoming or remaining thin. Large numbers of young women in high school report that they use maladaptive weight control techniques such as fasting (39.4%), appetite suppressants (8.1%), and skipping meals (33.5%) to lose weight (Tylka & Subich, 2002).

Adolescents are particularly vulnerable to eating disorders because anorexia nervosa has its highest incidence at the beginning of adolescence and bulimia nervosa has its highest incidence at the end (Emmons, 1992). From a psychodynamic perspective, the earlier scripts that are set in motion will have a powerful impact on behavior and cognition unless early information is replaced with new information. Arrival to adulthood does not ensure clarity about the existence or elimination of dysfunctional tapes. Thus, one task of adulthood is to unlearn many of the negative tapes received during childhood and adolescence and to replace them with messages that affirm the self and are more reflective of whom the individual has sculpted the self to be. The media, church, educational institutions, other women, family members, and men create an environment wherein men "construct the symbolic order" within which gender inequity and male supremacy are reproduced.

In this system, women and men (because of the price associated with the privilege of defining reality) become at war with their bodies. This is particularly true when a gap exists between body image perception and proximity to the socially constructed standard. Learning to define oneself as acceptable amid the aging process where one no longer fits the ideal of beauty is essential in combating appearance anxiety or fear-based thoughts that one's aging body is betraying them in a youth-obsessed culture (Saucier, 2004). Intense body dissatisfaction and a sense of disembodiment can ensue when one's body does not conform to the standard. Hutchinson (1982) stated, "The body is experienced as alien and lost to awareness ... The body has broken away or has been severed from the mind and is experienced as a foreign object, an albatross, or a hated antagonist" (pp. 59–60).

An area that has been understudied is the growing phenomenon of eating disorders among women 35–55 years of age. With a sample of 101 35–55 year old women, Slevec and Tiggemann (2011) found that television was positively related to body dissatisfaction and disordered eating but magazine exposure was not positively correlated. The researchers reason that the natural deviation from thin and youthful standards of beauty among middle-aged women may make them particularly vulnerable to the media's promulgation of beauty, contributing to aging anxiety and appearance investment.

Alienation from the body hampers appreciation and acceptance of multiple identities. Perceptions of the body amid parts that cause pain, create difficulty, or are defined by society as unattractive and unacceptable can be transformed through paradigm shifts. New discourses or ways of bringing meaning to bear on the value of the body can emerge and take root interpersonally.

Oppressive stereotypes about women of color are pervasive throughout the media. For instance, Root (1990) identified that

> Women of color are either fat and powerless (African American and Latina women); fat, bossy, and asexual; corrupt and/or evil (Asian/Pacific Island Americans and African Americans); obedient, quiet, and powerless (Latinas and Asian/Pacific Americans); exotic (Asian Americans, mixed race); or hysterical and stupid. (p. 530)

Gunn Allen (1992) observed that American society would be different if various traditions from Native American culture were followed, saying, "if American society judiciously modeled the traditions of the various Native Nations, the ideals of physical beauty would be considerably enlarged to include 'fat' strong-featured women, gray-haired, and wrinkled individuals, and others who in contemporary American cultured are viewed as 'ugly'" (p. 211).

Race and skin color are variables in the beauty business. American standards of beauty are based on White or White-approximating ideals. Lewis et al. (2011) explored African women's motivations for bleaching their skin. The six themes were a) removal of pimples, rashes, and skin disease; b) to have soft skin; c) to be White, beautiful, and more European looking; d) to remove the adverse effects of extended skin bleaching use on the body; e) to satisfy one's partner and to attract male mates; f) to satisfy and impress peers. The authors conclude that their findings provide support for the link between skin bleaching, self-objectification, colonialism, and Westernization. The physical features of many White women, as well as those of women of color, differ from socially constructed rigid and often unattainable beauty standards. In an effort to conform to accepted standards of beauty, many women of color will seek to fulfill Eurocentric beauty standards equated with status, acceptance, and legitimacy. Some Asian women have undergone plastic surgery to make their eyes appear more round or double-folded, as opposed to single-folded, for a more Western look. This drastic physical change may be fueled by Uba's (1994) statement, "There is evidence that Asian Americans have lower self-concepts than Euro-Americans do when it comes to physical appearance" (p. 83).

Rhinoplasty is a surgical procedure many Jewish women have undergone to obtain a smaller, narrower, and finer nose. Black women spend an inordinate amount of time, psychic energy, and money on the monumental issue of hair. Many, along with their Jewish sisters, have for decades been relaxing their hair by applying chemicals or a hot metal comb to naturally curly and coily hair to make it straight. Alice Walker (1987) refers to this relaxing process as "oppressing" the hair.

Emmons's (1992) research points to an erroneous assumption about eating disorders—that they are rare among people of color. She found that African American teenage girls were more likely than any other race and gender group examined to use laxatives as a dieting ploy. In contrast,

European Americans were more likely to vomit to lose weight. Cultural factors, values, and institutional variables such as racism and religious discourses all converge to influence the presence and diagnosis of eating disorders in women. Among Black women, stress associated with the struggle to deal with acculturation, success, racism, and family responsibilities may trigger bingeing and purging behavior in some who did not evidence disordered eating during adolescence.

Mastria (2002) maintains that cultural components of Latina culture predispose girls to defer and sacrifice themselves. She said, "From childhood, females are taught to repress sexual desires, and conditioned to be extremely modest and 'virginal' in terms of their bodies, which may cause conflict and shameful feelings about their bodies" (p. 71). Research conducted by Lester and Petrie (1998) on 139 female Mexican American college students found evidence of bulimia nervosa among 1.4% to 4.3% of the sample. Despite strongly entrenched beliefs about the protective aspects of race, a relationship may exist between increasing opportunities for social mobility for women of color and increasing vulnerability to disordered eating (Root, 1990).

The desire to bring honor and not disgrace to the family, coupled with the model minority myth, may contribute to disordered eating among Asian American girls (Mastria, 2002). The changing roles of women within the family and workforce have to be considered when understanding the etiology of eating disorders and its relationship with power and control. According to Chernin (1985), eating disorders "must be understood as a profound developmental crisis in a generation of women still deeply confused after two decades of struggle for female liberation, about what it means to be a woman in the modern world" (p. 17).

Familial factors play a pivotal role in the life of the girl who has an eating disorder. Brouwers (1990) reported that negative attitudes toward the body begin in the family and that, after self-body evaluation, the daughter's belief that the mother was critical of the daughter's body was the second biggest predictor of bulimia in female college students.

College campus factors or values may influence a girl's vulnerability to eating disorders. Salk and Engeln-Maddo (2011) conducted research with 152 undergraduate women on fat talk which refers to negative talk among women about the size and shape of their bodies. The researchers report that "nearly all college women reported that they engage in fat talk with friends and almost one third of these women described their fat talk as frequent or very frequent" (p. 25). An increase in body dissatisfaction and body surveillance was associated with women's good feelings about receiving appearance compliments within the context of engaging in fat talk.

Kashubeck, Walsh, and Crowl (1994) discovered that the literature on one college website emphasized physical appearance, attention to fashion, and participation in the sorority-fraternity system. Another college, a liberal arts institution, emphasized political activism and intellectual talent. The rate of eating disorders did not differ between the two schools, but the study found that at the first school, the factors associated with eating disorders were the perceived pressure to dress a certain way, to be smart, and to have a marginal grade point average. At the second school, being a girl and having low masculine gender role identity were the strongest predictors to disordered eating behaviors.

Research by Rogers and Petrie (2001) found that among 97 college women (27 non-White), dependency and assertion of autonomy were important in explaining the variance on the Eating Attitudes Test. It appears that symptoms of anorexia are characterized by dependency on and need for approval from a significant relationship, as well as the need to deny this reliance. Restricting food intake may be a way to assert one's sense of individualism within the gender role. Women's power comes from their beauty and physical allure as approved and esteemed by others.

In research with 200 Asian American college women, self-esteem, perceived pressure to be thin, ethnic identity, body shape, internalization of society's emphasis on appearance, and eating disorder symptomatology were assessed. The following were found: Asian American women's perceived pressure for thinness slightly predicted self-esteem and moderately predicted body preoccupation; self-esteem predicted body preoccupation; and body preoccupation strongly predicted eating disorder sympotomatology. Although ethnic identity predicted self-esteem, ethnic identity did not predict internalization of the thin ideal, body preoccupation, and disordered eating. Ethnic identity only influenced internalization of the thin ideal and body preoccupation through its association with self-esteem (Phan & Tylka, 2006).

Despite African American youths' positive self-esteem (Gibbs, 1985; Gibbs, Huang, & Associates, 1989; Ward, 1989), feeling enormous pressure to look according to European ideals adversely affects self-concept among this group as well as other women of color. They may feel compelled to change hairstyles, dress, body size, and makeup to be accepted and thus keep the doors of opportunity wide open. Robinson and Ward (1991) indicated that obesity among many African American women may be a quick-fix resistance strategy to negotiate the pressures and frustrations of daily racism and sexism.

African American women have been known to bleach their skin, but skin-color issues are connected to broader themes of identity and an awareness of the sociopolitical context of race in America. As people of African descent celebrate various hues, skin color as a status variable may hopefully take on less prominence.

Storytelling: No Choice

I was flipping through *National Geographic* recently and saw a picture of a newborn baby being washed in a bucket by a young girl. A toddler was sitting next to her. What caught my eyes was how very small this newborn baby was, as well as how young the girl was who was taking care of baby. As I read on, I came to understand that the young girl was actually the mother—both of the newborn and of the toddler playing nearby. This 14-year-old girl had just given birth to her second child. Still ill from the delivery, weak, and bleeding, she was responsible for taking care of her brand new baby and her toddler, even though she had no idea how to care for herself. This girl was one of many in Haijah (Northwest Yemen), where girls are required to marry at a very early age.

GENDER AND EXPERIENCES IN THERAPY

Qualitative research was conducted with 16 counselors to address how counselors conceptualize and address privilege and oppression within counseling and understand their perceptions of their training with respect to these constructs. Specifically, two research questions were asked: how do practitioners see privilege and oppression influencing and interacting in counseling, and what changes in training and practice related to these constructs do they see as necessary to better serve clients? Two themes emerged from the data: (1) the intersection between counselor process and cultural power and (2) transitions in counselor training practice. More specifically, interactions with clients were facilitative in counselors' awareness of privilege and oppression. In addition, counselors felt they lacked a sense of preparedness to address power issues in counseling (Hays, Dean, & Change, 2007).

Bernardez (1987) found three specific reactions to women in therapy: (1) the discouragement and disapproval of behavior that did not conform with traditional role prescriptions, such as mother; (2) the disparagement and inhibition of expression of anger and other "negative" affects, such as hatred and bitterness; and (3) the absence of confrontation, interpretation, and exploration of passive-submissive and compliant behavior in the client. Despite these reactions from therapists, Bernardez reported that female therapists showed greater empathy and ability to facilitate self-disclosure than males. There are exceptions; male therapists may be more inclined to reproduce the dominant-subordinate position by unconscious encouragement of the female's compliance, submissiveness, and passivity.

Fauth and Hayes (2006) investigated the applicability of a transactional theory of stress to understanding countertransference with male clients. Therapists' positive appraisals were linked with more positive diagnostic evaluation of their client. Negative appraisals were linked with increased distance from and hesitance with the client. "Counselors who felt more efficacious in managing their feelings and value conflicts with the client tended to avoid him less" (p. 436). The authors did not find that counselors' male gender role attitudes and male clients' gender role conformity interacted to predict the counselors' stress appraisals and countertransference.

A problem for both sexes is the strong gender role prohibition against female anger, criticism, rebellion, or domination. Anger is often equated with hatred, destructiveness, or bitterness. Helping clients realize that they have the right to take care of themselves, even if those in their environment tell them they are hurting others, is an important step on the road to self-mastery. Some clients "may exclude information that they assume the counselor will not understand or include details designed to counteract the counselor's presumed prejudices" (Hays, 1996, p. 36). The very exploration of bitterness and resentment can lead to the identification of sources of dissatisfaction.

The female counselor–male client dyad represents the typical caregiving pattern in society. Most men would feel very challenged entering therapy and abdicating power to a woman. If a woman is uncomfortable with her power, given her proximity to discourses that sing the power-of-men-over-women song, she may acquiesce her power and view men as greater authorities than herself.

Female counselor–female client is probably one of the most emotionally intense dyads. This dyad was found to allow for a fuller exploration of childhood experiences. Female clients, because of socialization, may challenge the female counselor and question her competence. Because of gender role socialization, therapists of both genders have difficulties with a whole array of aggressive behaviors in their women clients (Kaplan, 1987). When both the client and counselor are lesbian, the therapeutic relationship is shaped by the intersections of gender and sexuality in that both parties attempt to honor the mutuality inherent in empathic counseling (Slater, 1997). The very process of the counselor "coming out" to her client is an act of mutuality, and yet lesbian therapists should not be the only therapists engaging in this type of self-disclosure. It is also the task of the heterosexual counselor to disclose. Robinson and Watt (2001) summarized this point and stated, "The socially endorsed experience of heterosexuality and the unconscious and unearned privilege afforded heterosexuals often deems them unaware of the importance to transition through sexual identity formation. It is presumed that sexual identity formation pertains to gay people only" (p. 594). People who are heterosexually identified are sociopolitically advantaged and privileged (Mohr, 2002). Hoffman (2004) argued that lack of attention to identity development for majority group members is the inadvertent perpetuation of the need for minority group members to explain their realities.

Regardless of the gender of the counselor and the client, empathy is the key ingredient in therapy (Pinderhughes, 1989). **Empathy** is the ability of the therapist to surrender himself or herself to the affect of another while cognitively structuring that experience so as to comprehend its meaning in terms of other aspects of the client's psyche (p. 13). It requires that the counselor be comfortable and familiar with the world of affect and the nature of connections between people

(Kaplan, 1987). Empathy allows for a merger of people's experiences and understanding—not toward enmeshment but attunement. "In true empathic exchange, each is both object and subject, mutually engaged in affecting and being affected, knowing and being known" (Jordan, 1997a, p. 15). There are power differentials within counseling that are part of the professional relationship, yet empathy and mutuality are impeded by unacknowledged hierarchies within the counseling event when they reinforce hegemonic power dynamics (Mencher, 1997).

Therapists may disapprove of women who show power and controlling, competitive, and autonomous behavior while disliking behavior typically regarded as feminine (e.g., self-depreciation, submissiveness). Some male therapists may subconsciously dread women dominating them and fear their own vulnerability to female aggression. Female therapists may also fear the eruption of their own anger toward men, which can have an adverse impact on the therapeutic relationship. It is also possible that some therapists are afraid to experience the powerlessness that comes with examining social injustice, racism, and oppression (Bernardez, 1987).

Independent of race, ethnicity, and sexual orientation, male and female children and adolescents receive similar gender-appropriate messages. Poor White men and upper-class men of color are socialized to function and be in positions of control (whether they actually *are* is a different matter). For this reason, seeking help is incompatible with the masculine role. Middle-class White women and poor women of color are socialized to emphasize the needs and wants of others, usually before their own. Despite the similarities, more research is needed on the specific effects of class and other sources of differences as mediating traditional gender role messages.

Depression among college men and the low likelihood of their seeking out psychological services suggests that college counseling centers are in a prime position to do outreach (residence halls, orientations, classrooms, student development). Helping people reclaim the parts of themselves they have forfeited to conform to society's role expectations, both at home and at work, is a form of healing. In addition, men can be encouraged to reframe their notions of counseling. Good and Wood (1995) said that "changing men's view of counseling might consist of efforts to emphasize that participating in counseling is an activity involving personal courage and strength that is displayed through facing and sharing one's concerns" (p. 73).

A primary theme articulated throughout this work is that more differences are found within groups than between them. The need for mental health professionals to be aware of the salience of physical attractiveness as a status variable in everyday life is crucial to understanding clients as whole beings. Narrow definitions of physical attractiveness have implications for mental health attitudes, body validation, and the development of coping strategies to cope meaningfully with both unanticipated and normal maturational changes in physical appearance and ability. Integrated into this discussion is an examination of the culture's clear preference for the able-bodied and intolerance for persons with disabilities.

GENDER IDENTITY MODELS

The Womanist Model

Ossana, Helms, and Leonard's (1992) womanist identity model, adapted from Cross's four-stage Nigresence model, is helpful in illuminating the process of self-awareness. The first stage in the womanist identity model is *preencounter*, which maintains that women at this stage accept traditional or stereotypical notions of womanhood. Such notions are often steeped in women's reliance on others for approval and legitimacy. Naturally, the locus of control for women in this stage would be external. The second stage, *encounter,* occurs when a woman has an experience wherein she begins to question notions of womanhood and becomes aware of the prevalence of sexism in society. A woman's discovery that her male colleague with less education and experience is paid significantly more than she is could be described as an encounter. In the third stage, *immersion/emersion,* the woman surrounds herself with other women and literature about and by women. She is critical of the patriarchal context of society and may experience turbulent emotions, such as guilt and anger, toward herself for having been selfless for so long and at society for its history of promoting gender inequity. During the fourth and last stage, *internalization,* the woman defines womanhood on her own terms and is not bound by external definitions or dictates about what it means to be a woman. Research conducted by Carter and Parks (1996), using the womanist scale on Black and White women, found a relationship between womanist identity attitudes and mental health. No relationships were found among African American women, but they were found among European American women. More specifically, White women (*n* = 147) who were not at the highest or internalization stage of womanist identity were more likely to feel depressed, anxious, and scrutinized or under attack. These findings suggest that White women pay a psychological tax for pushing back against the dictates of hegemony. They also pay for their dependence upon hegemony.

White Male Identity Development Model

Scott and Robinson (2001) presented a circular White male racial identity model. According to the model, movement occurs in multiple directions; however, one type, a term preferred over stage, is most descriptive. It is a theoretically driven model and influenced by Helms (1995), Myers et al. (1991), and Sue and Sue (1990). This model addresses "the convergence of race and gender attitudes that White men exhibit as a result of socially constructed attitudes regarding appropriate displays of manhood" (p. 418). It could be used when counseling White men to help them gain insight into how race and gender intersect and contribute to problem presentation.

Type I, Noncontact, describes men who represent the status quo, deny racism, and seek power and privilege. Type II, Claustrophobic, characterizes the man who feels that other races are closing in on him. Men whose lives are characterized by this type are disillusioned by the American dream. There is a feeling that power and privilege are going to other races. Type III, Conscious Identity, describes the man who is in dissonance and feels this dissonance between existing belief systems and realities. The Type IV, Empirical, is a man who questions his role in racism and oppression. Finally, Type V, Optimal, describes the man who understands how his struggle for power and privilege has contributed to racism and oppression.

IMPLICATIONS FOR COUNSELORS AND PSYCHOLOGISTS

One reverberating point throughout this text is that U.S. society is highly gendered and has rather rigid notions about appropriate modes of being for men and women (Kaplan, 1987). Thus, the power of the therapeutic event is found in the interpersonal relationship between client and therapist. The importance of clinical skills and training is not being minimized; however, the relational bond based on mutuality and trust is primary.

Over time, women and men maintain and modify their sex role–related perceptions, attitudes, and behaviors. Sex role typology is complicated. Individual differences in determining sex roles must be allowed so as not to stereotype people, yet it is important to incorporate gender role socialization in working with clients. For instance, educating women about the relationship between perceived discrimination, collective self-esteem, personal self-esteem, and psychological distress may provide tools for understanding their own experiences (Fischer & Holz, 2007).

Gender dyad makes a difference in the counseling event. Often, the male and client roles are rather discontinuous. For instance, the personal characteristics of the male role often focus on physical strength and accomplishment, whereas the client role emphasizes acknowledgment of weakness. In the male role, men are often punished for seeking help, whereas in the client role, help seeking is reinforced (Skovholt, 1993).

Gender can add another dimension to the therapeutic process. Good and Mintz (1990) found that between two men, a male counselor and a male client, restricted emotionality and homophobia present themselves as issues. As unfortunate as it is, homophobia may prevent male clinicians from showing concern and care for male clients. A male client may feel tremendous angst and fear if he experiences warmth toward a male counselor. It is also likely that a male counselor could be embarrassed at his feelings toward another man's intense emotional expressions. The client could also be ashamed to disclose. When the counselor is male and the client is female, a different dynamic can surface. One form of bias is for male counselors to respond to female clients as sex objects. Moreover, because of socialization, a male counselor may adopt a one-up type of position with the client. The client may also have difficulty expressing to the counselor emotions that she may subconsciously feel are intolerable. Kaplan (1987) found that women with male therapists saw themselves as less self-possessed, less open, and more self-critical than did women with female therapists.

More researchers are conducting rich qualitative research to better understand gender themes. Phillips and Daniluk (2004) tape-recorded interviews with seven women between the ages of 30 and 57 who had been sexually abused as children. Women were asked questions such as:

1. How would you describe your recovery process?
2. What aspects of who you are as a person do you feel have remained constant or stable throughout your life?
3. In what ways do you think your past abuse experiences inform your sense of who you are today?
4. How has this changed over time?

Several themes emerged:

1. An increasing sense of visibility, congruence, and connection
2. An emerging sense of self-definition and self-acceptance
3. A shift in worldview
4. A sense of regret over what has been lost
5. A sense of resiliency and growth

In examining the constructs of race and gender among college students, Cokley (2001) conducted research on academic self-concept, racial centrality, and academic motivation of 257 African American college students. Ninety-two were male and 165 were female. Packets were given to these students during summer school at two historically Black colleges. The purpose of the study was to examine gender as an important variable in understanding the psychosocial development of African American students. The researchers found that women scored significantly higher on one of the extrinsic motivation scales (the Extrinsic Motivation Identified Regulation scale). Men had significantly higher scores on the Atrinsic Motivation scale, which represents neither intrinsic nor extrinsic motivation. The researchers concluded that Black female students were more motivated about being in college than were Black male students, who evidenced a lack of motivation. In tandem with the larger society, the college experience for many Black males is perceived as alienating. The number of Black males enrolling in and graduating from college has fallen off sharply over the years (Cokley, 2001). The lack of difference in race centrality scores between males and females may suggest that for both genders, race is a central and dominant construct.

The socialization differences for men and women have been widely documented. Men continue to be socialized toward assertiveness, power, and independence—to restrict emotion. Women are socialized toward nurturance, compliance, and direct achievement through affiliation with others, particularly men (Mintz & O'Neil, 1990). Such socialization patterns in early childhood have implications for relationships and can enhance a client's vulnerability to selflessness or excessive individualism. Because humans have myriad emotions, it is important for therapists to confront clients' beliefs about rigid gendered emotions while having the ability to hold women's intense anger and men's overwhelming sadness and fear (Brown & Gilligan, 1992).

The role of women in multicultural counseling and psychology is being explored in greater depth. Initially, the literature took a monolithic approach to counseling that failed to show how gender interacts with other identities as well as forces such as racism, sexism, class elitism, and homophobia. Gender similarities do not negate racial differences, nor do racial similarities negate gender differences.

CASE STUDY

BUILDING RAPPORT

Alena is 15. She is Mexican American and lives with her parents, who brought her to counseling because Alena appears anxious and often has panic attacks. Her mom says she cries at the drop of a hat. Alena likes her therapist, Lima. Alena confides in Lima that she enjoys smoking and that although she is a virgin, she has been pressured by her friends (boys and girls alike) to have sex. Lima asks Alena if she is personally interested in being sexually active; Alena replies that she does not know. Lima explores Alena's relationship with her parents to assess the connections that are there and to ascertain what might be driving Alena's restlessness and feelings of insecurity. Alena says that her father is rather sarcastic with her and that she feels "stupid" in his presence. She says her father smokes but would be livid if he found out Alena smokes as well. Alena remarks that her mother is mousey and does not stand up to her father when he yells at either one of them. Alena wishes that her mother was not such a wimp when it came to dealing with her husband. Alena feels bored a lot—she and her parents don't really spend time together. She likes a boy at her school who is two years older than she is. Lima asks Alena what she likes about him. Alena is not sure, other than she thinks he is cute. Lima discovers over several therapy sessions that the boy Alena likes uses drugs and alcohol. He has been pressuring Alena to have sex with him. In July, Alena comes into one of her sessions with a turtleneck on. Lima asks why she is wearing a turtleneck when it is so hot out. Alena shrugs her shoulders. Lima lets the issue go, but during the session, Alena inadvertently moves the turtleneck down, and Lima sees hickies on her neck, as well as bruising. When she inquires, Alena blushes—she's deeply embarrassed. Alena says that she and Doug, the guy

(Continued)

she has had a crush on, are having sex. Lima asks Alena why she decided to have sex. Alena said that she did not mean to, but Doug said they did it because Alena got him so excited that he couldn't stop himself.

QUESTIONS

1. What appear to be the critical issues facing Alena?
2. What DSM–IV–TR diagnosis might be missed for Alena?
3. What are some of the gender dynamics operating in Alena's life?
4. What might help Alena's parents in parenting their child?

DISCUSSION AND INTEGRATION

Alena and Lima

A major gender script that both males and females receive is that men are entitled to their sexuality in ways that women are not. Part of this entitlement absolves men of responsibility, given the enormity and legitimacy of their desire. A huge burden is heaped on the woman to control the man's sexuality (Jordan, 1997a). Prior to Alena leaving the office, Lima needs to ascertain the meaning of Alena's statement about her initiation into sexual intercourse. Was Alena forced into unwanted sexual activity? If gender were more central to the analysis or if the intersections of race and gender were seen as relevant to the improvement of both men and women's lives, how would communities of color be transformed. (Cole & Guy-Sheftall, 2003).

For girls and women of color, race, culture, social class, and urbanization interact with gender and create female responses and positions that are diverse and fluctuating (Abrams, 2002). Often adolescents who are depressed exhibit irritable behavior that is mistaken for behavioral misconduct (e.g., oppositional defiant disorder) but is actually deep sadness. In some instances, there is a combination of conduct disturbance and a mood disorder; however, the context and the length of time that the child has had the symptoms needs to be known. Alena could be depressed for many valid reasons: she has a fractured relationship with her father and thus feels rejected by him, she lacks a circle of women with whom to confide about her multiple identities, she is 15, and she has questions about sex and boys and relationships yet she feels silenced by both of her parents. It is highly possible that Lima, a therapist who is old enough to be Alena's mother, is able to create a holding environment for Alena's sadness. Lima asked Alena's mother about Alena's early childhood. As a young child of 7, Alena was reserved yet tended to be oversocialized with somewhat negative appraisals of herself (intropunitive). Block and Block (2006) indicated in their 30-year longitudinal study that depressive tendencies identified in young adulthood are related to prior observer-based evaluations from parents and teachers.

Alena's parents love her. There are, however, narratives that Alena has to share that may be hard for her parents to hear. Women tend to be socialized not to express anger; sadness and fear are more readily tolerated. Alena needs to learn that anger is an acceptable emotion but there are positive and nondestructive ways to release it. Brown (2003) is critical of the culture and its suppression of girls' strong feelings. To mediate their frustrations, fears, marginalization, and anger, girls will fight with other girls. Alena's feelings of rejection and betrayal from her father contributes to her emotions.

Alena's parents and other wise people can offer Alena a circle of stones, a place to go and to be as healing occurs. Alena would benefit richly from a mentor, someone who can nurture her development and focus on the communal aspects of being in community with others (Portman & Garrett, 2005). It can be helpful for clients when counselors consult with colleagues concerning clinical matters. Hoffman et al. (2005) present a feminist and multicultural model of consulting wherein the consultant functions as a change agent with the goal of helping both the counselor and the client in a nonhierarchical manner. (p. 60)?

Summary

In this chapter, the construct of gender in women's and men's lives was considered. The socialization process, as well as biological dimensions, was explored. Counselors need to be aware of the consequences of gender socialization on their personal lives and on those of their clients. Not to do so is to ignore the powerful role of gender in life. Implications for the development of a healthy relationship with the body were presented. Multiple components of physical attractiveness exist and encompass facial beauty, skin color, body size, strength, visible signs of aging, height, weight, and hair length and texture. A case study examined multiple themes in the life of an adolescent teen. Issues in clinical diagnoses were discussed.

Converging
Socioeconomic Class

> *The belief that anyone, regardless of his or her socioeconomic
> history or social position, can make it to the top if he or she
> works hard is undoubtedly one of the most cherished beliefs
> in the United States. Evidence to the contrary seems
> to do little to deter this deeply held cultural belief.*
>
> APA Task Force

This chapter is dedicated to an examination of the intersections of socioeconomic class with other aspects of identity, such as race, sexuality, gender, and ethnicity. A case study is provided to facilitate the integration of the material discussed throughout the chapter. The implications of a middle-class bias on the training of students in graduate counseling programs are discussed.

THE INVISIBILITY OF CLASS AS A VARIABLE IN COUNSELING

Class is ubiquitous and yet it is largely understudied, particularly as it relates to counseling and therapeutic effectiveness (Liu et al., 2004). Social class position is largely determined by income, education, and occupation. According to Liu et al. (2004), "social class may be defined as an individual's position within an economic hierarchy that is determined by his or her income, education level, and occupation; the individual is also aware of his or her place in the economic hierarchy and of others who may share a similar position" (p. 8). A primary component of social class is power which exists across individual, institutional, and societal levels (Appleby, Colon, & Hamilton, 2001).

Disciplines such as sociology, public health, medicine, feminist psychology, and anthropology have devoted ample attention to class issues, particularly because class affects educational equity, access to health care, and collectivistic versus individualistic societies (Fine, 1991; Lareau, 1997; Ogbu, 1997; Institute of Medicine, 2003). In counseling, the investigation of class as a status variable has been largely neglected, although researchers are bridging this gap. Liu et al. (2004) conducted a content analysis of the frequency of use of social class in the empirical and theoretical literature in three counseling journals: *Journal of Counseling Psychology, Journal of Multicultural Counseling and Development*, and *Journal of Counseling and Development*. Results of social class were typically reported in the method section. In fact, of the empirical articles that used social class, 31% did so in the method section of the article, and only 4% used social class in the data analysis. Liu et al. (2004) stated, "although social class may have been regarded as an important demographic variable to measure in the method section, few studies analyzed the participant data or incorporated social class findings into the discussion section" (p. 15). It was concluded that social class is an infrequently used variable in empirical counseling research.

Myths about class might contribute to this neglect. One myth states that we are a classless society and a second that we are a middle-class nation. The third myth is that we are all getting richer, and the final myth is that everyone has an equal change to succeed (Appleby, Colon, & Hamilton, 2001). Meritocracy, fairness, equality, and beating the odds are part of the nation's cultural fabric, regardless of one's indebtedness or income.

Data on class, income, and poverty challenge prevailing discourses about justice and a level playing field for all Americans. The number of people in poverty in 2010 was 46.2 million. This is the largest number in the 52 years for which poverty estimates have been published (De-Navs, Proctor, & Smith, 2011). In 2010, the poverty rate for the nation was 15.1%, which reflects an increase from 14.4% in 2009. Women have higher poverty rates than men. In 2009, their poverty rate was 13.9%, compared to 10.5% for men (Legal Momentum, 2010). The highest poverty rates were among African Americans and Native Americans. The lowest were among White Americans and Asian Americans. (See Table 12.1.)

The working class is about 35% of the population, with mainly blue-collar jobs. Tenure is not a reality in most of these jobs; thus people contend with job insecurity and heavy production pressures. The middle class is roughly 50% of the nation, and the upper class is the wealthiest 20% of the nation, who own nearly 80% of the wealth (Appleby et al., 2001).

TABLE 12.1 Poverty Rates by Year and Race, 2009–2010		
	2009	2010
Nation	14.3	15.1
Male Householder	16.9	15.8
Female Householder	29.9	31.6
Whites	9.4	9.9
Blacks	25.8	27.4
Latinos	25.3	26.6
Asians	12.9	12.9

US Census Bureau, 2011

To cope with the loss of employment, underemployment, food insecurity, and fore-closed homes, during the Great Recession which began in December 2007 and ended in June 2009, millions of Americans "doubled-up" or moved in with family and non-relatives. This expression was not found in the 3rd edition of this text. Among adults, 61.7 million (27.7%) were doubled-up in 2007. In 2011, 69.2 million (30.0%) lived in doubled-up households. It is important to note that although the adult population increased by only 3.8% between 2007 and 2011, the number of doubled-up adults increased by 12.2% (DeNavas-Walt, Proctor, & Smith, 2011).

THE INTERSECTIONS OF CLASS

Social class is multifaceted and complex. In the social sciences, there has been a tendency to minimize race issues and esteem class, particularly in light of increases in the numbers of middle-class families of color. Class, particularly for people of color, does not operate as a primary status trait because race and gender tend to be more conspicuous than class and can override it. "In the race-class-gender-nexus, race constitutes more than a social construction. It is a permanent and salient identity marker, self-indicator, and status locator that defines one's being, along with gender, sexuality, and class" (Wilkinson, 1997, p. 270).

Within a materialistic and consumeristic society, the structural inequities that can work against a person's best efforts to be successful can be overlooked. It is perhaps easy to blame people for failing to transcend their situations despite structural and institutional forces. For instance, women systematically earn less money than men. Often, men in nontraditional jobs (e.g., nursing) earn more money than their female counterparts (Chusmir, 1990).

Ogbu (1997) argued that "the inequality between Blacks and Whites is one not of class stratification but of racial stratification" (p. 766). **Racial stratification** is "the hierarchical organization of socially defined 'races' or groups on the basis of assumed inborn differences in status, honor, or material worth, symbolized in the United States by skin color" (p. 768). Among the foreign born population, 44% were naturalized citizens. The poverty rate among this group was 11.3% in 2010. This was not statistically different from 2009, however, the number in poverty increased to 1.9 million in 2010 from 1.7 million in 2009. For those who were not citizens, the poverty rate actually rose to 26.7% in 2010 from 25.1% in 2009. The

2010 number in poverty which was 5.7 million was not statistically different from 2009 (De-Navas-Walt, Proctor, & Smith, 2011). Children's poverty rate is higher than any other age group. In 2010, the poverty rate for children was higher than for 18–64 year olds as well as those 65 and older. Children accounted for 35.5% of people in poverty, but only 24.4% of the total population. In one year, from 2009 to 2010, the poverty rate for children under age 18 increased to 22.0% from 20.7% (DeNavas-Walt, Proctor, & Smith, 2011). Children suffer because of the economic situation of their parents, across race, married and single alike. However, higher unemployment, underemployment, and incarceration rates of Black, Latino, and Native American men have an adverse impact on the social and economic profiles of women of color who are most likely to be in relationships with men from their same ethnic or racial background. In understanding women and children's poverty, it is important to consider socio-political variables (e.g., the unemployment rate among African Americans with college degrees is similar to the unemployment rate of Whites who are high school graduates (Newman & Newman, 2010). Not to do so is to run the risk of pathologizing people.

Membership in groups that are socially constructed as having more value is a mediating variable (Robinson, 1999a). Middle-class women share some of the experiences of poor women; however, educational status and occupational position afford benefits across a variety of sectors: living in a neighborhood without gun violence, having access to cancer-fighting fruits and vegetables (healthier food is more expensive), and having access to a doctor when one is sick. Class does not negate the effects of racism, although class may minimize these effects. People who are poor experience more chronic health problems, live in crowded places, contend with noise and injury on the job, and are more likely to engage in behaviors associated with chronic disease. Over time, these experiences contribute to lower life expectancy (Newman, 1999).

In American society, success is defined and measured by material acquisition. Homes, cars, boats, jewelry, and other possessions are indicators of income and occupation; wealth also serves as a proxy variable for moral attributes such as being honest, hard-working, smart, and morally good. The socialization practices that most men are exposed to tie manhood to being a provider and having success in one's chosen career (Swanson, 1993). The inability to be successful in this fashion has historically and continues to have far-reaching implications for men who, for a variety of personal and systemic reasons, are unable to attain success as measured by high income.

CLASS: AN IDENTITY CONSTRUCT

Wealth does not automatically translate to feelings of power, security, and privilege, or low-income to feelings of anxiety, depression, and low self-esteem. Class has psychological effects on people's lives. For instance, McLoyd and Wilson (1992) found that working- and lower-class parents placed less emphasis on happiness during the rearing of their children. In the case of these parents, survival issues took precedence over happiness. Robinson (1990) found in her analysis of Black student persistence that the students who were most likely to graduate from college in four years came from two-parent households and had participated in anticipatory socialization experiences such as Future Teachers of America and Future Business Leaders while in high school. These variables, associated with persistence and success, and as measured by graduation, are representations of class but not necessarily income yet support the effects of class on career commitment and vocational identity. Race affects gender- and class-linked messages. Renzetti and Curran (1992) cited research that stated

Storytelling: Small House

A friend of mine was talking about her school age daughter who was the only child of color in her school. I asked her if her daughter struggled with being the only brown child. She said, "Somewhat—in the beginning, the children would want to touch her hair or asked her why her skin was so dark". To her surprise, my friend noticed that her daughter was mostly influenced by class. She had taken her child to visit a classmate and after the visit, her child asked, "Mommy, why is their house so small?"

Black boys and girls tend to be more independent than White boys and girls. Parents' strong emphasis on hard work and ambition and the less frequent gender stereotyping and exposure to strong mothers that characterizes the lives of many Black children may explain this finding (Cole & Guy-Sheftall, 2003).

Storck (1998) proposed that the definition of social class be expanded to include psychosocial class, which is "defined by a person's education and occupation, and correlated behaviors, thoughts, and feelings" (p. 102). Storck also observed that a working-class person tends not to be defined as college educated and is typically employed as a factory worker, with thoughts such as, "life starts after working hours," or "psychotherapy means that they will lock you up." Storck also stated that "both 'lower' and 'higher' ranking individuals and groups may feel disadvantaged or disempowered, in different contexts" (p. 101). However, a person from a lower psychosocial class may have higher feelings of marginalization or feel ignored and denied access. These class-determined feelings, according to Storck, are important contributors to depressive symptoms.

People can have similar jobs, incomes, and educational levels and have a different perspective about money as a function of environment and context. (See Storytelling: *Small House*.) Counselors are encouraged to take a contextualized approach to clients and consider multiple issues: sociohistorical, or the ways in which people's histories have been silenced and misrepresented; sociostructural, which includes legal, economic, and educational systems; and sociopolitical, or the distribution of power (Liu & Arguello, 2006).

MIDDLE-CLASS BIAS AND COUNSELOR TRAINING

Counseling students receive very little information about socioeconomic class as it relates to influences on identity development and subsequent implications for counseling. Moreover, the training caters to the haves, as opposed to other social classes (e.g., working and lower classes). A client's discussions about economic exploitation and oppression can be extremely difficult for a counselor to hear if the counselor is a member of the very group about which the client is talking/bemoaning (Cardemil & Battle, 2003). The therapist's inability to hear should not be the client's problem, but it becomes the client's problem when the counselor is unavailable emotionally.

Part of middle-class bias is related to the nature of graduate education itself, which is steeped in privilege. Graduate students are college graduates who have distinguished themselves from others in the general population as capable of meeting the rigors of an academic program. Having status as a graduate student is an esteemed position in society that carries middle-class connotations, independent of students' class-linked childhood socialization experiences or limited incomes.

The graduate school environment acculturates its members to a middle-class orientation given the emphasis on success, competition, control, and individualism. In addition, there is an expectation of future employment and class mobility. Graduate students are preparing themselves for positions that will designate their middle-class social standing and prestige. It is hoped that students' future salaries will reflect their elite standing. The pay can be modest, but the significance of the professional service and high status are evident.

Despite the privileged status of graduate school, some students make considerable financial sacrifices (e.g., working and going to school, borrowing money from family, securing substantial school loans) to attend school. Currently at Northeastern University, institution, each credit costs over $1,000. Graduate students spend over $60,000 for their two-year master's degree. The majority of graduate students in the United States could be described as embodying traditional values anchored within a middle-class framework: success, motivation, perseverance, self-reliance, Standard English, hard work, and delayed gratification. For some first-generation college and graduate students, the delayed gratification and financial indebtedness may not make sense to working-class family members. The family member who has received an education and physically moved away from the family of origin may be perceived by working-class siblings or parents as not belonging anymore due to different ways of speaking and life experiences. (See Storytelling: *You're Just Going to Have Kids Anyway*.)

What does it mean for a middle-class bias to pervade the training of counselors? Is it possible that the effects of socioeconomic class on psychosocial identity have been neglected in the counseling literature because the middle-class bias is so pervasive and has rendered the profession oblivious to itself? Sue and Sue (1990) identified two aspects of middle-class bias within counselor training. The first pertains to the emphasis on Standard English within society at large. The second refers to the 50-minute counseling sessions that typically characterize the counseling event.

Standard English represents a class issue because dialect, accent, and use of English are often used in drawing conclusions about a person's educational, occupational, income, intellectual, legal, and ultimately class status. Standard English operates as a form of power and access within society. Delpit (1997) discussed the power embodied in language and dialect. She argued against obliterating the unique cultural or speaking style of a group, yet she advocated educating people about the sociopolitical context in which standards and rules regarding the status quo exist. She advocates speaking honestly to children about the beauty and value of

Storytelling: You're Just Going to Have Kids Anyway

About 20 years ago, I got engaged. My fiancé had found a job on the West coast. I was on the East coast. I was in the throes of trying to figure out what to do. I wanted to be with my fiancé, but I had worked very hard to finish my doctoral degree. I had a good job as an Assistant Professor, and I was up for tenure. I did not have a job on the West coast, and I had no intention of going to California jobless. I was speaking with a family member, the one who told me to get a job as I was telling her I had been accepted into Harvard. She said earnestly, "You should just go to California with him. You're just going to have babies anyway." This family member was speaking from her position as a woman who had been taught by family and society that a woman's career was not nearly as important as a man's. I did not go to California, and our engagement did not result in marriage. I stayed on the East coast and was promoted and tenured.

their language and cultural style while helping them understand the political power games at stake. Delpit demonstrates the dialectic: a "both/and" perspective, in which on the one hand the cultural style is embraced and esteemed, while on the other hand students understand that others perceived as powerful (e.g., teachers, prospective employers) may denigrate it. This means having knowledge of two realities: appropriate contexts in which one's language can be celebrated and inappropriate contexts in which it will not.

Cultural encapsulation, or defining reality on the basis of a limited unidimensional cultural orientation (Wrenn, 1962), contributes to counselors' bias toward normative standards: being White, able-bodied, heterosexual, and using standard English (Reynolds & Pope, 1991). Schofield's (1964) use of the acronym YAVIS (young, attractive, verbal, intelligent, and successful) may enable counselors to see their tendency to favor this type of client. Perhaps it is related to the counselor's perception that the client is more similar to the counselor's actual or imagined sense of self.

Noticeable differences in communication and behavioral styles (e.g., the use of slang, street talk, or non-Standard English) between the client and counselor can contribute to counselors' discomfort with clients from lower socioeconomic groups. If the counselor is bothered that the client is on a sliding scale, countertransference can present a clinical obstacle.

Some counselors from middle-class backgrounds may not be equipped to deal with the multiple challenges and life problems that characterize some of their poor clients' lives, such as homelessness, pregnancy, appalling living conditions, hunger, mistreatment by the police and schools, crime, transience, and chronic violence or the threat of violence (Boyd-Franklin, 2003).

Another middle-class bias in counseling identified by Sue and Sue (1990) is the 50-minute counseling session. Neither the American Psychological Association (APA) nor the American Counseling Association (ACA) ethics codes dictate 45- or 50-minute therapy sessions. Some clients have work schedules that fluctuate from week to week. This disallows having a fixed day and time for therapy weekly. For example, a client may work the 11:00 p.m. to 7:00 a.m. shift at a gas station one week. The next week, their work schedule might be from 3:00 p.m. to 11:00 p.m. Pulling double shifts is a way for people to make considerable overtime—the cost is seen in disordered sleep, which reeks havoc on wakefulness. For some workers, their schedules may not be posted until a few days prior to the beginning of a new shift.

To accommodate each unique client, particularly in the absence of third-party reimbursement schedules that are strict in their requirement of 50-minute sessions, 90-minute sessions every other week might be preferable and should be offered if it is consistent with the clinician's schedule. A flexible schedule applies to a variety of clients across socioeconomic groups, from highly paid physicians on call to shift workers receiving minimum wage.

Which privileges are professionals willing to relinquish to better accommodate a diverse clientele? Wachtel (2002) stated, "It is extremely difficult to be successful in therapeutic work with patients outside the White middle class if one maintains traditional notions about 'the frame'" (p. 205).

Class issues are not discussed in counselor training largely because the context in which class occurs is normative and reflective of an American value. An implicit expectation that clients have jobs and conventional work hours based on standard work fuels this oversight. What about clients who do not own cars, live in cities where reliable public transportation is nonexistent, are unable to leave 15 minutes early from their jobs without being docked, or spend an entire afternoon catching and waiting for buses while having to walk as well? Some clients experience obstacles in their efforts to receive therapy as a direct result of the ways class shapes people's lives, including our own. Do we subtract the time from the client's hour, even if another client is not scheduled immediately, because of the middle-class cultural adage that "time is money"? As mental health professionals, we need to make a living. Recruiting full-paying clients to balance those who are on a sliding scale is a way to make our professional services more accessible to all people. Conversely, if clients drive up for their appointments in expensive cars and wear expensive clothing, how are we affected by these indicators of wealth or debt? Components of class include art, music, tastes, religion, food, and furniture (Bourdieu, 1984). When high-status clients appear, how self-conscious do we become of our work environments and other indicators of our proximity to middle-class status? How might our personal reactions, intimidation or admiration, affect our ability to extend our best professional practice to wealthy clients? Counselors need to look beneath the glamour of socioeconomic class and privilege to avoid being blinded by its allure. There are clients with financial means who come to therapy in great pain.

THE FLUIDITY OF CLASS-STATUS

Neither affluence nor poverty erases the effects of early conditioning. Middle-class persons can move into a lower income level because of unemployment, physical and mental illness, violence, divorce or loss of another significant relationship, disability, death of the primary provider, or traumatic event. Class is fluid, and this issue can be overlooked if it is assumed that clients and their counselors have had similar and consistent class socialization experiences from childhood to adulthood. A change in income does not translate into a loss of values to which one has become accustomed.

In 2010, real median household income was $49,445, a 2.3% decline from 2009 when it was $50,599 (see Table 12.2). Since 2007, median household income has declined 6.4% (from $52,823) and is now 7.1% below the median household income peak ($53,252) that occurred in 1999 (De-Navas, Proctor, & Smith, 2011). In 2007, the median annual income for all groups was higher than it was in 2008. Among White, non-Hispanic male full-time workers 15 years of age or older, the 2007 median was $38,809 compared with $22,520 for White, non-Hispanic women, $25,390 for Latino men, $17,392 for Latinas, $26,814 for Black men, and $20,511 for Black women (US Census Bureau, 2008). In 2008, the median annual income for White, non-Hispanic male full-time workers 15 years of age or older was $37,409 compared with $21,749 for White, non-Hispanic women, $24,003 for Latino men, $16,417 for Latinas, $25,254 for Black men, and $20,197 for Black women (US Census Bureau, 2008). (See Table 12.3.)

TABLE 12.2 2009 and 2010 Median Income of Householder by Race

	2009	2010
Nation	$50,599	$49,445
Asian	$66,550	$64,308
Black	$33,122	$32,068
Latino	$38,667	$37,759
White	$52,717	$51,846

TABLE 12.3 2007 and 2008 Median Income by Race and Gender				
	2007		**2008**	
	M	**F**	**M**	**F**
Asian	$38,622	$25,291	$36,607	$23,109
Black	$26,814	$20,511	$25,254	$20,197
Latino	$25,390	$17,392	$24,003	$16,417
White	$38,809	$22,520	$37,409	$21,749

MIDDLE-CLASS BIAS AND ETHICAL STANDARDS

The roots of a middle-class cultural bias are reflected in the official documents used to standardize the profession and provide its membership with rules and guidelines for professional practice. For example, the ACA Code of Ethics (Section A.10.d) approaches bartering for services with caution. However, it has become flexible in its position from just 10 years ago when it stated that counselors "refrain from accepting goods or services in return for counseling services because such arrangements create inherent potential for conflict, exploitation, and distortion of the professional relationship" (1995, Section A.10.c). The 2005 ethical code reads as follows:

> Counselors may barter only if the relationship is not exploitive or harmful and does not place the counselor in an unfair advantage, if the client requests it, and if such arrangements are in accepted practice among professionals in the community. Counselors consider the cultural implications of bartering and discuss relevant concerns with clients and document such agreements in a clear written contract. (Section A.10.c)

In rural, cultural/ethnic, and/or agricultural communities, money may not be as readily available or esteemed as currency. A woman may not be able to afford $140 an hour for therapy (or even a greatly reduced amount based on a sliding scale), but she may value doing housework, gardening, or providing child care as a means of paying for the therapy services rendered to her. This sounds like bartering and understandably is problematic. Zur (2006) said, "Bartering of goods is more likely to constitute a boundary crossing but not usually a dual relationship; bartering of services always creates dual relationships" (p. 19).

The APA (2002) Code of Ethics does not refute bartering within the context of psychotherapy. Section 6.06 states, "barter is the acceptance of goods, services, or other non-monetary remuneration from clients/patients in return for psychological services. Psychologists may barter only if (1) it is not clinically contraindicated, and (2) the resulting arrangement is not exploitative." Again, in certain contexts, dual relationships may not be readily avoidable and are the "hallmark of interconnected, rural settings" (Zur, 2006, p. 12). In a small town, dual relationships can look like the therapist shopping at a store that a client owns or going to the same church or temple, or children attending the same school. It is a middle-class bias that presumes such avoidance is preferred. Collectivistic communities are dependent on overlapping relationships where role diffusion cannot be avoided. Counselors, themselves, may be involved in conflicting roles (Pedersen, 1997). If there are few counselors of color in a community (urban and rural), it is likely that clients of color and the select counselors will frequent the same churches and community and recreational activities and may even have the same employer. Thus, the clear division of roles assumes an abundance of resources that are diverse enough so as not to intersect. The assumption is that clients and their counselors function and live out their lives in different social and political circles. This simply is not the case in some rural communities, communities of color, and ethnic communities—where, for instance, the family rabbi might be the marriage counselor and the child's Hebrew tutor.

ACA and APA are concerned with clients' well being and mental health professionals adhering to ethical codes with professional integrity. At the same time, APA recognizes the nature of multiple relationships and says in Section 3.05,

a. A multiple relationship occurs when a psychologist is in a professional role with a person and (1) at the same time is in another role with the same person, (2) at the same time is in a relationship with a person closely associated with or related to the person with whom the psychologist has the professional relationship, or (3) promises to enter into another relationship in the future with the person or a person closely associated with or related to the person.

   A psychologist refrains from entering into a multiple relationship if the multiple relationship could reasonably be expected to impair the psychologist's objectivity, competence, or effectiveness in performing his or her functions as a psychologist, or otherwise risks exploitation or harm to the person with whom the professional relationship exists.

   Multiple relationships that would not reasonably be expected to cause impairment or risk exploitation or harm are not unethical.

b. If a psychologist finds that, due to unforeseen factors, a potentially harmful multiple relationship has arisen, the psychologist takes reasonable steps to resolve it with due regard for the best interests of the affected person and maximal compliance with the Ethics Code.

c. When psychologists are required by law, institutional policy, or extraordinary circumstances to serve in more than one role in judicial or administrative proceedings, at the outset they clarify role expectations and the extent of confidentiality and thereafter as changes occur.

The current ACA Code of Ethics does not discourage dual relationships and has changed the ethical guidelines to respect healthy and therapeutic interactions between client and counselor.

A middle-class bias is seen in the very basic tenets of therapy, such as confidentiality. Students learn early in their programs that mental health professionals can be sued for violating a client's confidentiality. For example, Pedersen (1997) reminded us that in individualistic contexts personal space is in essence a commodity, but in collectivistic cultures, personal privacy might be viewed as being selfish.

Another middle-class bias exists in the expectation that clients will self-disclose. Actually, this is a hallmark of Rogerian counseling, which assumes that after disclosure, people experience a measurable and identifiable benefit and catharsis. Clearly, the roots of positivism are at work. Some clients may find therapy imbalanced due to the unidirectional nature of the exchange. It could be perceived as inconsistent with community, kinship, and mutuality. Another assumption embedded in disclosure is that an individual will be articulate (in Standard English) and be able to match affective experiences to words. It is a tall order for some clients to disclose personal details about themselves and their families with a professional stranger. Many low-wage earners, because of limited education and/or immigrant status, do not speak Standard English. Inability to speak Standard English is not synonymous with illegal status, limited intelligence, or the ability to learn.

Storytelling: Coming Down the Mountain

A small group of Americans were climbing Mt. Kilimanjaro in Tanzania. We were outfitted with our sturdy sneakers—some of us had hiking boots. I had my fanny pack with my water and energy bars, along with my layered, moisture-licking, wool clothing that you pay too much for at Outdoor shops. We were enjoying the splendor of our hike—the birds, the flowers, the monkeys. At the same time we were tired and challenged by the rigor of this uphill climb. All of sudden, two Tanzanian youths appeared carrying a long and heavy log balanced on both of their shoulders as they came down the mountain. They were wearing flip-flops. They smiled and warmly greeted us as they scampered past. We were sobered at how nimble they were and without all of the provisions (water, food, and special footwear) that we privileged Americans had.

An examination of core and dominant cultural values allows one to see why a middle-class bias prevails in the training of counselors. Competition, the Protestant work ethic, and self-reliance all stem from an individualistic and Western culture (Sue & Sue, 1990). Yet, some communities are more collective, wherein greater dependence on others is the norm. Perceptions of dependence also seem to be fostered by class status. (See Storytelling: *Coming Down the Mountain*.) Perhaps it is easier to live without cultivating a relationship with neighbors if one is not financially interdependent on others. The California community in which I was reared was collective and collaborative in orientation. In my community, neighbors depended on one another. We borrowed household flour and sugar from one another and helped raise and discipline each other's children. Class may dictate one's ability to provide for personal material needs independent of others. Having middle-class status, particularly within an individualistic context, may make it easier not to be in relationships with persons in close proximity to oneself. This is most likely different from poor or collectivistic communities (independent of class differences), where value is placed on kinship networks. Within collectivistic contexts seen among many Arab, African, Asian, Native American, Latino, and agrarian and religious White families, an extension of the personal self is part of the culture or tribe.

CLASSISM

The media plays a role in depicting poor people as invisible and yet responsible for their predicament. They tend to be presented as unworthy and not deserving of more. In American society, being poor and staying poor are not valued because poverty does not mirror the American values of competition, success, change, progress, rising above and transcending one's situation, and controlling one's life. The inability to significantly alter one's station in life is inconsistent with core American values.

Classism is a form of oppression against the poor. Smith (2005) defines *classism* as "an interlocking system that involves domination and control of social ideology, institutions, and resources, resulting in a condition of privilege for one group relative to the disenfranchisement of another. Members of both dominant and subordinated groups are capable of prejudice, but only dominant groups have the institutional and cultural power to enforce their prejudices via oppression" (p. 688).

APA (2007) defines classism as "the network of attitudes, beliefs, behaviors, and institutional practices that maintain and legitimatize class-based power differences that privilege middle and higher income groups at the expense of the poor and working classes" (p. 7). Starting out poor and becoming rich through marriage, promotion, business, and even winning the lottery are admired. The values of hard work and/or good fortune, pulling oneself up by one's bootstraps, and a belief in a just society are all at work as is the ability to, despite the odds, overcome one's situation.

Socioeconomic class is fluid, which means the so-called lines between class groups are not solid. Many working-class families are governed by middle-class values, such as education as a means of self-help, hard work, money management, perseverance, and delayed gratification. Ogbu (1997) reminded us that membership in class groups is transient since people move in and out of class which is an open entity without clear boundaries. Ogbu and the most recent recession, acknowledge that the white-collar worker can quickly become the blue-collar laborer. Newman (1999), an anthropologist and researcher on poverty, said, "The working poor are perpetually at risk for becoming the poor of the other kind; they are one paycheck away from what is left of welfare, one sick child away from getting fired, one missed rent payment short of eviction" (p. xiv).

Within the home there are cultural experiences that assist children in their adjustment to school, such as being read to, seeing people read books, waiting in line, and organizing one's work or play. Bourdieu (1984) referred to such experiences as cultural capital that have middle-class connections. The home environment, along with a host of other agents (e.g., school, church, neighborhood, extracurricular activities), socializes children toward a middle-class perspective. Linguistic structures, styles of interacting, and authority patterns characterize cultural resources that can be turned into highly beneficial and socially lucrative cultural capital.

Kenway (1988) conducted research on privileged girls in private schools in Australia. She was interested in looking at self-esteem within an educational context. In talking with the girls about their experiences, Kenway found they used words such as *proper, right, perfect, education, manners,* and *success* to describe their status as upper class and said, "Self-esteem may be bought via the right 'casual-chic' designer label. In the culture of consumption within which private schools are immersed, success also can be bought alongside approval, acceptance, and social honour" (p. 155). Kenway encouraged her readers to see the costs to these young girls in their efforts to maintain an image based on elite class distinctions as measured by an exclusive school environment.

IMPLICATIONS FOR COUNSELORS AND PSYCHOLOGISTS

Schnitzer (1996) asks, "How might clinicians best integrate knowledge about the impact of poverty on mental health into their practice?" (p. 577). Unraveling the effects of class on one's life is not easy and can be difficult. Dominant discourses within society and particularly within the nation's training programs connect class and self-worth. More often than not, the poor are seen as lazy, unmotivated, and intellectually inferior.

The middle class represents the referent for society. Counselors need to hear the prevalence of class conditioning when listening to their clients' stories and, when necessary, help their clients make important connections between their identity and the effects of class on their lives. For example, an adult client from a working-class family might be reluctant to take certain occupational risks because of socialization experiences that emphasize security, saving for a rainy day, and being practical about the future. "What is the effect of growing up poor on your willingness now to change jobs?" or "What kinds of messages did you receive about being poor or taking risks?" are questions that could further the client's exploration of the relationship between early family experiences and staying at a job that is unfulfilling.

Anxiety about change and risk-taking might be higher among clients who, as children and now as adults, have difficulty meeting basic needs. This is not to say that middle-class clients are prepared to embrace uncertainty or change, but having access to financial safety nets that augment one's existing resources may make it more psychologically comfortable and financially possible to engage in risk-taking behavior. Such resources include, but are not limited to, a trust fund, a family loan, the family home, the beach house, an inheritance, transportation and furniture.

Addressing the structural, social, and economic issues that affect clients' lives is essential. In doing so, we approach our clients from an ecological perspective. A focus on personal relationships and the clients' insights are critical to therapy, however, a broader view is warranted (Schnitzer, 1996). The following questions may encourage introspection about class:

1. Was there an event that you did not attend because you did not have the appropriate attire or accessories?
2. Were there sporting events or clubs that you could not participate in because your family did not have the money?
3. Were there friends you did not invite to your home because you were ashamed of where you lived and how your home looked?
4. What are your experiences with low-wage-earning people?
5. Have you consciously downplayed your wealth by dressing in attire or brands that did not display your wealth?
6. Did you choose friends or shun others because of their income or how they looked or what they drove or ate or wore?
7. Have you ever worked hard to convince people that although you had wealth, you were still a kind person?
8. Did you not date a person you were interested in because you did not think he or she would fit into your life because they had inadequate resources or did not come from the "right" family?
9. Were you ever told that you "just did not fit in," even if the criteria for fitting in was not necessarily related to money but perhaps other dimensions of identity, such as race or sexuality or body size?

CASE STUDY

CLASS DIVIDE

June is a 35-year-old African American single mother of five children. Two of the children in her care are her sister's. Her sister is in a federal prison for murder. June is a nurse's aid. She has been in therapy for 8 months and attends faithfully. She and her therapist, Candace, have decided on a sliding payment scale. June does not have health insurance. Several times, June was not able to make it to therapy because the car that her boyfriend had purchased for her had been repossessed. Her boyfriend has an unstable work history due to time spent in jail for drug charges. In therapy, June wants to strengthen her relationships and be a more involved parent. June receives weekly calls from the school regarding her oldest child who is frequently absent, is disruptive in class, and is known to be inappropriate with the teachers (yelling and disregarding their requests of her). June feels that the teachers and counselors do not understand her, and she feels angry after most interactions with them. June's mother and sister do not understand why she is going to a perfect stranger to discuss private family business. June appreciates the time in therapy to work on herself and get a break from all of the care she provides for everyone else around the clock. Her challenges are multiple, but Candace, her therapist, notices her commitment to therapy. June says it is one of the only times in her life where she can focus on herself. June also does not have dental insurance. If she did, she would get implants. All of her top teeth are missing.

QUESTIONS

1. What do psychologists and counselors need to understand in their work with clients who are low-wage-earning?
2. What are June's strengths?
3. How and when do therapists advocate for their clients?

DISCUSSION AND INTEGRATION

The Client, June

Despite the multiple challenges that describe June's life—poverty, single parenting, a significant other's legal problems and substance addiction, and a child with behavioral and learning difficulties—tenacity, hope, and commitment to her personal development describe June's strengths. Many people who start out poor as children and remain poor as adults have learned to "roll with the punches," use humor to "keep from crying," and shout up a prayer to God for help in times of trouble. They have also learned to hustle and make do with a system that often renders them invisible, pathological, and peripheral.

Socioeconomic status is a major component of biological processes, such as higher blood pressure, greater blockage of coronary arteries, and more rapid progression of HIV infection (Anderson, 2003). June, like others who are poor, does not have health insurance. The number of uninsured people increased to 49.9 million in 2010 from 49.0 million in 2009. In 2010, 9.8% of children under age 18 (7.3 million) were without health insurance. This is not statistically different from the 2009 estimates. The uninsured rate for children in poverty (15.4%) was greater than the rate for all children (9.8%). In 2006, 28.3% of female-headed households with no husband present were at the poverty line. In addition, the percentage and the number of people without health insurance increased from 16.1% in 2009 to 16.3% in 2010. (DeNavas-Walt, Proctor, & Smith, 2011). Among Latinos, 30.71% were uninsured, compared with 20.8% of Black people. Whites and Asians had the lowest rates of uninsured, at 11.7% and 18.1%, respectively. Among people who were foreign-born, 34.1% were not covered by health insurance. For native-born Americans, the uninsured health care rate was 13.8%.

It is inaccurate to assume that low-wage-earning people do not care about their children. June, like many other clients dealing with just "one more thing," may react with muted affect or numbing. "Class and racial differences between therapist and client may mean experiences with emotional and physical assault so profoundly variant that the therapist cannot adequately envision the impact on the human psyche" (Schnitzer, 1996, p. 575).

(Continued)

(Continued)

June's boyfriend experiences depression and frustration due to irregular employment. Regarding Black men, Washington (1987) said, "Economic stressors such as unemployment, underemployment, job losses, health catastrophes, loss of personal property, and gross indebtedness also exert an unacceptable level of chronic stress" (p. 194). The stress is tied into not being able to achieve society's clear standards about manhood, which are synonymous with career and material success. At the same time, addiction grossly impairs one's ability to seek work and maintain positions once offered. June's current relationship with her boyfriend is without physical violence—in the past others have been fraught with frequent physical and verbal altercations.

Like June, many unskilled parents leave the training and education of their children to teachers while valuing educational success and achievement. Lareau (1997) conducted research on two very different school populations. At the first school, 60% of parents were professionals, compared with 1% at the other. The majority of the professional parents had college degrees, and many fathers had advanced degrees. Parents in the unskilled jobs had either a high school education or had dropped out of high school. Only 1% of parents at the first school were unskilled workers, compared with 23% at the second one. Lareau found that interactions between professional parents and teachers were more frequent and comfortable. Professional parents were also more involved in the academic preparation of their children. Parents at the school at which the majority of parents were semiskilled or unskilled tended to have uncomfortable and infrequent interactions with teachers. Lareau wrote, "In the middle-class community, parents saw education as a shared enterprise and scrutinized, monitored and supplemented the school experience of their children" (p. 712). Children from middle-class families had greater cultural capital than children from lower income families. This is not to say that the family–school relationship among the middle class was better than that of the working class. Lareau stated, however, that "the social profitability of middle-class arrangements is tied to the school's definition of the proper family-school relationship" (p. 713).

June reported that her interactions with the school counselor left her feeling worst. It may be helpful for the therapist to attend such a meeting with her client. School counselors need to be aware of the ways in which culture can work against parents' perception of schools as accessible, particularly for working-class parents and their children. What may appear to be apathy from June may actually be feelings of powerlessness. For June and others like her, the quality of interactions with school personnel is linked to the discourses predominant from her educational contexts that were alienating and fraught with shame and difficulty. Brantlinger (1993) interviewed low-income parents. She found that many continue to carry the mental baggage from their early school experiences, which detracted from their ability, in some instances, to discuss their children's school experiences.

The Therapist, Candace

Jackson (2005) makes a distinction between *poor women* and *low-wage-earning women*, which, she says, "helps us to always keep an eye trained on the economic conditions that create and/or maintain the challenges that many women and their families to seek our services" (p. 238). Low-wage-earning people are more vulnerable within institutional structures, including school, courts, and police (Robinson, 1999a). For example, interest rates on credit cards are often near 30%. When making the minimum monthly payment, getting out of debt is nearly impossible. An important skill for June's therapist to have is the ability to engage in introspection and to ask questions toward gaining insight into the effects of class on her identity. No standard for training about social class and classism exists in counselor training. Because of this dearth, "counselors in training must seek experiences where they can explore their own social class worldviews and be challenged in a supportive environment" (Liu & Arguello, 2006, p. 9).

What is it about interactions with low-wage-earning people that may feel awkward or confining or familiar? What are the indicators of Candace's own privileged financial position that may be a point of disclosure to June, albeit unintentionally? Candace wants to nurture an egalitarian relationship with all of her clients, yet, there is an inherently unequal power dynamic. Feelings of guilt can contribute to a counselor's acquiescence of her power. This is defeating to both the therapist and the counseling event. As an identity construct, class has a significant impact on development. Like culture, people are often oblivious to it.

Garcia-Coll (1997) identified that White women have a difficult time holding Black women's anger and will go to great lengths to suppress, deny, and repress expressions of this anger. White women's historical role in the oppression of Black women and their enjoyment of present-day privileges earned as a function of that history discourage Black and White women from coming together and bearing witness to one another's anger, shame, and guilt. Good and effective therapy is not possible with all of this unspoken angst. June should neither have to pay for nor wait on Candace to work through her unresolved issues that leave her feeling uncomfortable and/or ill-prepared. It is common for women who are currently being battered or who have histories with domestic violence not to have adequate social support. In qualitative research with six Black and five White women who had survived battering, eight had earlier experiences of abuse (Hage, 2006). Experiences of abuse are a risk factor for further abuse. Fortunately, June has actively decided to be in a relationship free from the violence that characterized her life when her children were very young and when she was a child.

To facilitate the process of becoming more aware of her own class experiences and worldview, Candace could recall memories from her childhood and adulthood that were connected to class and that evoked feelings of pride, embarrassment, guilt, superiority, inferiority, and shame. It is important for Candace—regardless of race, class, sexuality, ability, or gender—to endorse mutuality, reciprocity, and sensitivity in her work. (Jordan & Romney, 2005). She recognizes that June has limited resources but also understands the importance of June meeting her financial obligations for therapy. Respecting June's situation, she asks, "What do you think you are able to pay for psychotherapy?" Candace asks June to ponder this question until their next session.

Summary

This chapter on class explored the neglect of class within the literature as a psychosocial variable. The middle-class bias in graduate counseling training programs was discussed at length. Work conducted by sociologists on school inequity was an important link in this discussion. A case was presented of a client from a low-income background with multiple strengths and challenges. Implications for counselors and psychologists were explored and questions presented for beginning the personal process of interrogating the dynamic of socioeconomic class in one's life.

Converging Sexuality

> *"Our nation will finally close the door on a fundamental unfairness for gays and lesbians, and indeed affirm equality for all Americans"*
>
> REP. NANCY PELOSI ON SEPTEMBER 20, 2011, DISCUSSING THE END OF THE 18 YEAR-OLD "DON'T ASK, DON'T TELL" LAW THAT PROHIBITED GAY AND LESBIAN MILITARY SERVICE WOMEN AND MEN FROM DIVULGING THEIR SEXUAL ORIENTATION.

This chapter focuses on sexuality. From the beginning, it should be noted that language is in flux and has changed over time. Terms will be used in this chapter that admittedly are contested, such as *gay, lesbian*, and *bisexual* (Eliason & Schope, 2007). Sexuality exists on a continuum representing variations within and between homosexuality, bisexuality, and heterosexuality.

There are people who have lived part of their lives with a particular sexual orientation and have come to question that sexuality. Persons who are transgendered do not fit into the binary of woman or man, gay or straight. This chapter recognizes the fluidity of sexuality over the developmental cycle and recognizes sexuality as part of a developmental system. A person's "sexual landscape might change, thus creating new opportunities for self description while transforming or eliminating existing possibilities" (Rust, 2006, p. 174). A possible outcome of this discussion is that the reader will become more conscious of a heterosexual bias that continues to exist in the culture at large and the profession in particular. An assumption of heterosexuality can be silencing and offensive to lesbian, gay, and questioning clients. As clinicians increase their awareness of their biases and their proximity to heterosexist discourses, service delivery will hopefully improve. Far too often, graduate counseling programs do not provide adequate training in this area. Unpacking personal biases and receiving knowledge about gay, lesbian, bisexual, intersexual, and transgendered clients provides therapists with the skills and competencies needed for this and other nondominant populations. At the same time, working outside of areas of expertise is a violation of the ethical standards of the American Counseling Association (ACA) and the American Psychological Association (APA).

Definitions are provided, and a case study concludes the chapter.

DEFINITIONS AND TERMINOLOGY

Hunt (1993) said, "As with any group, language has a strong impact on gay and lesbian culture. As times change and as words develop new connotations some words fall out of favor" (p. 2). The following terms are considered nonbiased and accepted terminology among people who identify as gay men, lesbians, or bisexuals. Intersexuality and transgendered will also be discussed. These terms are used as the standard terminology in this chapter. (See Storytelling: *Language*.)

Heterosexism is the belief that everyone is heterosexual and that heterosexual relationships are preferred and necessary for the preservation of the family, particularly the nuclear family.

Storytelling: Language

The terms *transsexual, transgender, transvestite,* and *gay* are not well understood. As I lectured in class one night, I mentioned that the majority of men who were transvestites were not gay but heterosexual and that people can be transgendered but not gay. The silence was intense. The confused looks on students' faces told me that they did not understand what I had just said. Another way to look at transgender was defined by Towle and Morgan (2002), who said that *transers* "has sometimes replaced third gender to designate gender roles and practices which are not definable in terms of local understandings of gender normativity" (p. 473). The term *third gender* was introduced in 1975 by M. Kay Martin and Barbara Voorhies and drew attention to the ethnographic evidence that gender categories in some cultures (as well as our own here in the West) could not be adequately explained in a two-gender framework. The heterosexual man who loves his body and has a girlfriend refers to himself as transgendered because he refuses to restrict his clothing choices to pants only. He wears skirts. At the same time, there are people who are transgendered who are gay or bisexual or questioning their sexuality. Transgendered does not mean gay. Transsexuals may not define themselves as gay but have had or plan to undergo reconstructive surgery to match hormone treatments or electrolysis for men who are transitioning to becoming women. Women who are transitioning to becoming men may have hysterectomies and/or mastectomies. Counselors and therapists have a responsibility to be informed of the correct language so as not to be insensitive or misinformed.

Heterosexism is institutionalized through religion, education, and the media and leads to homophobia (Robinson & Watt, 2001). It describes the institutionalization of antigay, antilesbian, and antibisexual beliefs, attitudes, and behaviors. Heterosexism is the deeply ingrained notion that heterosexuality is the superior sexual orientation (Wall & Evans, 1992). Pharr (1988) stated that heterosexism has been defined as a worldview, a value system that prizes heterosexuality, assumes it is the only appropriate manifestation of love and sexuality, and devalues homosexuality and all that is not heterosexual. Dines and Humez (2002) described heterosexism as the heterosexual predisposition that is encoded into and characteristic of the major social, cultural, and economic institutions of our society.

Although similar to heterosexism, **homophobia** is regarded as a sense of dread of being in close quarters with people who are lesbian, bisexual, or gay (Worthington, Dillon, & Becker-Schutte, 2005). *Homophobia* comes from the Latin *homo,* meaning "same" (in this case, referring to same-gender attraction), and *phobia,* meaning "fear of"; thus, the term's original application to individuals was an extreme and persistent fear and loathing of homosexuals (Pharr, 1988). Fear, hatred, and dislike tied to cultural socialization and religious beliefs are often present with homophobia. **Homonegativity** has been defined as negative feelings and thoughts about lesbian, gay, or bisexual orientations or individuals (Worthington et al., 2005). Pharr (1988) said that homophobia is a weapon of sexism because it works to keep men and women in rigidly defined gender roles. **Homosexuality** is attraction to the same sex for physical and emotional nurturance and is one orientation on the continuum from homosexuality to bisexuality to heterosexuality. This term has become associated with the historical belief that homosexuality is unnatural, sinful, and sick. For this reason, females who are homosexual/gay often prefer the term **lesbian** to describe their sexual orientation. The difference in terminology, which arose during the feminist movement, reflects the difference between gay men and lesbians. The term *lesbian* gets its origins from the Greek poet Sappho (c. 600 BCE), who lived on the Greek island of Lesbos in the Aegean Sea. Sappho's poems are exclusively about women.

Someone who acknowledges his homoerotic orientation and incorporates this knowledge into his identity and carries this identity into interpersonal relationships is defined as **gay**. The term *gay* signifies more self-awareness, self-acceptance, and openness than the term *homosexual.* Often, in developmental literature, the process of coming to terms with one's sexuality involves moving from being homosexual to becoming gay. One consequence of homophobia is **internalized homophobia**. It is produced by the negative messages about homosexuality that lesbians and gay men hear throughout their lives. Because gay men and lesbians are stereotyped, uninformed, or fed inaccurate, distorted information about homosexuality, the messages are internalized and result in low self-esteem. Internalized homophobia can lead to self-hatred and other psychological problems (Dworkin & Gutierrez, 1991).

Rust (2006) aptly pointed out that people sometimes misrepresent their identities to avoid judgment and disapproval. She said, "Lesbians and gay men often misrepresent their sexual locations when in heterosexual contexts, and bisexual women often misrepresent their location when in lesbian contexts" (p. 179). **Bisexuality** represents a shifting and dynamic sexual landscape that can be misunderstood, not only among heterosexually identified people but among gay men and lesbian women.

Transgender refers to persons who may be biologically one sex but may identify within their bodies, souls, and minds as the other sex. People may refer to themselves as transgender and still consider themselves gay, lesbian, bisexual, or heterosexual. A male-to-female transsexual might put it this way, "I see myself being with a man, but I did not see myself as a man with a man. I saw myself as a woman with a man." (See Storytelling: *Living Authentically*.)

Storytelling: Living Authentically

I once knew someone of color who had a wife and two children. This person, who I'll refer to as Hailey, served many years in the military. Although Hailey had an outward appearance that was masculine, in terms of style of dress, mannerism, and voice, Hailey felt that being male was not accurate, that an error had occurred. Hailey also was attracted to men but as a person who identified as female. Hailey felt paralyzed. On one hand, Hailey loved the woman with whom Hailey had two children and had shared a life together for a long time. On the other hand, Hailey felt that the denial was a death sentence. Denial was no longer an option. Hailey decided to get therapy to explore sexuality and identity as well as how to live authentically. Hailey had always felt different because there had been an attraction to men but not as a gay man but as a woman attracted to a man. Hailey did not want to hurt anyone and said in therapy, "My wife has always been good to me and she is such a kind soul." It took Hailey a while to find a suitable counselor. The first therapist, upon learning Hailey was struggling with sexuality issues, suggested Hailey see another counselor, citing Catholicism and Hailey's issues as conflicting with the counselor's personal and religious values. Feeling deflated and defeated, Hailey waited before searching again for a suitable professional with whom to work. After nearly a year, Hailey found a skilled and nonjudgmental counselor. After therapy for almost a year, Hailey decided to tell the wife the truth: a divorce was necessary and to live authentically meant living life as a woman. Therapy helped Hailey realize that no one was going to emerge from this situation without being hurt. Hailey had spent so much of her life hiding and denying what she knew to be true. Because she started to feel her own hurt and pain, she was able to recognize that her coming out would be hurtful to her wife and children. Hurt was one thing but deception was another. Therapy also helped her think about what it meant to be transsexual and a woman of color. Throughout her life, she had been battling not only heterosexism but also racism and sexism. At the same time, she was committed to being honest, answering people's questions, and staying connected to family.

For as long as Hailey could remember, she felt different, and yet words failed to fully express the nature and extent of this difference, which contributed to Hailey's sense of isolation and confusion about who she was. Not having people in whom Hailey could confide contributed to her loneliness. It was a significant step for Hailey to disclose her struggles with a therapist. In doing so, words again failed her in that she did not have the language to explain who she was: a genetically normal XY male who felt that her gender assignment was wrong and yet did not identify as gay because she saw herself as a female who was attracted to men. Growing up in a rural part of the Midwest only fueled Hailey's self-perception that she was abnormal. Therapy helped Hailey understand the stigma associated with not aligning with the gender binary. It also helped her see how she had internalized oppression and that racism, sexism, and homophobic attitudes were prevalent throughout her life. Hailey's authenticity was noted in deciding to no longer live a lie.

A tremendous amount of oppression and isolation exists within communities of color around homosexuality. A man's expression of interest in another man is construed as homosexuality. In a heterosexist society, homosexuality is often feared. Kimmel (2006) said homophobia is interwoven with sexism and racism. Hailey, as a young man, exaggerated his masculinity and interest in things male: fighting and hypersexuality. Persons of color who are transsexual differ from White people who have similar experiences. Fortunately, Hailey's therapist was attentive to her multiple identities particularly within the context of multiple sources of discrimination (Greene, 1994).

The first counselor Hailey interacted with did not want to work with Hailey because the presenting problem related to sexuality. Hailey's sexuality conflicted with her values and beliefs. While mental health professionals are not supposed to function outside of their scope of training or competence, counselors are encouraged to "gain knowledge, personal awareness, sensitivity, and skills pertinent to working with a diverse client population" (ACA, 2005, C.2.a). The first counselor clearly exhibited biased, inadequate, and inappropriate practice (Garnets, Hancock, Cochran, Goodchilds, & Peplau, 1991).

(Continued)

Hermann and Herlihy (2006) caution counselors about refusing to treat clients because of sexuality issues. In citing the case of *Bruff vs. North Mississippi Health Services, Inc.,* in 2001, they explained that "the most significant legal aspect of the Bruff case is the court's holding that an employer's legal obligation to make reasonable accommodations for employees' religious beliefs does not include accommodating a counselor's request to refer homosexual clients who ask for assistance with relationship issues" (p. 416). In short, counselors cannot use their religious practices and beliefs to defend discriminating based on sexual orientation.

Intersexual refers to people who are (pseudo) hermaphrodites (Kitzinger, 1999), or persons born with genitalia that is different or ambiguous enough to raise concerns as it deviates from a normative appearance. However, intersexuality is not always evident from an external evaluation. A newborn might have genitalia that resemble a very large clitoris and/or male genitalia that have a more masculine appearance. Intersexuality may be caused by congenital adrenal hyperplasia, mixed gonadal dysgenesis, androgen insensitivity syndrome (complete or partial), 5-alpha reductase deficiency, and many other conditions (Chase, 2003). The narrow construction and bifurcation of gender, which translates into males having a designated sized penis and testicles and females not having a clitoris that is too large and a vagina and uterus, does not apply to all children born in the United States and throughout the world (Sterling, 1992).

Queer Theory: There are three main points to Queer Theory: (1) a refusal of heterosexuality as the benchmark for all sexual formations; (2) interrogation of the frequent assumptions that lesbian and gay studies is a single homogeneous object; and (3) an insistence on the multiple ways in which race crucially shapes sexual subjectives. Queer Theory, which emerged in the early 1900s, is a study in which traditional sexual norms are rejected (Klages, 1997).

Coming out happens when gay men and lesbians come to accept being gay or lesbian as a salient component of their identities. Numerous developmental models describe the stages of the coming-out process, such as those of Cass (1979) and Coleman (1982). Gay and lesbian people have struggled throughout history with the notion that their sexual identity was a choice—and the *wrong* choice. Because of socialization, some gay men and lesbians have behaved heterosexually even though their identity was gay or lesbian. Many remember feeling different at an early age and see this as stemming from their gay and lesbian orientation. For this reason, the term **sexual orientation**, rather than *sexual preference,* is preferred. By owning this orientation, gay men and lesbians make a conscious choice to let their behavior conform to their orientation.

Heterosexism affects everyone, covertly and overtly, in this society. It is not only harmful to the victims but to the perpetrators as well. According to Smith (1982), heterosexism is intimately associated with other discriminatory practices (e.g., classism, sexism, racism, and ageism) in our society. She stated that verbal and behavioral expressions of heterosexism are acceptable and go uncontested in contexts where other discriminatory comments or gesticulations (e.g., racist, sexist, or anti-Semitic remarks) would be challenged or prohibited.

Sexual politics ensures the dominance of males over females and the dominance of heterosexuals over persons who are gay and lesbian (Pleck, 1984). Within a system of **hegemony** (a historical situation in which power is won and held) and **androcentrism** (in which the complementary of women and men implies women's subordinate social position to men), homosexuality becomes a threat for heterosexual men. Heterosexual men are socialized into believing that they must oppress women to reject anything that remotely resembles homosexuality. For this reason, "any kind of powerlessness, or refusal to compete among men becomes involved with the imagery of homosexuality" (Pleck, 1984, p. 84). Within heterosexuality, a central dimension of the power that men exercise over women is found. Clearly, sexism and homophobia are interlocking paradigms.

Sexual inequality and heterosexuality cannot be discussed without addressing sociopolitical power dynamics within society, such as the suppression of women's sexuality, forced sexuality through incest and rape, the idealization of heterosexual marriage, and the contradicting and confusing roles of motherhood.

Traditionally, a healthy or ideal personality has included a concept of *sexual identity* with three basic components:

1. A sexual preference for members of the opposite sex
2. A sex role identity as either masculine or feminine, depending on one's gender
3. A gender identity that is a secure sense of one's maleness or femaleness

Bem (1993) set out to refute these components by stating that sexual preference ought to be considered orthogonal to notions of mental health. She also indicated that the terms *heterosexual* and *homosexual* should be used to describe acts rather than persons.

NARRATIVE QUESTIONS

It is often through exposure to other people's personal narratives that students gain insight into the lived experiences of others. Gaining insight into one's own personal stories and histories is essential to self-knowledge. Consider your responses to the following questions (Falco, 1991, p. 174):

1. What was the first reference to gays or lesbians you ever remember hearing?
2. What do you remember about the first person you ever saw or met who you identified as gay or lesbian?
3. What did your parents teach you about people who are gay and lesbian?
4. What type of treatment did gay and lesbian clients receive in your therapy or counseling course?
5. How were gay or lesbian student therapists treated in your training program? Gay or lesbian supervisors or instructors?
6. Do you currently have friends or acquaintances whom you know to be gay or lesbian? If not, why do you think this is so?
7. Who do you think might be gay or lesbian? What are they like? Do you think they are typical of gays or lesbians?
8. What is the most memorable same-sex experience of your life? The most traumatic? The most meaningful and/or eye-opening?

THE IMPORTANCE OF A FOCUS ON GAY, LESBIAN, BISEXUAL, AND TRANSGENDER ISSUES IN COUNSELING

To be effective, therapists need to receive adequate training in counseling persons who are gay, lesbian, bisexual, and transgender. First they must understand the terms briefly discussed earlier. Although people who are gay, lesbian, and bisexual are more likely than people who are heterosexuals to seek therapy, they tend to be more dissatisfied with treatment compared to heterosexuals.

A need exists to provide psychotherapy in the gay/lesbian community, however, many mental health professionals have not been provided the appropriate training to assist gay men, lesbians, and bisexuals effectively through their coming out or identity development process. Beals and Peplau (2006) found in their study of 144 gay men and lesbians that they have better relationships with people they have directly told about their sexuality compared with people to whom they have not disclosed. Clearly, disclosure of a stigmatized identity can have profound and lasting implications for relationships; nonetheless, this finding suggests that relationship quality is adversely affected when people have not revealed core information about their identity.

Survey and anecdotal literature reveals that the source of dissatisfaction often is the counselor's ignorance or prejudice toward people who are gay (Bell & Weinberg, 1978). Just as clinicians must be aware of their racial biases regarding cultural and racial groups, they must also assess their biases as they relate to gay, lesbian, and bisexual clients (Pope, 1995). Clinicians have been influenced by living in a society that socializes people toward racist and homophobic attitudes. For example, Caroline Pace (1991) conducted an in-depth study on the attitudes of mental health professionals and graduate students in training programs toward gay men and lesbians. She found "counselors, like other individuals socialized by heterosexist institutions in the United States, hold negative attitudes toward lesbians and gays" (p. 73). The mental health professionals and counselors-in-training scored in the "low grade homophobic" range of the Index of Attitudes toward Homosexuals Scale.

The 2010 Census included bisexual, lesbian, gay, and transgendered persons, not by asking about their sexual orientation but instead asking about marital status. For instance, a woman who is living with another woman to whom she is not married could check the "unmarried partner" box. However, according to Gates (2010), as many as 15% of same-sex couples will not be identified as such in Census 2010. Approximately 10% of same-sex couples described their relationship as "roommates" or "non-relatives" and not as "spouses" or "unmarried couples." When this was queried further, researchers learned that confidentiality was a concern among one-quarter, and one-third took issue with the fact that the Census did not ask about sexual orientation or gender identity and were offended by the options presented to them. Another 5% of couples were not "Person 1" on the Census form, thus it was not possible to identity their relationship.

Examining Census 2010 data, demographer Gary Gates (August 25, 2011) from the Williams Institute study reports that there are 901,997 same-sex couples in the United States, representing 99% of US counties. Bradford, Barrett, and Honnold (2002) report that as of the 2000 census, there were nearly 600,000 same-sex couples, or nearly 1.2 million people. Same-sex female couples comprise the largest percentage of these partnerships at 60%. Of same-sex couples, 22% are raising children. Interestingly, child-rearing among same-sex couples is most common in the Deep South and Mountain West regions where attitudes tend to be more socially conservative. In such instances, LGBT people are more likely to have come out in later life and are more likely to have a child from a previous relationship with a different-sex partner when younger.

Among cities with populations above 250,000, the list of the top 10 large cities for same sex couples includes (in this order): San Francisco, California; Seattle, Washington; Oakland, California; Minneapolis, Minnesota; Atlanta, Georgia; Portland, Oregon; Long Beach, California; Washington, DC; Boston, Massachusetts; and Denver, Colorado. The top small cities (populations below 100,000) include Provincetown, Massachusetts; Wilton Manors, Florida; Palm Springs, California; Rehoboth Beach, Delaware; Guerneville, California; West Hollywood, California; Pleasant Ridge, Michigan; New Hope, Pennsylvania; Rancho Mirage, California; and Oakland Park, Florida. Gates said, "Particularly among smaller cities, the data reflects that the LGBT community has dispersed beyond traditional enclaves as social stigma eases, couples are more comfortable coming out, and a generation of aging and out same-sex couples begin to retire."

In another press release, Gates (April 7, 2011) examined four recent national and two state-level population-based surveys. The analyses suggest that there are more than 8 million adults in the United States who are lesbian, gay, or bisexual. This represents 3.5% of the adult population. There are also nearly 700,000 transgender individuals in the United States. When these numbers are combined, the study suggests that approximately 9 million Americans identify as LGBT. Among adults who identify as lesbian, gay, or bisexual, bisexuals comprise a slight majority (1.8% compared to 1.7% who identify as lesbian or gay); women are more likely than are men to identify as bisexual. Estimates of persons who report any lifetime same-sex sexual behavior and any same-sex sexual attraction are substantially higher than estimates of those who identify as lesbian, gay, or bisexual. The distinction between behavior and identity may help to explain these data. An estimated 19 million Americans (8.2%) report that they have engaged in same-sex sexual behavior, and nearly 25.6 million Americans (11%) acknowledge at least some same-sex sexual attraction.

Gay, lesbian, bisexual, and transgender people experience homophobia not only in the counselor's office, which should be a safe place to explore identity issues, but from the general public as well. In a study of 1,669 students, staff, faculty, and administrators at 14 private and public colleges and universities, 29% of respondents reported that they had been harassed because of their sexual orientation or gender identity. Harassment was defined as "conduct that has interfered unreasonably with your ability to work or learn on this campus or has created an offensive, hostile, intimidating working or learning environment" (Rankin, 2002, p. 26). The harassment was most likely, at 57%, to occur in public space on campus or while people were walking or working on campus. The harassment most frequently occurred through derogatory remarks, at 89%; verbal harassment or threats, 48%; graffiti, 39%; and pressure to be silent about sexual orientation/gender, 38%. This study also found that the majority of respondents, 71%, perceived transgender people to be the most likely to be harassed on campus. The actual percentage of harassment that occurred against transgendered people was 41%. In an environment that should support the universe of expression, ideas, and exploration, colleges and universities have been bastions of heterosexist and homophobic activity.

New research shows that lesbians, gay men, and bisexuals (LGB) are at increased risk for physical health problems due to prejudice-related stress. Frost, Lehavot, & Meyer (2011) found that LGB people who had experienced prejudice-related major life events were about three times more likely to have suffered a serious physical health problem over a one-year follow-up period than those who had not experienced such events. The effects of prejudice-related events remained statistically significant even after controlling for the experience of other stressful events, as well as other factors known to affect physical health, such as age, gender, employment, and lifetime health history.

Other crucial issues that face the gay population are substance abuse, depression, running away, HIV and AIDS, partner abuse, and attempted suicide. Goldberg, Bos, and Gartrell (April 2011) found that compared to matched adolescents from a national probability sample, the 17-year-old offspring of lesbian parents from the largest, longest-running, longitudinal study of same-sex parented families were more likely to report occasional substance use. However, they were not more likely to report heavy use. No associations were found between substance use and homophobic stigmatization or life satisfaction.

Researchers maintain that substance abuse among lesbians and gay men is high. The gay bar may be the most accessible and visible place to persons who are "out" to interact with others who are also "out" (Rothblum, 1994). Gay men and lesbians attempt suicide two to seven times more often than heterosexual comparison groups (Durby, 1994; Hammelman, 1993). Gay youth have a plethora of problems during adolescence, such as intensified feelings of isolation, depression, and lack of healthy role models (Browning, Reynolds, & Dworkin, 1994). School counselors should be aware of, and be prepared to work with, a diversity of youth because an estimated 3 million adolescents across the country are gay, lesbian, or bisexual. Due to the lack of role models and sympathetic support systems, another 20% to 35% of these young individuals attempt suicide (O'Connor, 1992). Gay youth are vulnerable and need caring adults. Racism and other sources of discrimination heighten this vulnerability among gay youth (Greene & Herek, 1994).

Asian American gay people find themselves "caught between two conflicting cultural values, between Asian and Western influences" (Chan, 1992, p. 116). Asian American and Native American gay men and lesbians also contend with strong traditional family roles, subsequent expectations, and community values that are often collectivistic, as opposed to individualistic, in orientation (Greene, 1994).

In qualitative and quantitative research conducted by Thompson and Morgan (2008), "mostly straight" women were discussed. An analysis of sexual behavioral measures revealed that mostly straight women were oriented more towards other women, in same-sex relationships than exclusively straight women, but they were less same-sex oriented than were bisexual women and lesbians with respect to sexual attraction as well as their fantasies. Through narratives about identity development, mostly straight women disclosed that sexual identity exploration was complex and uncertain. It was suggested that other researchers need to use "mostly straight" as a sexual identity subtype.

DEVELOPMENTAL PROCESSES

Everyone has sexuality. Sexuality interacts with other aspects of the self, such as race, age, class, and geography. The need to develop a clear sense of one's sexuality is not limited to GLBTIQQ (gay, lesbian, bisexual, transgender, intersexual, questioning, and queer people) only. Robinson and Watt (2001) argued that "the socially endorsed experience of heterosexuality and the unconscious and unearned privilege afforded heterosexuals often deems them unaware of the importance to transition through sexual identity formation" (p. 594). Not thinking about oneself as a sexual being (similar to not thinking about oneself as having race) has implications for therapists' ability to hear their clients talk about matters related to sexuality. Several themes of identity evolution, which is different from formation as it suggests an endpoint, have been identified by Eliason & Schope (2007): differences, confusion, exploration, disclosure, labeling, cultural immersion, distrust of the oppressor, degree of integration, internalized, oppression, managing, stigma, identity transformation, and, authenticity. (See Storytelling: *Living Authentically*).

Several linear models of gay and lesbian identity development exist. There are limitations associated with these models. Not all people progress through the stages as prescribed in that they may skip a stage or recycle back through them in the face of a significant event. There are older adults who experience their sexuality differently from youth. Some of the models do not account for development after adolescence. In addition, the experience of being bisexual and/or transgender is different from being gay or lesbian. Being a lesbian is a very different experience from being a gay male.

Erwin (2006) argues that lesbians are frequently overlooked by researchers, except when they are open about their identity, do not conform to societal gender role expectations, or have concerns about their sexual orientation. Being a feminine lesbian does not describe the experience of a woman who is butch in her appearance (Eliason & Schope, 2007). Despite the limitations of stage models, they do provide some understanding of where people might be in their evolution. The models can also help therapists and student development professionals with understanding the questions and themes that describe certain stages or phases. Cass's model is described below. Troiden's and Sullivan's models are also mentioned.

Cass's Model of Gay, Lesbian, and Bisexual Sexual Identity Formation

Vivian Cass (1979) developed a model to assess the growth, development, and awareness of gay, lesbian, and bisexual individuals. Most counselors will work with a gay, lesbian, or bisexual client at some juncture during their professional careers. The Cass model is provided as a guideline for assessing a client's level of development. It is important to note that the client may foreclose at a given stage, skip certain levels, or regress from a higher stage to a lower stage, depending on the events that occur in his or her life.

Coping strategies vary for gay, lesbian, bisexual, and transgender (GLBT) clients. Often, a therapist can assess the gay client's level of identity development in the coming-out process. According to the Cass model (1984), the gay identity formation process occurs in six stages, beginning with the individual having a sexual self-portrait that is heterosexual. For example, if the client were talking about a female, the female would see herself and her behavior as heterosexual as well as perceive others to view her as heterosexual. For the most part, the person's sexual self-portrait is consistent or congruent with heterosexuality. At some point in life, however, a change occurs. It might happen in childhood, in adolescence, in early adulthood, in middle age, or even very late in life.

Stage 1: Identity Confusion   Identity confusion is characterized by a growing awareness of thoughts, feelings, or behaviors that may be homosexual in nature. These self-perceptions are incongruent with earlier assumptions of personal heterosexuality and constitute the first developmental conflict of this model. Entrance into this stage begins with the conscious awareness that information regarding homosexuality is somehow personally relevant. When the continuing personalization of this information can no longer be ignored, the individual's sexual self-portrait feels inconsistent, or incongruent. The process of gay identity formation has begun.

Examples of questions a person in Stage 1 may be asking are "Who am I?", "Am I homosexual?", and "Am I really a heterosexual?" The individual sometimes feels, thinks, or acts in a homosexual way but would rarely, if ever, tell anyone about this. The individual is fairly sure that homosexuality has something to do with him personally.

With continuing personalization of information regarding homosexuality, the person begins privately to label his own behavior (or thoughts or feelings) as possibly gay. Publicly, the person maintains a self-image as heterosexual and perceives others as maintaining the same image. To deal with this incongruity, the person adopts one or more of the following three strategies (Berzon, 1988). The first is the *inhibition strategy* and describes the person who regards the definition of his behavior (thoughts, feelings) as correctly gay, but who finds this definition undesirable and unacceptable. Several actions are taken: the person restricts information regarding homosexuality (e.g., I don't want to hear, read, or know about it) or inhibits behavior (e.g., It may be true, but I'm not going to do anything about it). Denying the personal relevance of information regarding homosexuality is also an action taken (e.g., It has nothing to do with me). Other possible behaviors include becoming hypersexual (e.g., within the context of heterosexual interactions) or becoming asexual, wherein the person seeks a "cure." Another action is to become an antigay moral or religious crusader. If the inhibition strategies employed are successful in enabling the person to inhibit, redefine, or disown responsibility for gay behavior, a foreclosure of gay/lesbian identity will occur at Stage 1.

Personal innocence strategy is a second strategy. Here, the person rejects either the meaning or the context of the homosexual behavior so as not to have to own it. He then redefines the meaning or context of the behavior. For example, in US society, genital contact between males is acceptable in a variety of situations without the participating individuals being defined as gay. Little boys have "circle jerks." Men confined for long periods of time without access to women, such as in prison or other confined situations, have genital contact with one another, and they are not defined as gay. The shift occurs in the contextual meaning when males develop emotional attachments to the other males with whom they are having sex or when they have repeated contacts with the same male, increasing the possibility of emotional involvement.

For females in US society, just the opposite is true. Girls can be inseparable, experience deep emotional involvement with one another, and spend more time with each other than they do with the men in their lives, even into adulthood, and this behavior is not regarded as gay or unusual. For this reason, it may be easier for girls and women to hide their lesbian behavior or identities longer. The shift occurs when they have genital contact in addition to their emotional involvement, which is more likely to be considered lesbianism but may not be. Quite a bit of same-sex sexual experimentation occurs in adulthood among persons who had been or currently are in heterosexual marriages. Qualitative research is needed in this area to understand this phenomenon.

Another personal innocence strategy is categorized as redefining context. The individual disowns responsibility for his homosexual behavior by redefining the context in which it occurred. Examples of these rationalizations are "I was just experimenting," "I was drunk," "I just did it for the money," "I did it as a favor for a friend," "It was an accident," and "I was taken advantage of."

Success in the use of the inhibition and personal innocence strategies depends on the individual's ability to avoid provocative situations and to employ the psychological defense of denial. It is impossible to avoid erotic dreams and physiological responses to persons of the same sex to whom the individual is attracted. In this instance, these strategies will be only partially successful, and the individual may very well experience the beginning of a negative or self-rejecting sexual identity.

The person in the *information-seeking strategy* is likely to adopt this third strategy if the meaning attributed to his homosexual behavior is perceived as correct, or at least partially acceptable. Now the individual seeks more information in books, in therapy, or in talking with anyone who might have expertise or experience related to this topic. The question being addressed is "Am I homosexual?" How individuals perceive these characteristics or behaviors will influence the way they seek to resolve the incongruence, either through repression (identity foreclosure) or by moving into Stage 2. This strategy of seeking more information moves the person along to Stage 2.

Stage 2: Identity Comparison   Individuals begin to investigate those qualities first experienced in Stage 1. As they begin to gather information and seek out contacts with gay others, there is increased congruence between self-perceptions and behaviors but increased conflict with others. Stage 2 statements of *identity comparison* would include "I feel like I probably am gay, although I am not definitely sure." "I feel different. I think I may want to talk with someone, maybe someone gay about feeling different, but I'm not sure if I really want to or not."

As the person accepts the possibility that he may be gay, the individual begins to examine the wider implications of being gay. Whereas in Stage 1 the task was to handle the self-alienation that occurs with the first glimmerings of homosexuality, the main task of Stage 2 is to handle the social alienation that is produced by feeling different from peers, family members, and society at large. A particularly troubling aspect of relinquishing one's heterosexual identity is the giving up of behavioral guidelines and the expectations for one's future that accompany them. If marriage and family are not in one's future, then what is? What will give form, structure, and a sense of normalcy to one's life? With the letting go of a perception of a self that is clearly heterosexual, one can experience a profound feeling of loss. Here the person is able to see a gap between the identity of which they themselves are aware and the identity presented to others.

Certain conditions heighten the feeling of alienation from others, such as living in geographic isolation with no other gay people or resources available and being from a family that is deeply religious and with strong convictions about homosexuality as a sin.

Here are four strategies the individual may employ to reject homosexual self-definition while continuing homosexual behavior:

1. *Special case.* The person characterizes what is happening as the product of a liaison with one person and this one person only.
2. *Ambisexuality.* The person says he can be sexual with anybody; it doesn't matter what gender the other person is.
3. *Temporary identity.* The person regards his homosexuality as only temporary: "I could be heterosexual again any minute."
4. *Personal innocence.* The person blames his homosexuality on anyone or everyone else.

As conflict heightens, individuals may move to Stage 3.

Stage 3: Identity Tolerance   *Identity tolerance* is marked by increased contact with the gay community, leading to greater empowerment. At this point, individuals hold an increasingly strong gay self-image but continue to present themselves (outside the community) as heterosexual. There is dissonance, and the person is characterized as reluctantly adopting a gay self-concept based on the stigma associated with this identity and their own internalized oppression: "I'm gay and I tolerate (put up with) it." "I see myself as homosexual for now, but I'm not sure about the future." These are statements that a person would make at this stage. It occurs when the person has come to accept the probability that he is gay and recognizes the sexual, social, and emotional needs that come with being homosexual.

With more of a commitment to a gay identity, the person is now free to pursue social, emotional, and sexual needs. Doing this accentuates the difference between the person and heterosexuals even more. To deal with the increased social alienation from heterosexuals, the person seeks out gay people and the gay subculture. Involvement in the gay/lesbian community has distinct advantages in terms of movement toward a more positive gay/lesbian identity. According to Berzon (1988), it (1) contributes to a ready-made support group that understands and shares the individual's concerns; (2) provides opportunities to meet a partner; (3) gives access to positive gay and lesbian role models; and (4) provides opportunities to practice feeling more at ease as a lesbian or a gay man. However, if the person has poor social skills, is very shy, has low self-esteem, has strong fear of exposure (of sexual identity), or has a fear of the unknown, positive contacts are made more difficult.

A negative experience may occur if the person encounters gay men and lesbians who are still employing the inhibition and denial strategies of Stages 1 and 2. These lesbians and gay men will be perceived as unhappy, self-rejecting individuals with whom one would not want to be affiliated. However, individuals at this stage will be empowered by people who are accepting of their own gay and lesbian identities. A shift occurs when the individual's significant others are gay rather than heterosexual.

If the contacts made are experienced as negative, a reduction of involvement with gay subculture is probable, resulting in a foreclosure at Stage 3. If contacts are perceived as positive, it is likely that the strategies employed have broken down and that the individual will want to explore further. This breakdown of strategies will result in movement into Stage 4. In any case, the commitment to gay identity is now sufficient for the person to say, "I am gay."

Stage 4: Identity Acceptance   At this point, the conflict between the self and nongay others' perceptions is at an intense level. This conflict may be resolved through passing as "straight," having limited contact with heterosexuals, or selectively disclosing to significant (heterosexual) others. A person at this stage may say, "I am quite sure that I am gay/lesbian." "I accept this fairly happily." "I am prepared to tell a few people about being gay/lesbian (e.g., friends, family members), but I carefully select whom I tell." Identity acceptance occurs when the person accepts, rather than tolerates, a gay self-image and contact with the gay/lesbian subculture continues and increases.

The individual now has a positive identification with other gay people. The questions of earlier stages (What am I? Where do I belong?) have been answered. Attitudes toward sexual orientation of the gay men and lesbians with whom the person becomes associated are crucial at this point. If these individuals regard being gay as partially legitimate (being gay is acceptable in private, but being public about it is not acceptable), then the person is likely to adopt this attitude as his own philosophy and to live a compartmentalized, "passing" gay life.

To reduce the stress involved in interfacing with a homophobic society, the person has less and less to do with heterosexuals. Some selective disclosure of gayness to nongay family, friends, and coworkers occurs, but as much control as possible is exercised over the potentially discrediting information. The emphasis is on fitting into society and not making waves. If, on the one hand, this strategy is successful, the person forecloses at this identity acceptance stage. If, on the other hand, the person comes to associate with people who regard being gay as fully legitimate (in private and public), this attitude is likely to be adopted. Greater acceptance of one's gay orientation tends to increase the distance the person now feels from a society that is still homophobic. Homophobic attitudes are now particularly offensive to the person characterized by this stage.

To deal with the anger toward a rejecting society, in combination with the increasing self-acceptance that is occurring, the person moves into Stage 5. Those who find that the strategies described effectively manage the conflict may stay at this level comfortably; otherwise, the continuing conflict pushes them onward.

Stage 5: Identity Pride   Identity pride is marked not only by strong pride in the gay community and in identity, but also by intense anger directed toward, and isolation from, the heterosexual society. The conflict is managed through fostering a dichotomized homosexual (valued) and heterosexual (devalued) worldview. How others, particularly those who are not gay, respond to the expression of these feelings influences whether individuals move to the final stage. Persons who have arrived at this stage may say, "I feel proud to be a gay/lesbian and enjoy living as one." "I am prepared to tell many people about being gay/lesbian and make no attempt to hide this fact." "I prefer to mix socially with other gay men/lesbians because heterosexuals are typically antigay." This stage occurs when, accepting the philosophy of full legitimization, the person becomes immersed in the gay/lesbian subculture and has less and less to do with heterosexual others.

As identification with the gay/lesbian community deepens, pride in accomplishments of the community increases. Daily living still requires continuing encounters with the heterosexual world and its homophobic attitudes. These encounters produce feelings of frustration and alienation. The combination of anger and pride energizes the person into action against the heterosexual establishment and creates "the activist."

Confrontation with the heterosexual establishment brings the person more into public view, and earlier strategies to conceal sexual orientation must be abandoned. Doing so precipitates disclosure crises with significant heterosexuals, such as family and coworkers. It is better to tell the folks yourself than to let them hear that you are gay as you are interviewed on a news program.

What becomes crucial at this point is whether those significant heterosexuals in the gay person's life react negatively to the disclosure as expected or react positively. If the reaction is negative, confirming the person's expectations that it would be so, the view of the world as being divided into gays (who are okay) and nongays (who are not okay) gets reinforced. In this instance, the person forecloses at the identity pride stage. If the reactions of the heterosexuals to whom the person discloses are positive and inconsistent with his negative expectations, the person tends to change those expectations, which moves him into Stage 6.

Stage 6: Identity Synthesis   Movement to identity synthesis most likely occurs when individuals experience positive reactions from heterosexual others. The need to dichotomize the world into gays who are okay and nongays who are not is gone. The gay/lesbian aspect of one's identity can now be integrated with all other aspects of self.

Sexuality is regarded as one part of the individual's total identity. There is some conflict, but it is at the lowest and most manageable point. The person at this stage says, "I am prepared to tell anyone that I am gay/lesbian." "I am happy about the way I am but think that being gay/lesbian is not the most important part of me." "I mix socially with fairly equal numbers of gay men/lesbians and heterosexuals and anyone who is accepting of gay men and lesbians." The individual now acknowledges that some nongay people are as supportive of his gay identity as other gay people are. Because heterosexuals as a class are no longer seen as hostile, it is no longer necessary to sustain the high level of anger seen at Stage 5. Increasing contact with supportive nongays produces more trust.

Troiden's Homosexual Identity Developmental Model

Troiden (1989) also developed a nonsequential model of homosexual identity. *Sensitization* is the first stage and occurs before puberty. Here the child is more concerned with gender identification than with sexuality. *Identity confusion* is the next stage. Movement occurs during adolescence, around the age of 18 for females and 17 for males. There is a shift to sexuality and conflict exists between the identity developed during childhood and the identity demanded during adolescence.

Often adolescents struggle tremendously in this stage because they are ill-prepared from their heterosexual socialization to deal with these feelings and perceptions. *Identity assumption* is the third stage and occurs around ages 19 to 21 for males and 21 to 23 for females. One of the key tasks here is learning to make sense out of and negotiate social stigma. *Commitment* is the final stage and occurs around ages 21 to 24 for males and 22 to 23 for females. It includes commitment to a same-sex love marked by identifying oneself as gay, lesbian, or bisexual. There is less dependence on passing strategies here.

Sullivan's Model of Sexual Identity Development

Sullivan's (1998) model has five stages that include active and passive phases. It is relevant for both gay and heterosexual people. The first stage is *naivete* and reflects little awareness of sexual orientation. The second stage, *acceptance*, is characterized by a predominance of heterosexist thinking. *Resistance,* the third stage, as is consistent with many identity development models, reflects a state of dissonance. Oppression is now seen. *Redefinition* is the fourth stage. Here the person is reformulating his notions of heterosexuality not dictated by the discourses of heterosexism. The final stage is *internalization* and reflects the person's efforts to integrate newfound values into all aspects of his life.

COUNSELING GAYS, LESBIANS, AND BISEXUALS OF COLOR

Within generally supportive gay and lesbian social communities, people of color who are gay, lesbian, bisexual, and transgender are often oppressed and do not receive the affirmation that White GLBT people receive (Loiacano, 1989). Battle, Cohen, Warren, Fergerson, and Audam (2002) conducted a study in conjunction with the National Gay and Lesbian Task Force with 2,465 Black GLBT people—58% men, 43% women, and 3% transgendered. They found that two thirds indicated that homophobia was a problem within the Black community. Half of the respondents agreed that racism is a problem for Black GLBT people in their relations with White GLBT people. Gender differences were found regarding the most important issues facing Black GLBT people. Approximately 72% of the men stated that HIV/AIDS was the most important issue facing Black GLBT people, while 55% of the women responded the same way. Women were more likely, at 50%, to say that hate crime violence was the most pressing issue; less than 40% of the men responded in this way. In addition to contending with hate crime, there is the pressing issue of domestic violence in same-sex relationships, which the National Coalition Against Domestic Violence estimates at 25% to 33% (Peterman & Dixon, 2003). Gay families struggle with many of the same issues that heterosexual families contend with and need support and appropriate intervention (Laird, 2003).

The racism and oppression faced by gay men and lesbians of color often urge them to turn to their same-race communities for the development of coping techniques, help with maintaining a positive identity, and potential support (Icard, 1986). Because of the level of homophobia, few gay men and lesbians of color actually find needed support psychologically and socially. The African American community often reflects the attitude that homosexuality is inconsistent with being Black (Riggs, 1994).

Black gay males are faced with a problem of complying with male role expectations that include propagating the race and holding allegiance to the African American community, which generally maintains an anti-homosexual attitude (Icard, 1986). Similarities are found within the Native American and Asian American cultures. Greene (1994) said that "bearing some similarity to Asian cultures, gender roles are clearly delineated among Indian families, and obedience to parents is expected" (p. 247).

In working with Native American gay clients, the devastation of colonialism and Western influences need to be considered in interpreting sexuality. It is crucial that Spirit, and not the material world, be held as sacred in traditional Native American cultures. Gunn Allen (1992) talked about the gynocentric societies, which value the centrality of women, honor the young, and revere all of life that is part of the whole. In traditional society, there were sacred places for men and women who were embodied by Spirit and did not want to marry persons of the other gender, and there were men who dressed and lived like women. Among Native Americans, the term *berdache* has been misapplied to both gay men and lesbians. It is an Arabic word meaning "sex-slave boy" and has no relevance to American men or women (Gunn Allen, 1992). Concerning contemporary Native Americans who are gay, Greene (1994) stated that acceptance may be less on reservations than in large urban centers. Gunn Allen pointed to acculturation and fundamentalist Christianity as major influences on homophobic attitudes among some Native people.

The Policy Institute of the National Gay and Lesbian Task Force interviewed 912 Latino gay men drawn from New York, Miami, and Los Angeles as part of a project called Nuestras Voces (Our Voices). The men reported widespread experiences with oppression (homophobia, racism, and poverty). Sixty-four percent were verbally insulted as children for being gay or effeminate, 31% reported experiences of racism in the form of verbal harassment as children, 35% reported having been treated rudely as adults on account of their race or ethnicity, and 61% experienced a shortage of money for basic necessities, with 54% borrowing money to get by during the last 12 months before the interview (Diaz & Ayala, 2002). The report found that men who were high risk (less likely to use protection when engaging in anal intercourse with a non-monogamous partner) had higher rates of oppression when compared with low-risk men. To survive or cope with the pain of societal oppression and accompanying feelings of powerlessness, many men turn to drugs or alcohol as aids and comforters. Diaz and Ayala stated, "Substances are used to cope not only with homophobic messages but also with the anger and frustration caused by poverty, racism and many other forms of social discrimination and abuse" (p. 16). The authors proposed that HIV prevention programs must also help men learn to cope with (*and resist*—emphasis mine) the toxic forces of racism, poverty, sexism, and homophobia because these social forces weigh heavily on Latino gay men's lives. It is important for therapists who work with gay immigrant, ethnic, and other clients of color to ask the following questions:

1. Is the client an immigrant or American born?
2. To what ethnic group does the client belong?
3. What are the specific cultural values of this group? Of the client's family? Of the client?
4. How strongly does the client follow traditional customs?
5. What is the client's socioeconomic status?
6. What is the client's level of bilingualism?

IMPLICATIONS FOR COUNSELORS AND PSYCHOLOGISTS

The American Psychological Association (2006) issued 16 guidelines for psychotherapy with lesbian, gay, and bisexual clients organized across four areas: attitudes, relationships and families, diversity issues, and education. Guidelines 1 through 4 stipulate that psychologists recognize bisexuality and assessment and treatment of LGBT populations, that homosexuality is stigmatized in society, and that psychologists' prejudicial attitudes can adversely affect the LGBT clients' level of disclosure. The second four guidelines suggest that psychologists strive to respect the important role that relationships have for LGBT people, that parenting can be particularly challenging, that family ties need not be defined by biology only, and that sexuality can have an impact on relationships and communication within one's family of origin. Guidelines 9 through 13 encourage psychologists to understand the struggles that many LGBT people experience, particularly youth, people with disabilities, and persons of color, and that the population as a whole is very diverse. The last three guidelines pertain to education and state that psychologists support training and knowledge development on LGBT issues and are aware of community resources for this population.

Several helping strategies that counselors can employ in their work with LGBTIQQ people are as follows:

1. Be aware of personal feelings toward gay men, lesbians, and people who are transgendered.
2. Validate confusion.
3. Provide a safe, supportive environment conducive to the exploration of this struggle and confusion.
4. Explore what it means to be gay.
5. Dispute myths about homosexuality and bisexuality.
6. Suggest readings.
7. Help the client move beyond the grief by acknowledging and expressing the loss of a heterosexual blueprint for life.
8. Become familiar with local resources for gay men, lesbians, bisexuals, and transgendered people, and suggest supportive organizations to assist the client in building a support structure within the gay community.
9. Assist the client in overcoming barriers to positive socialization.
10. Be sensitive to the impact a gay/lesbian, bisexual, or transgendered identity may have on the context surrounding the problems and issues faced by the individual.
11. Encourage the client to create a support system within the gay/lesbian/bisexual/transgender community before coming out to heterosexual significant others.
12. Have some type of gay, lesbian, or bisexual literature on the bookshelf.
13. Display something as small as a pin (one pin available for heterosexuals says "Straight but not narrow"), a poster, or a quote that depicts a multicultural and nonbiased view of the world.
14. Attend workshops on counseling gay men, lesbians, bisexuals, and transgendered people.
15. Stay informed of local gay events that can serve as a resource to clients.
16. Personally and honestly assess one's level of sexual identity development.
17. Be aware of sexual identity models for heterosexuals as well as models for GLBT clients.

Chojnacki and Gelberg (1995) connected Cass's model to developmental stages of heterosexual counselors. A counselor who is at Stage 1 (confusion) may not clearly comprehend the oppressive contexts in which gay, lesbian, and bisexual persons live. Therefore, such a counselor may not understand the need for clients to be in a support group. Counselors in the latter stages, such as Stage 5 (identity pride), begin to feel pride about the quality of the services they provide to their clients and recognize the importance of understanding "the history, culture, ethics, jargon, and sense of community that define the gay and lesbian culture" (Pope, 1995, p. 302). Counselors at this stage also begin to experience greater alienation from colleagues perceived to be homophobic. Many gay and lesbian clients are cautious about entering therapy because they are aware of the homoprejudice among society at large and even among members of the helping profession (Rothblum, 1994). Gay, lesbian, or bisexual persons are disadvantaged when the helping professional is ignorant of sexual orientation, developmental processes, identity development, counseling techniques, and overall challenges with which this population contends on a daily basis. Referring a client to a different counselor who can be more effective may be an option, particularly when the first counselor is unable or inadequately trained to provide the necessary support to the client. However, counselors need to ascertain whether their unwillingness to work with persons who are gay and lesbian is indicative of an intolerance for other sources of diversity, such as race, class, and ability.

CASE STUDY

ASSIGNING GENDER

Justin and Kaitlin are both 25 years old and have been married for two years. They were both excited to learn that Kaitlin was pregnant. After nine months of eating well, exercising, and regular prenatal visits, Kaitlin goes into labor. Justin is with her throughout the 17-hour process. When their baby is born, there is silence in the delivery room. Upon inquiring about the gender of their baby, the doctor says that tests have to be run. After a harrowing wait, their doctor informs them that their baby was born with ambiguous genitalia, more specifically a micropenis. Because the doctors doubt the functionality of the penis with respect to urination and having intercourse, they recommend that their child be assigned a gender of female after reconstructive surgery. Their child has a 46 XY karatype. Justin and Kaitlin agree with their doctor's recommendation and consent to the surgery. When friends and family call to inquire about the gender of their baby, they tell everyone they had a baby girl and that her name is Katherine. Three weeks later their daughter has surgery (a bilateral gonadectomy and labial skin biopsy). After a few days of recovery, Kaitlin and Justin are relieved that the last month is now behind them. The doctors informed them that prior to puberty, Katherine will need to begin estrogen replacement and have future surgery to create a functional vagina.

QUESTIONS

1. What are the factors that influence doctors' recommendation to perform gender reconstructive surgery at birth?
2. If Justin and Kaitlin had presented for therapy prior to making their decision, what would have been helpful for them to hear?
3. Should Katherine be told of her parents' decision?
4. What type of concerns might arise for Katherine later in life with respect to her reconstructive surgery?

(*Continued*)

(Continued)

DISCUSSION AND INTEGRATION

Kaitlin and Justin

It is estimated that approximately 1 in 1,000 to 2,000 newborns are considered ambiguous enough to be candidates for genital surgery (Phornphutkul, Fausto-Sterling, & Cruppuso, 2000). There are several principles that guide doctors' decision to perform reconstructive surgery. A few of them were mentioned in the case study. Phornphutkul, Fausto-Sterling, and Cruppuso also report that doctors are seeking to avoid stigmatization of the patient and that gender assignment should be made as quickly as possible and prior to the child's discharge from the hospital. In addition, the future potential for sexual function and fertility are considered. That gender identity is fairly malleable at birth and a long-standing position that ambiguous genitalia should be avoided has influenced the medical profession's thinking on this topic. Even today, a phallus size of less than 1.5 cm at term is considered inadequate for development of a functional penis. A functional penis is defined as the ability to have intercourse and to urinate standing up. The authors stated, "given that reconstructive surgery aimed at achieving functional female genitalia is considered the more effective alternative, XY intersexual patients with microphallus and testes are often assigned female gender" (p. 135).

Kaitlin and Justin as new and young parents did not anticipate the outcome they encountered and most likely do not have a frame of reference for dealing with this situation. Therapy would have encouraged the new parents to express their fears and anxieties about the life of their child with ambiguous genitalia. Taking time to do some research or secure a second opinion would also be recommended. Having support while making such a decision is extremely helpful. Hormonal therapy has been known to have a positive impact on the length of the phallus during puberty. Phornphutkul et al. (2000) take the position that sexual assignment should be based on the underlying diagnosis "even if sex of rearing may not coincide with size and functionality of the phallus. Whenever possible, reconstructive genital surgery should be delayed until the patient's gender identity can be incorporated into the decision making process" (p. 136).

What would it mean for children to be left alone at birth and live their lives as intersexuals? All persons should have an opportunity to receive the services of a well-trained, qualified, and empathic mental health professional. These services should not be offered by a few sympathetic counselors in the field, but rather be available from therapists who seek to empower their clients. What might it mean for a person's mental health, body image, and sexual satisfaction to have as an adult the body they were born with? The couple in the case study did not have a place to hear or work through these questions, and this is a problem. The dichotomization of gender through society—from bathrooms, to sports teams, to dressing rooms—is not respectful or allowing of intersexuality. Therapists working with intersexuals or parents grappling with this enormous decision for their children need to be prepared to help clients merge with a support system within the intersexual community as a way of lessening feelings of isolation and normalizing one's attributes in the event the parents leave their infants' bodies alone. Ultimately, parents want their children to have a good life, to find meaningful work and love. If they were counseled that such a life was possible without surgical reassignment, they may think differently about the finality of surgery.

Summary

This chapter examined sexual orientation and acknowledged that it exists on a continuum. Definitions were provided, and developmental processes, identity models, and implications for mental health professionals working with gay, lesbian, and bisexual clients were discussed. A case study that dealt with intersexuality exposed readers to an issue that is not often covered in the discussion of gender or even sexuality.

Converging Disability

> *There is no design reason that wheelchairs need be so "medicalized"*
> *in their appearance (the classic heavy metal look).*
>
> IRVING KENNETH ZOLA

If we are fortunate to live long and prosper, disability will visit each of us in some way, shape, or form. (See Storytelling: *Not Enough*.) This chapter has been influenced by the literature on disability studies and feminist disability theory (Garland-Thomas, 2002; Olkin & Pledger, 2003; Olkin, 2004). The status of the lived body, the politics of appearance, the medicalization of the body, the privilege of normalcy, multiculturalism, sexuality, the social construction of identity, and the commitment to integration are all aspects of a feminist disability theory, which also includes genetics, beauty, health, prosthetics, and reproductive technologies (Garland-Thomas, 2002).

Storytelling: Not Enough

A woman with a "facial difference" told a story in Zitzelsberger (2005) about walking down the street and being approached by a man who upon looking at her said, "You are so ugly." The woman took the message to mean she did not belong, that she was too ugly to participate. I hear it as his castigation of her for having failed to be appropriate—appropriate would mean looking much better than she did). Privileges of "normative femininity" are often denied to women with disabilities (Garland-Thomas, 2002). From a very early age, girls and boys are conditioned, in both subtle and overt ways, to believe that fulfillment in life is hugely dependent on a girl's physical beauty. One of the discourses associated with disability is that people with a disability are defined by the all-encompassing disability and that who they are in their other identities—a loyal friend, lover of mystery novels, collector of teapots, or jazz music aficionado—is irrelevant. Personal beauty is far too often considered the most important virtue a woman can possess. Lakoff and Sherr (1984) said, "Beauty is power." Due to their heightened levels of vulnerability, women with disabilities are more likely to experience abuse and violence (Hunt, Matthews, Milsom, & Lammel, 2006).

UNDERSTANDING DISABILITY

In 2007, nearly 15% of the population, or over 41.2 million people, had some level of disability (Brault, 2009). Disability encompasses a variety of internal and external conditions, capabilities, and limitations. It can involve the physical, such as muscular dystrophy, systemic (lupus), cognitive (e.g., traumatic brain injury), visual (blindness), hearing (e.g., deafness), developmental (e.g., autism), psychiatric (e.g., bipolar disorder), or multiple impairment (Olkin, 2004, p. 333). A person has a disability if any of the following conditions apply: used a wheelchair, crutches, or a walker; had difficulty performing one or more functional activities such as seeing, hearing, walking, or grasping; had difficulty with or needed assistance with one or more activities of daily living such as bathing, dressing, eating, or toileting; had a developmental delay or learning disability; had difficulty walking, playing, or moving arms; had a specific condition, such as mental retardation, cerebral palsy, or Alzheimer's disease; had a mental or emotional condition that seriously interfered with everyday activities; or had a condition that made it difficult to remain employed.

Tremendous heterogeneity exists among the disabled. Given the differences, defining this group as a collective is challenging (Smits, 2004). There are people with non-visible disabilities who do not self-identify or claim an identity that includes having a disability. There are also persons with noncongenital or medically defined disabilities. Due to advances in technology, some people with disabilities are able to work from home and earn a living, whereas for others, technology costs are prohibitive.

Gender, race, and the nature of the disability also contribute to the diversity among the disabled. Persons of color with disabilities represent those with the highest poverty and unemployment rates (Marini, 2001). Among Asians or Pacific Islanders, the rate for the presence of a disability was 11.5%. Asians also had the lowest prevalence both of a severe disability and of the need for assistance. Blacks had the highest rate for the presence of a disability, 19.8%, and the highest rate of a severe disability and the need for assistance. Among non-Hispanic Whites, the rate for the presence of a disability was higher than Asians, at 19%. More than half of people aged 21 to 64 with any type of disability (55.9%) had some employment in the 12 months prior to data collection. In 2010, median earnings for a householder with a disability was $25,550 compared with $58,736 for a householder without a disability. Between 2009 and 2010, the income of households maintained by a householder with a disability declined by 8.5%, compared with a 2.1% decline for households maintained by a householder without a disability. The majority of people with disabilities are female and they earn less than their disabled male counterparts and they earn less than women without a disability. In 2010, earnings of full-time, year-round workers aged 15 and older with a disability were, on average, lower than earnings of persons who did not have a disability. Men with a disability had median earnings of $41,506 in 2010, compared with $48,031 for men without a disability. Women with a disability had median earnings of $31,851, compared with $37,028 for women without a disability. Among persons 18–64 years of age with a disability between 2009 and 2010, the poverty rate rose from 25% to 27.9% or from 3.7 million people to 4.2 million people. Among people aged 18 to 64 without a disability, 12.5% and 22.0 million were in poverty in 2010. This represents an increase from 12.0% and 21.0 million in 2009. People with disabilities bear more of the burden of poverty than people without disabilities. Persons aged 18 to 64 with a disability represented nearly 16% (15.9 %) of people aged 18 to 64 in poverty compared to 7.8% of all people aged 18 to 64 (DeNavas-Walt, Proctor, & Smith, 2011). Poverty rate increases with the severity of the disability. The poverty rate for people 25 to 64 years of age with a severe disability is 25.9%, compared with 11.2% among people with a nonsevere disability. According to the APA (2011), there are two Federal government programs that provide assistance to persons with disabilities. Supplemental Security Disability Insurance (SSDI) is an insurance program for workers who have become disabled and are not able to work after having paid Social Security taxes for a number of years. A higher income is related to higher SSDI earnings. The other program is Supplemental Security Income (SSI), which is a welfare program for people who have low income and limited resources. Despite the assistance of these two programs, persons with disabilities are more likely to be unemployed and live in poverty. Persons who are blind and visually impaired have unemployment rates that exceed 70% (American Psychological Association Task Force on Socioeconomic Status, 2007). Among older veterans who live below the poverty level, 50% have a disability.

Within the psychology curriculum, graduate students are more likely to receive instruction on race, gender, class, sexuality, and other dimensions of diversity then they are on disability (Olkin & Pledger, 2003; Pledger, 2003). Although disability pervades all aspects of culture 20 years after the passage of the Americans with Disabilities Act (ADA), "the modal number of required courses on disability was still zero, as it was in 1989" (Garland-Thomas, 2002, p. 297). The individualistic frame that represents the majority of mental health professionals in the West tends to focus studies of disability on the individual instead of expanding the scope to include the family, the community, and even a political context. With less of an emphasis on a medical model of disability, mental health professionals are encouraged to collaborate with other disciplines when conducting disability research in order to approach the study from a multidisciplinary perspective (Tate & Pledger, 2003).

DISABILITY STUDIES

Disability studies is an interdisciplinary field that incorporates sociology, history, medical anthropology, politics, law, feminist psychology, and literature (Olkin & Pledger, 2003). Important to the foundation of disability studies is a shift in the paradigm regarding people with disabilities as consumers and as part of the independent living movement. A grounding in the social model of disability that recognizes power, oppression, and economic issues must be included in this discussion. Disability is not just a component of identity but "essential to the exploration of humanness" (p. 297), and that disability studies do not reproduce the oppressive discourses that exist in the larger culture is included.

This new and emerging field is not without its critics. Thomas (2004) argued that disability studies as a distinct area of study might lead to segregation of people with disabilities from the rest of society. It was also argued that the name—*disability studies*—placed emphasis on individuals' disabilities and not on their abilities.

Disability studies have shone a light on the traditional theoretical constructions of disability. The biomedical model of disability has predominated. This model is rooted in the scientific method and defined disability in the language of medicine. A focus is on the disability existing within the individual and not on the person's environment, policy considerations, or structural issues. More recently, a sociopolitical model has emerged that defines people with disability as members of a minority group given the prejudice and discrimination that accompany this identity. Smart and Smart (2006) defined three dimensions of this model: (1) definitions about disability must be from an insider's perspective, from persons with disabilities; (2) people with disabilities must advocate for themselves and not allow "experts" to define disability for them; and (3) people with disabilities resist the labels that align them and their bodies with deviance and pathology. This work is in support of the sociopolitical model.

One of the outcomes of disability studies is a new and holistic paradigm of disability that emphasizes new models of research. The integration of participatory action research methods and person–environment conceptualization of disability encourages researchers and clinicians to move away from the limitations of medically oriented definitions and measures of disability (Tate & Pledger, 2003). This emerging research paradigm means collaboration with members of the disability community and involving them in research that is accessible. It is important not to use research participants for the purpose of one's research effort without offering anything back to the community.

Olkin (2003) identified several avenues for recruiting research participants from the disability community. She recommended disability magazines and newsletters, independent living centers, support groups, disability events, and disability-specific Internet sites. Survey Monkey is also a way for persons with disabilities to participate in research. An alternative research format should also be used, such as very large and dark print.

THE SOCIAL CONSTRUCTION OF DISABILITY

Many of the barriers that people with disabilities face are reinforced through language. (APA, 2007), encouraged human service providers to be mindful of their use of language. For instance, it is less appropriate to refer to people with disabilities as "disabled people." Stating that a person *uses* a wheelchair is different from the statement that a person is *confined* to a wheelchair.

Disability is a broad term. Garland-Thomas (2002) critiqued the definition, which, she said, "clusters ideological categories as varied as sick, deformed, crazy, ugly, old, maimed, afflicted, mad, abnormal, or debilitated—all of which disadvantage people by devaluing bodies that do not conform to cultural standards: its structuring institutions, social identities, cultural practices, political positions, historical communities, and the shared human experience of embodiment" (p. 5). Our individualistic and capital-driven culture equates normalcy with bodily control and perfection. Garland-Thomas (2002) saw similarities across marginalized identities and said, "female, disabled, and dark bodies are supposed to be dependent, incomplete, vulnerable, and incompetent bodies...women and the disabled are portrayed as helpless, dependent, weak, vulnerable, and incapable bodies" (p. 7). Having an able body and mind are not just valued in society, but are considered blessings. The ability to control, produce, reproduce, and master nature are constructed as biological and, for some, as spiritually superior. Fowler, O'Rourke, Wadsworth, and Harper (1992) said, "When one's physical and/or mental abilities are considered as the primary status for characterizing individuals, the resulting polarity implicitly divides all persons into two groups: the able and the unable" (p. 14). Much like race and gender, physical disability is elevated to and exists as a status-determining characteristic, overriding other dimensions of the self. Even achieved traits are eclipsed by immutable characteristics as a function of birth or through injury or a medical condition. Relationships are often constituted on the basis of similarity, not just with respect to race and class but also with disability.

Dominant discourses associated with disability are that people with disabilities are helpless, childlike, dependent, unattractive, asexual, and low-income wage earners. People with visible disabilities encounter hostility in society due to their physical and mental differences that violate deeply held cultural values about productivity, beauty, control, youth, and mastery over nature. Persons with disabilities are discriminated against, stereotyped, ignored, and in many instances presumed to be biologically inferior, particularly if the disability is congenital as opposed to acquired (Marini, 2001).

Just as physical attractiveness has been linked to assumptions of moral character, intelligence, marital satisfaction, dating frequency, and quality of life (Dion, Berschid, & Walster, 1972; Webster & Driskell, 1983), so has disability. In fact, disability is constructed within the context of physical unattractiveness. The socialization process equates self-worth with mobility, thinness, beauty, and not being disabled. Hahn (1988a) said, "The most salient features of many disabled persons are bodily traits similar to skin color, gender, and other attributes that have been used as a basis for differentiating people for centuries and without which discrimination would not occur" (p. 26). Zola (1991) stated that preference for specific body types over others represents another societal "ism." In this work, this form of discrimination has been termed "ableism." Considerable silence surrounds the experiences of those who have disabilities. (See Storytelling: *Campus Access*.) This is particularly relevant among able-bodied persons who assume that lack of membership in the disability community entitles them to ignorance or apathy.

Real-life stories in which people experience dramatic and sudden changes in their bodies are numerous. (See Case Study: *Rethinking Manhood* at the end of this chapter.) Wendell (1989), for example, wrote powerfully about the sudden overnight process of going from being able-bodied to being disabled as a result of a disabling chronic disease. "In 1985, I fell ill overnight with what turned out to be a disabling chronic disease. In the long struggle to come to terms with it, I had to learn to live with a body that felt entirely different to me—weak, tired, painful, nauseated, dizzy, unpredictable" (p. 63). Waiting to return to her original state was indeed dangerous because the likelihood of this occurrence was remote. So, in time, Wendell was required to learn how to identify and coexist with her new disabled body but not without struggle. "I began slowly to identify with my new, disabled body and to learn to work with it" (p. 63). Within a culture where normalcy and disability are regarded as antonyms, she wrote, "Disabled women struggle with both the oppressions of being women in male-dominated societies and the oppressions of being disabled in societies dominated by the able-bodied" (p. 64).

Both Wendell (1989) and Zola (1991) maintained that a theory on disability and the body is needed. Because of the strong cultural assumptions of able-bodiedness and physical attractiveness, such a theory is beneficial to all, regardless of current or, better yet, temporary physical status.

Many people with disabilities experience their bodies through pain. Wendell (1989) stated that persons who live with chronic pain can teach the general public what it means to share space with chronic discomfort. Crucial questions emerge, such as how a person welcomes pain into

Storytelling: Campus Access?

In my role as a faculty senator, I received a call from a colleague who was disappointed and angered by her inability to get the campus to provide her with temporary public transportation from her office to her classroom during recovery from foot surgery. She stated she was not treated well by the various offices with whom she came into contact. I pursued her concerns and there was nothing available to her—she could have taken short-term disability and stayed at home recovering but as a dedicated teacher, she wanted to be on campus and teaching. Even with ADA, many spaces are not accessible to persons in scooters or wheelchairs, and even to mothers pushing their children in strollers. Our culture privileges those who are mobile, which is ironic. We are an aging society in which more and more people will face various forms of disability.

his or her life, especially if it is feared. In turn, are people with chronic pain feared and loathed by those who are reminded of their own vulnerability? Feeling the pain, as opposed to medicating it away (Wendell, 1989), meditating on the pain, engaging in visual imagery, and making peace with it are examples of being in, listening to, and embracing one's body. This increased consciousness is a gift from pain. Such a gift can move a person to a place of unconditional acceptance of her body despite the circumstances. Writer Audre Lorde (1994) said, "There is a terrible clarity that comes from living with cancer that can be empowering if we don't turn aside from it" (p. 36). It is in the not turning away, the bold and yet humble confrontation of the source of pain, that strength is found for the journey. All can benefit from this truth. Pain, in its various forms, is a feature of living and is independent of physical ability status.

The wisdom among some people with disabilities may benefit persons without disabilities. The tendency to regard people who are different as "other" impedes benefiting from people who do not look normal. "If disabled people were truly heard, an explosion of knowledge of the human body and psyche would take place" (Wendell, 1989, p. 77). Persons with disabilities have much to teach the able-bodied about acceptance, dignity, and empowerment.

PERFECTION, BEAUTY, AND THE ABLE BODY

Despite the valiant and noble efforts of the women's movement, negative body image continues into the 21st century. According to Hutchinson (1982), "Body image is not the same as the body, but is rather what the mind does to the body in translating the experience of embodiment into its mental representation" (p. 59). Birtchnell, Lacey, and Harte (1985) indicated three aspects of body image: (1) *physiological*, which involves the brain's ability to detect weight, shape, size, and form; (2) *conceptual*, which is the mental picture of one's own body; (3) and *emotional*, which refers to the feelings about one's body weight, shape, and size. A survivor of breast cancer (Elder, 2000) spoke movingly about the impact of the disease, but noted the silence around attractiveness and desirability. She worried about her appearance and how the mastectomy would affect her married life. Her husband was more concerned about her than the loss of her breast.

A physically active and able-body is a valued commodity within society. (See Storytelling: *Wrong Type of Groom*). Discourses concerning the female body's function as a site for others' approval and scorn predisposes girls and women to diminished self-esteem. Adult women are incapable of helping young women celebrate their bodies when they themselves are unable to honor their own bodies. The socialization of young girls to see their primary role in life as pleasing others encourages the development of anxiety, depression, and an unhealthy reliance

Storytelling: Wrong Type of Groom?

In Sharon Anderson and Valerie Middleton's *Explorations in Privilege, Oppression, and Diversity*, a young man tells a story of his approaching wedding day. Being Catholic he approached his priest to marry him and his bride. The priest would not marry the groom. Why? Because he was divorced? No. The priest would not marry the man because the man had a disability. The priest suspected that the man would not be able to reproduce (the purpose of marriage), which led the priest to question why the man wanted to get married in the first place.

on others for approval. Brouwers (1990) argued that the emotional aspect of body image is at the crux of bulimia, characterized by recurrent episodes of binge eating and subsequent feelings of lack of control. Intense dissatisfaction with body image and strong hatred of one's body is correlated with bulimia.

Dissatisfaction with one's body is reinforced in the face of unattainable standards of perfected beauty. Restricting and denying one's movement and comfort are handicapping, but this is what women do regularly to appear beautiful to others. Social desirability is aligned with wearing fashions that are uncomfortable (stilettos), tight (jeans), unflattering (muffin top jeans) and inappropriate (exposure of one's anatomy due to pelvic resting jeans), painful, and even harmful to the body. Stilettos are worn because they add height, slenderize the legs, and elongate the body. They also restrict movement and interfere with normal walking. Bunions, corns, and other serious foot problems suffered by millions of women result from the mantra that pain comes with beauty.

More and more women are opting for expensive and risky plastic surgery to achieve the perfect breasts, nose, and buttocks. Garland-Thomas (2002) noted that "the beautiful woman of the 21st century is sculpted surgically from top to bottom" (p. 10). Aging and obesity are big business. The attitude is that beauty is something to be acquired and at any cost (Okazawa-Rey, Robinson, & Ward, 1987). Liposuction, abdominoplasty, face lifts, breast augmentation, and other forms of plastic surgery are commonplace. A relationship exists among beauty, thinness, success, power, acceptance, and self-worth moreso for girls and women than it does for boys and men. In fact, one study found that overall body dissatisfaction was higher among girls than among boys (Paxton et al., 1991). This finding may explain why 87% of those who undergo plastic surgery are women (Steinem, 1992).

Billions of dollars are spent annually on products and services in Herculean efforts to beautify, freshen, deny, and defy the aging process. Looking good is not denounced. The maniacal emphasis placed on physical attractiveness as synonymous with having an able body is problematic. Hahn (1988a) discussed beauty power and its association with mate selection and sexual intimacy. She said, "As long as physical beauty determines sexual choices, human relations will be guided by fortuitous pleasing compositions of bone, muscle, and skin" (p. 27). Hahn observed that inner beauty and character will take a back seat in the competition for partners. Perceived as a prized commodity, beauty operates to "snare a mate who can give her the opportunity to live out her biological and social destiny" (Hutchinson, 1982, p. 60). Rockquemore (2002) said it well: "for women, appearances are power in the mating market" (p. 492).

Age is the one identity construct that has the greatest bearing on beauty. *Ageism*, or discrimination against middle-aged and elderly people, differs between men and women. According to Nuessel (1982), "Ageism is distinct from other forms of discrimination because it cuts across all of society's traditional classifications: gender, race, religion, and national origin" (p. 273).

Ageism affects women in that in the normal and inevitable maturational process, men mature and become refined; women wilt and wither. The devaluation of women's bodies among a male-dominated medical community cannot be divorced from lucrative and costly hysterectomies and other surgeries for women. The medical community has used estrogen against women to support a belief that this hormone is essential for femininity and youth. Now women are discouraged from using hormone replacement therapy unless indicated. Although there are benefits, such as relief from the symptoms of menopause, cancer is a risk.

As women mature and develop a sense of personal power and an internal locus of control, they come to perceive their beauty differently. Powerful women recognize that responsible self-care and respect for others is superior to selflessness and that becoming older is a privilege.

IMPLICATIONS FOR COUNSELORS AND PSYCHOLOGISTS

Mental health professionals have a responsibility to address disability issues in addition to having the psychological skills and expertise to assist the client (Pledger, 2003). Towards this end, APA's Committee on Disability in Psychology is dedicated to: (1) promoting the psychological welfare of people with disabilities; (2) promoting the development and implementation of psychological service delivery models responsive to the needs of people with disabilities; (3) promoting the awareness of disability issues in psychological research as well as specific research activity in disability areas; and (4) promoting inclusion of knowledge about disabilities and disability issues in education, training programs, and professional development of psychologists.

Helping professionals are not exempt from attitudes that favor attractive children and adults over those regarded as unattractive (Ponzo, 1985). Guidance counselors need to be particularly mindful of the power of words in shaping children's constructions of themselves. Lerner and Lerner (1977) wrote, "Evidence suggests that when compared to the physically attractive child, the unattractive child experiences rejecting peer relations, the perception of maladjustment by teachers and peers, and the belief by teachers of less educational ability" (p. 586).

Professionals are encouraged to ascertain their own beliefs about body image and physical attractiveness. Some may be more inclined to gravitate toward able-bodied and attractive clients. This is biased behavior and discredits a profession that should be oriented toward empowerment and respect. Due to worldview, gender, culture, and/or individual differences, some clients may not value and thus may not strive for independence or mastery over their environments. Refusing to do so is not a form of pathology, but such attitudes have to be examined in the context of culture (Marini, 2001).

Mental health professionals need to assess the impact of the culture's messages about beauty, perfection, and disability on their self-esteem and on their perceptions, favorable and otherwise, of others. Smart and Smart (2006) warn, "If the counselor views disability as a tragic inferiority, then he or she will more likely experience a negative, emotional response to the client with a disability" (p. 37). Knowledge about a client's disability and accompanying functional limitations is part of multicultural competence (Marini, 2001).

To improve compliance with the Americans with Disabilities Act and to serve the needs of individuals with disabilities, it is recommended that mental health professionals:

1. Do not deny services to a client with a disability.
2. Do not provide unequal service to clients with disabilities. Different service to respond effectively to a client's needs is not the same as unequal.
3. Provide auxiliary aids such as large print materials, Braille, notepads, and pencils.

4. Evaluate the structural and architectural environment (ramps, curb cuts, elevator control buttons) to ensure access into the building.
5. Involve the services of a contractor when building a new office so that ADA requirements can be followed. (APA, 2007).

CASE STUDY

RETHINKING MANHOOD

Reese is a 24-year-old Latino male from a low-wage-earning family. At the age of 14, he joined a gang and eventually became a person with a VASCI (violence-acquired spinal cord injury). During a gun fight with a rival gang, Reese was shot two times in the back. One of the bullets nicked his spinal cord. Reese survived the gunshot blasts and is now a quadriplegic. The brush with death was sobering for him and has allowed him to redirect his life. He is now going through peer mentoring training, has a stable relationship with his fiancé, and looks forward to starting college some day in the future. Part of Reese's role as a peer mentor is to discuss sex following a spinal cord injury. Reese realizes he needs help in addressing these issues and receives assistance from his mentor.

QUESTIONS

1. How can a mentor assess where Reese is in his own recovery?
2. How does Reese's status as a quadriplegic affect his masculinity and, more specifically, his sexuality?
3. Could a female mentor help Reese?

DISCUSSION AND INTEGRATION

The Mentor, Reese

Disability intersects with gender. In a society where masculinity is equated with virility, strength, sexuality, and self-reliance, it is understandable that men with physical disabilities are perceived as contradictions to hegemonic masculinity. Gerschick and Miller (1994) stated that "men with physical disabilities are marginalized and stigmatized because they undermine the typical role of the body in United States culture . . . Men's bodies allow them to demonstrate the socially valuable characteristics of toughness, competitiveness, and ability" (p. 35). To arrive at a place of acceptance of one's body, there has to be (1) a confrontation of the societal standard that maintains that masculinity is not only narrowly defined but also in contradiction to the disabled man's body; (2) repudiation of this socially constructed norm; and (3) affirmation of the self through a recognition that the norms and discourses, and not the person, are problematic (Collins, 1989). From this perspective, the man is able to reconstruct, for himself and for others, alternative gender roles and practices (Gerschick & Miller, 1994).

Myers et al. (1991) stated that, in society today, with all of its isms, "the very nature of the conceptual system is itself inherently oppressive and that all who adhere to it will have a difficult time developing and maintaining a positive identity" (p. 55). A suboptimal system operates when self-worth is attached to factors separate from the self. Optimally, self-worth is intrinsic to the self. Accidents and illness suddenly change the ability and control over one's body.

Core American values—the Protestant work ethic, individualism, capitalism, and self-reliance—are inextricably bound to notions of physical attractiveness, power, mobility, strength, and dominance over one's body. Vulnerability and uncertainty simply do not coexist well in a society that values domination and conquest and believes that illness and subsequent disability are a result of the individual's doing. Wendell (1989) stated, "The demand for control fuels an incessant search for the deep layered explanations for causes of accidents, illness, and disability" (p. 72).

A client who experiences a traumatic loss needs time and space to mourn and process the loss. After being shot, Reese's life can be meaningful; first, however, he has to redefine some of the dimensions of manhood, such as success, attractiveness, masculinity, sexual activity, and function. Because "a disability carries sufficient conceptual power to stereotype an individual, regardless of whether the disability was present at birth or acquired later in life" (Fowler et al., 1992, p. 102), Reese's conceptualization of self across multiple identities has shifted. Part of this shifting self-conceptualization encompasses what it means to be a man.

A multiculturally competent mentor is not reluctant to explore the violence in Reese's past and how he makes meaning of it in the present. Reese did not fall asleep while driving and hit a tree. He was involved in gang-related violence and so was the man who shot him. Where is Reese with feelings of anger and fantasies of retaliation? In Hernandez's (2005) qualitative study of 16 men with newly acquired spinal cord injury from gunshot trauma, she found three main themes: disability was viewed as a wake-up call or blessing, disability was viewed as a turning point, and disability was viewed as identity transforming.

Reese does not have a disease. His disability is from a violent injury, and he is healthy within the context of his disability. Seeing Reese as sick does not encourage the mentor to view him as active, able, and alive—all words that tend not to be associated with the experience of having a disability (APA, 2007). Garland-Thomas (2002) identifies resistance to claiming a disability identity as partly influenced by limited ways to talk about disability that are not oppressive.

At the appropriate time, the mentor can help Reese critique traditional and oppressive notions of masculinity for all men, regardless of ability or disability. Boys are socialized to believe that masculinity is synonymous with being a protector, provider, and worker. Athleticism and body strength create the basis for virility. Men with physical disabilities struggle with internalized notions of masculinity that are inconsistent with the presence of disability. Men with disabilities are not perceived by society as strong because a large part of this strength and manhood equation is having an able body, which is synonymous with the ability to achieve an erection. There are different types of strength, physical as well as character, that are not typically identified by society.

Asking for psychological help is a form of self-reliance and control (Roberts, Kisselica, and Frederickson, 2002). Research has shown that supportive social networks are associated with psychological well-being and adjustment to one's disability (Belgrave, 1991; Swanson, Cronin-Stubbs, & Sheldon, 1989). Prior to the accident, Reese had a very active, albeit dangerous, life involving the full use of his legs. Although Reese's mobility has been improved by his wheelchair, which is controlled by mouth, a measure of Reese's

(*Continued*)

(*Continued*)

healing is his physical, social, and mental activity. The mentor will want to know what Reese's identity means to him, particularly as he will be helping men who are grappling with a loss of identity.

Recently, Reese has noticed his ability to move two of his fingers on his right hand. This change in functional limitation gives him hope that he will be able to do more in the future. Reese's ability to perform is by no means static but fluctuates across situations and environments—this variation in function is known as the enablement/disablement phenomenon (Pledger, 2003). Through journaling, within small groups, and by providing assistance to others, Reese can continue to unravel the strongholds of socially constructed notions of desirability, attractiveness, and worthiness that have had an enormous impact on his self-concept. Reese's mentor reframes meanings of strength, realizing that Reese can exhibit strength through his lived experiences of dignity, interdependence, competitiveness, and wisdom.

Many of the issues Reese and other men grapple with are related to sexual impotence. A woman could be an appropriate mentor to the extent that she is comfortable with the client's transference and is able to frankly discuss sex. When possible, clients should be asked what their preferences are. They should not have to contend with a counselor who remains uncomfortable with intimate conversation the client needs as part of his recovery. Reese has major concerns about his sexual activity and its expression, given his inability to achieve an erection. How will he experience sexual gratification? How will he provide sexual pleasure? A series of technological devices are available that assist couples with achieving satisfying sex lives in the event of spinal cord injuries, medication-induced impotence, and other barriers to erection. Penile implants made of silicone or polyurethane can be surgically installed. One type consists of two semirigid but bendable rods; the other type consists of a pump, a fluid-filled reservoir, and two cylinders into which the fluid is pumped to create an erection. Vacuum devices can also be used to increase blood flow to the penis. Problems have been reported with both vacuum and inflatable devices (Balch, 2006, p. 509).

Reese's body, mind, spirit, and heart are sources of giving and receiving intense pleasure. Notions of what constitutes a normal sex life had to be altered for Reese to find the meaning that is now a part of his life. Genital sex is one way to give and receive pleasure but it is not the only way.

Finally, it is crucial to remember that what is perceived as attractive is a socially constructed cultural dictate mediated and perpetuated by society. Many Native Americans do not regard disability as punishment for having sinned and tend not to judge or stigmatize people (Marini, 2001).

Summary

This chapter examined the culture's fascination and preoccupation with physical attractiveness. A case study examined able-bodyism in a male client who had become disabled as a result of a violent incident. Implications for counselors were discussed with respect to the convergence of physical attractiveness, race, age, ability, disability, and gender. Demographic data were presented on the number of Americans with disabilities.

Converging Spirituality

> *When the student is ready, the Master will come.*
>
> JAPANESE BUDDHIST PROVERB

A case study is presented first and discussed throughout this chapter. Definitions of spirituality and religion are provided. Spirituality as a component of diversity, as an identity construct and as an integral part of the therapy process, is discussed.

SPIRITUALITY AND RELIGION DEFINED

Religion and spirituality are interrelated, but important differences exist. Religion comes from the Latin root *religio*, which means a "bond between humanity and the gods" (Ingersoll, 1995, p. 11). Religion is the practice of one's beliefs with respect to a higher being. Involved are behaviors, rituals, and routines related to the worship experience (Robinson & Watt, 2001). Spirituality is understood as the "outward expression of the inner workings of the human spirit" (Swinton, 2001, p. 20).

CASE STUDY

CRISES OF FAITH

Tim is a 36-year-old African American man. He has been married for six years to Geri, also 36. They met while they were in college and are both from the Northwest. They reside in Seattle, Washington. They regularly enjoy a variety of outdoor activities throughout the year: cross-country skiing, horseback riding, and marathons. Tim is a youth pastor and feels that his work with teenagers is a calling from God. Geri is Director of Music at the church. Tim had been noticing a mild ache in his lower abdomen and pain in his genital area. He figured it was due to a rigorous weekend of cross-country skiing, as well as simply getting older. When the pain did not go away, he stopped doing strenuous exercise for a while. Geri noticed that Tim was limping slightly and was more reluctant to have intercourse. Geri pleaded with Tim to go to the doctor, but he was resistant and embarrassed. Once the pain increased, Tim could not ignore it any longer.

Tim had a physical, and during the exam, Dr. Wilson noticed that Tim's left testicle was enlarged. Tests confirmed the doctor's suspicions. Tim was diagnosed with advanced testicular cancer. The doctor recommended the use of radioactive rods and chemotherapy in order to give Tim the highest chances for survival. This technique did not eliminate the cancer, and the removal of both testicles was recommended. After much prayer, and second and third opinions, Tim decided to proceed with the procedure.

Six months later, Tim is cancer free and is back to work as a minister. He does not have the same passion for the ministry as he once did. He feels lost when talking with the teens about dating, marriage, and sexuality. As a result of the surgery, Tim is unable to have an erection and is on testosterone replacement therapy to avoid a feminizing direction to his body: weight gain, loss of muscle tone, and an upward shift in voice pitch. Dr. Wilson encourages exercise that requires less risk of bodily injury, such as walking, gardening, and cycling. He has also recommended medical techniques that would assist Tim and Geri sexually. Tim is really turned off at doing something that was meant to be natural. In the last year, Tim has struggled with depression, irritability, and overwhelming feelings of inadequacy. Because they desire children, Geri has suggested they pursue adoption. Tim is not interested in thinking about this issue. On a weekly basis since the surgery, Geri has heard Tim ask, "What have I done that is so terrible that God would punish me like this?" On the advice of his senior minister, Tim reluctantly goes for counseling. His counselor is Michael Grant, a licensed professional European American counselor who specializes in men's issues. He is Jewish.

QUESTIONS

1. How can Michael integrate Tim's spirituality into the therapy?
2. What are the implications of Michael's spirituality on his work with Tim?
3. How do counselors address crises of faith within therapy?

DISCUSSION AND INTEGRATION

The Therapist, Michael

Among many people, faith helps them cope with stress while making meaning in life, particularly when seeking to answer questions such as, "What will become of me?" or "What am I going to do?" Spirituality provides hope, particularly in the face of distress and uncertainty, and can give some a sense of meaning and purpose in life (Ganje-Fling & McCarthy, 1996). When this belief system fails to provide hope and purpose, a crisis of faith is said to result. Professionals need to first assess their own cultural and spiritual faith and belief systems to help clients navigate this oftentimes uneven terrain.

It is impossible to help clients explore anxiety producing and keep you up at night issues around spirituality, death, and sexuality if we, as mental health professionals, have not begun this narrative personally, intrapsychically (Robinson-Wood & Braithwaite-Hall, 2005). Michael cannot afford to overlook faith as key to Tim's identity and recovery. Dissimilarity in religious and spiritual values between Tim and Michael can explain Michael's hesitance to explore religion or self-disclose his values. If Michael lacks knowledge about Tim's culture and/or religion, it is crucial that he close this knowledge gap.

During their first session, Michael discloses that he is Jewish and does not go to temple regularly, but that his faith is important to him. Wiggins-Frame and Braun (1996) wrote of the importance of mental health professionals clarifying their values and religious beliefs in order to deal with such issues successfully in therapy. Michael also tells Tim that he is comfortable discussing religion and that many of his clients are not Jewish but Christians, Protestants, and Muslims, and some are atheists. Through the process of Michael's skillful questioning, he asks Tim to describe his spirituality. Tim became aware that he had subscribed to a belief that punishment came to those who had strayed from God's will and had shown disobedience. According to Sutherland and Moodley (2010), many African Americans believe that the mind, body, and soul are connected—and that what affects one affects the other. Tim was characterized by this belief system. From his vantage point, he was deliberate about cultivating a physically active lifestyle and maintaining a spiritual connection with God. Tim, prior to the cancer diagnosis, was a peaceful man. Because he saw himself as faithful to God's call on his life to pursue a divinity degree, commit his life to the ministry, and marry his wife, he felt lost in his ability to make sense out of the tragedy that had befallen him.

Michael had a clinical hunch that Tim held fast to some religious beliefs that were a source of oppression and did not contribute to his experiencing God's protection in his life (Robinson & Watt, 2001). Rather than interpret Tim's difficulty with cognitive restructuring as pathological, Michael understood that Tim's position was largely influenced by his religious beliefs. Michael's understanding of Christianity, along with his awareness of the overlap between his own religion and Christianity, aided him in disentangling spiritual themes from pathology in Tim's life (Schultz-Ross & Gutheil, 1997).

Age impacts religious identity and affiliation. According to the Pew Research Center (2010), one-in-four members of the Millennial generation, those who were born after 1980 and came of age at the beginning of the 21st century are not affiliated with any particular faith. They described their religion as "atheist," "agnostic" or "nothing in particular." This compares with less than one-fifth of people in their 30s (19%); 15% of people in their 40s; 14% of those in their 50s and 10% or less among those 60 and older. About two-thirds of young people (68%) say they are members of a Christian denomination and 43% describe themselves as Protestants. Among adults, 81% of adults 30 and older associate with Christianity and 53% who are Protestants. Older people are more likely to be involved religiously and to identify themselves as Christians. Young adults do not pray as often as their elders, yet the number of young adults who state that they pray daily is comparable to the proportion reported among young people in prior decades.

In their work with African American survivors of breast cancer, Halbert et al. (2007) saw spirituality "as having a personal relationship with a higher power and faith and may be a process used to find meaning in one's life, while religion is defined as a set of practices and beliefs (e.g., dogma) that are shared by a community or group" (p. 282). Spirituality is associated with a transcendent and sacred dimension (Robinson-Wood & Braithwaite-Hall, 2005) and includes a "capacity for creativity, growth, and development of a value system" (Young, Wiggins-Frame, & Cashwell, 2007, p. 48).

Ingersoll (1995) identified spirituality as having seven dimensions:

1. One's conception of the divine or a force greater than oneself
2. One's sense of meaning or what is beautiful and worthwhile
3. One's sense of a relationship with Divinity and other beings
4. One's tolerance or negative capability for mystery
5. Peak and ordinary experiences engaged to enhance spirituality (may include rituals or spiritual disciplines)
6. Spirituality as play or the giving of oneself
7. Spirituality as a systemic force that acts to integrate all the dimensions of one's life. (p. 11)

It is possible to be spiritual and not religious and to be religious and not spiritual (Burke & and Miranti, 2001). Religion is often associated with an institutionalized set of beliefs "by which groups and individuals relate to the ultimate" (Burke, 1999, p. 252). It is defined as the specific organized and codified form through which individuals may express their spirituality (Young et al., 2007, p. 48). Miller and Thoresen (2003) conceptualized religion as associated with the social phenomenon and spirituality understood at the level of the individual; nonetheless, spirituality and religion overlap and are related constructs in that they share some characteristics and do not share others.

Hall and Pargament (2003) caution against the polarization of religion and spirituality, which "ignores the fact that all forms of spiritual expression unfold in a social context and that virtually all organized faith traditions are interested in the ordering of personal affairs" (p. 64). These authors also site other consequences association with a bifurcation of religion and spirituality:

1. There is a risk that spirituality emerges as good and religion as bad. The truth is that there are helpful and harmful aspects related to each.
2. Most people experience spirituality within a religious context and frankly do not see a distinction between the two.
3. The polarization could lead to duplication of concepts and measures used in research.

CLINICAL SKILLS IN INTEGRATING SPIRITUALITY AND PSYCHOTHERAPY

Effective therapy does not deny differences between client and therapist but respects completely the multiple identities that comprise the self. Multiculturally competent therapy emphasizes an ecological framework wherein the person and environment interaction is considered along with culture, ethnicity, family, structural issues, history, and spirituality, which is seen as fundamental to who the client is in therapy (Robinson-Wood & Briathwaite-Hall, 2005). Spirituality is a core dimension of life, along with friendship, love, work, and self-regulation (Witmer & Sweeney, 1992), but there are barriers to an inclusion of spirituality into therapy.

The lack of training about spirituality within therapeutic contexts is a key issue for many therapists, particularly given that spirituality has emerged as a dimension of multiculturalism (Hall, Dixon, & Mauzey, 2004). Unresolved issues in the therapist's life, lack of clarity about spirituality as a mysterious and deep phenomenon, and fear of imposing values may lead a therapist to maintain silence. The misguided belief that spirituality cannot and should not be studied has contributed to its absence in research (Miller & Thoresen, 2003).

The connections between spirituality and therapy are strong. "Both psychological growth and spiritual conversion draw the person out of old ways of being, through the deaths such letting go requires, and into liberation forms of life consistent with one's true self" (Berliner, 1995, p. 113). Both spirituality and therapy are oriented to helping the client do the following:

1. Learn to accept himself in relationship to the environment and with the people in one's environment.
2. Forgive oneself and others. Sometimes not forgiving others makes sense, thus allowing the client to release toxic and debilitating resentment and hurt.
3. Acknowledge personal shortcomings and those of others as part of the human experience.
4. Confront corrective and destructive guilt.
5. Modify patterns of thinking, behaving, and feeling that are self-destructive and contribute to a lesser life. (Burke & Miranti, 2001)

Skills that may help Michael and other clinicians approach spirituality as a topic for clinical insight have been identified:

1. The ability to examine one's own prejudice and biases around spirituality and religion, both positive and negative
2. Becoming familiar with the various literature regarding spiritual experiences
3. Exploring religion from a different culture than one's own and assessing the relevance of the spiritual domains in the client's therapeutic issues
4. Using a client's spiritual beliefs in the pursuit of the client's therapeutic goals (Cashwell & Young, 2004; West, 2000)

Braithwaite-Hall (2011) found in her research with 106 African American Christian women that 71% had scores that indicated presence of depressive symptoms, whereas 29% (n = 36) had scores that indicated clinical levels of depression. Contrary to the researcher's hypothesis, there was a high prevalence of depression in the sample. Among some Christians, there is a belief that faith in God means not having to succumb to depression, which can be problematic for Christians who experience the very human depths of depression at some point in life. Michael realizes that Tim is undergoing a crisis of faith. And although such a crisis can lead to spiritual growth and personal transformation, it is disorienting and painful, nonetheless. Parker (1985) saw faith and development as integrated: "The idea that active participation and struggle is necessary is common not only to discussions of religious development but to discussion of other forms of cognitive growth and change" (p. 45). Michael demonstrates many of these skills as shown in his skillful questioning. Some of these questions convey his understanding of basic principles of Christianity. To facilitate a discussion of spirituality, Michael asks Tim the following:

1. Has spirituality failed you?
2. How has spirituality helped you in the past?
3. Would you perceive God as punishing if you did not have to have an orchiectomy?

4. How do you make spiritual sense of your cancer-free diagnosis?
5. Do you experience God's presence during prayer and worship?
6. Does your faith affect the way you look at your suffering?
7. Does Jesus' suffering help you make sense of your suffering?
8. How does the orchiectomy affect your sense of your manhood as a Black man?

SPIRITUALITY, THERAPY, AND CULTURAL CONSIDERATIONS

Psychologists can find themselves surprised that among many African Americans, therapy is regarded as anti-spiritual (Boyd-Franklin, 2010). Tim and Michael have racial and religious differences between them. Michael's multicultural competence has equipped him with the ability to consider Tim's cultural worldview. One of the significant contributions of multicultural counseling and psychology has been to transition from a narrow focus on the individual to viewing the self in relation to a broader cultural context (Wiggins-Frame & Braun, 1996). Concerning African Americans and other groups of color, the authors said, "this shift has prompted recognition of spiritual and healing systems indigenous to racial-ethnic American cultures ... standards for multicultural counseling competencies all include a call for practitioners to be knowledgeable about and to use religious and spiritual healers and leaders" (p. 22).

Michael is mindful that Tim presents with spiritual issues related to a surgical procedure to treat his cancer. As a multiculturally competent clinician, Michael considers Tim's race and the impact on him, not only as a man but as a young, African American man who has not yet fathered children. Michael is mindful of the press of dominant discourses on himself and Tim. One of these discourses is that manhood and virility are synonymous, particularly for Black men within a culture that objectifies them sexually.

Vontress (2004) reminds mental health professionals not to impose race on clients but attend to the significance that the client attaches to race as an important issue in their lives. In time, after rapport and trust have developed and Michael has been instrumental in alleviating Tim's depressive symptoms, he might introduce race through a question such as, "What is the effect of the surgery on your sense of your manhood as a Black man?"

Tim's crisis of faith, although understandable and functional, can have adverse implications for his well-being and quality of life. Although spirituality can play a role in moderating health and well-being (Miller & Thoresen, 2003), the converse seems true. In their review of nine hypotheses about the link between religion or spirituality and mortality, morbidity, disability, or recovery from illness, Powell, Shahabi, and Thoresen (2003) concluded, "religious people who become upset by the belief that God has abandoned them or who become dependent on their faith, rather than their medical treatment for recovery, may inadvertently subvert the success of their recovery" (p. 50).

Having visited a Black church on several occasions, Michael understands the crucial role that the Black church has played in the lives of African Americans. From civil rights organizing to social activism in the form of feeding programs, prison ministries, and educational centers (Adkison-Bradley, Johnson, Sanders, Duncan, & Holcomb-McCoy, 2005), the Black church has been a beacon of hope and light for Black Americans. Michael displays a multicultural competency of integrating appropriate interventions into the therapeutic event. He is comfortable with the use of scripture in therapy, the therapeutic benefit of Tim sharing his prayers for a miracle of healing, and Tim's conclusion that his earnest prayers went unanswered.

According to Boyd-Franklin (2010), psychologists need to expand the subject of spirituality and religion to ascertain its relevance in the client's life. Because one of Tim's goals is to restore his relationship with God, Michael queries Tim about whether his church has prayed for him. Michael is familiar with "prayer as an integral part of the process for relieving the pain and suffering often associated with their everyday life experience" (Adksion-Bradley et al., 2005).

As a Youth Pastor, Tim feels enormous guilt for not being a man of greater faith. The cathartic process of being listened to and speaking one's truth without censor or judgment help Tim. He eventually appreciates that the pressure he put on himself to accept his cancer and loss of his testicles as God's will exacerbated his feelings of powerlessness and did not allow him to express his anger at the unthinkable, God. Halbert et al. (2007) said, "... discussing of religious and spiritual beliefs with heath care providers is important to African Americans diagnosed with prostate cancer" (p. 282).

Michael communicates to Tim that surrendering to a situation is not the same as condoning it. This difference was a critical one for Tim, who saw that many of the ministers in his spiritual community took the stances that his cancer was God's will, that his survival was a manifestation of God's faithfulness, and that Tim needed to approach God with a grateful heart. To join with his client, Michael acknowledges that Tim's disappointment in and doubts about God's provision and care have been expressed through the ages by the Old Testament prophets, Jesus himself, and other people of faith across religions.

Unpacking religious teachings is hard and daunting work. Messages such as "don't question God" or "just pray about it and the problem will take care of itself" do not encourage people to get underneath the emotions that contribute to their crises of faith and extreme disappointment in God. Tim feels deprived of God's grace, which, if present, would have meant healing of his cancer. Michael asks Tim to consider if people can pray for healing, die anyway, and yet still be whole, healed, and benefactors of God's grace. (See Storytelling, *Grace?*)

Tim's religious beliefs are gendered in nature as well: part of his depression is feeling that he has failed his wife by not giving her children. Tim is also concerned that due to his operation his wife looks at him differently, with less desire. In time, Michael will encourage Tim and his wife to undergo couples' therapy.

One of the helpful interventions for Tim was bibliotherapy (reading books, particularly autobiographies of people who have survived similar challenges in life) to reduce his feelings of aloneness. Another intervention for Tim was to eventually join a support group of men who had survived prostate and testicular cancers. Because Tim is a private man, he resisted this suggestion from Michael. For this reason, Michael did not introduce this suggestion until he felt that Tim might be more supportive of it. Michael knew of a support group that was facilitated by a man of color, given the disproportionate rates of prostate and testicular cancer among men of color.

Storytelling: Grace?

Years ago, I was talking with one of my dearest friends about a mother and her young son who were traveling on a stretch of highway when their car stalled at a dangerous place. Other motorists would be unable to see them in time to avoid an accident. Before help arrived, their car was hit by another vehicle approaching at a high rate of speed. The mother died. Her son survived. My friend told me that she and her mother, just a few weeks prior to this fatal accident, had broken down near that same spot but shortly afterward, a police officer pulled up behind them, flashed his blue lights, and radioed for a tow truck. In the meantime, he put flares down to alert oncoming cars to go around the stalled car. "There but for the grace of God go I," said my friend as she compared her outcome with that of the mother's. I asked, "Do you think the mother who died benefited from God's grace?" My friend answered, "Yes, I do." I said, "So do I." Survival and rescue are not the only examples of God's grace, provision, and protection.

In one study, cancer survivors described helpful communication as empathic listening, allowing the client to talk and weep without interjecting helpful advice or cheerleading, and offering gentle encouragement. Unhelpful communication included admonishing people to overcome their illness, avoidance, and forced cheerfulness (Curtis & Juhnke, 2003). In another study by Ussher and Perz (2010), both men and women who were caregivers (carers) of loved ones with cancer tended to self-silence themselves. Women saw self-silencing as a requisite for coping, as they connected their caregiving with the natural place of being a woman. Men saw self-silencing as normal aspect of masculinity. Women carers also had high levels of anxiety and depression. It is critical that Geri seek therapy as she cares for husband and herself.

DIVERSE HEALING STRATEGIES

Essential as relationships are to well-being, they can be stressful. Each of us could benefit from therapy. The majority of people, however, will not seek the services of a counselor and/ or psychologist. Church, temple, synagogue, and community groups, in consultation with mental health professionals, can and do offer paraprofessional sensitivity training to leaders. Individuals, couples, or groups who are experiencing transition and need support can benefit greatly from these low-cost, highly effective services. Training can also review when to refer people if and when problems exceed the paraprofessional's scope of training. As people confront and recover from various emotional and psychological wounds, the support of a community is needed.

hooks (1993) said that if places of healing do not exist to help people process their grief, they must be created because "bottled-in-grief can erupt into illness" (p. 104). In healing, balance and harmony are restored (Shore, 1995). "Home psychoanalysis" (Hooks, 1993), or informal spaces where people feel free to share their stories and receive nonjudgmental support, is not inconsistent with professional help when necessary. Authentic spaces need to be created so that people may heal and move forward, catch their breath, regain and create new rhythms, and reclaim their voices. Granted, therapists and counselors provide valuable service to people in need, but other havens can and do promote healing.

Effective Lay-Led Healing

Toward strengthening intrapersonal and interpersonal relationships, the following may be helpful:

- *Book and film circles* describe the gathering of people, not just to talk about the books and films they are reading and seeing, but to think reflectively about the connections between the written texts and the motion pictures on their lives and the lives of others. Feelings of isolation are also minimized, and people can see their life stories mirrored in another's.
- *Storytelling* allows people to think of their own personal stories or those told by another person and reflect on their meaning and importance. Alice Walker tells the story of growing up in a family where there were limited financial resources. Although it seemed like there was nothing to eat in the house, her mother, with creativity and care, would prepare the most delicious and nutritious food in beautiful blue bowls. It is empowering for clients to realize that they can author their own lives and live the stories they choose.
- *Affirmations* written on a daily basis provide ritual and rhythm to life while promoting positive thinking. Shinn (1989) offers wonderful examples: (1) my supply is endless, inexhaustible, and immediate and comes to me under grace in perfect ways; (2) rhythm,

harmony, and balance are now established in my mind, body, and affairs; and (3) infinite Spirit, give me wisdom to make the most of my opportunities. Never let me miss a trick.

- *Poetry*—others and one's own. Iyanla Vanzant's (1998) poem, "Yesterday I Cried," is really a story about a woman who cried over losses and disappointment. She ends the poem on a triumphant note, embracing her wisdom, resistance, and power.
- *Kitchen table talk* is an informal gathering of friends around the kitchen table to eat and to talk about whatever is on people's minds. An adaptation of this activity can take place in therapy. (See Storytelling: *Movement*.)
- *Burning bowls.* I used to participate in this on New Year's Eve at my church. The minister would direct each of us to write down on a piece of paper that what we did not want to take into the new year. Finances, relationships, physical health, and spirituality were topic areas to consider. We would then place the pieces of paper in a bowl and burn them. People do not have to wait for the end of the year to participate in this activity of literally incinerating the pieces of paper that reflect what is no longer desired. They could be encouraged to think about what they do not want to take with them into the next day, or the next hour. Vanzant (1998) identified several "lessons" one could burn: (1) making decisions in fear, (2) being afraid to say no (or yes), (3) believing that I should not get angry, (4) being afraid to trust myself, (5) not asking for help when I need it, (6) not telling the truth, (7) being afraid to make a mistake, and (8) feeling afraid that I want too much.
- *Letters to oneself.* I have asked my students to write a letter to themselves at an earlier point in their lives. In this letter, they need to offer support, forgiveness, understanding, and wisdom to the younger person they are. A graduate student once wrote to herself as a high school student. She had made a decision to attend a college closer to her home to accommodate her boyfriend who had moved to another state to attend college. He expected her to stay home (as did her mother and sister) in order to receive him during holidays and breaks, thus not wanting her to attend the college of her choice several states away. As a graduate student, she came to realize that she forfeited her desires for his and had been encouraged to do so by both women and men alike.
- *Massage* is a loving way to affirm oneself, relax, and experience soothing human touch.

Storytelling: Movement

A client shared her story of being sexually brutalized by her father and "family friends" for years. Her single-parent mother battled with her own addictions and was not available to this defenseless girl child. Her therapist said, "It was not your fault. You deserved better than what you received and as a little girl you should have been protected." The client began to cry. As she did, the raw, but healing skin cut with a razor from her own hands whispered that this woman's heart and soul were healing as well. We as therapists and counselors must listen. We must not distract or silence, but must hear the storied lives of our clients. It is meaningful that we have told the painful and disappointing stories from our lives to our own therapists and counselors. This would represent a gigantic step in the direction of a social justice agenda—for the healers to become healed. Mental health professionals bring themselves into the counseling room. They bring their pain, disappointment, success, arrogance, insensitivity, and empathy. They bring their attitudes about race, gender, class, sexual orientation, culture, abortion, politics, gender roles, and interracial marriages. Some counselors will find it difficult to bear witness to certain stories or emotions from their clients. The stories themselves are not the problem nor is the difficulty that a therapist encounters in hearing them. It is only problematic when we as professionals are unwilling or are unable to hear.

- *Latin and swing dancing* are high touch, and the music is soulful and stirring.
- *Metaphor and Narrative* can be very therapeutic with clients who may have a difficult time naming and articulating intense feelings. A client who has a conflicted relationship with her mother could be asked, "What color is the relationship you have with your mother?" "What shape is it?" "Is it an ocean, river, pond, stream, or gutter?" "How does it sound?" and "Who are its friends?" Such questions enable the client to externalize the pain and conflict.
- *Tell me when to stop* is an activity that I have done with clients who have a difficult time clarifying their feelings around conflicting issues. I have asked them to tell me to stop when the width of my hands arrives at a point that represents the depth of their feelings. I had one client who told me that my arms were not wide enough to describe how angry she was at her husband. It was not until that moment that she became aware of the extent of her rage at his infidelity during her pregnancy.

Other Approaches

Other approaches that are instrumental in healing include physical exercise, prayer, meditation, yoga, journaling, aromatherapy, and hydrotherapy. There are times when drug therapy or antidepressants under the careful supervision of a psychiatrist, medical doctor, or nurse practitioner are warranted and can assist people along their journeys.

Creative Arts

Creative arts can be very helpful to the therapeutic event. According to Gladding (1997), "Creative arts refers to any art form, including visual representations (paintings, drawings, sculpture), poetry, drama, and music, that helps individuals become more aware of themselves or others" (p. 354). The National Coalition of Art Therapies Association (NCATA) is an interdisciplinary organization that supports all art therapies. Drawings, photography, cartooning, drama, cinema, games, poetry/metaphor, bibliotherapy, working with sand, writing, and music and movement all fall under the umbrella of creative therapies. It helps for counselors to understand the importance of the creative process as a part of the healing taking place. Shore (1995) said, "When clients become artists they have tools for activating their own compost and fertilizing their inner lives" (p. 93).

Wellness

To encourage healing, whether using creative therapies or more traditional ones, a holistic and multidimensional approach in which mind and body are seen as one is essential. Myers, Sweeney, and Witmer (2001) proposed a Wheel of Wellness. Five life tasks for healthy functioning are depicted and include spirituality, self-direction, work and leisure, friendship, and love. There are additional components for self-direction such as sense of humor, physical fitness, sense of worth, and cultural identity. This ecological model interacts dynamically with other life forces including religion, education, family, and community.

IMPLICATIONS FOR COUNSELORS AND PSYCHOLOGISTS

Therapy is a gift in that it can help people move toward wisdom, peace, and sanity following tragedy and crises. Therapists who are able to usher spirituality into the therapy room and critique cultural patterns about religion and gender allow clients to experience the healing benefits of spirituality within therapy. What counselors-in-training are being taught about spirituality represents a significant gap in the research (Young et al., 2007). Toward the articulation of competencies that mental health professionals need in their work with spirituality, nine competencies identified 13 years ago during an initial Summit on Spirituality are provided for both counselors-in-training and seasoned practitioners:

1. The ability to explain the relationship between religion and spirituality, including similarities and differences.
2. The ability for the counselor to describe religious and spiritual beliefs and practices within a cultural context.
3. Personal exploration of one's religious and spiritual beliefs.
4. An understanding of various models of religious/spiritual development across the lifespan.
5. Sensitivity to and acceptance of a variety of religious and spiritual expressions in the client's communication.
6. An ability to identify the limits of one's understanding of a client's spiritual expression and demonstrate appropriate referral skills.
7. The ability to assess the relevance of the spiritual domains in the client's therapeutic issues.
8. Sensitivity to and respect of the spiritual themes in the therapeutic process.
9. The ability to use the client's spiritual beliefs in the pursuit of the client's therapeutic goals.

Summary

This chapter began with a case study that was discussed throughout. An African American man's crises of faith following testicular cancer diagnosis, treatment, and finally an orchiectomy were presented. His therapist was also a male but was racially and religiously different. Multicultural competencies for mental health professionals when integrating spirituality and religion into therapy were highlighted. Definitions were provided as were the challenges associated with bifurcating these terms.

EPILOGUE

**If you ask me what I came to do in this world, I will tell you,
I came to live out LOUD.**

ÉMILE ZOLA

As a girl growing up, I listened to the Beattles a lot. I am so glad I did. I dream of a world where people, irrespective of skin color, hair texture, body size, income, age, sexuality, gender, and ability, can truly live as one.

It is my hope that as you read the text, you will think critically and talk about the cases—about the models, the research, the census data, and the stories. I hope you will let me know what resonated with you and helped you to think about your world differently—and what you did not like or agree with or understand. I have attempted to present a way for the therapeutic event to embrace the multiple, shifting, and simultaneous identities in all of our lives.

Thank you for reading. I am grateful.

Sincerely,
Tracy Robinson-Wood

REFERENCES

Abernathy, A. D. (1995). Managing racial anger: A critical skill in cultural competence. *Journal of Multicultural Counseling and Development, 23*, 96–102.

Abrams, L. S. (2002). Rethinking girls "at-risk": Gender, race, and class intersections and adolescent development. *Journal of Human Behavior in the Social Environment, 6*, 47–64.

Abudabbeh, N. (1996). Arab families. In M. McGoldrick, J. K. Pearce, & J. Giordano (Eds.), *Ethnicity and family therapy* (pp. 333–346). New York: Guilford Press.

Abudabbeh, N. (2005a). Arab families: An overview. In M. McGoldrick, J. Giordano, & N. Garcia-Preto (Eds.), *Ethnicity and family therapy* (pp. 423–436). New York: Guilford Press.

Abudabbeh, N. (2005b). Palestinian families. In M. McGoldrick, J. Giordan, & N. Garcia-Preto (Eds.), *Ethnicity and family therapy* (pp. 487–498). New York: Guilford Press.

Abudabbeh, N., & Nydell, M. K. (1993). Transcultural counseling and Arab Americans. In J. McFadden (Ed.), *Transcultural counseling: Bilateral and international perspectives* (pp. 261–284). Alexandria, VA: American Counseling Association.

Adherents.com. (2007). *Major religions of the world ranked by number of adherents*. Retrieved September 18, 2011, from http://www.adherents.com/

Adksion-Bradley, C., Johnson, D., Sanders, J. L., Duncan, L., & Holcomb-McCoy, C. (2005). Forging a collaborative relationhsip between the Black church and the counseling profession.*Counseling and Values, 49*, 147–154.

Ahnallen, J. M., Suyemoto, K. L., & Carter, A. S. (2006). Relationship between physical appearance, sense of belonging and exclusion, and racial/ethnic self-identification among multiracial Japanese European Americans. *Cultural Diversity and Ethnic Minority Psychology, 12*, 673–686.

Alba, R. D. (1990). *Ethnic identity: The transformation of White America*. New Haven, CT: Yale University Press.

Alinsky, S. D. (1990). *Rules for radicals: A primer for realistic radicals*. New York: Random House.

Al-Krenawi, A., & Graham, J. R. (2000). Culturally sensitive social work practice with Arab clients in mental health settings. *Health Social Work, 25*(1), 9–22.

American Cancer Society. (1989). A summary of the American Cancer Society report to the Nation: Cancer in the poor. *CA Cancer Journal for Clinicians, 39*, 263–265.

American Counseling Association. (1995). *Code of ethics*. Alexandria, VA: American Counseling Association.

American Counseling Association. (2005). *Code of ethics*. Alexandria, VA: American Counseling Association.

American Psychological Association. (2002). *Code of ethics*. Washington, DC: Author.

American Psychological Association. (2003). Guidelines on multicultural education, training, research, practice, and organizational change for psychologists. *American Psychologists, 53*, 377–402.

American Psychological Association. (2006). *Guidelines for psychotherapy with lesbian, gay, and bisexual clients*. Washington, DC: American Psychological Association.

American Psychological Association. (2007a). *Disability issues in psychology: Enhancing your interactions with people with disabilities*. Washington, DC: American Psychological Association.

American Psychological Association. (2007b). *Report of the APA task force on socioeconomic status*. Washington, DC: American Psychological Association.

American Psychological Association. (2008). *Resolution on the Americans with Disability Act*. Adopted by the APA Council of Representatives, February 2008. Washington, DC: National Academies Press.

American Psychological Association. (2011). *Disability and Socioeconomic Status*. Retrieved August 10, 2011, from http://www.apa.org/pi/ses/resources/publications/factsheet-disability.pdf.

Ancis, J. R., Sedlacek, W. E., & Mohr, J. J. (2000). Student perceptions of campus cultural climate by race. *Journal of Counseling and Development, 78*, 180–185.

Andersen, A. E. (1986). Males with eating disorders. In F. E. F. Larocca (Ed.), *Eating disorders* (pp. 39–46). San Francisco: Jossey-Bass.

Anderson, N. B. (2003). *Unraveling the mystery of racial and ethnic health disparities: Who, what, when, where, how and especially, why?* Boston: Institute on Urban Health Research, Northeastern University.

Anderson, S. K., & Middleton, V. A. (2004). *Explorations in privilege, oppression, and diversity*. Belmont, CA: Wadsworth.

Anderson, S. K., & Middleton, V. A. (2011). *Explorations in diversity: Examining privilege and oppression in a multicultural society* (2nd ed.). Belmont, CA: Brooks/Cole.

ANRED. (2006). *Anorexia and related eating disorders*. Retrieved September 28, 2007, from http://www.anred.com/stats.html

ANRED. (2011). Retrieved December 5, 2011, from http://Anred.org

Appleby, G. A., Colon, E., & Hamilton, J. (2001). Culture, social class, and social identity development. In G. Appleby, E. Colon, & J. Hamilton (Eds.), *Diversity, oppression and social functioning: Person-in-environment assessment and intervention* (pp. 16–34). Needham Heights, MA: Allyn & Bacon.

Aprahamian, M., Kaplan, D. M., Windham, A. M., Sutter, J. A., & Visser, J. (2011). The relationship between acculturation and mental health of Arab Americans. *Journal of Mental Health Counseling, 33*, 80–92.

Arab American Institute. (2006). *Arab Americans*. Retrieved September 15, 2007, from http://www.aaiusa.org/

Arab American Institute. (2011). *Quick facts about Arab Americans*. Retrieved December 15, 2011, from http: aai.3cdn.net/63c6ecf052bdccc48f_afm6ii3a7.pdf7b

Arndt, L., & Davies, A. (2011). Warrior Spirit: Soul wound and coping among American Indians in law enforcement. *The Counseling Psychologist, 39*(4), 527–569. DOI: 10.1177/0011000010389827

Arredondo, P. (1992). *Latina/Latino value orientations: Tape 1. Cultural considerations for working more effectively with Latin Americans*. Amherst, MA: Microtraining and Multicultural Development.

Arredondo, P., & Arciniega, G. M. (2001). Strategies and techniques for counselor training based on the multicultural counseling competencies. *Journal of Multicultural Counseling and Development, 29*, 263–273.

Arredondo, P., Psalti, A., & Cella, K. (1993). The woman factor in multicultural counseling. *Counseling and Human Development, 25*(8), 1–8.

Arredondo, P., & Rodriguez, V. (2005). Working with contemporary Latino immigrants. *Counseling and Human Development, 38*, 1–12.

Arredondo, P., Toporek, R., Brown, S. P., Jones, J., Locke, D. C., Sanchez, J., et al. (1996). Operationalization of the multicultural competencies. *Journal of Multicultural Counseling and Development, 24*, 42–78.

Assaud, R., & Roudi-Fahimi, F. (2007). *Youth in the Middle East and North Africa: Demographic opportunity or challenge?* Washington, DC: Population Reference Bureau. Retrieved December 29, 2011, from http://www.prb.org/pdf07/youthin-MENA.pdf

Atkinson, D. R., & Hackett, G. (1995). *Counseling diverse populations*. Madison, WI: Brown and Benchmark.

Atkinson, D. R., Morten, G., & Sue, D. W. (1983). *Counseling American minorities: A cross cultural perspective*. Dubuque, IA: William C. Brown.

Avakian, M. (2002). *Atlas of Asian-American history*. New York: Checkmark Books.

Awad, G. (2010). The impact of acculturation and religious identification on perceived discrimination for Arab/Middle Eastern Americans. *Cultural Diversity and Ethnic Minority Psychology, 16*(1), 59–67. doi: 10.1037/a0016675.

Balch, P. A. (2006). *Prescription for nutritional healing* (4th ed.). Garden City Park, NY: Avery.

Ballentine, B., & Ballentine, I. (1993). *The Native Americans: An illustrated history*. Atlanta, GA: Turner.

Battle, J., Cohen, C. J., Warren, D., Fergerson, G., & Audam, S. (2002). Say it loud. I'm Black and I'm Proud. *Black Pride Survey 2000*. New York: The Policy Institute of the National Gay and Lesbian Task Force. Retrieved August 8, 2003, from http://www.ngltf.org/pi/blackpride.htm

Beals, K. P. M., & Peplau, L. A. (2006). Disclosure patterns within social networks of gay men and lesbians. *Journal of Homosexuality, 51*, 101–117.

Beals, M. J., & Beals, K. L. (1993). Transcultural counseling and the Hispanic community. In J. McFadden (Ed.), *Transcultural counseling: Bilateral and international perspectives* (pp. 213–238). Alexandria, VA: American Counseling Association.

Becerra, R. M. (1988). The Mexican American family. In C. H. Mindel, R. W. Habenstein, & R. Wright (Eds.), *Ethnic families in America: Patterns and variations* (3rd ed., pp. 141–159). New York: Elsevier.

Becvar, S. B., & Becvar, R. (1993). *Family therapy: A systematic integration* (2nd ed.). Boston: Allyn & Bacon.

Begley, S. (1995, February 13). Three is not enough. *Newsweek,* 67–69.

Belgrave, F. Z. (1991, January–March). Psychosocial predictors of adjustment to disability in African Americans. *Journal of Rehabilitation,* 37–40.

Bell, A., & Weinberg, M. (1978). *Homosexuality: A study of human diversity among men and women*. New York: Simon & Schuster.

Bem, S. L. (1993). *The lenses of gender: Transforming the debate on sexuality inequality*. New Haven, CT: Yale University Press.

Bennett, L., Jr. (1982). *Before the Mayflower: A history of Black America*. Chicago: Johnson.

Berliner, P. M. (1995). Soul healing: A model of feminist therapy. In M. Burke & J. Mirant (Eds.), *Counseling: The spiritual dimension* (pp. 113–125). Thousand Oaks, CA: Sage.

Bernardez, T. (1987). Gender-based countertransference of female therapists in the psychotherapy of women. In M. Braude (Ed.), *Women and therapy* (pp. 25–39). New York: Haworth Press.

Berry, J. W., & Kim, U. (1988). Acculturation and mental health. In P. R. Dasen, J. W. Berry, & N. Sartorius (Eds.), *Health and cross-cultural psychology: Toward applications* (pp. 207–236). Newbury Park, CA: Sage.

Berry, J. W., & Sam, D. L. (1997). Acculturation and adaptation. In J. Berry, M. Segall, & C. Kagitcibasi (Eds.), *Cross-cultural psychology* (Vol. 3, pp. 291–326). Boston: Allyn & Bacon.

Berzon, B. (1988). *Permanent partners: Building gay and lesbian relationships that last*. New York: E. P. Dutton.

BIA. (2011). *U.S. Department of the Interior*. Retrieved December 9, 2011, from http://www.bia.gov/WhoWeAre/index.htm.

Birchnell, S. A., Lacey, J. H., & Harte, S. (1985). Body image distortion in bulimia nervosa. *British Journal of Psychiatry, 47*, 408–412.

Black, L. (1996). Families of African origin. In M. McGoldrick, J. Giordano, & J. K. Pearce (Eds.), *Ethnicity and family therapy* (pp. 57–65). New York: Guilford Press.

Black Women's Health Imperative. (2011). *Black women and HIV/AIDS*. Retrieved July 12, 2011, from http://www.blackwomenshealth.org/issues-and-resources/black-women-and-hiv-aids.

Block, J., & Block, J. H. (2006). Venturing a 30-year longitudinal study. *The American Psychologist, 61*, 315–327.

Bourdieu, P. (1984). *Distinction: A social critique of the judgment of taste.* Cambridge, MA: Harvard University Press.

Bowman, V. E. (1996). Counselor self-awareness and ethnic self-knowledge as a critical component of multicultural training. In J. L. DeLucia-Waack (Ed.), *Multicultural counseling competencies: Implications for training and practice* (pp. 7–30). Alexandria, VA: Association for Counselor Education and Supervision.

Boyd-Franklin, N. (1989). *Black families in therapy: A multisystems approach.* New York: Guilford Press.

Boyd-Franklin, N. (2003). Race, class, and poverty. In F. Walsh (Ed.), *Normal family process* (pp. 260–279). New York: Guilford Press.

Boyd-Franklin, N. (2010). Incorporating spirituality and religion into the treatment of African Americans. *The Counseling Psychologist, 38,* 976–1000. doi:10.1177/0011000010374881.

Bradford, J., Barrett, K., & Honnold, J. A. (2002). *The 2000 Census and same-sex households: A user's guide.* New York: The Policy Institute of the National Gay and Lesbian Task Force. Retrieved from http://www.thetaskforce.org/downloads/reports/reports/FamilyPolicy.pdf

Bradley, C., & Hawkins-Leon, C. G. (2002). The transracial adoption debate: Counseling and legal implications. *Journal of Counseling & Development, 80,* 433–440.

Bradshaw, C. (1994). Asian and Asian American women: Historical and political considerations in psychotherapy. In L. Comas-Diaz & B. Greene (Eds.), *Women of color: Integrating ethnic and gender identities* (pp. 72–113). New York: Guilford Press.

Braithwaite-Hall, M. (2011). *Standing in the need of prayer: Beliefs about depression and treatment held among African American Christian women of prayer.* Unpublished dissertation, Northeastern University, Boston, MA.

Brantlinger, E. A. (1993). *Politics of social class in secondary schools: Views of affluent and impoverished youth.* New York: Teachers College Press.

Brault, M. (2008, December). *Americans with disabilities: 2005 Household Economic Studies Current Population Study.* Retrieved September 14, 2011, from http://www.census.gov/prod/2008pubs/p70–117.pdf

Brault, M. (2009). *Review of changes to measurements of disability in the 2008 American Community Survey.* Retrieved September 14, 2011, from http://www.census.gov/hhes/www/disability/2008ACS_disability.pdf

Brittingham, A., & de la crz, G. P. (2005, March). *We the people of Arab ancestry in the United States.* Special Census Reports. 2000. CENSR-21. U.S. Department of Commerce. Economics and Statistics Administration. U. S. Census.

Bronstein, P., & Quina, K. (1988). *Teaching a psychology of people.* Washington, DC: American Psychological Association.

Brookins, C. B., & Robinson, T. L. (1995). Rites of passage as resistance to oppression. *Western Journal of Black Studies, 19*(3), 172–185.

Brouwers, M. (1990). Treatment of body image dissatisfaction among women with bulimia nervosa. *Journal of Counseling and Development, 69,* 144–147.

Brown, D. (1981). *Bury my heart at Wounded Knee.* New York: Henry Holt & Company.

Brown, L. (1994). *Subversive dialogues: Theory in feminist therapy.* New York: Basic Books.

Brown, L. M. (2003). *Girlfighting: Betrayal and rejection among girls.* New York: New York University Press.

Brown, L. M., & Gilligan, C. (1992). *Meeting at the crossroads: The landmark book about the turning points in girls' and women's lives.* New York: Ballantine Books.

Browning, C., Reynolds, A. L., & Dworkin, S. H. (1994). Affirmative psychotherapy for lesbian women. *Counseling Psychologist, 19,* 177–196.

Brunsma, D. L. (2006). Mixed messages: Doing race in the color-blind era. In D. Brunsma (Ed.), *Mixed messages: Multiracial identities in the "color-blind" era* (pp. 1–11). Boulder, CO: Lynne Reinner.

Brunsma, D. L., & Rockquemore, K. A. (2001). The new color complex: Appearances and biracial identity. *Identity: An international journal of theory and research, 1*, 225–246.

Bryant, A., & LaFromboise, T. D. (2005). The racial identity and cultural orientation of Lumbee American Indian high school students. *Cultural Diversity and Ethnic Minority Psychology, 11*, 82–89.

Burck, C., & Speed, B. (1995). *Gender, power, and relationships.* New York: Routledge.

Burke, M. T., Hackney, H., Hudson, O., Miranti, J., Watts, G. A., & Epp, L. (1999). Spirituality, religion, and CACREP curriculum standards. *Journal of Counseling & Development, 77*, 251–257.

Burke, M. T., & Miranti, J. (2001). The spiritual and religious dimensions of counseling. In D. Locke, J. Myers, & E. Herr (Eds.), *Handbook of counseling* (pp. 601–612). Thousand Oaks, CA: Sage.

Burnett, J. W., Anderson, W. P., & Heppner, P. P. (1995). Gender roles and self-esteem: A consideration of environmental factors. *Journal of Counseling and Development, 73*, 323–326.

Byrd, W. M., & Clayton, L. A. (2003). Racial and ethnic disparities in healthcare: A background and history. In Institute of Medicine (Ed.), *Unequal treatment: Confronting racial and ethnic disparities in healthcare* (pp. 455–527). Washington, DC: National Academies Press.

Cameron, S. C., & Turtle-Song, I. (2003). Native American mental health: An examination of resilience in the face of overwhelming odds. In F. Harper & J. McFadden (Eds.), *Culture and counseling: New approaches.* Boston: Allyn & Bacon.

Cao, L., & Novas, H. (1996). *Everything you need to know about Asian-American history.* New York: Penguin.

Carballo-Dieguez, A. (1989). Hispanic culture, gay male culture, and AIDS: Counseling implications. *Journal of Counseling and Development, 68*, 26–30.

Cardemil, E. V., & Battle, C. L. (2003). Guess who's coming to therapy? Getting comfortable with conversations about race and ethnicity in psychotherapy. *Professional Psychology: Research and Practice, 34*, 278–286.

Carpenter, K. M., & Addis, M. E. (2000). Alexithymia, gender, and responses to depressive symptoms. *Sex Roles: A Journal of Research, 42*, 629–638.

Carrigan, T., Connell, B., & Lee, J. (1987). Toward a new sociology of masculinity. In H. Brod (Ed.), *The making of masculinities: The new men's studies* (pp. 63–100). Boston: Allen and Unwin.

Carroll, L., & Gilroy, P. J. (2002). Transgender issues in counselor preparation. *Counselor Education & Supervision, 41*, 233–242.

Carter, R. T., & Parks, E. E. (1996). Womanist identity and mental health. *Journal of Counseling and Development, 74*, 484–489.

Cashwell, C. S., & Young, J. S. (2004). Spirituality in counselor training: A content analysis of syllabi from introductory spirituality courses. *Counseling and Values, 48*, 96–109.

Cass, V. C. (1979). Homosexual identity formation: A theoretical model. *Journal of Homosexuality, 4*, 219–235.

Cass, V. C. (1984). Homosexual identity: A concept in need of definition. *Journal of Homosexuality, 9*, 105–126.

CDC. (2011). *HIV among Latinos.* Retrieved December 19, 2011, from http://www.cdc.gov/hiv/latinos/index.htm.

Chae, M. H. & Foley, P. F. (2010). Relationship of ethnic identity, acculturation, and psychological well-being among Chinese, Japanese, and Korean Americans. *Journal of Counseling & Development, 88*(4), 466–476.

Chan, C. S. (1992). Cultural considerations in counseling Asian American lesbians and gay men. In S. H. Dworkin & F. J. Gutierrez (Eds.), *Counseling gay men and lesbians: Journey to the end of the rainbow* (pp. 115–124). Alexandria, VA: American Association for Counseling and Development.

Chang, E. C. (1996). Cultural differences in optimism, pessimism, and coping: Predictors of subsequent adjustment in Asian American and Caucasian American college students. *Journal of Counseling Psychology, 43*, 113–123.

Chang, J., & Sue, S. (2005). Culturally sensitive research: Where have we gone wrong and what do we need to do now? In M. Constantine & D. Sue (Eds.), *Strategies for building multicultural competence in mental health and educational settings* (pp. 229–246). Hoboken, NJ: John Wiley & Sons.

Chang, P. (2000). Treating Asian/Pacific American addicts and their families. In J. Krestan (Ed.), *Bridges to recovery: Addiction, family therapy, and multicultural treatment* (pp. 192–218). New York: Free Press.

Chang, P. Y. (2002) *Asian American Immigration and Identity Transformation: The History of the Chinese, Japanese and Koreans in America.* Stanford University, Department of Sociology, Unpublished Powerpoint Presentation, from http://www.stanford.edu/dept/lc/efs/ALC/ppt/alc_AAid_8.15.07.ppt

Chao, R. (2006). Counselors' multicultural competencies: Race, training, ethnic identity, and color-blind racial attitudes. In G. R. Waltz and R. Yep (Eds.), *VISTAS: Perspectives on counseling 2006* (pp. 73–76). Alexander, VA: American Counseling Association.

Chao, R. C., Wei, M., Good, G. E., & Flores, L. Y. (2011). Race, color-blind racial attitudes, and multicultural counseling competence: The moderating effects of multicultural counseling training. *Journal of Counseling Psychology, 58,* 72–82.

Chase, C. (2003). *The child with an intersex condition: Total patient care* [Video]. Seattle: Intersex Society of North America.

Chen, G. A., LePhuoc, P., Guzman, M. R., Rude, S. S., & Dodd, B. G. (2006). Exploring Asian American racial identity. *Cultural Diversity and Ethnic Minority Psychology, 12,* 461–476.

Chernin, K. (1985). *The hungry self: Women, eating, and identity.* New York: Harper & Row.

The Children's Partnership. (2000). *Tomorrow's youth: A changing demographic.* Retrieved December 15, 2003, from http://www.childrenspartnership.org/AM/Template.cfm?Section=Home&Template=/CM/ContentDisplay.cfm&ContentFileID=1010

Chin, J. L. (2003). Multicultural competencies in managed health care. In D. Pope-Davis, H. Coleman, W. Liu, & R. Toporek (Eds.), *Handbook of multicultural competencies in counseling & psychology* (pp. 347–364). Thousand Oaks, CA: Sage.

Choi, Y., Harachi, T. W., Gillmore, M. R., & Catalano, R. F. (2006). Are multiracial adolescents at greater risk? Comparisons of rates, patterns, and correlates of substance use and violence between monoracial and multiracial adolescents. *American Journal of Orthopsychiatry, 76,* 86–97.

Chojnacki, J. T., & Gelberg, S. (1995). The facilitation of a gay/lesbian/bisexual support-therapy group by heterosexual counselors. *Journal of Counseling and Development, 73,* 352–354.

Choudhuri D. D. (2005). Conducting culturally sensitive qualitative research. In M. Constantine and D. W. Sue (Eds.), *Strategies for building multicultural competence. In mental health and educational settings* (pp. 269–282). Hoboken, NJ: Wiley.

Chow, E. N.-L. (1991). The development of feminist consciousness among Asian American women. In J. Lorber & S. A. Farrell (Eds.), *The social construction of gender* (pp. 255–268). Newbury Park, CA: Sage.

Chow, E. N.-L. (1994). The feminist movement: Where are all the Asian American women? In R. Takaki (Ed.), *From different shores: Perspectives on race and ethnicity in America.* New York: Oxford University Press.

Christian, B. (1989). But who do you really belong to— Black studies or women's studies? *Women's Studies, 17,* 17–23.

Christian, C. M. (1995). *Black saga: The African American experience (a chronology).* Boston: Houghton Mifflin.

Chung, R. C.-Y. (2005). Women, human rights, and counseling: Crossing international boundaries. *Journal of Counseling & Development, 82,* 262–268.

Chusmir, L. H. (1990). Men who make nontraditional choices. *Journal of Counseling and Development, 69*(1), 11–16.

Clark, R., Anderson, N. B., Clark, V. R., & Williams, D. R. (2002). Racism as a stressor for African Americans: A biopsychosocial model. In T. LaVeist (Ed.), *Race, ethnicity and health* (pp. 319–339). San Francisco: Jossey-Bass.

Clutter, A. W., & Nieto, R. D. (n.d.). *Understanding the Hispanic culture.* Ohio State University fact sheet. Family and Consumer Sciences. Retrieved September 25, 2007, from http://ohioline.osu.edu/hyg-fact/5000/5237.html

Cokley, K. O. (2001). Gender differences among African American students in the impact of racial identity on academic psychosocial development. *Journal of College Student Development, 42*, 480–487.

Cokley, K. O. (2005). Racial (ized) identity, ethnic identity, and Afrocentric values: Conceptual and methodological challenges in understanding African American identity. *Journal of Counseling Psychology, 52*, 517–526.

Cole, J. B., & Guy-Sheftall, B. (2003). *Gender talk: The struggle for women's equality in African-American communities.* New York: Random House.

Coleman, E. (1982). Developmental stages of the coming out process. *American Behavioral Scientist, 25*, 469–482.

Collins, J. F. (2000). Biracial Japanese American identity: An evolving process. *Cultural Diversity and Ethnic Minority Psychology, 6*, 115–133.

Collins, P. H. (1989). The social construction of Black feminist thought. *Signs, 14*, 745–773.

Comas-Diaz, L. (1993). Hispanic Latino communities: Psychological implications. In D. Atkinson, G. Morten, & D. W. Sue (Eds.), *Counseling American minorities: A cross-cultural perspective* (pp. 245–263). Madison, WI: Brown and Benchmark.

Comas-Diaz, L., & Greene, B. (1994a). Overview: An ethnocultural mosaic. In L. Comas-Diaz & B. Greene (Eds.), *Women of color* (pp. 3–9). New York: Guilford Press.

Comas-Diaz, L., & Greene, B. (1994b). Women of color with professional status. In L. Comas-Diaz & B. Greene (Eds.), *Women of color: Integrating ethnic and gender identities in psychotherapy* (pp. 347–388). New York: Guilford Press.

Comstock, D. L., Hammer, T. R., Strentzsch, J., Cannon, K., Parsons, J., & Salazar, G. (2008). Relational-cultural theory: A framework for bridging relational, multicultural, and social justice competencies. *Journal of Counseling and Development, 86*, 279–287.

Cook, D. A. (1994). Racial identity in supervision. *Counselor Education and Supervision, 34*, 132–241.

Cook, E. P. (1987). Psychological androgyny: A review of the research. *Counseling Psychologist, 15*, 471–513.

Cooper, R. (2002). A note on the biological concept of race and its application in epidemiological research. In T. A. LaVeist (Ed.), *Race, ethnicity, health: A public health reader* (pp. 99–114). San Francisco: Jossey-Bass.

Corey, G. (1991). *Theory and practice of counseling and psychotherapy.* Pacific Grove, CA: Brooks/Cole.

Cornell, S., & Hartmann, D. (1997). *Ethnicity and race: Making identities in a changing world.* Thousand Oaks, CA: Pine Forge Press.

Cose, E. (1993). *The rage of a privileged class.* New York: HarperCollins.

Cosgrove, L. (2006). The unwarranted pathologizing of homeless mothers: Implication for research and social policy. In R. Toporek, L. Gerstein, N. Fouad, G. Roysircar, & T. Israel (Eds.), *Handbook for social justice in counseling psychology* (pp. 200–214). Thousand Oaks, CA: Sage.

Cottone, R. R., & Tarvydas, V. M. (1998). *Ethical and professional issues in counseling.* Upper Saddle River, NJ: Merrill/Prentice Hall.

Crockett, L. J., Iturbide, M. I., Stone, R. A. T., McGinley, M., Raffaelli, M., & Carlo, G. (2007). Acculturative stress, social support, and coping: Relations to psychological adjustment using Mexican American college students. *Cultural Diversity and Ethnic Minority Psychology, 13*, 347–355.

Crose, R., Nicholas, D. R., Gobble, D. C., & Frank, B. (1992). Gender and wellness: A multidimensional systems model for counseling, *Journal of Counseling & Development, 71*, 149–156.

Cross, W. E. (1991). *Shades of black: Diversity in African American identity.* Philadelphia: Temple University Press.

Curtis, R. A., & Juhnke, G. A. (2003). Counseling the client with prostate cancer. *Journal of Counseling & Development, 81*, 160–167.

Dana, R. H. (1993). *Multicultural assessment perspectives for professional psychology.* Boston: Allyn & Bacon.

Dana, R. H. (2000). The cultural self as locus for assessment and intervention with American Indians/Alaska Natives. *Journal of Multicultural Counseling and Development, 28*, 66–81.

Dana, R. H. (2002). Examining the usefulness of DSM–IV. In K. Kurasaki, S. Okasaki, & S. Sue (Eds.), *Asian American mental health: Assessment theories and methods* (pp. 29–46). New York: Kluwer.

D'Andrea, M., & Daniels, J. (1991). Exploring the different levels of multicultural counseling training in counselor education. *Journal of Counseling and Development, 70*, 78–85.

Darwin, C. (1859). *The origin of species by means of natural selection.* New York: Modern Library.

Day-Vines, N. L., Wood, S. M., Grothaus, T., Craigen, L., Holman, A., Dotson-Blake, K., et al. (2007). Broaching the subjects of race, ethnicity, and culture during the counseling process. *Journal of Counseling and Development, 85*, 401–409.

DeJong, J., & El-Khoury, G. (2006, October 21). Reproductive health of Arab young people. *British Medical Journal, 333*, 849–851.

de las Fuentes, C. (2007). Latina/o American populations. In M. Constantine (Ed.), *Clinical practice with people of color: A guide to becoming culturally competent* (pp. 46–60). New York: Teachers College Press.

Delpit, L. (1997). The silenced dialogue: Power and pedagogy in educating other people's children. In A. Halsey, H. Lauder, P. Brown, & A. Wells (Eds.), *Education: Culture, economy, society* (pp. 582–594). Oxford, UK: Oxford University Press.

DeNavas-Walt, C., Proctor, B. D., & Smith, J. (2007). *Income, poverty, and health insurance coverage in the United States: 2006.* Washington, DC: U.S. Department of Commerce, Current Population Reports.

DeNavas-Walt, C., Proctor, B. D., & Smith, J. C. (2011). *Income, poverty, and health insurance coverage in the United States: 2010.* P-60-239. Current Population Reports. Washington, DC: U.S. Department of Commerce, U.S. Census Bureau.

Devoe, D. (1990). Feminist and nonsexist counseling: Implications for the male counselor. *Journal of Counseling and Development, 69*, 33–36.

Dey, J. G., & Hill, C. (2007). *Behind the pay gap.* Washington, DC: American Association of University Women Foundation.

Diaz, R. M., & Ayala, G. (2002). *Social discrimination and health: The case of Latino gay men and HIV risk.* New York: The Policy Institute of the National Gay and Lesbian Task Force. Retrieved July 31, 2003, from http://www.thetaskforce.org/downloads/reports/reports/SocialDiscriminationAndHealth

Dilworth-Anderson, P., Boswell, G., & Cohen, M. D. (2007). Spiritual and religious coping values and beliefs among African American caregivers: A qualitative study. *Journal of Applied Gerontology, 25*, 355–369.

Dines, G., & Humez, J. M. (2002). *Gender, race, and class in media: A text-reader.* Thousand Oaks, CA: Sage.

Dinsmore, J. A., & England, J. T. (1996). A study of multicultural counseling training at CACREP-accredited counselor education programs. *Counseling Education and Supervision, 36*(1), 58–76.

Dion, K., Berschid, E., & Walster, E. (1972). What is beautiful is good. *Journal of Personality and Social Psychology, 14*, 94–108.

Dobbins, J. E., & Skillings, J. H. (1991). The utility of race labeling in understanding cultural identity: A conceptual tool for the social science practitioner. *Journal of Counseling & Development, 70*, 37–44.

Duerk, J. (1994). *Circle of stones: Woman's journey to herself.* San Diego, CA: Lura Media.

Dulany, P. (1990). On becoming empowered. In J. Spurlock & C. Robinowitz (Eds.), *Women's progress: Promises and problems* (pp. 133–142). New York: Plenum Press.

Durby, D. D. (1994). Gay, lesbian, and bisexual youth. *Journal of Gay and Lesbian Social Services, 1*(3/4), 1–37.

Dwairy, M. (2004). Individuation among Bedouin versus urban Arab adolescents: Ethnic and gender differences. *Cultural Diversity and Ethnic Minority Psychology, 10*, 340–350.

Dwairy, M. (2005). *Culturally sensitive counseling and psychotherapy: Working with Arabic and Muslim clients.* New York: Teachers College Press.

Dworkin, S. H., & Gutierrez, F. J. (1991). *Counseling gay men and lesbians: Journey to the end of the rainbow.* Alexandria, VA: American Association for Counseling and Development.

Efthim, P. W., Kenny, M. E., & Mahalik, J. R. (2001). Gender role stress in relation to shame, guilt, and externalization. *Journal of Counseling & Development, 79*, 430–438.

Elder, P. (2000). An entirely routine test. In M. Clark (Ed.), *Beating our breasts: Twenty New Zealand women tell their breast cancer stories* (pp. 29–35). New Zealand: Cape Catley Limited.

Eliason, M. L., & Schope, R. (2007). Shifting sands or solid foundation. Gay, lesbian, bisexual, and transgender identity formation. In I. H. Meyer & M. E. Northridge (Eds.), *The health of sexual minorities: Public health perspective on lesbian, gay, bisexual, and transgender health* (pp. 3–26). New York: Springer.

Ellis, C. M. (2004). Putting race on the table: Counselors addressing race. *Counseling and Human Development, 37*(1), 1–8.

Emmons, L. (1992). Dieting and purging behavior in Black and White high school students. *Journal of the American Dietetic Association, 92*, 306–312.

Ennis, S. R., Rios-Vargas, M., & Alpert, N. G. (2011). *The Hispanic population.* 2010. Census Briefs. C2010BR-04. U.S. Census Buruea. Washington, DC: U.S. Department of Commerce.

Enns, C. Z. (1991). The "new" relationship models of women's identity: A review and critique for counselors. *Journal of Counseling and Development, 69*, 209–217.

Enns, C. Z. (1994). On teaching about the cultural relativism of psychological constructs. *Teaching on Psychology, 21*, 205–212.

Equal Employment Opportunity Commission. (1991). *Americans with Disabilities Act handbook.* Washington, DC: Government Printing Office.

Erickson, C. D., & Al-Timimi, N. (2001). Providing mental health services to Arab Americans: Recommendation and considerations. *Cultural Diversity and Ethnic Minority Psychology, 7*, 308–327.

Erikson, E. (1968). *Identity: Youth and crisis.* New York: Norton.

Erwin, T. M. (2006). A qualitative analysis of the *Lesbian Connection's* discussion forum. *Journal of Counseling & Development, 84*, 95–107.

Evans, K. M., Kincade, E. A., Marbley, A. F., & Seem, S. R. (2005). Feminism and feminist therapy: Lessons from the past and hopes for the future. *Journal of Counseling & Development, 83*, 269–277.

Evans, L., & Davies, K. (2000). No sissy boys here: A content analsysis of the representation of masculinity in elementary school reading textbooks. *Sex Roles: Journal of Research, 42*, 255–270.

Exum, H. A., & Moore, Q. L. (1993). Transcultural counseling from African-American perspectives. In J. McFadden (Ed.), *Transcultural counseling: Bilateral and international perspectives* (pp. 193–212). Alexandria, VA: American Counseling Association.

Falbo, T., & De Baessa, Y. (2006). The influence of Mayan education on middle school students in Guatemala. *Cultural Diversity and Ethnic Minority Psychology, 12*, 601–614.

Falco, K. L. (1991). *Psychotherapy with lesbian clients: Theory into practice.* New York: Brunner/Mazel.

Fauth, J., & Hayes, J. A. (2006). Counselors' stress appraisals as predictors of countertransference behavior with male clients. *Journal of Counseling & Development, 84*, 430–439.

Fenell, D. L., & Weinhold, B. K. (1996). Treating families with special needs. *Counseling and Human Development, 28*(7), 1–10.

Ferdman, B. M., & Gallegos, P. I. (2001). Racial identity development and Latinos in the United States. In C. Wijeyesinghe & B. Jackson III (Eds.), *New perspectives on racial identity development: A theoretical and practical anthology* (pp. 32–66). New York: New York University Press.

Fine, M. (1991). Invisible flood: Notes on the politics of "dropping out" of an urban public high school. *Equity and Choice, 8*, 30–37.

Fine, M. A., & James-Myers, L. (1990). The development and validation of an instrument to assess an optimal Afrocentric worldview. *Journal of Black Psychology, 17*(1), 37–54.

Fischer, A. R., & Holz, K. B. (2007). Perceived discrimination and women's psychological distress: The roles of collective and personal self-esteem. *Journal of Counseling Psychology, 54*, 154–164.

Fitzpatrick, L. (2010, April 20). Why do women still earn less than men? *Time U.S.* http://www.time.com/time/nation/article/0,8599,1983185,00.html.

Fowler, C., O'Rourke, B. O., Wadsworth, J., & Harper, D. (1992). Disability and feminism: Models for counselor exploration of personal values and beliefs. *Journal of Applied Rehabilitation Counseling, 23*, 14–19.

Fowler, J., & Keen, S. (1978). *Life maps: Conversations on the journey of faith.* Waco, TX: Word Books.

Frieden, T. R. (2011, January 14). Foreword. Center for Disease Control and Prevention. *Morbidity and Mortality Weekly Report, 60*, 1. U. S. Department of Health and Human Resources.

Friedman, C., & Leaper, C. (2010). Sexual-minority college women's experiences with discrimination: Relations with identity and collective action. *Psychology of Women Quarterly, 34*, 152–164.

Frisbie, W. P., Cho, Y., & Hummer, R. A. (2002). Immigration and the health of Asian and Pacific Islander adults in the United States. In T. A. LaVeist (Ed.), *Race, ethnicity, health: A public health reader* (pp. 231–251). San Francisco: Jossey–Bass.

Frost, D. M., Lehavot, K., Meyer, I. H. (2011). *Minority stress and physical health among sexual minorities.* Poster Presented at the American Psychological Association, Washington, DC. Retrieved from: http://williamsinstitute.law.ucla.edu/wp-content/uploads/Frost-Lehavot-Meyer-APA-2011.pdf

Ganje-Fling, M. A., & McCarthy, P. (1996). Impact of childhood sexual abuse on client spiritual development: Counseling implications. *Journal of Counseling & Development, 74*, 253–262.

Gans, H. J. (1992, January 8). Fighting the biases embedded in social concepts of the poor. *Chronicle of Higher Education*, p. A56.

Garcia-Coll, C. (1997). Building connection through diversity. In J. Jordan (Ed.), *Women's growth in diversity: More writings from the Stone Center* (pp. 176–182). New York: Guilford Press.

Garcia-Preto, N. (1996). Latino families: An overview. In M. McGoldrick, J. Giordano, & J. Pearce (Eds.), *Ethnicity and family therapy* (pp. 141–154). New York: Guilford Press.

Garland-Thomas, R. (2002). Integrating disability, transforming feminist theory. *NWSA, 14*, 1–32.

Garnets, L., Hancock, K. A., Cochran, S. D., Goodchilds, J., & Peplau, L. A. (1991). Issues in psychotherapy with lesbians and gay men: A survey of psychologists. *American Psychologist, 46*, 964–972.

Garrett, J. T., & Garrett, M. W. (1994). The path of good medicine: Understanding and counseling Native American Indians. *Journal of Multicultural Counseling and Development, 22*, 134–144.

Garrett, J. T., & Garrett, M. W. (1996). *Medicine of the Cherokee: The way of right relationship.* Sante Fe, NM: Bear.

Garrett, J. T., & Herring, R. D. (2001). Honoring the power of relation: Counseling Native adults. *Journal of Humanistic Counseling, Education, and Development, 40*, 139–160.

Garrett, J. T., & Pichette, E. C. (2000). Red as an apple: Native American acculturation and counseling with or without reservation. *Journal of Counseling & Development, 78*, 3–13.

Garrett, M. (1998). *Walking on the wind: Cherokee teachings for harmony and balance.* Santa Fe, NM: Bear.

Garrett, M. T., Garrett, J. T., Torres-Rivera, E., Wilbur, M., & Roberts-Wilbur, J. (2005). Laughing it up: Native American humor as spiritual tradition. *Journal of Multicultural Counseling and Development, 33*, 194–204.

Garrett, M. T., Torres-Rivera, E., Brubaker, M., Portman, T. A. A., Brotherton, D., West-Olatunji, C., et al. (2011). Crying for a vision: The Native American Sweat Lodge Ceremony as therapeutic intervention. *Journal of Counseling & Development, 89*, 318–325.

Gates, G. (2011a). *United States Census 2010: Same sex couples per 1000 households.* Los Angeles, CA: The Williams Institute, UCLA School of Law.

Gates, G. J. (2011b). How many people are lesbian, gay, bisexual, and transgender? Williams Institute, UCLA, School of Law. Retrieved August 7, 2011, http://williamsinstitute.law.ucla.edu/wp-content/uploads/Census2010Snapshot-US-v2.pdf. Retrieved August 7, 2011.

Gates, G. J., & Cooke, A. M. (2010). *U.S. Census Snapshot: 2010. Same-sex couples.* Williams Institute, UCLA, School of Law. Retrieved from http://williamsinstitute.law.ucla.edu/wp-content/uploads/Census2010Snapshot-US-v2.pdf

Gerschick, T. J., & Miller, A. S. (1994). Gender identities at the crossroads of masculinity and physical disability. *Masculinities, 2*, 34–55.

Gertner, D. M. (1994). Understanding and serving the needs of men. *Counseling and Human Development, 27*, 1–16.

Gibbs, J. T., & Hines, A. M. (1992). Negotiating ethnic identity: Issues for Black-White biracial adolescents. In M. P. P. Root (Ed.), *Racially mixed people in America* (pp. 223–238). Newbury Park, CA: Sage.

Gibbs, J. T., Huang, L. N., & Associates. (1989). *Children of color: Psychological interventions with minority youth.* San Francisco: Jossey-Bass.

Gillem, A. R., Cohn, L. R., & Throne, C. (2001). Black identity in biracial Black/White people: A comparison of Jacqueline who refuses to be exclusively Black and Adolphus who wishes he were. *Cultural Diversity and Ethnic Minority Psychology, 7*, 182–196.

Gilligan, C. (1982). *In a different voice.* Cambridge, MA: Harvard University Press.

Ginther, D. K., Schaffer, W. T., Schnell, J., Masimore, B., Liu F., Haak, L. L., et al. (2011). Race, ethnicity, and NIH awards. *Science, 333*, 1015–1019.

Gladding, S. T. (1997). *Community and agency counseling.* Upper Saddle River, NJ: Merrill/Prentice Hall.

Gloria, A. M., & Ho, T. A. (2003). Environmental, social, and psychological experiences of Asian American undergraduates: Examining issues of academic persistence. *Journal of Counseling & Development, 81*, 93–105.

Gloria, A. M., & Peregoy, J. J. (1995). Counseling Latino alcohol and other substance users/abusers: Cultural considerations for counselors. *Journal of Substance Abuse Treatment, 13*, 1–8.

Gloria, A. M., & Peregoy, J. J. (1996). Counseling Latino alcohol and other substance users/abusers: Cultural considerations for counselors. *Journal of Substance Abuse Treatment, 13*, 119–126.

Goldberg, N. G, Bos, H. M. W., & Gartrell, N. K. (2011). Substance use by adolescents in the USA. *Journal of Health Psychology,* 16(8), 1231–1240. doi: 10.1177/1359105311403522.

Goldenberg, I., & Goldenberg, H. (1996). *Family therapy: An overview* (4th ed.). Pacific Grove, CA: Brooks/Cole.

Gone, J. (2010). Psychotherapy and Traditional Healing for American Indians: Exploring the prospects for therapeutic integration. *The Counseling Psychologist, 38* (2), 166–235. doi: 10.1177/0011000008330831

Gonzalez, M., Castill-Canez, I., Tarke, H., Soriano, F., Garcia, O., & Velasquez, R. J. (1997). Promoting the culturally sensitive diagnosis of Mexican Americans: Some personal insights. *Journal of Multicultural Counseling and Development, 25,* 156–161.

Good, G. E., Dell, D. M., & Mintz, L. B. (1989). Male role and gender role conflict: Relations to help seeking in men. *Journal of Counseling Psychology, 36,* 295–300.

Good, G. E., & Mintz, L. B. (1990). Gender role conflict and depression in college men: Evidence for compounded risk. *Journal of Counseling and Development, 69*(1), 17–21.

Good, G. E., Robertson, J. M., Fitzgerald, L. F., Stevens, M., & Bartels, K. M. (1996). The relation between masculine role conflict and psychological distress in male university counseling center clients. *Journal of Counseling and Development, 75*(1), 44–49.

Good, J. J., & Sanchez, D. (2010). Doing gender for different reasons Why gender conformity predicts positive and negative self-esteem. *Psychology of Women Quarterly, 34,* 203–214.

Good, G. E., & Wood, P. K. (1995). Male gender role conflict, depression, and help seeking: Do college men face double jeopardy? *Journal of Counseling and Development, 74*(1), 70–75.

Good, M. J. D., James, C., Good, B. J., & Becker, A. E. (2003). The culture of medicine and racial, ethnic, and class disparities in health care. In Institute of Medicine (Ed.), *Unequal treatment: Confronting racial and ethnic disparities in healthcare* (pp. 594–625). Washington, DC: National Academies Press.

Gorney, C. (2011, June). Too young to wed: The secret world of child brides. *National Geographic, 219*(6), 78–96.

Gossett, T. (1963). *Race: The history of an idea in America.* New York: Schocken.

Graves, J. L. (2003). *The emperor's new clothes. Biological theories of race at the new millennium.* New Jersey: Rutgers University Press.

Greene, B. (1994). Ethnic-minority lesbians and gay men: Mental health and treatment issues. *Journal of Consulting and Clinical Psychology, 62,* 243–251.

Greene, B., & Herek, G. M. (1994). *Lesbian and gay psychology: Theory, research, and clinical applications.* Thousand Oaks, CA: Sage.

Grubb, H. J. (1992). Intelligence at the low end of the curve: Where are the racial differences? In A. Burlew, W. Banks, H. McAdoo, & D. Azibo (Eds.), *African American psychology: Theory, research, and practice* (pp. 219–228). Newbury Park, CA: Sage.

Gunn Allen, P. (1992). *The sacred hoop: Recovering the feminine in American Indian traditions.* Boston: Beacon Press.

Gunn Allen, P. (1994). Who is your mother? Red roots of White feminism. In R. Takaki (Ed.), *From different shores: Perspectives on race and ethnicity in America* (2nd ed., pp. 192–198). New York: Oxford University Press.

Gushue, G. V., & Sciarra, D. P. (1995). Culture and families: A multidimensional approach. In J. G. Ponterotto, J. M. Casas, L. A. Suzuki, & C. M. Alexander (Eds.), *Handbook of multicultural counseling* (pp. 586–606). Thousand Oaks, CA: Sage.

Hacker, A. (1992). *Two nations: Black and White, separate, hostile, unequal.* New York: Ballantine Books.

Haddock, S. A., Zimmerman, T. S., & Lyness, K. P. (2003). Changing gender norms: Transitional dilemmas. In F. Walsh (Ed.), *Normal family process* (pp. 301–336). New York: Guilford Press.

Hage, S. M. (2006). Profiles of women survivors: The development of agency in abusive relationships. *Journal of Counseling & Development, 84,* 83–94.

Hahn, H. (1988a, Winter). Can disability be beautiful? *Social Policy,* pp. 26–32.

Hahn, H. (1988b). The politics of physical differences: Disability and discrimination. *Journal of Social Issues, 44*(1), 39–47.

Haider, R. (1995). *Gender and development.* Cairo, Egypt: American University in Cairo Press.

Halbert, C. H., Bary, F. K., Weathers, B., Delmoor, E., Coyne, J., Wileyto, O., et al. (2007). Differences in cultural beliefs and values among African American and European American men with prostate cancer. *Cancer Control, 14*, 277–284.

Hall, C. R., Dixon, W. A., & Mauzey, E. (2004). Spirituality and religion: Implications for counselors. *Journal of Counseling & Development, 82*, 504–507.

Hall, P. C., & Pargament, K. I. (2003). Advances in the conceptualization and measurement of religion and spirituality. *American Psychologist, 58*(1), 64–74.

Hall, R. E. (1992). Bias among African-Americans regarding skin color: Implications for social work practice. *Research on Social Work Practice, 2*, 479–486.

Hall, R. E. (2001). Identity development across the lifespan: A biracial model. *The Social Sciences Journal, 38*, 119–123.

Hall, R. E. (2005). From psychology of race to issues of skin color: Western trivialization and people of African descent. *International Journal of Psychology and Psychological Therapy, 5*, 125–134.

Hall, R. E., & Livingston, J. N. (2006). Mental health practice with Arab families: The implications of spirituality vis-à-vis Islam. *American Journal of Family Therapy, 34*(2), 139–150.

Hamilton, J., Powe, B., Pollard, A. B., Lee, K., & Felton, A. M. (2007). Spirituality among African American cancer survivors: Having a personal relationship with God. *Cancer Nursing, 30*, 309–316.

Hammelman, T. L. (1993). Gay and lesbian youth: Contributing factors to serious attempts or considerations of suicide. *Journal of Gay and Lesbian Psychotherapy, 2*(1), 77–89.

Hanna, S. M., & Brown, J. H. (1995). *The practice of family therapy: Key elements across models.* Pacific Grove, CA: Brooks/Cole.

Hardiman, R. (1982). *White identity development: A process-oriented model for describing the racial consciousness of White Americans.* Unpublished doctoral dissertation, University of Massachusetts, Amherst, MA.

Hardiman, R. (2001). Reflections on White identity development theory. In C. Wijeyesinghe & B. Jackson III (Eds.), *New perspectives on racial identity development: A theoretical and practical anthology* (pp. 108–128). New York: New York University Press.

Hare-Mustin, R. T. (1988). Family change and gender differences: Implications for theory and practice. *Family Relations, 37*, 36–41.

Harper, F. E. (1854). *The slave auction.* National Endowment for the Arts & Poetry Foundation. Retrieved January 17, 2008, from http://www.poetryfoundation .org/poem/177157

Harris, D. R., & Sims, J. J. (2002). Who is multiracial? Assessing the complexity of lived race. *American Sociological Review, 67*, 614–627.

Harris, K. (1995). Collected quotes from Albert Einstein. Retrieved September 1, 2007, from http://rescomp .stanford.edu/~cheshire/EinsteinQuotes.html

Harrison, P. M., & Beck, A. J. (2005). Prisoners in 2004. *Bureau of Justice Statistics Bulletin.* Washington, DC: U. S. Department of Justice, Office of Justice Programs.

Harrison, P. M., & Beck, A. J. (2006, November). Prisoners in 2005. *Bureau of Justice Statistics Bulletin.* Washington, DC: U.S. Department of Justice, Office of Justice Programs.

Hartung, P. J. (1996). Transforming counseling courses: From monocultural to multicultural. *Counseling Education and Supervision, 36*(1), 6–13.

Harvey, R. D., LaBeach, N., Pridgen, E., & Gocial, T. M. (2005). The intragroup stigmatization of skin tone among Black Americans. *Journal of Black Psychology, 31*, 237–253.

Hays, D. G., Dean, J. K., & Chang, C. Y. (2007). Addressing privilege and oppression in counselor training and practice: A qualitative analysis. *Journal of Counseling & Development, 85*, 317–324.

Hays, P. A. (1996). Addressing the complexities of culture and gender in counseling. *Journal of Counseling and Development, 74*, 332–338.

Healey, J. F. (1997). *Race, ethnicity, and gender in the United States: Inequality, group conflict, and power.* Thousand Oaks, CA: Pine Forge Press.

Heinrich, R. K., Corbine, J. L., & Thomas, K. R. (1990). Counseling Native Americans. *Journal of Counseling and Development, 69*, 128–133.

Helms, J. E. (1984). Toward a theoretical explanation of the effects of race on counseling: A Black and White model. *Counseling Psychologist, 12*(3), 153–165.

Helms, J. E. (1990). *Black and White racial identity: Theory, research, and practice.* New York: Greenwood Press.

Helms, J. E. (1995). An update of white and people of color racial identity model. In J. G. Ponterotto, J. M. Casa, L. A. Suzuki, & C. M. Alexander (Eds.), *Handbook of multicultural counseling* (pp. 181–198). Thousand Oaks, CA: Sage.

Helms, J. E. (2003). A pragmatic view of social justice. *The Counseling Psychologist, 31*, 305–313.

Helms, J. E. (2007). Some better practices for measuring ethnic and racial identity constructs. *Journal of Counseling Psychology, 54*, 235–246.

Helms, J. E., & Parham, T. A. (1984). *Racial Identity Attitude Scale.* Unpublished manuscript.

The Henry J. Kaiser Foundation (2011, December). *Fact Sheet: HIV/AIDS Epidemic in the United States.* Retrieved December 20, 2011, from http://www.kff.org/hivaids/upload/3029-12.pdf

Herman, M. (2004). Forced to choose: Some determinants of racial identification in multiracial adolescents. *Child Development, 75*, 740–748.

Hermann, M. A., & Herlighy, B. R. (2006). Legal and ethical implications of refusing to counsel homosexual clients. *Journal of Counseling & Development, 84*, 414–418.

Hernandez, B. (2005). A voice in the chorus: Perspectives of young men of color on their disabilities, identities, and peer-mentors. *Disability & Society, 20*, 117–133.

Hernandez, M. (1996). Central American families. In M. McGoldrick, J. Giordano, & J. Pearce (Eds.), *Ethnicity and family therapy* (pp. 214–224). New York: Guilford Press.

Herring, R. D. (1992). Understanding Native American values: Process and content concerns for counselors. *Counseling and Values, 34*, 134–137.

Herrnstein, R. J., & Murray, C. (1994). *The bell curve: Intelligence and class structure in American life.* New York: Free Press.

Hines, P. M., & Boyd-Franklin, N. (1996). African American families. In M. McGoldrick, J. Giordano, & J. K. Pearce (Eds.), *Ethnicity and family therapy* (pp. 66–84). New York: Guilford Press.

Hirata, L. C. (1979). Free, indentured, enslaved: Chinese prostitutes in Nineteenth-Century America. *Signs, Women in Latin America, 5*(1), 3–29.

Hixson, L., Hepler, B. B., & Kim. M. O. (2011). The White Population: 2010. C2010-BR05. *2010 Census Briefs.* U.S. Washington, DC: Department of Commerce, U.S. Census Bureau.

Ho, A. K., Sidanius, J., Levin, D. T., & Banaji, M. (2011). Evidence for hypodescent and racial hierarchy in the categorization and perception of biracial individuals. *Journal of Personality and Social Psychology*, 492–506.

Hochschild, A. R. (2003). *The second shift.* New York: Penguin Books.

Hochschild, J. L., & Weaver, V. (2007). The skin color paradox and the American racial order. *Social Forces, 86*(2), 643–670.

Hoffman, M. A., Phillips, E. L., Noumair, D. A., Shullman, S. Geishler, C., Gray, J., et al. (2005). Toward a feminist and multicultural model of consultation and advocacy. *Journal of Multicultural Counseling & Development, 34*, 116–128.

Hoffman, R. M. (2001). The measurement of masculinity and femininity: Historical perspective and implications for counseling. *Journal of Counseling & Development, 79*, 472–485.

Hoffman, R. M. (2004). Conceptualizing heterosexual identity development: Issues and challenges. *Journal of Counseling & Development, 82*, 375–380.

Holcomb-McCoy, C. C. (2000). Multicultural counseling competencies: An exploratory factor analysis. *Journal of Multicultural Counseling and Development, 28*, 83–97.

Hong, G. L., & Domokos-Cheng Ham, M. (2001). *Psychotherapy and counseling with Asian American clients: A practical guide.* Thousand Oaks, CA: Sage.

Hooks, B. (1993). *Sisters of the yam: Black women and self-recovery.* Boston: South End Press.

Hoopes, D. S. (1979). Intercultural communication concepts: Psychology of intercultural experience. In M. D. Psych (Ed.), *Multicultural education: A cross-cultural training approach.* LaGrange Park, IL: Intercultural Network.

Horse, P. G. (2001). Reflections on American Indian identity. In C. Wijeyesinghe & B. Jackson III (Eds.), *New perspectives on racial identity development: A theoretical and practical anthology* (pp. 91–197). New York: New York University Press.

Horst, E. A. (1995). Reexamining gender issues in Erikson's stages of identity. *Journal of Counseling and Development, 73*, 271–278.

Howden, L., & Meyer, J. (2011, May). *Age and Sex Composition: 2010. 2010 Census Briefs.* Retrieved November 8, 2011, from http://www.census.gov/prod/cen2010/briefs/c2010br-03.pdf

Hoxie, F. E. (Ed.). (1996). *Encyclopedia of North American Indians: Native American history, culture, and life from paleo-Indians to the present.* Boston: Houghton Mifflin.

Hsu, F. L. K. (1953). *American and Chinese: Two ways of life.* New York: Abeland-Schuman.

Hughes, E. C. (1945). Dilemmas and contradictions of status. *American Journal of Sociology, 50*, 353–357.

Humes, K., Jones, N., & Ramirez, R. (2011, March). *Overview of Race and Hispanic Origin: 2010. 2010 Census Briefs.* Retrieved May 20, 2011, from www.census.gov/prod/cen2010/briefs/c2010br-02.pdf.

Hunt, B. (1993). What counselors need to know about counseling gay men and lesbians. *Counseling and Human Development, 26*(1), 1–12.

Hunt, B., Matthews, C., Milsom, A., & Lammel, J. A. (2006). Lesbians with physical disabilities: A qualitative study of their experiences with counseling. *Journal of Counseling & Development, 84*, 163–173.

Hutchinson, M. G. (1982). Transforming body image: Your body—friend or foe? In Women & Therapy, 1(3), 59–67. doi: 10.1300/J015V01N03_08.

Icard, L. (1986). Black gay men and conflicting social identities: Sexual orientation versus racial identity. In J. Gripton & M. Valentich (Eds.), Social work practice in sexual problems [Special issue]. *Journal of Social Work and Human Sexuality, 4*(1–2), 83–93.

Ingersoll, R. E. (1995). Spirituality, religion, and counseling: Dimensions and relationship. In M. Burke & J. Mirant (Eds.), *Counseling: The spiritual dimension* (pp. 5–18). Thousand Oaks, CA: Sage.

Ingrassia, M. (1993, August 30). Endangered family. *Newsweek,* pp. 17–29.

Institute of Medicine (Ed.). (2003). *Unequal treatment: Confronting racial and ethnic disparities in healthcare.* Washington, DC: National Academies Press.

Ivey, A. E., & Collins, N. M. (2003). Social justice: A long-term challenge for Counseling Psychology. *The Counseling Psychologist, 31*, 290–298.

Ivey, A. E., Ivey, M. B., & Simek-Morgan, L. (1997). *Counseling and psychotherapy: A multicultural perspective* (4th ed.). Boston: Allyn & Bacon.

Jackson, A. (1908). Second annual message. In J. D. Richardson (Ed.), *A compilation of the messages and papers of the presidents 1789–1902* (Vol. II). Retrieved January 10, 2003, from http://www.pbs.org/wgbh/aia/part4/4h3437t.html

Jackson, L. A., Sullivan, L. A., & Rostker, R. (1988). Gender, gender role, and body image. *Sex Roles, 19*, 429–443.

Jackson, V. (2005). Robbing Peter to pay Paul: Reflections on feminist therapy with low-wage earning women. In M. Mirkin, J. Suyemoto, & B. Okun (Eds.), *Psychotherapy with women: Exploring diverse contexts and identities* (pp. 237–246). New York: Guilford Press.

Joe, J. R. (2003). The rationing of healthcare and health disparity for the American Indians/Alaskan Natives. In Institute of Medicine (Ed.), *Unequal treatment: Confronting racial and ethnic disparities in healthcare*. Washington, DC: National Academies Press.

John, R. (1988). The Native American family. In C. H. Mindel, R. W. Habenstein, & R. Wright (Eds.), *Ethnic families in America: Patterns and variations* (3rd ed., pp. 325–366). New York: Elsevier.

Johnson, T., & Vriens, L. (2011). *Islam: Governing under Sharia. Council on Foreign Relations Law.* Retrieved January 11, 2012, from http://www.cfr.org/religion/islam-governing-under-sharia/p8034

Jones, H. L., Cross, W. E., & DeFour, D. C. (2007). Race-related stress, racial identity attitudes, and mental health among Black women. *Journal of Black Psychology, 33*, 208–231.

Jones, J. (1985). *Labor of love, labor of sorrow*. New York: Vintage Books.

Jones, N. A. (2005). We the people of more than one race in the United States. *Census 2000 special reports*. Washington, DC: U.S. Department of Commerce, U.S. Census Bureau.

Jones, N. A., & Symens Smith, A. (2001). The two or more races population: 2000. *Census 2000 brief*. U.S. Department of Commerce. Washington, DC: U.S. Department of Commerce, U.S. Census Bureau.

Jordan, J. V. (1997a). Relational development: Therapeutic implications of empathy and shame. In Judith V. Jordan (Ed.), *Women's growth in diversity: More writings from the Stone Center* (pp. 136–161). New York: Guilford Press.

Jordan, J. V (1997b). A relational perspective for understanding women's development. In Judith V. Jordan (Ed.), *Women's growth in diversity: More writings from the Stone Center* (pp. 9–24). New York: Guilford Press.

Jordan, J. V (1997c). Clarity in connection, empathic knowing, desire, and sexuality. In Judith V. Jordan (Ed.), *Women's growth in diversity: More writings from the Stone Center* (pp. 50–73). New York: Guilford Press.

Jordan, J., & Romney, P. (2005). Women in the workplace: An application of relational-cultural theory. In M. Mirkin, J. Suyemoto, & B. Okun (Eds.), *Psychotherapy with women: Exploring diverse contexts and identities* (pp. 198–214). New York: Guilford Press.

Jourdan, A. (2006). The impact of the family environment on the ethnic identity development of multiethnic college students. *Journal of Counseling & Development, 84*, 328–340.

Kagitcibasi, C. (1997). Individualism and collectivism. In J. Berry, M. Segall, & C. Kagitcibasi (Eds.), *Cross-cultural psychology: Social and behavioral applications* (Vol. 3, pp. 1–49). Boston: Allyn & Bacon.

Kaplan, A. G. (1987). Reflections on gender and psychotherapy. In M. Braude (Ed.), *Women and therapy* (Vol. 6, pp. 11–24). New York: Haworth Press.

Karenga, M. (1980). *Kawaida theory*. Los Angeles: Kawaida.

Kashubeck, S., Walsh, B., & Crowl, A. (1994). College atmosphere and eating disorders. *Journal of Counseling and Development, 72*, 640–645.

Kegan, R. (1982). *The evolving self*. Cambridge, MA: Harvard University Press.

Kenway, J. (1988). *High-status private schooling in Australia and the production of an educational hegemony*. Unpublished doctoral dissertation, Murdoch University, Western Australia.

Kerwin, C., Ponterotto, J. G., Jackson, B. L., & Harris, A. (1993). Racial identity in biracial children: A qualitative investigation. *Journal of Counseling Psychology, 40*, 221–231.

Kich, G. K. (1992). The developmental process of asserting a biracial, bicultural identity. In M. P. P. Root (Ed.), *Racially mixed people in America* (pp. 304–317). Newbury Park, CA: Sage.

Kim, B. S. K. (2011). Client motivation and multicultural counseling. *The Counseling Psychologist, 39*, 267–275. doi: 10.1177/0011000010375310.

Kim, B. S. K., Li, L. C., & Liang, C. T. H. (2002). Effects of Asian American client adherence to Asian cultural values, session goal, and counselor emphasis of client expression on career counseling process. *Journal of Counseling Psychology, 49*, 342–354.

Kim, B. S. K., & Lyons, H. Z. (2003). Experiential activities and multicultural counseling competence training. *Journal of Counseling & Development, 81*, 400–408.

Kim, J. (2001). Asian American identity development theory. In C. Wijeyesinghe & B. Jackson III (Eds.), *New perspectives on racial identity development: A theoretical and practical anthology* (pp. 67–90). New York: New York University Press.

Kimmel, M. S. (2006). Masculinity as homophobia: Fear, shame, and silence in the construction of gender identity. In T. E. Orr (Ed.), *The social construction of difference and inequality: Race, class, gender, and sexuality* (pp.133–150). Boston: McGraw-Hill.

King, N. (1988). Teaching about lesbians and gays in the psychology curriculum. In P. A. Bronstein & K. Quina (Eds.), *Teaching a psychology of people: Resources for gender and sociocultural awareness* (pp. 168–174). Washington, DC: American Psychological Association.

Kitano, H. H. L. (1988). The Japanese American family. In C. H. Mindel, R. W. Habenstein, & R. Wright (Eds.), *Ethnic families in America: Patterns and variations* (3rd ed., pp. 258–275). New York: Elsevier.

Kitzinger, C. (1999). Intersexuality: Deconstructing the sex/gender binary. *Feminism & Psychology, 9*(4), 493–498.

Klages, M. (1997). *Queer theory*. Retrieved July 2, 2011, from http://english252-005.wikidot.com/queer-theory

Kliman, J. (2005). Many differences, many voices: Toward social justice in family therapy. In M. Pravder, K. Suyemoto, & B. Okun (Eds.), *Psychotherapy with women: Exploring diverse contexts and identities* (pp. 42–63). New York: Guilford Press.

Kluckhohn, F. R., & Strodtbeck, F. L. (1961). *Variations in value orientations*. Evanston, IL: Row, Peterson.

Kocarek, C. E., Talbot, D. M., Batka, J. C., & Anderson, M. A. (2001). Reliability and validity of three measures of multicultural competence. *Journal of Counseling & Development, 79*, 486–496.

Kochhar, R. (2007). *1995–2005: Foreign-born Latinos make progress on wages*. Washington, DC: Pew Hispanic Center.

Kogan, M. (2000, July/August). Course exposes hidden racial prejudices: Students confront their hidden biases to better prepare for psychology practice. *Monitor on Psychology, 31*(7). Retrieved September 1, 2007, from http://www.apa.org/monitor/julaug00/prejudice.html

Kreider, R. (2003). Adopted children and stepchildren 2000. *Census 2000 special reports*. Washington, DC: U.S. Department of Commerce, Economics and Statistics Administration. Retrieved October 20, 2007, from www.census.gov/prod/2003pubs/censr-6.pdf

Ladany, N., Brittan-Powell, C. S., & Pannu, R. K. (1997). The influence of supervisory racial identity interaction and racial matching on the Supervisory Working Alliance and Supervisee Multicultural Competence. *Counselor Education and Supervision, 36*, 284–304.

Laird, J. (2003). Lesbian and gay families. In F. Walsh (Ed.), *Normal family processes* (pp. 176–209). New York: Guilford Press.

Lakoff, R. T., & Scherr, R. L. (1984). *Face value: Politics of beauty*. Boston: Routledge, Kegan, & Paul.

Lamb, M. E. (1982). Parental behavior and child development in nontraditional families. In M. E. Lamb (Ed.), *Nontraditional families: Parenting and child development*. Hillsdale, NJ: Erlbaum.

Landry, B. (2007). *Race, gender and class: Theory of methods of analysis*. Upper Saddle River, NJ: Pearson Prentice Hall.

Lane, J. M., & Addis, M. E. (2005). Male gender role conflict and patterns of help seeking in Costa Rica and the United States. *Psychology of Men & Masculinity, 6*, 155–168.

Lareau, A. (1997). Social-class differences in family-school relationships: The importance of cultural capital. In A. Halsey, H. Lauder, P. Brown, & A. Wells (Eds.), *Education: Culture, economy, society* (pp. 703–717). Oxford, UK: Oxford University Press.

LaVeist, T. A. (2002). Why we should study race, ethnicity, and health. In T. A. LaVeist (Ed.), *Race, ethnicity, health: A public health reader* (pp. 1–7). San Francisco: Jossey-Bass.

Le, C. N. (2007). Interracial dating & marriage. *Asian-Nation: The landscape of Asian America.* Retrieved October 21, 2007, from http://www.asian-nation.org/interracial.shtml

Le, C. N. (2008). *Adopted Asian Americans. Asian-Nation: The landscape of Asian America.* Retrieved January 27, 2008, from http://www.asian-nation.org/adopted/shtml

Leach, M. M., Behrens, J. T., & LaFleur, N. K. (2002). White racial identity and white racial consciousness: Similarities, differences, and recommendations. *Journal of Multicultural Counseling and Development, 30*, 66–80.

Leaper, C., & Brown, C. S. (2008). Perceived experiences with sexism among adolescent girls. *Child Development, 79*, 685–704.

Lee, C. (2001). Defining and responding to racial and ethnic diversity. In D. Locke, J. Myers, & E. Herr (Eds.), *Handbook of counseling* (pp. 581–588). Thousand Oaks, CA: Sage.

Lee, D., & Ahn, S. (2011). Racial Discrimination and Asian Mental Health: A Meta Analysis. *The Counseling Psychologist, 39*(3), 463–489. doi: 10.1177/0011000010381791.

Lee, J., & Beal, F. D. (2007). Reinventing the color line immigration and America's new racial/ethnic divide. *Social Forces, 86*(2), 561–586.

Lee, R. M. (2003). Do ethnic identity and other-group orientation protect against discrimination for Asian Americans? *Journal of Counseling Psychology, 50*, 131–141.

Legal Momentum. (2010). Retrieved October 29, 2011, from http://www.legalmomentum.org.

Lemkau, J. P., & Landau, C. (1986). The "selfless syndrome": Assessment and treatment considerations. *Psychotherapy, 23*, 227–233.

Leong, F. T. L., Wagner, N. S., & Kim, H. H. (1995). Group counseling expectations among Asian American students: The role of culture-specific factors. *Journal of Counseling Psychology, 42*, 217–222.

Lerner, R. M., & Lerner, J. L. (1977). Effects of age, sex, and physical attractiveness on child-peer relations, academic performance, and elementary school adjustment. *Developmental Psychology, 13*, 585–590.

Lesiak, C., & Jones, M. (1991). *In the White man's image* [The American Experience Series]. Alexandria, VA: Public Broadcasting Source.

Lester, R., & Petrie, T. A. (1998). Prevalence of disordered eating behaviors and bulimia nervosa in a sample of Mexican American female college students. *Journal of Multicultural Counseling and Development, 26*, 157–165.

Levitt, H., Butler, M., & Hill, T. (2006). What clients find helpful in psychotherapy: Developing priniciples for facilitating moment-to-moment change. *Journal of Counseling Psychology, 53*, 314–324.

Lewis, K. M., Rubkin, N., Gaska, K., & Njaki, C. L. (2011). Investigating motivations for women's skin bleaching in Tanzania. *Psychology of Women Quarterly, 35*(1), 29–37.

Lin, J. C. H. (1994). How long do Chinese Americans stay in psychotherapy? *Journal of Counseling Psychology, 41*, 288–291.

Lipsitz, G. (2005). The possessive investment in Whiteness: Racialized social democracy and the "White problem in American studies." In T. Ore (Ed.), *The social construction of difference and inequality: Race, class, gender and sexuality* (pp. 402–413). Boston: McGraw-Hill.

Liu, W. M., & Arguello, J. L. (2006). Using social class and classism in counseling. *Counseling and Human Development, 39*, 1–9.

Liu, W. M., Saba, R. A., Soleck, G., Hopps, J., Dunston, K., & Pickett, T. (2004). Using social class in counseling psychology research. *Journal of Counseling Psychology, 51*, 3–18.

Livneh, H., & Sherwood, A. (1991). Application of personality theories and counseling strategies to clients with physical disabilities. *Journal of Counseling and Development, 69*, 525–538.

Loewen, J. W. (1995). *Lies my teacher told me: Everything your American history textbook got wrong.* New York: Simon & Schuster.

Loiacano, D. K. (1989). Gay identity issues among Black Americans: Racism, homophobia, and the need for validation. *Journal of Counseling and Development, 68,* 21–25.

Lorde, A. (1994). Living with cancer. In E. C. White (Ed.), *The Black women's health book: Speaking for ourselves* (pp. 27–37). Seattle, WA: Seal.

Lott, B. (1994). *Women's lives: Themes and variations in gender learning* (2nd ed.). Pacific Grove, CA: Brooks/Cole.

Lou, E., Lalonde, R. N., & Wilson, C. (2011). Examining a multidimensional framework of racial identity across different biracial groups. *Asian American Psychology, 2*(2), 79–90. doi: 10.1037/a0023658.

Mackun, P., & Wilson, S. (2011, March). *Population Distribution and Change: 2000 to 2010.* U.S. Department of Commerce Economics and Statistics Administration. Retrieved from www.census.gov/prod/cen2010/briefs/c2010br-01.pdf

Maffly-Kipp, L. (2000). *African-American religion in the nineteenth century.* University of North Carolina, Chapel Hill. Retrieved January 15, 2004, from http://www.nhc.rtp.nc.us/tserve/nineteen/nkeyinfo/nafrican.htm

Mahalik, J. R., Lagan, H. D., & Morrison, J. A. (2006). Health behaviors and masculinity in Kenyan and U.S. male college students. *Psychology of Men & Masculinity, 7,* 191–202.

Marini, I. (2001). Cross-cultural counseling issues of males who sustain a disability. *Journal of Applied Rehabilitation Counseling, 32,* 36–44.

Mass, A. I. (1992). Interracial Japanese Americans: The best of both worlds or the end of the Japanese American community. In M. P. P. Root (Ed.), *Racially mixed people in America* (pp. 265–279). Newbury Park, CA: Sage.

Mastria, M. R. (2002). Ethnicity and eating disorders. *Psychoanalysis and Psychotherapy, 19*(1), 59–77.

McBride, M. (1990). Autonomy and the struggle for female identity: Implications for counseling women. *Journal of Counseling and Development, 69,* 22–26.

McCarthy, J. (2005). Individualism and collectivism: What do they have to do with counseling? *Journal of Multicultural Counseling and Development, 33,* 108–117.

McCarthy, J., & Holliday, E. L. (2004). Help-seeking and counseling within a traditional male gender role: An examination from a multicultural perspective. *Journal of Counseling & Development, 82,* 25–30.

McDonald, A. L. (1990). Living with our deepest differences. *Journal of Law and Religion, 8,* 237–239.

McFadden, J. (1993). *Transcultural counseling: Bilateral and international perspectives.* Alexandria, VA: American Counseling Association.

McIntosh, P. (1988). *White privilege and male privilege: A personal account of coming to see correspondences through work in women's studies* (Working Paper No. 189). Wellesley, MA: Wellesley College Center for Research on Women.

McIntosh, P. (1989, July/August). White privilege: Unpacking the invisible knapsack. *Peace and Freedom,* pp. 10–12.

McIntosh, P. (1990). *Interactive phases of curricular and personal revision with regard to race* (Working Paper No. 219). Wellesley, MA: Wellesley College Center for Research on Women.

McKelley, R. A., & Rochlen, A. B. (2007). The practice of coaching: Exploring alternatives to therapy for counseling-resistant men. *Psychology of Men & Masculinity, 8*(1), 53–65.

McLoyd, V. C., & Wilson, L. (1992). Telling them like it is: The role of economic and environmental factors in single mothers' discussions with their children. *American Journal of Community Psychology, 20,* 419–444.

McWhirter, E. H. (1991). Empowerment in counseling. *Journal of Counseling and Development, 69,* 222–227.

Mencher, J. (1997). Structural possibilities and constraints of mutuality in psychotherapy. In J. Jordan (Ed.), *Women's growth in diversity: More writings from the Stone Center* (pp. 110–119). New York: Guilford Press.

Mercado, M. M. (2000). The invisible family: Counseling Asian American substance abusers and their families. *The Family Journal: Counseling and Therapy for Couples and Families, 8,* 267–272.

Middle East Institute. (2004). Retrieved September 10, 2007, from www.mideast.org

Miller, W. R., & Thoresen, C. E. (2003). Spirituality, religion, and health: An emerging research field. *American Psychologist, 58*(1), 24–35.

Min, P. G. (1988). The Korean American family. In C. H. Mindel, R. W. Habenstein, & R. Wright (Eds.), *Ethnic families in America: Patterns and variations* (3rd ed., pp. 199–229). New York: Elsevier.

Mindel, C. H., Habenstein, R. W., & Wright, R. (1988). *Ethnic families in America: Patterns and variations.* New York: Elsevier.

Mintz, L. B., & O'Neil, J. M. (1990). Gender roles, sex, and the process of psychotherapy: Many questions and few answers. *Journal of Counseling and Development, 68,* 381–387.

Minuchin, S. (1974). *Families and family therapy.* Cambridge, MA: Harvard University Press.

Minuchin, S. (1984). *Family kaleidoscope.* Cambridge, MA: Harvard University Press.

Minuchin, S. (1991). The seductions of constructivism. *The Family Networker, 15*(5), 47–50.

Mio, J. S. (2005). Academic mental health training settings and the multicultural guidelines. In M. Constantine & D. Sue (Eds.), *Strategies for building multicultural competence in mental health and educational settings* (pp. 129–144). Hoboken, NJ: John Wiley & Sons.

Miranda, A. O., & Matheny, K. B. (2000). Psychosociological predictors of acculturative stress among Latino adults. *Journal of Mental Health Counseling, 22,* 306–317.

Mishkind, M. E., Rodin, J., Silbersein, L. R., & Striegel-Moore, R. H. (1987). The embodiment of masculinity: Cultural, psychological, and behavioral dimensions. In M. S. Kimmel (Ed.), *Changing men: New directions in research on men and masculinity* (pp. 37–52). Newbury Park, CA: Sage.

Miville, M. L., Constantine, M. G., Baysden, M. F., & So-Lloyd, G. (2005). Chameleon changes: An exploration of racial identity themes of multiracial people. *Journal of Counseling Psychology, 52,* 507–516.

Mohatt, G. (2010). Moving toward an Indigenous Psychotherapy. *The Counseling Psychologist, 38,* 236–242. doi: 10.1177/0011000009345532.

Mohr, J. J. (2002). Heterosexual identity and the heterosexual therapist: An identity perspective on sexual orientation. *The Counseling Psychologist, 30,* 532–566.

Moir, A., & Jessel, D. (1991). *Brain sex: The real difference between men and women.* New York: Delta.

Moradi, B., DeBlaere, C., & Huang, Y. (2010). Centralizing the experience of LGBT people. *The Counseling Psychologist, 38,* 322–330. doi: 10.1177/0011000009346325.

Moradi, B., & Hasan, N. T. (2004). Arab Americans persons' reported experiences of discrimination and mental health: The mediating role of personal control. *Journal of Counseling Psychology, 51,* 418–428.

Moradi, B., van den Berg, J. J., & Epting, F. R. (2006). Intrapersonal and interpersonal manifestation of antilesbian and gay prejudice: An application of personal construct theory. *Journal of Counseling Psychology, 53,* 57–66.

Mullins, E., & Sites, P. (1984). Famous Black Americans: A three-generational analysis of social origins. *American Sociological Review, 49,* 672.

Murphy, B. C., & Dillon, C. (2008). *Interviewing in action in a multicultural world.* Belmont, CA: Thomson. Brooks Cole.

Myers, J. E., Sweeney, T. J., & Witmer, J. M. (2001). Optimization of behavior: Promotion of wellness. In D. Locke, J. Myers, & E. Herr (Eds.), *The handbook of counseling* (pp. 641–652). Thousand Oaks, CA: Sage Publications.

Myers, L. J. (1991). Expanding the psychology of knowledge optimally: The importance of world view revisited. In R. Jones (Ed.), *Black psychology* (3rd ed., pp. 15–28). Berkeley, CA: Cobb and Henry.

Myers, L. J., Speight, S. L., Highlen, P. S., Cox, C. I., Reynolds, A. L., Adams, E. M., et al. (1991). Identity development and worldview: Toward an optimal conceptualization. *Journal of Counseling and Development, 70*, 54–63.

Napholz, L. (1994). Sex role orientation and psychological well-being among working Black women. *Journal of Black Psychology, 20*, 469–482.

Nassar-McMillan, S. C., & Hakim-Larson, J. (2003). Counseling consideration among Arab Americans. *Journal of Counseling & Development, 81*, 150–159.

National Campaign to Prevent Teen Pregnancy. (2010). *Preventing unplanned and teen pregnancy: Why it matters.* Retrieved November 19, 2011, from http://www.thenationalcampaign.org/about-us/wim.aspx

National Center for Mental Health Promotion and Youth Violence Prevention. (2011). *Meeting the needs of Latino children: Part 1: Risk.* Retrieved August 17, 2011, from http://www.promoteprevent.org/publications/prevention-briefs/meeting-needs-latino-youth-part-i-risk.

National Conference of State Legislatures. (July 14, 2011). *Same-sex marriage, Civil Unions and Domestic Partnerships.* Retrieved August 28, 2011, from http://www.ncsl.org/default.aspx?tabid=16430.

National Poverty Center. (2011). *Poverty in the United States.* The University of Michigan. Gerald Ford Public Policy Center. Retrieved November 2, 2011, from http://www.npc.umich.edu/poverty/#5

Neal, A. M., & Wilson, M. I. (1989). The role of skin color and features in the Black community: Implications for Black women and therapy. *Clinical Psychology Review, 9*, 323–333.

Nelson, H. L. (1997). *Feminism and families.* New York: Routledge.

Nelson, M. C. (1996). Separation versus connection: The gender controversy. *Implications for Counseling Women, 74*, 339–344.

Neville, H., Spanierman, L., & Doan, B. (2006). Exploring the association between color-blind racial ideology and multicultural counseling competencies. *Cultural Diversity and Ethnic Minority Psychology, 12*, 275–290.

Neville, H. A., Lilly, R. L., Duran, G., Lee, R. M., & Browne, L. (2000). Construction and initial validation of the Color-Blind Racial Attitudes Scale (CoBRAS). *Journal of Counseling Psychology, 47*, 59–70.

Newman, B. M., & Newman, P. R. (2009). *Development through life: A psychosocial approach* (10th ed.). Belmont, CA: Wadsworth.

Newman, D. M. (2007). *Identities and inequalities: Exploring the intersections of race, class, gender, and sexuality.* Boston: McGraw-Hill.

Newman, J. L., Fuqua, D. R., Gray, E. A., & Simpson, D. B. (2006). Gender differences in the relationship of anger and depression in a clinical sample. *Journal of Counseling & Development, 84*, 157–162.

Newman, K. S. (1999). *No shame in my game: The working poor in the inner city.* New York: Vintage Books and Russell Sage Foundation.

Nhat Hanh, T. (1998). *The heart of the Buddha's teaching.* Berkeley, CA: Parallax Press.

Nichols, L. M., & Hunt, B. (2011). The significance of spirituality for individuals with chronic illness: Implications for mental health counseling. *Journal of Mental Health Counseling, 33*, 51–66.

Nicholson, L. (1997). The myth of the traditional family. In H. L. Nelson (Ed.), *Feminism and families* (pp. 27–42). New York: Routledge.

Nicolau, S., & Santiestevan, S. (1990). *The Hispanic almanac.* New York: Hispanic Policy Development Project.

Nisbett, R. (1995). Race, IQ, and scientism. In S. Fraser (Ed.), *The bell curve wars: Race, intelligence, and the future of America.* New York: Basic Books.

Nobles, W. (1972). African philosophy: Foundations for Black psychology. In R. H. Jones (Ed.), *Black psychology.* New York: Harper & Row.

Novas, H. (1994). *Everything you need to know about Latino history.* New York: Penguin.

Nuessel, F. H. (1982). The language of ageism. *Gerontologist, 22*, 273–276.

Nugent, H. (2007). Race row Nobel scientist James Watson scraps tour after being suspended. Retrieved October 19, 2007, from www.timesonline.co.uk/tollnews/uk/article2694632.ece

Obermeyer, C. M. (2006). HIV in the Middle East. *British Medical Journal, 333*, 851–854.

O'Connor, M. F. (1992). Psychotherapy with gay and lesbian adolescents. In S. H. Dworkin & F. J. Gutierrez (Eds.), *Counseling gay men and lesbians: Journey to the end of the rainbow* (pp. 3–22). Alexandria, VA: American Association for Counseling and Development.

Ogbu, J. U. (1997). Racial stratification and education in the United States: Why inequality persists. In A. Halsey, H. Lauder, P. Brown, & A. Wells (Eds.), *Education: Culture, economy, society* (pp. 765–778). Oxford, UK: Oxford University Press.

Okazawa-Rey, M., Robinson, T. L., & Ward, J. V. (1987). Black women and the politics of skin color and hair. *Women and Therapy, 6*, 89–102.

Olkin, R. (2004). Making research accessible for people with disabilities. *Journal of Multicultural Counseling and Development, 32*, 332–343.

Olkin, R., & Pledger, C. (2003). Can disability studies and psychology join hands? *American Psychologist, 58*, 296–298.

Olson, M. J. (2003). Counselor understanding of Native American spiritual loss. *Counseling and Values, 47*, 109–117.

Omni, M., & Winant, H. (2006). Racial formations. In T. Ore (Ed.), *The social construction of difference and inequality: Race, class, gender, and sexuality* (pp. 19–29). Boston: McGraw-Hill.

Opoku, J. A. (April 3, 1994). Personal communication. Accra, Ghana.

Ore, T. E. (2006). Constructing differences. In T. Ore (Ed.), *The social construction of difference and inequality: Race, class, gender, and sexuality* (pp. 1–18). Boston: McGraw-Hill.

Ossana, S. M., Helms, J. E., & Leonard, M. M. (1992). Do "womanist" identity attitudes influence college women's self-esteem and perceptions of environmental bias? *Journal of Counseling and Development, 70*, 402–408.

Pace, C. (1991). *A description of factors affecting attitudes held by mental health professionals and students toward lesbians and gays.* Unpublished master's thesis, University of Florida, Gainesville.

Padilla, A. M. (1984). Synopsis of the history of Chicano psychology. In J. Martinez & R. Mendoza (Eds.), *Chicano psychology* (pp. 1–19). Orlando, FL: Academic Press.

Palmer, P. J. (1999). A vision of education as transformation. In S. Glazer (Ed.), *The heart of learning: Spirituality in education* (pp. 15–32). New York: Putnam.

Parham, T. (Presenter), (1992). *Counseling African Americans* [Video]. Amherst, MA: Microtraining and Multicultural Development.

Parker, M. S. (1985). Identity and the development of religious thinking. In A. S. Waterman (Ed.), *Identity in adolescence* (pp. 43–60). San Francisco: Jossey-Bass.

Parker, W. M., & Schwartz, R. C. (2002). On the experience of shame in multicultural counseling: Implications for White counselors-in-training. *British Journal of Guidance and Counseling, 30*, 311–318.

Passel, J. S., Wang, W., & Taylor, P. (2010, June). Marrying Out: One in seven new U.S. Marriages in interracial or interethnic. *Pew Research Center*. Retrieved June 15, 2011, from http://pewresearch.org/pubs/1616/american-marriage-interracial-interethnic

Paxton, S. J., Wertheim, E. H., Gibbons, K., Szmukler, G. I., Hillier, L., & Petrovich, J. L. (1991). Body image satisfaction, dieting beliefs, and weight-loss behaviors in adolescent girls and boys. *Journal of Youth and Adolescence, 20*, 361–379.

Pedersen, P. B. (1990). The constructs of complexity and balance in multicultural counseling theory and practice. *Journal of Counseling and Development, 15*, 16–24.

Pedersen, P. B. (1997). The cultural context of the American Counseling Association code of ethics. *Journal of Counseling and Development, 76*, 23–28.

Peregoy, J. J. (1993). Transcultural counseling with American Indians and Alaskan Natives: Contemporary issues for consideration. In J. McFadden (Ed.), *Transcultural counseling: Bilateral and international perspectives* (pp. 163–191). Alexandria, VA: American Counseling Association.

Peterman, L. M., & Dixon, C. G. (2003). Domestic violence between same sex partners: Implication for counseling. *Journal of Counseling & Development, 81*, 40–47.

Petrie, T. A., & Rogers, R. L. (2001). Extending the discussion of eating disorders to include men and athletes. *The Counseling Psychologist, 29*, 743–753.

Pew Forum U.S. Religious Landscape Survey. (2008). A religious portrait of African-Americans. *Pew Forum on Religion and Public Life*. Retrieved November 2, 2011, from http://www.pewforum.org/A-Religious-Portrait-of-African-Americans.aspx

Pew Research Center. (2010). The Pew Forum on Religion and Public Life. *A Project of the Pew Research Center*. Retrieved December 5, 2011, from http://www.pewforum.org

Pew Research Center Publications. (2011). *Muslim Americans: No Signs of Growth in Alienation or Support for Extremism Mainstream and Moderate Attitudes*. Retrieved November 22, 2011, from http://pewresearch.org/pubs/2087/muslim-americans-islamic-extremism-911-attacks-mosuqes

Phan, T., & Tylka, T. L. (2006). Exploring a model and moderators of disordered eating with Asian American college women. *Journal of Counseling Psychology, 53*, 36–47.

Pharr, S. (1988). *Homophobia: A weapon of sexism*. Little Rock, AR: Chardon.

Phillips, A., & Daniluk, J. C. (2004). Beyond "survivor": How childhood sexual abuse informs the identity of adult women at the end of the therapeutic process. *Journal of Counseling & Development, 82*, 177–184.

Phillips, M. A., & Murrell, S. A. (1994). Impact of psychological and physical health, stressful events, and social support on subsequent mental health help seeking among older adults. *Journal of Consulting and Clinical Psychology, 62*, 270–275.

Phinney, J. S. (1989). Stages of ethnic identity development in minority group adolescents. *Journal of Early Adolescence, 9*, 34–49.

Phinney, J. S. (1990). Ethnic identity in adolescents and adults: Review of research. *Psychological Bulletin, 198*, 499–514.

Phinney, J. S. (1992). The Multi-group Ethnic Identity Measure: A new scale for use with adolescents and young adults from diverse groups. *Journal of Adolescent Research, 7*, 156–176.

Phinney, J. S. (1997). Ethnic and American identity as predictors of self-esteem among African American, Latino, and White adolescents. *Journal of Youth and Adolescence, 26*,165–185.

Phinney, J. S., & Flores, J. (2002). "Unpackaging" acculturation: Aspects of acculturation as predictors of traditional sex role attitudes. *Journal of Cross-Cultural Psychology, 33*, 320–331.

Phinney, J. S., & Rosenthal, P. A. (1993). Ethnic identity in adolescence: Process, context, and outcome. In F. Adams, R. Montemayor, & T. Oulotta (Eds.), *Advances in adolescent development* (Vol. 4, pp. 145–172). Newbury Park, CA: Sage.

Phornphutkul, C., Fausto-Sterling, A., & Gruppuso, P. A. (2000). Gender self-reassignment in an XY adolescent female born with ambiguous genitalia. *Pediatrics, 106*, 135–137.

Pieterse, A. L., & Carter, R. T. (2007). An examination of the relationship between general life stress, racism-related stress, and psychological health among Black men. *Journal of Counseling Psychology, 54*, 101–109.

Pinderhughes, E. (1989). *Understanding race, ethnicity, and power: The key to efficacy in clinical practice*. New York: Free Press.

Pinderhughes, E. (1995). Empowering diverse populations: Family practice in the 21st century. *Families in Society: The Journal of Contemporary Human Services, 76*(3), 131–140.

Pleck, J. H. (1984). Men's power with women, other men, and society: A men's movement analysis. In P. P. Ricker & E. H. Carmen (Eds.), *The gender gap in psychotherapy: Social realities and psychological processes* (pp. 79–89). New York: Plenum Press.

Pledger, C. (2003). Discourse on disability and rehabilitation issues. *American Psychologist, 58*, 279–284.

Ponterotto, J. G., Alexander, C. M., & Grieger, I. (1995). A multicultural competency checklist for counseling training programs. *Journal of Multicultural Counseling and Development, 23*, 11–20.

Ponterotto, J. G., & Casas, J. M. (1991). *Handbook of racial/ethnic minority counseling research.* Springfield, IL: Charles C. Thomas.

Ponzo, Z. (1985). The counselor and physical attractiveness. *Journal of Counseling and Development, 63*, 482–485.

Pope, M. (1995). The "salad bowl" is big enough for us all: An argument for the inclusion of lesbians and gay men in any definition of multiculturalism. *Journal of Counseling and Development, 73*, 301–304.

Pope-Davis, D. B., Liu, W. M., Toporek, R., & Brittan-Powell, C. S. (2001). What's missing from multicultural competency research: Review, introspection, and recommendations? *Cultural Diversity and Ethnic Minority Psychology, 7*, 121–138.

Pope-Davis, D. B., & Ottavi, T. M. (1994). The relationship between racism and racial identity among White Americans: A replication and extension. *Journal of Counseling and Development, 72*, 293–297.

Portman, T. A. A. (2001). Sex role attributions of American Indian women. *Journal of Mental Health Counseling, 23*, 72–84.

Portman, T. A. A., & Garrett, M. L. (2005). Beloved women: Nurturing the sacred fire of leadership from an American Indian perspective. *Journal of Counseling & Development, 83*, 284–291.

Portman, T. A. A., & Herring, R. D. (2001). Debunking the Pocahontas paradox: The need for a humanistic perspective. *Journal of Humanistic Counseling, Education, and Development, 40*, 185–199.

Poston, W. S. C. (1990). The biracial identity development model: A needed addition. *Journal of Counseling and Development, 69*, 152–155.

Powell, L. H., Shahabi, L., & Thoresen, C. E. (2003). Religion and spirituality: Linkages to physical health. *American Psychologist, 58*(1), 36–52.

Race and the human genome: Researchers definitely trump the notion of race with DNA research. (2004). Retrieved January 30, 2004, from http://racerelations.about.com/library/weekly/aa021501a.htm

Rampage, C., Eovaldi, M., Ma, C., & Weigel-Foy, C. (2003). Adoptive families. In F. Walsh (Ed.), *Normal family processes: Growing diversity and complexity* (pp. 210–232). New York: Guilford Press.

Rankin, S. (2002). *Campus climate for gay, lesbian, bisexual, and transgender people: A national perspective.* New York: The Policy Institute of the National Gay and Lesbian Task Force. Retrieved August 3, 2003, from http://www.thetaskforce.org/downloads/reports/reports/CampusClimate.pdf

Rastogi, S., Tallese D., Johnson, T. D., Hoeffel, E. M., & Drewery, M. P., Jr. (2011, November 21). *Majority of Black population lived in the south. Random Samplings: The official blog of the U.S. Census Bureau.* Retrieved November 27, 2011, from http://blogs.census.gov/censusblog/2011/11/majority-of-the-black-population-lived-in-the-south.html

Rastogi, S., Tallese D., Johnson, T. D., Hoeffel, E. M., & Drewery, M. P., Jr. (2011, November 21). The Black Population: 2010. *2010 Census Briefs.* C2010BR-06. U.S. Department of Commerce Economics and Statistics Administration U.S. Census Bureau.

Rayle, A. D., Chee, C., & Sand, J. K. (2006). Honoring their way: Counseling American Indian women. *Journal of Multicultural Counseling and Development, 34*, 66–79.

Redfield, R., Linton, R., & Herskovits, M. J. (1936). Memorandum for the study of acculturation. *American Anthropologist, 38*(1), 149–152.

Reid-Trotman, P. (2011). Revisiting "Poor women: shut up and shut out." *Psychology of Women Quarterly, 35*, 189–192. doi: 10.1177/0361684310395917.

Rendon, L. I., & Robinson, T. L. (1994). A diverse America: Implications for minority seniors. In W. Hartel, S. Schwartz, S. Blue, & J. Gardner (Eds.), *Ready for the real world: Senior year experience series* (pp. 170–188). Belmont, CA: Wadsworth.

Renzetti, C. M., & Curran, D. J. (1992). *Women, men, and society.* Boston: Allyn & Bacon.

Reynolds, A. L., & Pope, R. L. (1991). The complexities of diversity: Exploring multiple oppressions. *Journal of Counseling and Development, 70,* 174–180.

Rice, V. H., Weglicki, L. S., Thomas, T., & Hammad, A. (2006, April). Predictors of Arab American Adolescent tobacco use. *Merrill-Palmer Quarterly, 52*(2), 327–342.

Richardson, T. Q., & Molinaro, K. L. (1996). White counselor self-awareness: A prerequisite for developing multicultural competence. *Journal of Counseling and Development, 71,* 238–242.

Ridley, C. R. (1989). Racism in counseling as an aversive behavioral process. In P. B. Pedersen, J. G. Draguns, W. J. Lonner, & J. E. Trimble (Eds.), *Counseling across cultures* (pp. 55–78). Honolulu: University of Hawaii Press.

Riggs, M. (Producer/Director). (1994). *Black is...Black ain't* [Video]. San Francisco: California Newsreel.

Roberts, S. A., Kisselica, M. S., & Fredrickson, S. A. (2002). Quality of life of persons with medical illnesses: Counseling & holistic contribution. *Journal of Counseling & Development, 80,* 422–432.

Robinson, T. L. (1990). Understanding the gap between entry and exit: A cohort analysis of Black student persistence. *Journal of Negro Education, 59,* 207–218.

Robinson, T. L. (1993). The intersections of gender, class, race, and culture: On seeing clients whole. *Journal of Multicultural Counseling and Development, 21,* 50–58.

Robinson, T. L. (1999a). The intersections of dominant discourses across race, gender, and other identities. *Journal of Counseling & Development, 77,* 73–79.

Robinson, T. L. (1999b). The intersections of identity. In A. Garrod, J. V. Ward, T. L. Robinson, &

B. Kilkenney (Eds.), *Souls looking back: Stories of growing up Black.* New York: Routledge.

Robinson, T. L. (2001). White mothers of non-White children. *Journal of Humanistic Counseling, Education and Development, 40,* 171–184.

Robinson, T. L., & Howard-Hamilton, M. (1994). An Afrocentric paradigm: Foundation for a healthy self-image and healthy interpersonal relationships. *Journal of Mental Health Counseling, 16,* 327–339.

Robinson, T. L., & Kennington, P. A. D. (2002). Holding up half the sky: Women and psychological resistance. *Journal of Humanistic Counseling, Education and Development, 41,* 164–177.

Robinson, T. L., & Ward, J. V. (1991). A belief in self far greater than anyone's disbelief: Cultivating resistance among African American adolescents. *Women & Therapy, 11,* 87–103.

Robinson, T. L., & Ward, J. V. (1995). African American adolescents and skin color. *Journal of Black Psychology, 21,* 256–274.

Robinson, T. L., & Watt, S. K. (2001). Where no one goes begging: Gender, sexuality, and religious diversity. In D. Locke, J. Myers, & E. Herr (Eds.), *Handbook of counseling* (pp. 589–599). Thousand Oaks, CA: Sage.

Robinson-Wood, T. L. (2008). Extending culture beyond race and ethnicity. In C. Lee (Ed.), *Elements of culture.* Boston: Allyn & Bacon.

Robinson-Wood, T. L. (2009). Love, school, and money: Stress and cultural coping among ethnically diverse Black college women: A mixed-method analysis. *The Western Journal of Black Studies, 33,* 77–86.

Robinson-Wood, T. L. (2010a). Is that your mom? A qualitative investigation of White mothers of non-White children in the United States and New Zealand. *Journal of Ethnographic and Qualitative Research, 22,* 226–238.

Robinson-Wood, T. L. (2010b). Privileging multiple converging identities in counseling and Clemmont E. Vontress. In R. Moodley & R. Walcott (Eds.), *Counseling across and beyond cultures: Exploring the work of Clemmont E. Vontress in clinical practice* (pp. 233–246). Toronto: University of Toronto Press.

Robinson-Wood, T. L., & Braithwaite-Hall, M. (2005). Spirit matters: Women, spirituality, and clinical contexts. In M. Mirkin, J. Suyemoto, & B. Okun (Eds.), *Psychotherapy with women: Exploring diverse contexts and identities* (pp. 280–296). New York: Guilford Press.

Rockquemore, K. A. (1999). Between Black and White: Understanding the "biracial" experience. *Race and Society, 2*, 197–212.

Rockquemore, K. A. (2002). Negotiating the color line: The gendered process of racial identity construction among Black/White biracial women. *Gender and Society, 16*, 485–503.

Rogers, J. A. (1967). *Sex and race.* St. Petersburg, FL: Helga Rogers.

Root, M. P. P. (1990). Disordered eating in women of color. *Sex Roles, 22*, 525–536.

Root, M. P. P. (1992). Within, between, and beyond race. In M. P. P. Root (Ed.), *Racially mixed people in America* (pp. 3–11). Newbury Park, CA: Sage.

Root, M. P. P. (1998). Experiences and processes affecting racial identity development: Preliminary results from the biracial sibling project. *Cultural Diversity and Mental Health, 4*, 237–247.

Rosenblum, K. E., & Travis, T. C. (2005). *The meaning of difference: American constructions of race, sex, and gender, social class, and sexual orientation.* Boston: McGraw-Hill.

Rothblum, E. D. (1994). "I only read about myself on bathroom walls": The need for research on the mental health of lesbians and gay men. *Journal of Consulting and Clinical Psychology, 62*, 213–220.

Rowley, S. J., Burchinal, M. R., Roberts, J. E., & Zeisel, S. A. (2008). Racial identity, social context, and race-related social cognition in African American middle school children. *Developmental Psychology, 44*, 1537–1546. doi:10.1037/a0013349.

Roysircar, G. (Ed.). (2003). *Multicultural counseling competencies: 2003.* Alexandria, VA: Association of Multicultural Counseling and Development.

Rudolph, J. (1990). Counselors' attitudes toward homosexuality: Selective review of the literature. *Journal of Counseling and Development, 65*, 165–168.

Ruelas, S. (2003). Objectively measures multicultural competencies: A preliminary study. In D. Pope-Davis, H. Coleman, W. Liu, & R. Toporek (Eds.), *Handbook of multicultural competencies & counseling* (pp. 283–300). Thousand Oaks, CA: Sage.

Russell, G. (1994). *A map of American Indian history.* Phoenix, AZ: Thunderbird Enterprises.

Rust, P. C. (2006). Sexual identity and bisexual identities: The struggle for self-description in a changing sexual landscape. In T. E. Orr (Ed.), *The social construction of difference and inequality: Race, class, gender, and sexuality* (pp. 169–186). Boston: McGraw-Hill.

Sadker, M., Sadker, D., & Long, L. (1993). Gender and educational equity. In J. Banks & C. McGee-Banks (Eds.), *Multicultural education* (pp. 111–128). Boston: Allyn & Bacon.

Salazar, C. F. (2006). Conceptualizing multiple identities and multiple oppressions in clients' lives. *Counseling and Human Development, 39*(1), 1–18.

Salk, R. H., & Engeln-Maddo, R. (2011). "If you're fat then I'm humongous": Frequency, content, and impact of Fat Talk Among college women. *Psychology of Women Quarterly, 35*(1), 18–28.

Sanchez, G. J. (2002). "Y tu, que?" (YzK): Latino history in the new millennium. In M. Suarez-Orozco & M. M. Paez (Eds.), *Latinos: Remaking America* (pp. 45–58). Berkeley, CA: University of California Press.

Sandhu, D. S. (1997). Psychocultural profiles of Asian and Pacific Islander Americans: Implications for counseling and psychotherapy. *Journal of Multicultural Counseling and Development, 25*, 7–22.

Santiago-Rivera, A. L. (2003). Latinos values and family transitions: Practical considerations for counseling. *Counseling and Human Development, 35*, 1–12.

Santiago-Rivera, A. L., Arredondo, P., & Gallardo-Cooper, M. (2002). *Counseling Latinos and la familia: A practical guide*. Thousand Oaks, CA: Sage.

Saucier, M. G. (2004). Midlife and beyond: Issues for aging women. *Journal of Counseling & Development, 82*, 420–425.

Sawy, N. E. (2005). Yes, I follow Islam, but I'm not a terrorist. In T. E. Ore (Ed.), *The social construction of difference and inequality: Race, class, gender, and sexuality* (pp. 570–571). Boston: McGraw-Hill.

Schliebner, C. T., & Peregoy, J. J. (1994). Unemployment effects on the family and the child: Interventions for counselors. *Journal of Counseling and Development, 72*, 368–372.

Schnitzer, P. K. (1996). "They don't come in." Stories told, lessons taught about poor families in therapy. *American Journal of Orthopsychiatry, 66*, 572–582.

Schofield, W. (1964). *Psychotherapy: The purchase of friendship*. Upper Saddle River, NJ: Prentice Hall.

Scholl, M. B. (2006). Native American identity development and counseling preferences: A study of Lumbee undergraduates. *Journal of College Counseling, 9*, 47–59.

Schoulte, J. (2011). Bereavement among African American and Latino/a Americans. *Journal of Mental Health Counseling, 33*, 11–20.

Schulte, E. (2002). More black men in jail than college. Retrieved September 25, 2007, from http://www.socialist worker.org/2002

Schultz-Rooss, R. A., & Gutheil, T. G. (1997). Difficulties in integrating spirituality into psychotherapy practice, *Journal of Psychotherapy Practice and Research, 6*, 130–138.

Schwartz, W. (1998). The identity development of multiracial youth. *Digest*, No.137, EDO-UD-98-7. Eric Clearinghouse on Urban Education.

Scott, D. A., & Robinson, T. L. (2001). White male identity development: The key model. *Journal of Counseling & Development, 79*, 415–421.

Sehgal, R., Saules, K. K., Young, A., Grey, M.J., Gillem, A.R., Nabors, N.A., Byrd, M.R., & Jefferson, S. (2011). Multicultural counseling competence among clinical psychology trainees and experienced multicultural psychologists: Do we practice what we know? *Cultural Diversity and Ethnic Minority Psychology, 17*(1), 1–10.

Sharfstein, D. J. (2007). Crossing the color line: Racial migration and the one-drop rule, 1600–1860. *Minnesota Law Review, 91*, 592–656.

Shiarev, E., & Levy, D. (2004). *Cross cultural psychology: Critical thinking and contemporary applications*. Boston: Pearson.

Shih, M., Bonam, C., Sanchez, D., & Peck, C. (2007). The social construction of race: Biracial identity and vulnerability to stereotypes. *Cultural Diversity and Ethnic Minority Psychology, 13*, 125–133.

Shih, M., & Sanchez, D. T. (2005). Perspectives and research on the positive and negative implications of having multiple racial identities. *Psychological Bulletin, 131*, 569–591.

Shinn, F. S. (1989). *The wisdom of Florence Scovel Shinn*. New York: A Fireside Book.

Shore, L. I. (1995). *Tending inner gardens: The healing art of feminist therapy*. New York: Harrington Park Press.

Simon, J. P. (1996). Lebanese families. In M. McGoldrick, J. K. Pearce, & J. Giordano (Eds.), *Ethnicity and family therapy* (pp. 364–375). New York: Guilford Press.

Skovholt, T. M. (1993). Counseling and psychotherapy interventions with men. *Counseling and Human Development, 25*, 1–6.

Slater, S. (1997). Contributions of the lesbian experience to mutuality in therapy relationships. In J. Jordan (Ed.), *Women's growth in diversity: More writings from the Stone Center* (pp. 119–126). New York: Guilford Press.

Slevec, J. H., & Tiggemann, M. (2011). Predictors of body dissatisfaction and disordered eating in middle-aged women: A test of the sociocultural model of disordered eating. *Psychology of women Quarterly, 35*(4), 617–627.

Smart, J. F., & Smart, D. W. (2006). Models on disability: Implications for the counseling profession. *Journal of Counseling and Development, 84*, 29–40.

Smith, B. (1982). Toward a Black feminist criticism. In G. Hull, P. Scott, & B. Smith (Eds.), *All the women are White, all the Blacks are men, but some of us are brave* (pp. 157–175). Old Westbury, NY: Feminist Press.

Smith, L. (2005). Psychotherapy, classism, and the poor. *American Psychologists, 60*, 687–696.

Smits, S. J. (2004). Disability and employment in the U.S.A.: The quest for best practices. *Disability & Society, 19*, 647–662.

Sodowski, G. R., Wai, E. W. M., & Plake, B. (1991). Moderating effects of sociocultural variables on acculturation attitudes of Hispanics and Asian Americans. *Journal of Counseling and Development, 70*, 194–204.

Souter, A., & Murthy, R. S. (2006, October 21). Relation between mental health care and general development. *British Medical Journal, 333*, 861.

Spanierman, L. B., Poteat, V. P., Beer, A. M., & Armstrong, P. I. (2007). Psychosocial costs of racism to Whites: Exploring patterns through cluster analysis. *Journal of Counseling Psychology, 53*(3), 434–441.

Spanierman, L. B., Todd, N. R., & Anderson, C. J. (2009). Psychosocial costs of racism to Whites: Understanding patterns among university students. *Journal of Counseling Psychology, 56*, 239–252.

Spence, J. T., & Helmreich, R. L. (1978). *Masculinity and femininity: Their psychological dimensions, correlates, and antecedents.* Austin: University of Texas Press.

Spickard, P. R. (1992). The illogic of American racial categories. In M. P. P. Root (Ed.), *Racially mixed people in America* (pp. 12–23). Newbury Park, CA: Sage.

Staples, R. (1988). The Black American family. In C. H. Mindel, R. W. Habenstein, & R. Wright (Eds.), *Ethnic families in America: Patterns and variations* (3rd ed., pp. 303–324). New York: Elsevier.

Stavans, I. (1995). *The Hispanic condition: Reflections on culture and identity in America.* New York: Harper Perennial.

Steinberg, S. (1989). *The ethnic myth: Race, ethnicity, and class in America.* Boston: Beacon Press.

Steinem, G. (1992). *Revolution from within: A book of self-esteem.* Boston: Little, Brown.

Steinmetz, E. (2006). *Americans with disabilities: 2002.* Washington, DC: U. S. Department of Commerce, U.S. Census Bureau.

Sterling, A. F. (1992). *Myths of gender.* New York: Basic Books.

Stevens, M. J., Pfost, K. S., & Potts, M. K. (1990). Sex role orientation and the willingness to confront existential issues. *Journal of Counseling and Development, 68*, 47–49.

Stewart, J. C. (1996). *1001 things everyone should know about African American history.* New York: Doubleday.

Stiver, I. P. (1997). A relational approach to therapeutic impasses. In J. Jordan (Ed.), *Women's growth in diversity* (pp. 288–310). New York: Guilford Press.

Storck, L. E. (1998). Social class divisions in the consulting room: A theory of psychosocial class and depression. *Group Analysis, 31*, 101–115.

Suarez-Orozco, M., & Paez, M. M. (2002). *Latinos: Remaking America.* Berkeley: University of California Press.

Sue, D. W. (Presenter). (1989). *Cultural identity development* [Video]. Amherst, MA: Microtraining and Multicultural Development.

Sue, D. W., Arredondo, P., & McDavis, R. J. (1992). Multicultural counseling competencies and standards: A call to the profession. *Journal of Counseling and Development, 70*, 477–483.

Sue, D. W., Bernier, J. E., Daran, A., Feinberg, L., Pedersen, P., Smith, C. T., et al. (1982). Cross-cultural counseling competencies. *Counseling Psychologist, 19*, 45–52.

Sue, D. W., Carter, R. T., Caas, J. M., Fouad, N. A., Ivey, A. E., Jensen, M., et al. (1998). *Multicultural counseling competencies: Individual and organizational development.* Thousand Oaks, CA: Sage.

Sue, D. W., Ivey, A. E., & Pedersen, P. B. (1996). *A theory of multicultural counseling and therapy.* Pacific Grove, CA: Brooks/Cole.

Sue, D. W., & Sue, D. (1990). *Counseling the culturally different: Theory and practice.* New York: John Wiley.

Sue, D. W., & Sue, D. (1995). Asian Americans. In N. Vaac, S. B. Devaney, & J. Witmer (Eds.), *Experiences and counseling multicultural and diverse populations* (3rd ed., pp. 63–90). Bristol, PA: Accelerated Development.

Sullivan, P. (1998). Sexual identity development: The importance of target or dominant group membership. In R. C. Sanlo (Ed.), *Working with lesbian, gay, bisexual, and transgender college students: A handbook for faculty and administrators* (pp. 3–12). Westport, CT: Greenwood Press.

Sutherland, P., & Moodley, R. (2010). Reclaiming the spirit: Clemmon E. Vontress and the quest for spirituality and traditional healing in counseling. In R. Moodley & R. Walcott (Eds.), *Counselling across and beyond cultures: Exploring the work of Clemmont E. Vontress in clinical practice* (pp. 263–277). Toronto: University of Toronto Press.

Sutton, C. T., & Broken Nose, M. A. (1996). American Indian families: An overview. In M. McGoldrick, J. Giordano, & J. K. Pearce (Eds.), *Ethnicity and family therapy* (pp. 31–44). New York: Guilford Press.

Suzuki-Crumly, J., & Hyers, L. L. (2004). The relationship among ethnic identity, psychological well-being, and intergroup competence: An investigation of two biracial groups. *Cultural Diversity and Ethnic Minority Psychology, 10,* 137–150.

Swanson, B., Cronin-Stubbs, D., & Sheldon, J. A. (1989). The impact of psychosocial factors on adapting to physical disability: A review of the research literature. *Rehabilitation Nursing, 14,* 64–68.

Swanson, J. L. (1993). Sexism strikes men. *American Counselor, 1,* 10–13, 39.

Swinton, J. (2001). *Spirituality and mental health care: Rediscovering a "forgotten" dimension.* London: Jessica Kingsley Publishers.

Syzmanski, D. M., & Sung, M. R. (2010). Minority stress and psychological distress among Asian American sexual minority persons. *The Counseling Psychologist, 38,* 848–872. doi: 10.1177/0011000010366167.

Takaki, R. (1993). *A different mirror: A history of multicultural America.* Boston: Back Bay Books.

Takaki, R. (1994a). *From different shores: Perspectives on race and ethnicity in America.* New York: Oxford University Press.

Takaki, R. (1994b). The myth of the "model minority." In R. C. Monk (Ed.), *Taking sides: Clashing views on controversial issues in race and ethnicity* (pp. 55–61). Guilford, CT: Dushkin.

Tate, D. G., & Pledger, C. (2003). An integrative conceptual framework of disability, *American Psychologist, 58,* 289–295.

Tatum, B. D. (1992). Talking about race, learning about racism: The application of racial identity theory in the classroom. *Harvard Educational Review, 61*(1), 1–24.

Tatum, B. D. (1997). Racial identity development and relational theory: The case of Black women in White communities. In J. Jordan (Ed.), *Women's growth in diversity* (pp. 91–106). New York: Guilford Press.

Thomas, K. T. (2004). Old wine in a slightly cracked new bottle, *American Psychologist, 59,* 274–275.

Thomas, M. B. (2006). Navigators guide patients through the continuum: Barriers include language, finance, transportation. *Hospital Case Management, 3,* 191–194.

Thomason, T. C. (2000). Issues in the treatment of Native Americans with alcohol problems. *Journal of Multicultural Counseling and Development, 28,* 243–252.

Thompson, E. M., & Morgan, E. M. (2008). "Mostly straight young women": Variations in sexual behavior and identity development. *Developmental Psychology, 44,* 15–21.

Toporek, R. L., & Williams, R. A. (2006). Ethics and professional issues related t the practice of social justice in counseling psychology. In R. Toporek, L. Gerstein, N. Fouad, G. Roysircar, & T. Israel. (Eds.), *Handbook for social justice in counseling psychology* (pp.17–36). Thousand Oaks, CA: Sage.

Towle, E. B., & Morgan, L. M. (2002). Romancing the transgender native: Rethinking the use of the "third gender" concept. *GLQ: A Journal of Lesbian and Gay Studies, 8*, 469–497.

Tran, T. V. (1988). The Vietnamese American family. In C. H. Mindel, R. W. Habenstein, & R. Wright (Eds.), *Ethnic families in America: Patterns and variations* (3rd ed., pp. 276–302). New York: Elsevier.

Trimble. (2010). The principled conduct of counseling research with ethnocultural populations. In J. G. Ponterotto, J. Manuel Casas, L. A. Suzuki, & C. M. Alexander (Eds.). *Handbook of multicultural counseling* (3rd ed., pp. 147–161). Los Angeles: Sage.

Troiden, R. R. (1989). The formation of homosexual identities. *Journal of Homosexuality, 17*, 43–73.

Trujillo, A. (2000). Psychotherapy with Native Americans: A view into the role of religion and spirituality. In P. S. Richards & A. E. Bergin (Eds.), *Handbook of psychotherapy and religious diversity*. Washington, DC: American Psychological Association.

Tsai, J. L., & Chensova-Dutton, Y. (2002). Models of cultural orientation: Differences between American-born and overseas-born Asians. In K. Kurasaki, S. Okasaki, & S. Sue (Eds.), *Asian American mental health: Assessment theories and methods* (pp. 95–106). New York: Kluwer Academic.

Tsai, M., & Uemura, A. (1988). Asian Americans: The struggles, the conflicts, and the successes. In P. Bronstein & K. Quina (Eds.), *Teaching a psychology of people* (pp. 125–133). Washington, DC: American Psychological Association.

Tsu, L. (1972). *Tao Te Ching* (G. F. Feng & J. English, Trans.). New York: Vintage.

Turner, C. W. (1997). Clinical applications of the Stone Center theoretical approach to minority women. In J. Jordan (Ed.), *Women's growth in diversity: More writings from the Stone Center* (pp. 74–90). New York: Guilford Press.

Tylka, T. L., Subich, L. M. (2002). Exploring young women's perceptions of the effectiveness and safety of maladaptive weight control techniques. *Journal of Counseling & Development, 80*, 101–110.

Uba, L. (1994). *Asian Americans: Personality patterns, identity, and mental health*. New York: Guilford Press.

Udry, J. R., Li, R. M., & Hendrickson-Smith, K. (2003). Health and behavior risks of adolescents with mixed-race identity. *American Journal of Public Health, 93*, 1865–1870.

Umaña-Taylor, A. J. (2004). Ethnic identity and self-esteem: Examining the role of social context. *Journal of Adolescence, 27*, 139–146.

Labor Force Characteristics by race and ethnicity, 2009. (2010). U.S. Department of Labor, U.S. Bureau of Labor Statistics, Offi ce of Employment and Unemployment Statistics, Division of Labor Force Statistics, Washington, D.C.

U.S. Census Bureau. (2000a). *America's families and living arrangements*. Washington, DC: U.S. Department of Commerce.

U.S. Census Bureau. (2000b). *Population by age, sex, and race and Hispanic origin: Current population survey*. Washington, DC: U.S. Department of Commerce.

U.S. Census Bureau. (2000c). *Profile of selected social characteristics: Current population survey*. Washington, DC: U.S. Department of Commerce.

U.S. Census Bureau. (2000d). *The Asian population: 2000*. Washington, DC: U.S. Department of Commerce.

U.S. Census Bureau. (2000e). U.S. Summary: 2000. *Census 2000 Profile*. Washington, DC: U.S. Department of Commerce.

U.S. Census Bureau. (2001a). Labor force participation for mothers with infants declines for first time, Census Bureau reports. *U.S. Department of Commerce News*. Retrieved September 1, 2007, from http://www.census.gov/Press-Release/www/2001/cb01-170.html

U.S. Census Bureau. (2001b). *Poverty in the United States*. Washington, DC: U.S. Department of Commerce, Annual Demographic Supplement.

U.S. Census Bureau. (2001c). *The Hispanic population in the United States. March 2000*. Washington, DC: U.S. Department of Commerce, Economics and Statistical Administration.

U.S. Census Bureau. (2001d). The nuclear family rebounds, Census Bureau reports. *U.S. Department of Commerce News*. Retrieved March 12, 2004, from http://www.census.gov/Press-Release/www/releases/archives/children/000326.html

U.S. Census Bureau. (2002). *Poverty in the United States*. Washington, DC: U.S. Department of Commerce.

U.S. Census Bureau. (2006). Americans with disabilities. *Household Economic Studies*. Washington, DC: U.S. Department of Commerce.

U.S. Census Bureau. (2007a). FactFinder, 2006. *American community survey data profile highlights*. Washington, DC: U.S. Department of Commerce.

U.S. Census Bureau. (2007b). The American community—American Indians and Alaska Natives: 2004. *American community survey reports*. Washington, DC: U.S. Department of Commerce.

U.S. Census Bureau. (2007c). The American community—Asians: 2004. *American community survey reports*. Washington, DC: U.S. Department of Commerce.

U.S. Census Bureau. (2007d). The American community—Blacks: 2004. *American community survey reports*. Washington, DC: U.S. Department of Commerce.

U.S. Census Bureau. (2007e). The American community—Hispanics: 2004. *American community survey reports*. Washington, DC: U.S. Department of Commerce.

U.S. Census Bureau. (2007f). The American community—Pacific Islanders: 2004. *American community survey reports*. Washington, DC: U.S. Department of Commerce.

U.S. Census Bureau. (2008). 2007 American Community Survey; B04006. *People reporting ancestry; using American FactFinder*. Retrieved September 29, 2008, from http://factfinder.census.gov.

U.S. Census Bureau. (2009). *Hispanic Americans by the numbers*. Retrieved January 15, 2012, from http://www.infoplease.com/spot/hhmcensus1.html.

U.S. Census Bureau. (2011). *2009 American Community Survey, BO4006*. People reporting Ancestry, from http://factfinder.census.gov.

U.S. Census Bureau, Current Population Survey. (2011). *Table 3. Detailed Years of School Completed by People 25 Years and Over by Sex, Age Groups, Race and Hispanic Origin: 2010 Annual Social and Economic Supplement*. Washington, DC: U.S. Census Bureau.

U.S. Census Bureau, Current Population Survey (2011, June). *Table 6. Households by Type, for Black Alone and White Alone, Not Hispanic Households: 2010 Civilian non-institutionalized population*. U.S. Census Bureau, Current Population Survey, Washington, DC: Annual Social and Economic Supplement, 2010.

U.S. Census Bureau News. (2005). Educational attainment. People 25 years old and over by total money earnings in 2004, work experience in 2004, age, race, Hispanic, origin. Retrieved August 1, 2007, from http://pubdb3.census.gov/macro/032005/perinc/new03_004.htm

U.S. Census Bureau News. (2007). Household income rises, poverty rate declines, number of uninsured up. Washington, DC: U.S. Department of Commerce.

U.S. Census Bureau News (2011, November 1). American Indian and Alaska Native Heritage Month: CB11-FF.22. U.S. Department of Commerce, Washington, DC.

U.S. Centers for Disease Control and Prevention. (2004). *HIV/AIDS among Hispanics: The body*. Retrieved September 1, 2007, from www.thebody.com

U.S. Department of Energy Genome Programs Genetic research confirms: There's only 1 human race (2003, July 15). St. Louis Post-Dispatch.http://genomics.energy.gov. http://www.ornl.gov/sci/techresources/Human_Genome/project/info.shtml

U.S. Department of Health and Human Services. (2001). *Mental health: Culture, race, and ethnicity—A supplement to mental health: A report to the Surgeon General*. Rockville, MD: U.S. Department of Health and Human Services, Public Health Service.

U.S. Department of the Interior. (2002). *Federal Register*. Washington, DC: Bureau of Indian Affairs.

Ussher, J. M., & Perz, J. (2010). Gender differences in self-silencing and psychological distress in informal cancer carers. *Psychology of Women Quarterly, 34*, 228–242.

Utsey, S., Walker, R. L., & Kwate, N. A. (2005). Conducting quantitative research in a cultural context: Practical applications for research with ethnic minority populations. In M. Constantine & D. Sue (Eds.), *Strategies for building multicultural competence in mental health and educational settings* (pp. 247–268). Hoboken, NJ: John Wiley & Sons.

VanBoven, A. M., & Espelage, D. L. (2006). Depressive symptoms, coping strategies, and disordered eating among college women. *Journal of Counseling & Development, 84*, 341–348.

Vandiver, B. J. (2001). Psychological nigrescence revisited: Introduction and overview. *Journal of Multicultural Counseling and Development, 29*, 165–173.

Vanzant, I. (1998). *Yesterday I cried*. New York: A Fireside Book.

Vasquez, H., & Magraw, S. (2005). Building relationships across privilege: Becoming an ally in the therapeutic relationship. In M. Mirkin, K. Suyemoto, & B. Okun (Eds.), *Psychotherapy with women: Exploring diverse contexts and identities* (pp. 64–83). New York: Guilford Press.

Vasquez, M. J. T. (1994). *Latinas*. In L. Comas-Dias & B. Greene (Eds.), *Women of color* (pp. 114–138). New York: Guilford Press.

Venner, K. L., Wall, T. L., Lau, P., & Ehlers, C. L. (2006). Testing of an orthogonal measure of cultural identification with adult mission Indians. *Cultural Diversity and Ethnic Minority Psychology, 12*, 632–643.

Vera, E. M., & Speight, S. L. (2003). Multicultural competence, social justice, and counseling psychology: Expanding our roles. *The Counseling Psychologist, 31*, 253–272.

Vernon, I. (2002). *Killing us quietly: Native Americans and HIV/AIDS*. Lincoln, NE: Bison Books.

Vontress, C. E. (1986). Social and cultural foundations. In R. Hayes & J. Lewis (Eds.), *In the counseling profession* (pp. 215–250). Itasca, IL: Peacock Publishers.

Vontress, C. E. (2004). Reactions to the multicultural counseling competencies debate. *Journal of Mental Health Counseling, 24*, 74–80.

Wachtel, P. L. (2002). Psychoanalysis and the disenfranchised: From therapy to justice. *Psychoanalytic Psychology, 19*, 199–215.

Waldman, C. (2000). *Atlas of the North American Indian*. New York: Checkmark Books.

Walker, A. (1987). Oppressed hair puts a ceiling on the brain. In *Living by the word: Selected writings, 1973–1983*. Retrieved January 27, 2008, from http://www.geocities.com/Hotsprings/Falls/8860/ceiling.html

Wall, V. A., & Evans, N. J. (1992). Using psychosocial development theories to understand and work with gay and lesbian persons. In N. J. Evans & V. A. Hall (Eds.), *Beyond tolerance: Gays, lesbians, and bisexuals on campus* (pp. 25–28). Alexandria, VA: American College Personnel Association.

Ward, J. V. (1989). Racial identity formation and transformation. In C. Gilligan, N. P. Lyons, & T. J. Hanmer (Eds.), *Making connections: The relational worlds of adolescent girls at Emma Willard School* (pp. 215–232). New York: Troy Press.

Ward, J. V. (2000). *The skin we're in: Teaching our children to be emotionally strong, socially smart, and spiritually connected*. New York: Free Press.

Warren, A. K., & Constantine, M. G. (2007). Social justice issues. In M. Constantine (Ed.), *Clinical practice with people of color* (pp. 231–242). New York: Teachers College Press.

Washington, C. S. (1987). Counseling black men. In M. Scher, M. Stevens, G. Good, & G. A. Eichenfield

(Eds.), *Handbook of counseling and psychotherapy* (pp. 192–202). Newbury Park, CA: Sage.

Watt, S. K., Robinson, T. L., & Lupton-Smith, H. (2002). Building ego and racial identity: Preliminary perspectives on counselors-in-training. *Journal of Counseling and Development, 80*, 94–100.

Webster, M., Jr., & Driskell, J. E., Jr. (1983). Beauty as status. *American Journal of Sociology, 89*, 140–164.

Weedon, C. (1987). *Feminist practice and poststructuralist theory.* New York: Blackwell Publishing.

Wehrly, B. (1995). *Pathways to multicultural counseling competence: A developmental journey.* Pacific Grove, CA: Brooks/Cole.

Weisman, L. K. (1992). *Discrimination by design: A feminist critique of the man-made environment.* Urbana: University of Illinois Press.

Wendell, S. (1989). Toward a feminist theory of disability. *Hypatia, 4*, 63–81.

West, A. E., & Newman, D. L. (2007). Childhood behavioral inhibition and the experience of social anxiety in American Indian adolescents. *Cultural Diversity and Ethnic Minority Psychology, 13*, 197–206.

West, C., & Zimmerman, D. H. (1991). Doing gender. In J. Lorber & S. A. Farrell (Eds.), *The social construction of gender* (pp. 13–37). Newbury Park, CA: Sage.

West, W. (2000). *Psychotherapy and spirituality: Crossing the line between therapy and religion.* London: Sage Publications.

Wester, S. R., Kuo, B. C. H., & Vogel, D. L. (2006). Multicultural coping: Chinese Canadian adolescents, male gender role conflict, and psychological distress. *Psychology of Men & Masculinity, 7*, 83–100.

Wester, S. R., Vogel, D. L., & Archer, J. (2004). Male restricted emotionality and counseling supervision. *Journal of Counseling & Development, 82*, 91–98.

Wester, S. R., Vogel, D. L., Wei, M., & McLain, R. (2006). African American men, gender role conflict, and psychological distress: The role of racial identity. *Journal of Counseling & Development, 84*, 419–429.

Wiggins-Frame, M., & Braun, C. (1996). Counseling African Americans: Integrating spirituality in therapy.*Counseling and Values, 41*, 16–28.

Wijeyesinghe, C. (2001). Racial identity in multiracial people: An alternative paradigm. In C. Wijeyesinghe & B. Jackson III (Eds.), *New perspectives on racial identity development: A theoretical and practical anthology* (pp. 129–152). New York: New York University Press.

Wikipedia. Retrieved October 5, 2007, from www.en. wikipedia.org/wiki/Queer_theory

Wilkinson, D. (1997). Reappraising the race, class, gender equation: A critical theoretical perspective. *Smith College Studies in Social Work, 67*, 261–276.

Wilson, T. P. (1992). Blood quantum: Native American mixed bloods. In M. P. P. Root (Ed.), *Racially mixed people in America* (pp. 108–126). Newbury Park, CA: Sage.

Wilson, W. J. (1994). The black community: Race and class. In R. Takaki (Ed.), *From different shores: Perspectives on race and ethnicity in America* (2nd ed., pp. 243–250). New York: Oxford University Press.

Wise, T. (2005). *White like me: Reflections on race from a privileged son.* Brooklyn, NY: Soft Skull Press.

Witmer, J. M., & Sweeney, T. J. (1992). A holistic model for wellness and prevention over the life span. *Journal of Counseling & Development, 71*, 140–143.

Wong, F., & Halgin, R. (2006). The "model minority": Bane or blessing for Asian Americans? *Journal of Multicultural Counseling and Development, 34*, 38–49.

Wong, M. G. (1988). The Chinese American family. In C. H. Mindel, R. W. Habenstein, & R. Wright (Eds.), *Ethnic families in America: Patterns and variations* (3rd ed., pp. 230–257). New York: Elsevier.

Worell, J., & Remer, P. (1992). *Feminist perspectives in therapy: An empowerment model for women.* New York: Wiley.

World Health Organization. (2005). *Tobacco free initiative.* Retrieved September 1, 2007, form http://www. who.int/tobacco/en/

World Health Organization Tobacco Free Initiative. (2005). Retrieved July 17, 2011, from http://www. who.int/tobacco/en/

Worthington, R. L., Dillon, F. R., & Becker-Schutte, A. M. (2005). Development, reliability, and validity of the lesbian, gay, and bisexual knowledge and attitudes scale for heterosexuals. *Journal of Counseling Psychology, 52*, 104–118.

Worthington, R. L., Soth-McNett, A. M., & Moreno, M. V. (2007). Multicultural counseling competencies research: A 20 year content analysis. *The Counseling Psychologist, 54*, 351–361.

Wrenn, C. G. (1962). The culturally encapsulated counselor. *Harvard Educational Review, 32*, 444–449.

Wu, F. (2002). *Yellow: Race in America beyond Black and White.* New York: Basic Books.

Yakushko, O., & Chronister, K. M. (2005). Immigrant women and counseling: The invisible others. *Journal of Counseling & Development, 83*, 292–298.

Yap, C. Y., Settles, I., H., & Pratt-Hyatt, J. S. (2011). Mediators of the relationship between racial identity and life satisfaction in a community sample of African American women and men. *Cultural Diversity and Ethnic Minority Psychology, 17*(1), 89–97. doi: 10.1037/a0022535.

Yeh, C., & Wang, Y. (2000). Asian American coping attitudes, sources, and practices: Implications for indigenous counseling strategies. *Journal of College Student Development, 41*, 94–103.

Ying, Y. (2002). The conception of depression in Chinese Americans. In K. Kurasaki, S. Okasaki, & S. Sue (Eds.), *Asian American mental health: Assessment theories and methods* (pp. 173–184). New York: Kluwer Academic.

Ying, Y., & Miller, L. S. (1992). Help-seeking behavior and attitude of Chinese Americans regarding psychological problems. *American Journal of Community Psychology, 20*, 549–556.

Young, J. S., Wiggins-Frame, M., & Cashwell, C. S. (2007). Spirituality and counselor competence: A national survey of American Counseling Association members. *Journal of Counseling & Development, 85*(1), 47–52.

Zane, N. W. S., & Huh-Kim, J. (1998). Addictive behaviors. In L. S. Lee & N. Zane (Eds.), *Handbook of Asian American psychology* (pp. 527–554). Thousand Oaks, CA: Sage.

Zetzer, H. A. (2005). White out. Privilege and its problems. In S. Anderson & V. Middleton (Eds.), *Explorations in privilege, oppression, and diversity* (pp. 3–16). Belmont, CA: Thomson, Cole.

Zia, H. (2000). *Asian American Dreams: The emergence of an American people.* New York: Farrar, Straus, and Giroux.

Zinn, H. (2003). *A people's history of the United States. 1492–present.* New York: HarperCollins.

Zitzelsberger, H. (2005). (In)visibility: Accounts of embodiment of women with physical disabilities and differences. *Disability & Society, 20*, 389–403.

Zola, I. K. (1991). Bringing our bodies and ourselves back in: Reflections on a past, present, and future "medical sociology." *Journal of Health and Social Behavior, 32*, 1–16.

Zuckerman, M. (1990). Some dubious premises in research and theory on racial differences. *American Psychologist, 45*, 1297–1303.

Zur, O. (2006). Therapeutic boundaries and dual relationships in rural practice: Ethical, clinical and standard of care considerations. *Journal of Rural Community Psychology, V. E9/1* (Online Journal).

Zwang, J. (2010, November 29). High school graduation rate is increasing, report shows. *eschool news.* Technology news for today's k-20 educator. Retrieved October 5, 2011, from: http://www.eschoolnews. com/2010/11/29/high-school-graduation-rate-is-improving-report-shows.

NAME INDEX

SUBJECT INDEX